PANDRO S. BERMAN

ONE OF THE GREATEST PRODUCERS OF HOLLYWOOD'S GOLDEN ERA

A FAMILY MEMOIR BY
MICHAEL BERMAN

Copyright © 2025 by Michael Berman
PANDRO S. BERMAN
ONE OF THE GREATEST PRODUCERS
OF HOLLYWOOD'S GOLDEN ERA
A FAMILY MEMOIR
by MICHAEL BERMAN

Cover Design: Joanna D'Angelo
Interior Book Design/Formatting: Joanna D'Angelo

This book is a work of non-fiction. The names, characters, places, and incidents are true from the author's associations. Names missing are those that could not be reached for permission or did not give permission. Permission was given for those names that are included. From the author's memory, any resemblance to actual events, business establishments, locales, or persons, living or dead, is entirely the truth.

All rights reserved. No part of this publication may be reproduced, stored in a retrieval system, or transmitted in any form or by any means (electronic, mechanical, photocopying, recording, or otherwise) without the prior written permission of both the copyright owner and the publisher. The only exceptions are brief quotations in printed reviews.

The scanning, uploading, and distribution of this book via the Internet or via any other means without the permission of the publisher is illegal and punishable by law. Please purchase only authorized electronic editions, and do not participate in or encourage electronic piracy of copyrighted materials.

Your support of the author's rights is appreciated.

For permission requests, write to the publisher at the email address: hmberman@sbcglobal.net

ISBN EBOOK: 979-8-9930663-0-1

ISBN PRINT BOOK: 979-8-9930663-1-8

I dedicate this book to my wonderful son Frank. It was to be your legacy. You graced all of our lives during the 24 precious years you were with us.

PANDRO S. BERMAN
ONE OF THE GREATEST PRODUCERS OF HOLLYWOOD'S GOLDEN ERA

A FAMILY MEMOIR

MICHAEL BERMAN

PROLOGUE

GUNGA DIN

The phone rang almost a dozen times before a noticeably out-of-breath production assistant finally answered. "*Gunga Din* Production Office... this is Marc Stein."

"This is Jane Loring in Pandro Berman's office at RKO... aren't you the young man I spoke with yesterday?"

"Yes, ma'am."

"I gave you instructions that George Stevens was to call Mr. Berman as soon as possible."

"Yes, ma'am... I sent your message right out to the location, and I reminded Mr. Stevens again after they wrapped."

"Well, he never called, and Mr. Berman is quite upset."

"I'm sorry, ma'am, but they didn't finish shooting until after eleven o'clock last night."

Jane was clearly annoyed. "Will they be shooting late again tonight?"

"Yes, ma'am... they're scheduled to wrap at ten o'clock."

"All right. Get a pencil and write this down."

"Yes, ma'am, I have a pencil."

"Crestview 64901... That's Mr. Berman's home phone number. And don't give it to anyone but George Stevens. He is to call Mr. Berman tonight no matter how late it is. I don't care if it's four o'clock in the morning. Do you understand me?"

"Yes, ma'am... I will tell him."

Jane slammed the phone down without saying goodbye. "Directors," she muttered. "They think they run the studios."

At seven o'clock the next morning, Pandro Berman arose from a restless sleep and turned to his wife, Vi.

"I'm going up to the location, and I want you to go with me."

She was not anxious to join him, knowing there would probably be fireworks, but she was committed to stand by her husband, who was going into battle. She would do everything in her power to help him through this difficult time.

"He never called last night, did he, Pan?"

Pandro shook his head and pulled back the covers. "Nope."

He went into his den adjacent to the bedroom and picked up the phone.

At eight o'clock sharp the doorbell rang, and Pandro opened the door to two uniformed studio cops, who had pulled an RKO Studio camera truck into the driveway behind the shiny black 1939 Packard. The studio had purchased it a few months earlier for their Head of Production. It was his reward for a remarkable series of hit movies he had produced over the last few years. America was just beginning to come out of the Great Depression, and these movies had elevated the stature of RKO to that of a major studio, albeit the smallest in Hollywood.

"Do you boys know how to get to the location?"

"Yes, Mr. Berman, we have a map."

"Good. I'll follow you. Let's go, Vi."

She wasn't quite ready to walk out the door, but she would put on her lipstick and the rest of her makeup in the car.

It was a three-and-a-half-hour drive from Los Angeles to Lone

Pine, California, where the sandy desert floor at the foot of Mt. Whitney most closely resembled the desert in northwest India. The British Army fought one battle after another with the rebel Hindu "Thugee" cult, losing almost as many as they had won. It is best described in the magical poetry of Rudyard Kipling.

Because it was early on a Saturday morning, there was very little traffic getting out of town and practically no cars on Highway 395, which leads directly into the little town of Lone Pine, about eighty miles east of Fresno. It was a popular location in the 1920s and '30s, used by many movie companies for shooting westerns because of its rugged barrenness. Early western stars made pictures there, followed by more familiar actors like Roy Rogers, Gene Autry, and Gary Cooper. Everyone's favorite childhood hero, William Boyd—known to his fans as *Hopalong Cassidy*—made multiple episodes of his western serials in this location. Now, RKO had mounted what was, at the time, the most elaborate and extravagant location shoot ever planned by any studio, for the production of *Gunga Din*.

After wrestling with this problem for several weeks, my father, Pandro S. Berman, head of RKO, finally made a critical decision. He knew exactly what he had to do...

I have a mental picture of my father, sitting in his office at RKO, trying desperately to find ways to shake dollars out of this mammoth budget before finally signing his name to it in approval of what could easily turn into a disaster.

Making matters even more critical was the fact that George Stevens was directing this epic. He was truly a great talent, but he was routinely slow and over budget on almost every picture he was associated with. RKO could ill afford him on a production of this magnitude, in spite of his reputation. In those days, RKO was one of the three smallest studios in Hollywood, along with Columbia and United Artists. It had a tiny stable of contract players, none of whom were big box office attractions. If they wanted an established star to be in their movie, they had to rent one from the big studios at a horrendous cost. And if the picture was a hit, and they wanted to rent that star again for a sequel, the cost would be even higher the second time around—unless the original deal had been made for a second role at the same price.

Cary Grant, a rising star in 1938, was an expensive rental from Columbia after his successful performance in *Topper*. Douglas Fairbanks Jr. and Victor McLaglen were under contract to RKO and much more affordable. Joan Fontaine was a contract player who had yet to establish herself, so she was a bargain.

In 1938, when *Gunga Din* went into production, the average cost of an RKO feature film was between $300,000 and $600,000. That figure—called the "Negative Cost"—included pre-production, production, and post-production expenses. It was called the Negative Cost because it included the expense of cutting the negative and making an Answer Print. It did not include the cost of multiple prints for the theaters or advertising, which were quite expensive and burdensome to a movie that was already over budget.

Before they could stop the bleeding, George Stevens had taken the picture more than two and a half times over budget, making it the most expensive movie in RKO history. The final Negative Cost reached a staggering $1.9 million. My father had been receiving calls from the New York corporate office insisting that he put the brakes on. Finally, the bank, which had been financing *Gunga Din*, announced there would be no more loans. That would have prevented completion of the movie, which still had a little more than two weeks left to shoot.

My parents and the studio cops arrived at the Lone Pine location just as the company had broken for lunch. Most of the actors and crew were seated at the outdoor lunch tables, but George Stevens and Cary Grant were nowhere in sight. They were having a private lunch in the director's trailer, so my father dispatched one of the studio cops to bring them outside with the rest of the company.

When they finally emerged, my father calmly and firmly announced that he was shutting down the production. Stevens went into shock.

"We have another two weeks of shooting to finish the picture."

Dad met him with a cold stare.

"No, you don't... You are finished now."

He ordered the studio cops to confiscate the cameras and the film, load them into the camera truck, and take them back to the studio and lock them up. The last day's shooting would be sent to the lab to be developed and printed and delivered to the editing room.

When everything was loaded, he turned back to my mother and said, "Let's go," and they started walking back to the car.

Stevens, who had been watching all of this in disbelief, ran after them, pleading with Dad not to do this and eventually threatening to file a lawsuit.

It was terribly embarrassing to my mother, who had become quite fond of George Stevens. He had previously directed several of Dad's pictures, including *Alice Adams* with Katharine Hepburn and *Swing Time*, one of the best of the Fred Astaire and Ginger Rogers musicals. My father ignored Stevens' threats and said nothing. He just started the car and sped off.

My mother was humiliated, and she asked my father why he couldn't have handled it a little more tactfully. He explained that it was much too late for tact or even polite conversation.

"There was no other way to handle it."

He was seriously concerned that *Gunga Din* could bankrupt the studio and that he would be out of a job. All the hard work he had put into the company would be washed away, and he would have to start over in the business.

Mom knew what a precarious situation they were in, but she also knew that my father was prone to imagining the worst-case scenarios. To him, gloom and doom were always just around the corner.

"What about all of your hit movies?" she offered. "Don't they count for anything? I'm sure any of the other studios would be thrilled to have you."

Dad was in one of his brooding moods. "Don't be so sure about that... In this business, you're only as good as your last picture, and this one could be my Waterloo."

They drove in silence for the next hour or so. By three o'clock, they were both hungry, so they stopped at a roadside restaurant for hamburgers and French fries. As they ate, things began to look a little brighter.

After giving it serious thought, Mom put a positive spin on the day's events. "You made a crucial decision, Pan... I'm sure it's the right one. Few people on your level would have had the stomach for what you did."

She scooted over in the front seat, and though they were going sixty miles an hour, she put her arms around him and gave him a warm hug. It was a loving embrace, and she knew it was just what he needed. His steely grip on the steering wheel eased and his tense shoulders finally relaxed.

TURNING THE CORNER

Not very many people in Hollywood had access to Pandro Berman's home phone number. It was given out on the condition that it would only be used in dire emergencies. It was like getting a top-secret clearance, which was, by nature, only temporary. The number was changed periodically, when it was determined that too many people had possession of it, including former employees who had worked with my father on earlier projects. There was a permanent list of friends and relatives who always had the number, and they were instantly updated every time it changed so they wouldn't feel cast out of favor.

One of those people who our home phone number was George Stevens. Having directed several of Dad's pictures, he was considered part of the inner circle. When he called that evening, my mother answered the phone and told him that her husband was sleeping and that he should call back on Monday at the studio. The tone in her voice told George that he'd better not pursue it any further.

Other people in the cast and crew who did not have the number waited until Monday morning and flooded my dad's office with calls. In addition to George Stevens, most of the calls were from the principal actors, including Cary Grant and Douglas Fairbanks Jr., both of whom had lost important scenes that could seriously elevate their performances.

Originally, Grant and Fairbanks were assigned each other's roles; Grant was to be the one leaving the army to marry Joan Fontaine's character, and Fairbanks the happy-go-lucky treasure hunter—since the character was identical to the legendary screen persona of Fairbanks' father.

According to Robert Osborne of Turner Classic Movies, when Grant had wanted to switch parts, director George Stevens suggested they toss a coin; Grant won, and Fairbanks Jr. lost his most important role.

On the other hand, according to a biography of George Stevens by Marilyn Ann Moss entitled *Giant: George Stevens, a Life on Film*, the role of Cutter was originally slated for comedy actor Jack Oakie until Grant requested the part because it would allow him to inject more humor into his performance, at which point Fairbanks Jr. was brought on board to replace Grant as Ballantine.

On a more recent showing of the film on TCM, Ben Mankiewicz contradicted the coin-flip story told by Osborne, stating that Grant was originally chosen to play Sergeant Ballantine and later decided to switch to the more comedic role of Sergeant Cutter. He claimed that after taking over the role Grant had recommended his friend Douglas Fairbanks Jr. for the part. Fairbanks Jr. himself claimed he was cast as Cutter by Howard Hawks, then asked to change.

We will never know the truth of what had really happened.

The great strength of this movie was in the writing, which

became a vehicle for these stars to advance their careers and possibly earn Oscar nominations.

The screenplay, based on a story developed by Ben Hecht and Charles MacArthur from Rudyard Kipling's wonderful narrative poem. Kipling, who died in 1936, had sold the screen rights to his poem to Edward Small and his Reliance Pictures for the sum of £4,700—about $20,000.

RKO acquired the rights as part of a production deal with Small when he moved to the company. William Faulkner did some preliminary script work on the project, which was eventually assigned to Howard Hawks. Hawks got Ben Hecht and Charles MacArthur to write the screenplay, and the film was set to start in 1937. However, Hawks was fired from the project following the commercial failure of *Bringing Up Baby*, and George Stevens was assigned to direct.

The story was a collaborative effort of three highly accomplished writers, including William Faulkner, one of America's greatest novelists. Hecht and MacArthur were two of Hollywood's finest screenwriters, and both were successful playwrights and journalists as well. MacArthur was married to the wonderful Broadway actress Helen Hayes.

In spite of their having collaborated on the story, neither Hecht nor MacArthur were involved in writing the actual screenplay. The reason had always been a mystery to me, and I'm sure I asked my father why they didn't do the screenplay as well as the story. But that was many years ago, and if he gave me the answer, I don't recall what it was. I don't know if there's anyone alive now who could.

Credit for the screenplay went to Joel Sayre Jr., a journalist and novelist, and Fred Guiol, a screenwriter and budding director. There were also uncredited contributions by Lester Cohen, John Colton, William Faulkner, Vincent Lawrence, Dudley Nichols, and Anthony Veiller.

My father had supervised the writing, making notable story contributions of his own, and he took great pride in the finished product. No one felt the loss of those important late scenes more than

Pandro himself, but he was between a rock and a hard place, and he had no choice except to leave them out.

When Dad arrived at the studio on Monday morning, he was handed the huge list of messages from the frantic calls that had come in. Returning them would have to wait until late in the afternoon. There was far more urgent business to attend to, namely, how they could possibly finish the picture without an ending.

As a former film editor, my father knew that an ending would have to be manufactured with film borrowed from other parts of the picture and used in a way that made the audience feel the story was approaching its natural conclusion. That proved to be no easy task, and several highly experienced film editors would be needed.

Dad's brother, Henry Berman, was the editor of record. He had been working on the picture since day one, and he was becoming recognized as one of the top editors in Hollywood. He would later go on to earn Oscars for editing and become a major studio producer.

Two more editors were then added to the project, including John Lockert, a seasoned RKO picture editor, and John Sturges, who would later become one of Hollywood's most notable directors of action movies like *The Great Escape, Gunfight at the O.K. Corral,* and *The Magnificent Seven.*

The editing rooms were off-limits to everyone, including George Stevens, which must have been particularly galling to a director of his stature. A studio cop was placed outside the door to the editing suite, and no one was allowed in.

Dad eventually returned George Stevens' phone calls and promised to allow him to attend the screening once the editors had a first cut ready. He also told him he would be involved in any further changes from that point forward. George could not believe he was being treated this way by a man for whom he had enormous respect —a man who had helped elevate him from cameraman to director— and was now cutting him off from his own picture. But there was nothing he could do except be patient. Eventually, he would be allowed to contribute once again.

Late Monday afternoon, my father began returning the many calls that had come in during the day from actors and others, begging him to change his mind and allow the shooting to continue. Pandro, as always, maintained the stoic calm for which he had become famous, which must have been infuriating to those who saw the picture as a shooting star that could launch their careers.

In a quiet voice, he explained why it was impossible to continue. He told them the financing had dried up, and that there was a very real possibility that RKO could go bankrupt. None of them really believed the studio would close, but they began to understand the gravity of the situation, and eventually, they stopped calling—except for one person.

She was one of Hollywood's biggest stars, and though she was already divorced from Douglas Fairbanks Sr., she tried to use her influence to convince Dad to relent and allow those final scenes to be shot. Mary Pickford argued that because of his wonderful performance in *Morning Glory*, her stepson deserved a chance to elevate his name as an actor. Pickford claimed it was one of the reasons he had accepted the part and that he had been looking forward to those final scenes for months.

My father understood and respected the power Pickford wielded in Hollywood. Even though the advent of sound proved to be her undoing, she was still highly admired for running her own studio and involving herself in every aspect of film production.

My father handled her diplomatically, listening respectfully and pretending to be flattered by her call. But he maintained his calm demeanor and found inoffensive ways to say no. He offered to arrange a special advance screening of the film for her and anyone she wanted to invite—but the bottom line was unchanged: There would be no more shooting.

Over the next month, the re-editing of *Gunga Din* went on at a frantic pace, often going late into the night. Although they were able to solve some major problems, it was evident, that in order to truly end the picture convincingly, they needed critical shots to sell the defeat of the rebels in the final battle and wrap up the movie on an upbeat note.

The edit was finally completed and screened to see if what had worked in the individual scenes, viewed in the editing room on the small screen of the Moviola, would also work in the continuity of the whole picture as seen on the big screen. George Stevens was invited to the screening to see what they had done to his movie. He came into the projection room with a sour look on his face, and at first, it was clear that he thought Dad and the editors had ruined everything. But, as he watched, he became as enamored with the film, as my father and all the editors were.

When the lights came up, they all congratulated each other, and Stevens was ecstatic. "I can't believe you made it work. This is a miracle."

It was about 9:30 p.m. when the screening ended, so they all went across the street to Lucy's, the famous Hollywood restaurant, where the employees of RKO and Paramount Studios used to hang out after work. A few drinks later they were all back to being friends. My father told me that when they were getting up to leave, Stevens gave him a huge bear hug and thanked him for all that he had done for the movie.

After another week of finishing touches in the cutting room, it was agreed that one or two more days of shooting would be required to make the ending more realistic. Stevens came up with some great ideas of how a limited number of specific shots would get the job done, and Dad and the editors agreed.

A couple of weeks later Stevens directed the critical shots that would give the picture the big ending they needed. With permission from the New York office, money for the shoot was borrowed from another RKO picture that was shooting on the lot, and the pick-up shots were made at the RKO ranch in Encino and at a second location near Lake Sherwood. It was much faster and easier not to return to the Lone Pine location, and much less expensive. It was early January and there was snow in the Sierras. Whatever new shots they took would not match what had been shot previously at Lone Pine in any case.

It was no surprise that all of Hollywood was watching the situation unfold with great interest. Everyone in the business thought that *Gunga Din* was a disaster that was well on its way to destroying RKO and sending hundreds of people out into the streets to look for new jobs.

Hollywood was a small town, and news traveled fast, particularly secrets. The paparazzi had reliable sources with the capability of uncovering almost anything. When it became evident that Pandro had "righted the ship," he began to get calls from the most important people in the business, people like Jack Warner and Sam Goldwyn and Daryl Zanuck and his high school buddy, David Selznick. They all thanked him for restoring order to the movie business and for doing things that they had been reluctant to do.

Since the earliest days of silent movies, which were run in empty retail stores at night for a few dozen people sitting in folding chairs, the director had always been king. Up to that point, no one, including heads of studios, had really challenged the authority of the director, even though they had the power to do so. But that had changed thanks to my father.

Even though the power of the director became diminished, it would make a strong comeback years later. With the emergence of independent movie production, and the end of the acting stables, the directors would again rise to power. Today, the best way to get a project off the ground is to attach a major star and a "heavyweight" director.

But back in 1939, my father became the heavyweight. He not only saved *Gunga Din* from box office disaster. He also saved RKO and his own position as production chief. The film earned $1,888,000 in the United States and Canada and $919,000 elsewhere, for a total of $2,807,000. But because of its high production cost, it recorded a loss of $193,000. It was, however, the sixth highest-grossing film nationally in 1939, and that loss would be quickly erased when the film was re-released.

Because of his efforts, my father gained the respect of many of Hollywood's major players, who felt that he had changed the power structure in Hollywood for the betterment of the entire movie industry.

In a later chapter, I will have more to say about the screenplay, the direction, and the performances that made this very controversial motion picture such a major hit. *Gunga Din* was one of many fine pictures released in 1939, which many people consider to be Hollywood's greatest year.

Ironically, my father was not the first studio executive to halt production on a movie before it finished shooting, even though all of Hollywood gave him credit for that. Dad's childhood friend, Irving Thalberg, had shut down a Universal picture many years earlier, but it did not make nearly as big a splash as *Gunga Din*.

In 1922 Erich von Stroheim was directing *Foolish Wives*, a movie about a con artist masquerading as Russian nobility, who attempts to seduce the wife of an American diplomat. Von Stroheim had angered Thalberg by ordering a considerable number of designer gowns for the actresses at outrageous prices. In addition to that, he was well over budget, so Thalberg halted the production. But it wasn't a critical situation like *Gunga Din*, and there were only a couple of days left on the shooting schedule.

There was no fear that Universal would go bankrupt because of the director's extravagance. Thalberg told von Stroheim that he had seen all the film and that there was more than enough footage to complete the picture, and that he was shutting down production.

Von Stroheim, of course, was outraged, and the feud between him and Thalberg quickly became juicy gossip. Everyone knew they hated each other, so Hollywood viewed this more as a personal vendetta than an actual crisis.

The following year, however, von Stroheim was directing another

Universal picture titled *Merry-Go-Round*. He and Thalberg had reached a tacit agreement that this production was not to go a penny over budget or there would be serious consequences. So, when von Stroheim violated the agreement, Thalberg fired him on the spot and hired actor-director Rupert Julian to finish the picture. That was a significant move that should have caused an earthquake in Hollywood. No director had ever been fired from a Hollywood movie before it was finished shooting. But the Hollywood elite viewed this as a natural consequence of the feud between Thalberg and von Stroheim, who was not particularly popular within the industry to begin with.

So *Gunga Din* became the symbol of a more cost-conscious Hollywood, and directors had been put into their proper place as employees, not gods of the cinema.

BRINGING UP BABY (HOLLYWOOD STYLE)

It was three years before the release of *Gunga Din* when my father cast me in a real-life role in one of his three major, non-celluloid productions. My mother had a great deal to do with it as well.

The most wanted baby in Hollywood has finally arrived. After nine years of waiting and hoping, Pandro and Vi Berman are the parents of a six-pound-eleven-ounce baby boy named Harry Michael... The announcement appeared in Louella Parsons' powerful column in the *Los Angeles Examiner* and about four hundred other newspapers in the Hearst syndicate on June 3, 1936. Consequently, I was more famous on my day of birth than on any ensuing day of my life to date.

In some sense, life is a card game, and you must play with the cards you're dealt. I was dealt a royal flush; not only was I born into wealth and privilege but also into the fantasy world of movies and celebrity, and it took years for me to really understand it and deal with it. When I was young, I was naïve enough to think that everyone lived like we did. But, with age and maturity and a broader perspective, I was able to look back more realistically on what it meant to grow up in Hollywood in the "Golden Era." As a child, it was a purple dream seen through rose-colored glasses... almost too good to be true.

Of course, the reason for all of this was that my father was one of Hollywood's three legendary boy-wonders. He had come west with nothing in his pockets and had rapidly ascended to the position of head of production of RKO Studios at the boyish age of twenty-eight.

He got there by producing many exceptional movies, many of which were big box office hits, including nine of the ten Fred Astaire–Ginger Rogers dance pictures.

Those movies uplifted the spirits of audiences in the 1930s when the country was mired in the Great Depression, and they brought money to RKO Studios in the hardest of times.

With the possible exception of sports such as roller skating, movies have always been the cheapest form of good entertainment. During difficult times in the 1930s, moviegoers were able to escape from their troubles, if only for a couple of hours. They fell in love with the beautiful footwork of Fred and Ginger, the brilliant choreography of Hermes Pan, and the wonderful music of Irving Berlin, George Gershwin, Jerome Kern, and other important composers.

My father produced or personally supervised the production of one hundred and thirteen films during his career, which is an unbelievable accomplishment. It's a feat that will never be duplicated, because, these days, it takes years to get a movie project off the ground. The entire career of a movie producer of today might only consist of seven or eight pictures, except, of course, for those at the very top.

If you are one of that small, elite group of power brokers, your phone never stops ringing. When I was a kid, I remember it ringing constantly in our home, even though our phone number was unlisted.

1

GENESIS

Pandro Berman was one of three Jewish boys who attended De Witt Clinton High School in the Bronx during the years 1918 through 1922. Those boys were in the minority at that school, and they had befriended each other in a time of serious need. All three were slight and slender, and the school playground proved to be a challenging—and often dangerous—environment. Squadrons of tough Irish and Italian boys took delight in chasing them down and beating them up. They had to find places to hide—dark niches under the eaves of the school building or the basement with the janitor—during lunch and after school, until it was safe to walk home.

The other two boy wonders were the illustrious Irving Thalberg and the great David O. Selznick, both of whom also emerged as boy geniuses in Hollywood and enjoyed spectacular careers. How they all managed to do it is a fascinating story, which I'll detail throughout this book. But first, there's some essential background I need to share.

The question I've been asked repeatedly throughout my life—by friends, strangers, and curious minds alike—is: "How did your father get the name Pandro?"

Well, it goes back to when our family emigrated from Poland to the United States, just before the turn of the 20th century.

Like many others, our ancestors came to America seeking refuge from oppression and antisemitism—and chasing the opportunity for a better life. My great-grandfather Szmuel (pronounced Shmule), his wife Eva, and five of their seven children arrived at Ellis Island in the late 1880s. My grandfather Harry Berman—Pandro's father—was among them.

They had traveled in steerage, and all were sick upon arrival. Eva was pregnant with the first of two more children, who would be born in the United States. The customs officers couldn't understand their last name—Pandrovitz—no matter how many times Szmuel repeated it. Finally, they asked him if he had any relatives already living in the United States.

He replied, "Berman… in Chicago."

And that was it. Our family officially entered the country as the Bermans.

We've done extensive research on all the Berman families living in Chicago at the time, but we've never been able to determine how—or even if—we were related to any of them. It's entirely possible that old Szmuel (Samuel) invented the name on the spot. He may have panicked in front of the customs officers and blurted it out to avoid risking rejection. Had he said Schnitzer, he would've been telling the truth—we had distant relatives by that name living in Philadelphia.

Years later, I asked my father why Szmuel hadn't mentioned the Schnitzer family. My dad said Szmuel didn't know much about them, and if any of them had been in trouble with the law, the entire family could have been denied entry.

I thought that was incredibly shrewd. I never would've thought of that.

Dad replied, "Szmuel was no dummy. He was a survivor."

He had uprooted his family and brought them to America with no money during unimaginably hard times.

My grandfather Harry, with the blessing of his parents Szmuel and Eva, married a girl from Pittsburgh named Julie Epstein. When they were deciding on a name for their firstborn, Julie thought it was a shame that their real family name had been lost due to the customs officers' ignorance. So, she came up with a way to honor it: she shortened Pandrovitz to Pandro and used it as a first name.

They named my father Pandro Samuel Berman, in honor of the man who brought his family to America and made a living pushing a cart through the Lower East Side of Manhattan.

That's the story I was told as a child when I first asked my father about his name—and I've repeated it many times to anyone with the same curiosity.

My father graduated from De Witt Clinton High School with honors and was accepted into the Wharton School of Business at the University of Pennsylvania. Even back then, it was recognized as the finest business school in America. But his father Harry—after whom I was named—died suddenly, and there was no money for college tuition.

Dad knew he had to go to work right away, but jobs were scarce. The country was slipping into the pre-Depression era. Small businesses were folding, and large companies were laying off workers by the thousands.

His old school chum, Irving Thalberg, had taken an entry-level job in the New York offices of Universal Pictures as secretary to Carl Laemmle, the head of the studio. Thalberg quickly impressed his boss and shot up through the ranks. Within a year, he was sent to Hollywood as studio manager, answering only to Laemmle himself.

In 1923, Thalberg produced the original *Hunchback of Notre Dame* starring Lon Chaney—and it put him on the map. Cecil B. DeMille tried to lure him away to Paramount with several generous offers. He raved about Thalberg, calling him a genius.

But Irving had other ideas. He turned down DeMille and joined

Louis B. Mayer, helping orchestrate the merger of Metro Pictures and Samuel Goldwyn Pictures to form Metro-Goldwyn-Mayer. Despite the inclusion of his name, Goldwyn had no role in MGM's management or production.

Thalberg, however, had an enormous role. He became a master star-maker, credited with launching or shaping the careers of Lon Chaney, Ramon Novarro, John Gilbert, Joan Crawford, Clark Gable, Jean Harlow, Wallace Beery, Luise Rainer, Greta Garbo, Lionel Barrymore—and Norma Shearer, who eventually became his wife.

Louis Mayer treated him like the son he never had. Mayer desperately wanted a son—but was only blessed with daughters.

When Thalberg arrived in Hollywood in 1923, he wrote to my dad, urging him to come west and promising great opportunities in the movie business. Pandro was keenly interested, but he had an agonizing decision to make. His father had left them with very little money. His mother, Julie—who had once worked as a court stenographer—now had to stay home to care for his younger brother Henry, who was nine years his junior.

Henry was a melancholy child, grieving not just the loss of his father but also his little brother Maxie, who had recently died of scarlet fever at the age of three.

Though it broke his heart to leave during such a painful time, my father knew the odds of finding decent work in New York were slim. He had to step up. And with a heavy heart, he packed his bags and headed to California to seek his fortune.

When he arrived, he found this letter tucked in his luggage. It's one of the most inspiring letters I've ever read. My father said it had moved him to tears when he'd read it the first time.

July 20, 1923

>*Pandro darling,*
>*It's terribly hard to give you up, for that's what I'm doing today. No one, but a mother or father could do it, because our love for you is so*

deep that we are willing to cut out our hearts and hand them over to you.

Pandro, I am not going to be sentimental, for you too are feeling this separation keenly. I only want to tell you that I have studied you carefully—far more so than you would think—in the past years, and aside from the fact that you are my son, I cannot help but admire the way you have met the problems that have confronted you.

You did take school very seriously. Your decisions were good, and everything you undertook was handled well by you. You have always been truthful with me, and now that I am giving you to the "mother of all living," I just want to say this: I shall not measure your success in dollars and cents as others will. I want more than that from you. I want, first of all, honesty, then kindness for all your fellow beings, and justice to all.

If—or rather when (for I know you will)—reach the high places, stoop down and lift others up with you. When you arise in the morning and start your day, thank God for your blessings. That will help more than anything else.

And one request before I close: Do not neglect your reading. Read no matter what—but read... and study the philosophers. You will never regret it. And never forget that you have had a wonderful start in life with a loving father—and above all, never forget him, or your brother Henry...

Your Loving Mother

That was the send-off my father received when he took his friend Thalberg's advice and came to Hollywood. He kept the letter in his pocket and read it over and over again, until it was ragged and falling apart. It was his inspiration to keep fighting through difficult times. My sisters and I each have old carbon-paper copies—blurred and barely legible—and even those are extremely worn. That letter is a classic. It still moves me to tears occasionally when I re-read it.

Thalberg was right about the opportunities that existed in Hollywood, but it took a while for my father to fully take advantage of them. Dad's other friend, David Selznick, eventually came to Hollywood as well, but like Thalberg, he began his film career in New York. He worked for his father, Lewis J. Selznick, who operated a small but not terribly successful film company, which went bankrupt in 1923. Still, it provided a valuable opportunity for David and his brother Myron to learn the rudiments of the motion picture business.

David served as corporate director of Lewis J. Selznick Pictures and dabbled in writing and producing. That experience—along with his father's connections—got him a job as an assistant story editor at Metro-Goldwyn-Mayer. Myron would go on to become one of Hollywood's most successful talent agents. He traveled to Europe and signed an impressive number of promising actors to personal contracts and sold them to Hollywood, where they became stars. One of his great acquisitions was Vivien Leigh, whom he brought to his brother David to play Scarlett O'Hara in *Gone with the Wind*.

A HUMBLE BEGINNING

My father's first job in Hollywood was something less than glamorous. He was an entry-level assistant in the camera department, tasked with driving a truck out to the Mojave Desert at five o'clock in the morning—before sunrise. There, he would load film into the camera magazines using a black bag in the back of the truck, to avoid exposing it to light. At sunrise, they began shooting the old Tom Mix and Ken Maynard Western serials, which were quite popular at the time.

How Dad got that job is not entirely clear, but his father, Harry, had been a crack film salesman at F.B.O. (Film Booking Office of America)—the company that eventually became RKO when it merged with Radio Corporation of America and the Keith-Albee and

Orpheum theater circuits. Harry was well-liked in the company, so it's possible that his goodwill helped Pandro get his foot in the door.

After that, though, it was all on Dad's shoulders, and he seized every opportunity that came his way. He found himself a small apartment in Hollywood near the RKO/Paramount studio lot at Melrose and Gower. In those days, both companies shared production facilities, though RKO was much smaller and occupied far less space.

Dad threw himself into the job and worked long hours. He told me he found people in California to be a lot nicer than New Yorkers, and he had no trouble making new friends.

He took most of his meals at Musso and Frank Grill on Hollywood Boulevard, which has been serving great food at reasonable prices since 1919. Since there was no commissary on the lot, many RKO and Paramount employees ate there, and the crowd was small enough that RKO executives often knew crew members by name—whether they were grips, script clerks, or makeup artists. My dad enjoyed the "small-town" atmosphere of that restaurant and became a regular.

He began working for very little money. RKO paid him a meager starting salary of $25 a week, which was difficult to live on—even in 1923. But he was also supporting his mother and younger brother, so he sent half of it back to New York every week. Somehow, they managed to live on it. Dad took pride in the fact that he never missed a Friday night wire payment at Western Union, no matter what sacrifices he had to make or what debt he had to incur.

Living up to that challenge was undoubtedly a character-building experience—and one I believe helped prepare him to handle the enormous responsibilities he would eventually face as the head of a Hollywood studio. I used to marvel at those stories as a boy and once asked him what kept him going under all that pressure.

His answer was always the same: "I had no choice."

I often wondered why Dad never went to Thalberg for help when he first arrived, but I hesitated to ask. Given the disparity in their careers during those early days, I thought it might be an embarrassing question—so I never brought it up.

The truth is, he didn't need help from Thalberg. He was fortunate to find a great mentor who took a liking to him and gave him the boost he needed. His name was William Le Baron, head of production at RKO and a producer of quality films—some of which were big hits.

Le Baron rescued my father from the camera department and placed him in the editing room, saying, "Now you will learn something about how to make a movie."

Dad wasn't particularly happy in the editing department, which required enormous patience and strong organizational skills to manage thousands of feet of film. But he stuck with it. Within two years, he'd moved from apprentice to assistant editor, and finally to picture editor—where he could truly show his creative side, even though most of the movies he worked on weren't exactly masterpieces.

He was credited with editing such cinematic treasures as *Stocks and Blondes*, *Texas Tornado*, and several other forgettable RKO titles. He always told me he learned a lot about filmmaking in the editing room, though I knew he truly hated the work.

At the end of 1929, Le Baron rescued him again. He called Dad into his office and told him talking pictures were the next big thing. Warner Brothers had just released *The Jazz Singer*, and Columbia was beginning to make "talkies." Le Baron wanted to bring sound to RKO, and he arranged a job for my father in the new sound department at Columbia.

Dad was to spend several months there learning everything he could about sound production. He would then return to RKO as Le Baron's assistant, with the title of associate producer on the films Le Baron personally produced or supervised.

He accepted the assignment and worked at Columbia for about six months. During that time, he compiled extensive notes to bring back to his mentor. When he finally returned, Le Baron was thrilled.

Dad's research became the foundation for sound film production at RKO. He began his new role with confidence, enthusiasm—and a substantial raise.

He threw himself into the work with such dedication that he became something of a "time and motion" study. He often worked late into the night without complaint. Overtime didn't exist in those days, but that didn't matter. The work fascinated him, and he was learning fast.

He had enormous respect for William Le Baron, who had been hired by Jesse Lasky to head production at Famous Players–Lasky—a merger of small film companies controlled by Adolph Zukor that eventually became Paramount Pictures. Making Le Baron head of production was seen as an impulsive and risky move by Hollywood insiders. After all, he had limited Broadway experience, mostly as a playwright, and no real film background. But it turned out to be a stroke of brilliance. Le Baron produced several successful pictures for Lasky and earned his credibility.

In 1929, he left Lasky to become head of production at FBO and stayed through the transitional mergers that created RKO by combining RCA, the Keith-Albee and Orpheum theater circuits, and FBO Studios. Le Baron was named head of production at the new studio.

That same year, he undertook an ambitious big-budget musical that became a huge hit. *Rio Rita* was the film adaptation of a popular Broadway musical that he co-produced with its creator, Florenz Ziegfeld Jr. The movie starred John Boles and the electrifying Bebe Daniels, along with the comedy team of Bert Wheeler and Robert Woolsey. It grossed $2.4 million on a $678,000 budget—the largest in the studio's history—and became the biggest hit of 1929. Le Baron was proud to have beaten *Broadway Melody of 1929*, Metro's first musical talkie, to release.

Le Baron also produced *Cimarron*, one of Hollywood's most celebrated Westerns, which won him the Oscar for Best Picture in 1931.

That was my father's first assignment as Le Baron's executive assistant, and he never forgot the thrill of getting that job.

I was twelve years old when he told me the story. We were driving down to Palm Springs one Friday evening, and I'd never seen him so animated. He described the assignment in vivid detail, saying it was his first real accomplishment since leaving New York. He'd already been a skilled assistant director and editor, but this was different. This was something he could be proud of. He beamed as he told the story.

Dad knew he was in good hands working directly with the head of the studio. He would go to Le Baron's office at the end of a long day, and the two of them would share a drink while reviewing plans for the next. Le Baron kept orange juice in the refrigerator and scotch in his desk drawer. They mixed the two—something that sounded to me like oysters with chocolate sauce—but Dad said he got used to it and even started to like it. Later, of course, he drank his scotch with soda—and always kept it locked up in the library bar, wary that the hired help might sneak a glass or two.

Following *Cimarron*, Dad worked on a great number of Le Baron's films as both assistant director and associate producer—including the original *King Kong*, collaborating with the legendary Merian C. Cooper. He also worked with famed director Tod Browning on the 1931 version of *Dracula*, starring Bela Lugosi.

Afterward, Browning tried to lure my father to MGM to work on *Freaks*, a film about a traveling circus filled with sideshow curiosities: midgets, limbless performers, pinheads, conjoined twins, a bearded lady, and a half-man/half-woman. Browning promised my father the moon—including producer status on all his upcoming projects. But Dad wouldn't leave his mentor at RKO.

Freaks was a wild, ambitious film featuring acts from circuses all over the world. It caused a stir, and everyone rushed to see these so-called human oddities. But in the end, *Freaks* was a box office disappointment, grossing only $289,000 in the U.S. and $52,000 internationally—for a total loss of $164,000.

Dad had made the right call by staying with Le Baron.

He threw himself into every new assignment with the same enthusiasm and discipline. He began to realize that Thalberg had been right—there was tremendous opportunity out West.

He sat in on production meetings with Le Baron and the other producers, learning all he could. He got to know the prominent agents, worked with every RKO-contracted director, and earned their trust. He was respectful, quiet, and reliable—and everyone knew he'd been chosen for good reason.

Years later, when I entered the business, he gave me the same advice someone had once given him when he started working with Le Baron:

"Keep your ears open and your mouth shut until you have the most brilliant idea to solve a dilemma. When you just can't hold it in any longer, deliver it in a few short words—and then shut your mouth again. At some point, they'll realize you might be valuable in an elevated position."

I smiled when he told me that. But I eventually found out how right he was.

In 1929, Le Baron gave Dad creative authority over the editing of *Rio Rita*, and, having cut seven RKO pictures himself, he made smart editorial decisions.

But in a shocking turn of events, my father's great mentor left RKO in 1931 after a dispute over his film *The Gay Diplomat*. That was the official reason given—but the real reason was disappointing box office returns. Most of Hollywood knew it.

Dad stepped in immediately, assuming his mentor's responsibilities. He finished Le Baron's unfinished films and supervised the rest of the studio's productions. By that time, he'd gained the experience to do the job—and he did it well enough to earn the support of several key executives back in New York.

2

STUDIO SHARKS AND POWER PLAYS

In 1931, when Pandro was appointed temporary Head of Production at RKO, the studio was being run by a group led by Benjamin Kahane. Kahane had been chief counsel for the Orpheum Theater circuit when it merged with the Keith-Albee theaters and RCA to form Radio-Keith-Orpheum. FBO—Film Booking Office of America—was a small silent-era studio that played a crucial role in that merger. It was the production facility the group needed to make movies.

Naturally, these various factions were locked in a fierce power struggle, each lobbying for their preferred candidate to become the permanent Head of Production. Pandro was a politically safe choice as a temporary appointee, but everyone knew there would be a battle ahead when it came time to fill the position permanently.

FBO owned 460 acres out in the Pacific Palisades near the ocean, where they filmed non-Western action pictures and romantic melodramas. But perhaps even more important was FBO's robust distribution wing, headed by my grandfather, Harry Berman. He had built a network of bookings with small-town theaters across America—FBO's bread and butter. Since they didn't have major stars under contract like the big studios did, FBO specialized in lower-budget "little pictures," and they didn't have to compete for big-city theater chains. Audiences in smaller towns were happy to watch films without famous names, and FBO was happy to supply them.

But after the merger, everything changed.

RKO set its sights higher. It moved into the big-studio marketplace and began producing more ambitious, "bigger pictures." It was a massive gamble, but my father believed it was necessary if RKO was going to be a serious player in the motion picture industry.

When the company needed a major star, they would rent one from a big studio—at an exorbitant cost. But it was a calculated risk. If the film was a hit, the borrowed star would have packed theaters. Eventually, RKO followed the major studio model and began signing its own contract players. A few of them became legitimate stars—and started bringing in real money for the company.

My grandfather had started to forge relationships with theater owners in larger cities, and thanks to those efforts—and my father's bold decisions—RKO's prestige began to rise in the industry. Eight years had passed since my grandfather died, and now his son was stepping up to lead the very company his father had helped build.

Around this time, Joseph Kennedy—the former champion of small-town movies and FBO's largest stockholder—began to get cold feet. As RKO pivoted toward bigger, riskier productions, Kennedy decided the gamble wasn't worth it. He sold off his shares and left the company altogether.

The movie business has always been a risky one, but the bold moves my father was making at RKO were on a whole other level. More than once, the executives back at the parent company in New York were left holding their breath.

PANDRO S. BERMAN

THE BIRTH OF A PRODUCER

My father's first challenge as acting Head of Production at RKO was to rescue *The Gay Diplomat*. LeBaron had exited the studio over creative clashes with the New York office, but the production was also running significantly over budget, and there were issues with the leading lady, Betty Compson, who was unhappy with how her role was developing. It was no small feat to smooth over objections from all sides and still try to make the picture a success.

One of Dad's greatest gifts was diplomacy. With his calm demeanor and intelligent problem-solving, he managed to appease both Betty Compson and the New York executives. He brought in screenwriter Alfred Jackson to punch up the dialogue and had the director reshoot several scenes with Compson—subtle changes that elevated her performance and satisfied the front office.

The film still wasn't a hit, but Dad limited the losses to $50,000—far better than the projected $150,000 deficit. It wasn't a success, but it also wasn't a disaster. And that alone was enough to convince the New York office they might have picked the right man—at least temporarily—to succeed LeBaron.

Dad oversaw other projects in 1931, but the first film he produced solo was *Bad Company*, a pre-Code gangster flick starring Ricardo Cortez and the fresh-faced Helen Twelvetrees. The film was a thinly veiled nod to Al Capone—both fascinating and terrifying to the public during the Great Depression. Directed by Tay Garnett, an RKO regular, the film featured strong performances and modest financial success. For my father, it was a step forward—and the beginning of bigger opportunities.

Impressed with Cortez's performance, Dad cast him opposite Irene Dunne in *Symphony of Six Million*, which became a major hit (more on that in a later chapter).

It took over a year to name a permanent replacement for LeBaron. That honor went to my father's old school friend, David Selznick—who promptly fired nearly everyone... except Dad.

Selznick made it clear that it wasn't nostalgia keeping him on board. It was merit. He respected Dad's work and believed they could collaborate effectively.

Selznick had rapidly risen through the story department at MGM, produced two films, and moved to Paramount before landing at RKO. Like my father, he had helped usher in the era of sound films, and he was pleased that Dad had already modernized RKO using Columbia's sound system.

With several pet projects of his own, Selznick let Dad keep running the slate. He reviewed the productions Dad was overseeing and saw no red flags. He left my father to manage day-to-day operations while focusing on his own pictures. Selznick hired an assistant to manage the details on his projects and trusted Dad to handle the rest.

He'd still screen all of Dad's films, occasionally offering edits before they were finalized, and he personally reviewed the answer prints to ensure quality before approving wide release. Other than that, Dad was free to sink or swim. Thankfully, he swam.

Selznick was married to Irene Mayer, daughter of MGM mogul Louis B. Mayer. Her sister, Edith, was married to William Goetz, later head of Universal and producer of classics like *Sayonara*. In Hollywood, those weren't just marriages—they were mergers, forging dynasties that shaped the industry.

The Berman and Selznick families were close socially, too. My mother and Irene Selznick were dear friends and pregnant at the same time. Irene's son, Danny, was born two weeks before me in May 1936. We were often playpen buddies—just like our fathers, we became lifelong friends.

The Selznicks lived atop Summit Drive in Benedict Canyon, with a panoramic view of Los Angeles. I spent many early days there with Danny while our mothers lunched and chatted. Summit Drive was "Celebrity Row" back then. The Selznick house was across the street from Charlie Chaplin, a wildly aggressive tennis player, who was constantly depositing tennis balls into the

Selznick's east garden, and it became Danny's least favorite task to return them.

Next door to Chaplin was Fred Astaire, who at the time was working with my dad on the beloved Astaire/Rogers musicals. Fred was deeply devoted to his wife, the elegant and reserved Phyllis Potter. They had two children—Fred Jr. and Ava. Ava was a classmate of my sister, Cindy, and a frequent guest at our Friday night movies and family dinners.

Phyllis and Fred often attended wrap parties at our home, which my mother hosted to celebrate Dad's film shoots. Both were quiet and charming, preferring conversations with familiar collaborators like George and Ira Gershwin and choreographer Hermes Pan.

Phyllis died tragically in 1954 at just 46. Fred was devastated. He stayed in the house alone with his children, heartbroken and reclusive. It wasn't until 1980, when both kids had left home, that he remarried—this time to Robyn Smith, a spirited young jockey. Fred couldn't bring himself to live in the same home he'd shared with Phyllis, so he bought the empty lot next door and built a new house with Robyn.

Just three doors down stood the legendary estate of Mary Pickford and Douglas Fairbanks: Pickfair. It was a palatial home atop a steep driveway, surrounded by a towering white wall and guarded by massive stone gateposts, each topped with a baby angel. The wrought-iron gates were as tall and impenetrable as a fortress.

Tour buses often cruised by, hoping for a glimpse of the couple dubbed "Hollywood royalty." Danny used to puzzle over those baby angels, thinking lions or eagles would've been more fitting. We eventually figured Mary Pickford imagined her home as a sort of heaven on earth—baby angels and all.

Across from Pickfair lived the powerhouse agent Sam Jaffe, who represented many of Hollywood's brightest stars. Sam and his wife, Mildred, were close friends with both our family and the Selznicks. Danny and I grew up alongside their daughters, and we all remain close to this day.

MICHAEL BERMAN

RISING THROUGH THE REELS...AND THE RANKS

In 1932, my father produced a screwball comedy titled *The Half-Naked Truth*. He didn't talk much about it, so I always assumed it wasn't a favorite. I hadn't seen it until years later, on Turner Classic Movies—and let's just say, it's far from a classic. The film has a certain wild charm but falls short of greatness.

The plot follows a washed-up carnival barker who reinvents a sideshow singer into a Broadway star. Lupe Vélez, the fiery Latina known as "The Mexican Spitfire," stars in the leading role. Though she appeared in 45 films, Vélez is arguably more remembered for her Hollywood romances—including a marriage to Johnny Weissmuller, the original and most iconic Tarzan, and a torrid relationship with Gary Cooper.

Her performance in *The Half-Naked Truth* veered into caricature—over-the-top and farcical. Lee Tracy, as the barker, was loud, smug, and constantly chuckling at his own jokes. Still, there were some memorable performances from beloved character actors like Franklin Pangborn and Frank Morgan. Morgan, who played the Broadway producer in the film, would go on to achieve cinematic immortality as the Wizard in *The Wizard of Oz*—utterer of the immortal line, "Pay no attention to the man behind the curtain."

Despite the chaos, director Gregory La Cava held the production together and, astonishingly, the film made a $50,000 profit. My father always listed it as one of "the worst pictures I ever made"—but a profitable flop still counts as a win in Hollywood math.

Gregory La Cava, however, was a different story. Dad held him in the highest regard. La Cava had started out as a cartoonist and animator, working with Walter Lantz on *The Katzenjammer Kids*. He transitioned into directing live-action films during World War I. Dad admired his ability to soothe difficult actors and credited him with taming the notoriously temperamental W.C. Fields—a feat few directors managed.

That same year, 1932, Dad produced the critically acclaimed *What Price Hollywood*, a film that would set the template for all future *A Star is Born* stories. It was written by journalist Gene Fowler, one of Hollywood's most amusing and acerbic characters and based on an original story by Adela Rogers St. Johns (which earned an Oscar nomination) It introduced my father's longtime collaboration with director George Cukor.

The film follows the well-worn but still poignant tale of a young actress on the rise and a once-great director in decline. Cukor coaxed a deeply nuanced performance from Constance Bennett, while Dad insisted on casting Lowell Sherman as the fading director—over Cukor's objections. Dad won the argument, and rightly so. Sherman's portrayal was layered and heartbreaking, and it practically stole the show.

With strong supporting roles from Gregory Ratoff and Louise Beavers, *What Price Hollywood* was a hit, and Selznick was impressed. He saw it as a validation of his decision to keep Dad on board.

The film's legacy is remarkable. Selznick remade it five years later at MGM as *A Star is Born* (1937), starring Janet Gaynor and Fredric March. Directed by William Wellman, it was a greater commercial success. In 1954, it was remade again—this time with Judy Garland and James Mason under Cukor's direction—and was heralded as a masterpiece. Then came Barbra Streisand and Kris Kristofferson in 1976, with the story reimagined for the rock 'n' roll era. Finally, in 2018, the story was told once more, starring Bradley Cooper and Lady Gaga, garnering awards and nominations—including an Oscar for Lady Gaga's original song and nominations for Cooper's direction and screenplay.

In 1933, Dad took a left turn into horror with *The Monkey's Paw*, co-produced with Merian C. Cooper. This was his one and only foray into the genre—and he had to be talked into it. Based on the famous cautionary tale about three wishes with dire consequences, it was a faithful adaptation of the story that had been staged and filmed multiple times since its origins in British fiction.

In this version, a young man is killed in a tragic freight accident. His parents receive the cursed paw and, predictably, wish their son back to life—inviting horrifying consequences. The film was successful, but Dad never returned to horror. When I mentioned it to him years later, he just shrugged: "Fantasies are not my cup of tea. I like real movies about real people. Let Walt Disney do the fantasies."

Later that year, Dad worked again with Cooper on *King Kong*, serving as associate producer—though his responsibilities on that film far exceeded the title.

1933 turned out to be a breakout year. Dad produced four major films—each critically acclaimed and financially successful.

One standout was *The Silver Cord*, adapted from a play by Pulitzer Prize-winner Sidney Howard. The film starred Joel McCrea and Irene Dunne, but the real star was Laura Hope Crews, who gave a powerhouse performance as a controlling, manipulative mother. The emotional stakes were high: two sons trying to start lives of their own, only to be emotionally throttled by their overbearing mother. Crews' portrayal was suffocating and brilliant—an avalanche of guilt in human form. It's among my father's finest works, though rarely remembered.

Howard, incidentally, also penned *They Knew What They Wanted*, which became the Broadway musical *The Most Happy Fella*, and his final screenplay was *Gone with the Wind*. Tragically, he died in a freak tractor accident before the film's release.

That same year, Dad paired Joel McCrea again—this time with Constance Bennett—in *Bed of Roses*. She played a reformed prostitute trying to live a respectable life after prison. Bennett, known for glamour, had to lean into grit and humor to sell the role. She pulled it off, crafting a performance both brassy and vulnerable. While not a top ten classic, it was a sharp, romantic comedy with heart.

But 1933's biggest success was *Symphony of Six Million*. Dad had been impressed by Ricardo Cortez in *Bad Company*, and here, he cast him as a Jewish doctor from New York's Lower East Side—breaking from the typical "Latin lover" typecast Cortez had been stuck in.

The story followed the doctor's rise to a posh Park Avenue practice and his estrangement from his roots and his childhood sweetheart—played by Irene Dunne—until a family crisis pulls him back to his humble origins. He must operate on his father to save his life, and in doing so, rediscovers his humanity and love. It was a classic tearjerker—and a huge hit with audiences.

Dad often said, "That was the first decent movie I ever made." A humble statement, but far from the truth. He was a self-critical perfectionist, even when he succeeded. I just wanted him to enjoy his victories.

Danny Selznick and I hadn't seen *Symphony of Six Million*—it was never aired on TV. So, in the early 1950s, his father arranged a private screening for us at Selznick International Pictures. Though a bit dated, the film held up beautifully. We laughed in a few unintentional places, but we both walked away knowing why it had been so beloved.

In my opinion, it was every bit as powerful as *What Price Hollywood*. When I told my father that, he smirked, rolled his eyes, and said, "You might be right about that." He had a wonderful sense of humor—a bright counterbalance to the quiet shadows he occasionally carried.

The final triumph of 1933 was *Morning Glory*. Starring Katharine Hepburn, Douglas Fairbanks Jr., and Adolphe Menjou, the film told the story of a hopeful young actress navigating heartbreak and hardship on her journey to Broadway success. Hepburn won her first Academy Award for the role—cementing her place in Hollywood. Dad would go on to produce fourteen films with her.

She became a frequent guest in our home. I adored listening to her speak. That crisp, mid-Atlantic accent—so uniquely "Hepburn"—was unmistakable and enchanting.

3

CLASHING EGOS AND CLENCHED FISTS

In 1933, David Selznick left RKO to return to MGM, where his father-in-law, Louis B. Mayer, established a second prestige production unit for David, parallel to the one he had created for his beloved Irving Thalberg. Hollywood insiders were quietly snickering at a cruel joke making the rounds. It was a parody of the Ernest Hemingway novel *The Sun Also Rises*. In reference to Selznick's move to MGM, it was mockingly retitled: *The Son-in-Law Also Rises*.

Not everyone in Hollywood thought it was funny—and my dad was one of those not laughing. He knew his childhood buddy was an exceptional talent as well as a savvy businessman, and he thought the joke was deeply unfair. It was undoubtedly born of jealousy, which is certainly no stranger to Hollywood.

Louis B. Mayer wasn't stupid. He surrounded himself with the best people in the business, which is why he lasted nearly forty years as the ruling monarch of MGM. His faith in his son-in-law paid off handsomely—right from David's first year on the lot. Selznick's early MGM output included the all-star ensemble *Dinner at Eight* (1933),

David Copperfield (1935), *Anna Karenina* (1935), and *A Tale of Two Cities* (1935), which was nominated for Best Picture and Best Editing. That last film also helped establish Ronald Colman as a major star.

Merian C. Cooper replaced Selznick as Head of Production at RKO later in 1933, with my dad staying on as his assistant. He worked with Cooper on *King Kong*, earning credit as associate producer. Although we never spoke about it directly, I knew that being passed over was one of my father's great disappointments. But fate had other plans. Cooper left RKO the following year, and my father was immediately appointed to replace him—this time as Head of Production, and this time, it was permanent. His appointment made front-page news in all the trades. I've proudly saved a copy of *The Hollywood Reporter* with Dad's picture beneath the headline.

My mother threw an enormous party to celebrate, inviting fifty or sixty of Hollywood's elite, all dressed to the nines in tuxedos and evening gowns. The champagne flowed like beer at a Polish wedding. Years later, she told me how proud she was of Dad that night—how much he deserved the recognition. She had an inner glow when she told me that story, something I rarely saw anymore, and I was touched to see how deeply she loved him. I would've given anything to have been at that party, to see her that happy. But I hadn't been born yet.

As I mentioned earlier, the year I was born, my father made *Swing Time*—which he considered the best of the Astaire/Rogers musicals, along with *Shall We Dance* and *Top Hat*. Sixty years after its release, critic Roger Ebert agreed. In his retrospective review for the *Chicago Sun-Times*, he wrote:

> Fred Astaire and Ginger Rogers headline Swing Time, the romantic spirit-lifter buoyed by a sublime Jerome Kern/Dorothy Fields score, nimble direction by Academy Award winner George Stevens, and Fred and Ginger's effortless dancing. The blithe "Pick Yourself Up," the Oscar-winning "The Way You Look Tonight," the moving "Never Gonna Dance" ode to love and loss, and Fred's "Bojangles of Harlem"

tap tribute to the great Bill "Bojangles" Robinson—they all stand out among the standouts in a film widely acknowledged as one of the pair's best.

Mom and Dad hosted another spectacular party for the release of *Swing Time*. George Stevens arrived with Ginger Rogers—they'd become great friends during the shoot. Jerome Kern and Dorothy Fields were there too, having just won a well-deserved Oscar for "The Way You Look Tonight." The guest list was packed with Hollywood royalty from every major studio, and the party made the trades—not just for its glamour, but because of a rather shocking incident that took place that night.

Unfortunately, I can't remember the name—though my father told it to me when I was old enough to appreciate the story—but some RKO executive, not a fan of George Stevens and definitely a few martinis deep, approached George and Ginger in the front hallway and slurred, "The problem with you, George, is that you've let Ginger's success go to your head."

Ginger bristled with fury. She slapped him—right across the face.

He responded, "Why don't you let your boyfriend do his own fighting?"

That's all George needed to hear.

He took off his jacket and shoved the executive out the front door and onto the lawn. There were several limousines parked in the driveway and on the street, and when the chauffeurs realized a fight was breaking out, they quickly formed a ring around the two men. For them, it was like ringside seats to Dempsey vs. Tunney.

Inside the house, my mother heard the commotion and ran outside to see what was happening. When she saw the two men locked in combat, she screamed at them to stop and threatened to call the police. They didn't stop—but Stevens ended the whole thing with a roundhouse punch that knocked the executive flat, face down in the muddy grass.

Then George walked over, took the champagne flute out of my mother's hand, and said, "Thanks, Vi... I could use a drink."

My father missed the entire thing. He was upstairs in his den at a large card table, playing poker with the Marx Brothers—and getting shellacked. Years later, he confessed to me that he'd lost more than $15,000 that night, and his accountant had been furious.

Before leaving the party, Chico Marx pulled my mother aside and said, "You really shouldn't let him play with us anymore." He grinned and added, "It's as easy as taking candy from a baby."

FROM BOX OFFICE BOOM TO BUST

In 1934, RKO acquired the rights to Somerset Maugham's heartbreaking novel *Of Human Bondage*, and my dad produced the film, borrowing a young contract player from Warner Bros. named Bette Davis to star opposite Leslie Howard. Bette earned an Oscar nomination for her performance, and the picture catapulted her to stardom. It also made a lot of money for RKO, which, at the time, was in serious need of a hit.

Jack Warner was thrilled to suddenly have a major box office attraction in Bette Davis and, in a fit of generosity (or shrewd business sense), offered my dad the entire stable of Warner contract players at discount rates—that is, all the players who weren't yet stars. The offer did not include names like Humphrey Bogart, Lauren Bacall, James Cagney, Edward G. Robinson... or Bette Davis, for that matter. Even though Dad had helped ignite her star, she was now off-limits.

Later that year, Dad finally made a real turkey—and I don't mean the one served at Thanksgiving dinner. It was an ill-fated picture called *Man of Two Worlds*, starring a handsome Czech actor named Francis Lederer, who had been a big deal in German films. In America, however, he never achieved true stardom, despite Irving Thalberg's best efforts to launch his career in Hollywood.

Man of Two Worlds certainly didn't help. Everyone at RKO and MGM was hoping it would introduce Lederer to American audiences in a big way, but my dad had misgivings even before the out-of-town sneak preview. He never truly liked the script—though he managed to talk himself into believing it was production-ready—and despite a fair amount of excitement around the studio about this new heartthrob, Lederer's performance left both Dad and the director a little cold.

When my parents arrived in Santa Barbara for the preview, the theater was sold out. That never happened on a weeknight unless a major production was being screened, and word had leaked out. In those cases, Hollywood folks might drive up just to get an early look, especially publicists or paparazzi.

But this wasn't a major picture. The packed house felt suspicious. Dad looked around for familiar faces—studio folks, columnists, friends—but found none. When the screening ended, the audience filed out quietly. There was no electric buzz of conversation, no excited chatter—the kind of energy you usually hear when people love what they've just seen.

Some audience members did stop to fill out preview cards, which offered a sliver of hope. Typically, if someone really dislikes a movie, they don't bother filling one out—they just want to leave.

The next morning, someone from publicity brought the cards to Dad's office. He and the director started reading them. Most had little to say about the story or direction—but they raved about Francis Lederer. Comments like: "This is not a great movie, but Francis Lederer is a great actor" and "Francis Lederer is Hollywood's next big star."

Dad was stunned by the outpouring of praise for such a mediocre performance. It plagued him for a day or two, but he eventually figured it out.

Lederer had packed the theater with at least fifty of his Hollywood pals and their dates—some actors, some extras—whom he'd instructed to quietly attend, sit through the movie, and then leave behind glowing preview cards. That's why no one in the audience looked familiar to Dad or to the publicity staff at the preview.

Despite Thalberg's efforts to turn him into a leading man, Lederer never reached that level of fame in Hollywood. His little stunt didn't quite work the way he'd hoped. Strangely enough, Dad still cast him in another RKO movie the following year—*Romance in Manhattan*, opposite Ginger Rogers. Because of Lederer's good looks, Ginger believed the film would turn them into a hot on-screen couple. It didn't. The movie wasn't a hit, and they never worked together again.

Still, Lederer continued to get work. He invested wisely in real estate and lived comfortably into his 100s in a Spanish-style villa with a stable in Canoga Park.

My father was furious with himself for making *Man of Two Worlds* against his better judgment. And to add insult to injury, he had another flop that same year.

It was an absurd musical comedy with the title *Down to Their Last Yacht*. I only found out about it when I was twelve, flipping through a yearly edition of *Fame Magazine* while waiting in Dad's office to go to lunch. The title made me laugh—it sounded like something I'd want to see. At that age, I wanted to watch every movie ever made.

When I asked my dad about it, he grimaced.

"I must have been out of my mind to make that picture," he said. "Selznick talked me into it. I should never have listened to him."

Two flops in a row might spell the end of a career in Hollywood. I often wondered if Dad felt vulnerable, if he feared that it was all over—but I never had the nerve to ask. I didn't need to. He bounced back quickly, with another string of hits—beginning with a very different kind of musical.

PANDRO S. BERMAN

TENORS, TIARAS, AND TINSELTOWN

In 1934, Columbia Pictures released a movie called *One Night of Love* starring the internationally renowned Metropolitan Opera soprano Grace Moore. It was a big risk—opera-themed films had traditionally flopped at the box office—but this one became a runaway hit. The film captured three Oscars and earned four additional nominations, including Best Picture and Best Actress for Grace Moore. With a beautiful score by Victor Schertzinger and lyrics by Gus Kahn, it charmed the critics and surprised the industry.

Riding that success, several studios scrambled to sign sopranos for their own operatic ventures. MGM already had Jeanette MacDonald, and they paired her with Nelson Eddy in *Rose Marie*, which turned into another major box office triumph. Meanwhile, my father signed Lily Pons—a celebrated coloratura soprano who had performed in opera houses across the globe. She was not only vocally gifted but also stunningly beautiful, with a smile that could light up a theater.

Dad cast her opposite a young Henry Fonda in *I Dream Too Much*, and together they were wonderful, borrowing a touch of glitter from the Fred Astaire and Ginger Rogers magic. Pons became especially famous for singing "The Bell Song" from *Lakmé* by Léo Delibes, and she delivered it to perfection in the film, hitting notes most sopranos could only dream of. She also performed lovely new songs by Jerome Kern and Dorothy Fields—and even danced under the direction of choreographer Hermes Pan. The film resonated with audiences in both America and Europe, leading to three more films for Lily Pons and a long, celebrated run at the Metropolitan Opera.

My mother was one of her biggest fans. Around the time the movie was released, we got a Doberman Pinscher puppy—and Mom named her "Pons" after the opera star. By the time I was four years old, Pons (the dog) was fully grown and became my playful guardian. She was gentle, protective, and the first family dog I can remember.

That same year, my father had another enormous hit: *The Gay*

Divorcee, one of the beloved Astaire/Rogers dance musicals—and always my personal favorite. In that film, Fred and Ginger introduced "The Continental," a dazzling seventeen-minute dance number that won the very first Academy Award for Best Original Song. With music by Con Conrad and lyrics by Herb Magidson, it was not only a spectacular performance but a major hit in record stores. The film also received three additional Oscar nominations, including Best Picture of 1934.

Cole Porter's haunting "Night and Day" was featured in the movie, as well as a charming cameo performance by a very young Betty Grable. She would later become the favorite pin-up girl of American soldiers during World War II—and my favorite pin-up, too. That blonde hair, creamy complexion, and those legs? Unforgettable.

The Gay Divorcee was a smash, earning $1,800,000 in worldwide theater rentals with a negative cost of just $520,000—a huge profit in the 1930s. Dad immediately began gearing up the studio to make more of those pictures.

Now, as I mentioned earlier, "negative cost" refers to the total of pre-production, production, and post-production expenses—including the cutting of the master negative—before prints are made. Advertising and distribution costs were not included. Back then, making physical prints was wildly expensive. Today, of course, those costs have been virtually eliminated. Everything is digital now: movies are streamed into theaters electronically or transferred to DVD or Blu-ray for home viewing.

One of the biggest challenges Dad faced with the Astaire/Rogers films was securing truly great music. Sure, there were plenty of capable Hollywood composers who could write a nice score—but very few could write hit songs like the Tin Pan Alley greats: Irving Berlin, George Gershwin, and the like. Those boys only wanted to write for Broadway. They saw movies as second-tier entertainment.

But my father had a way of winning people over. He could twist your arm so gently, you didn't even realize it was happening. Eventually, most of the big-name songwriters ended up composing for his movies.

One of the best results of that effort was *Roberta*, released in 1935. In addition to Fred and Ginger, it featured Irene Dunne and a young Randolph Scott, who was on the verge of stardom. The score—by Jerome Kern and Dorothy Fields, with extra lyrics by Otto Harbach—was one of the best they ever wrote. It included "Yesterdays," later re-recorded by The Beatles, and "Smoke Gets in Your Eyes," along with two massive radio hits that year: "I Won't Dance" and "Lovely to Look At." The latter was nominated for Best Song, with additional lyrics by Jimmy McHugh.

Roberta was another hit, raking in $2,335,000 at the box office. It also boosted the career of director William Seiter, one of Dad's best friends in the old days. I grew up with his kids. Seiter went on to direct several RKO films, including some of the classic Wheeler and Woolsey comedies and *Room Service*, the Marx Brothers film my father also produced.

Just as Dad was basking in this golden run of hits, disaster struck. His 1935 film *Sylvia Scarlett* turned out to be the worst financial failure in RKO's history. He was furious with himself for being talked into it. I remember him growling,

"That script had holes in it you could drive a truck through... What the hell was I thinking?"

The story followed Henry Scarlett, fleeing to England after being charged with embezzlement in France. He brings along his daughter Sylvia, disguised as a boy so they can continue their criminal schemes. But Sylvia soon meets a handsome artist, and surprisingly

sheds her disguise and reveals herself as a beautiful young woman, ready for romance.

Hepburn loved the story. She convinced director George Cukor to sign on, and together they talked my dad—against his instincts—into producing it.

My mother described the out-of-town preview as a total disaster. She could hear disgusted audience members walking out halfway through the screening—something she'd never seen at one of Dad's films.

Hepburn and Cukor were waiting with my mother in the lobby, but Dad didn't come out until the house had emptied. When he finally appeared, he was striding furiously toward the exit, scowl locked on his face. Hepburn and Cukor ran after him, apologizing frantically:

"We're so sorry, Pan. We'll make another movie for you... for free..."

Dad didn't stop.

"I never want to speak to either one of you again," he snapped, without even turning around.

My mother, mortified, said she wanted to crawl into the woodwork. She told me the look on Hepburn's face was heartbreaking.

Of course, Dad relented. Within a few weeks, he was working with Hepburn and Cukor again. But his behavior at that preview was undeniably childish. If you didn't know him, you might think he was a real monster.

Years later, I saw *Sylvia Scarlett* at a 1930s film festival in a little theater on Fairfax I wondered why Hepburn had fallen in love with that peculiar story, and I told my dad that she probably wanted to get in touch with her male side and see if she could play both a boy and a girl successfully in the same movie. Dad thought about it. "That's pretty observant of you, my boy... I think you're right about that."

The following year, he brought *Mary of Scotland*—Maxwell Anderson's acclaimed play—to the screen. I've always thought it was one of his finest achievements. Katharine Hepburn and Frederick March gave outstanding performances under the skilled direction of John Ford. The critics praised it, but the film lost money.

It was one of Dad's biggest disappointments, and he referred to it often as a cautionary tale about unhappy endings.

"*Audiences want to leave the theater with smiles on their faces,*" was what he used to say all the time, when he read a script that didn't have a happy ending.

FIRST COMES LOVE THEN COMES MARRIAGE...

When the hero and heroine meet in a romantic comedy it's called a "meet cute." My parents' "meet cute" happened back in 1919 when they were both living in Kansas City. Their families lived in the same apartment building. My maternal grandfather, Frank Newman, owned the Golden Horseshoe movie theater in that city, and my dad's father, a film distributor for FBO (Film Booking Office), was building up relationships with the theater owners in the area. My father and his family would only be in Kansas City for a couple of years before moving to another city, where Grandpa Harry would start over, building new connections.

It was a life of upheaval for Dad, who was born in Pittsburgh, but also lived in Cincinnati, St. Louis, Philadelphia, and Kansas City before settling in New York, where he attended high school. He told me that changing schools every two years was a difficult adjustment, but he eventually learned how to cope.

Living in the same building in Kansas City and being in essentially the same business, the two families saw a lot of each other. My mother developed a big crush on my father, who had become a good-looking boy in his early teens. He was about 5'7" and quite slender, with a handsome face and a beautiful head of dark brown hair. Mom told me his best feature was his penetrating brown eyes. When she looked into them, she would get goose flesh. She used to hang around on the front balcony of the apartment, waiting for Dad to come home from school, and did everything she could to get him to notice her.

She often came over to babysit my uncle Henry, who was nine years younger than Dad. Henry was a funny little boy of three who didn't speak much English. He had been raised by a nanny who spoke to him in German, and now that she was gone, the family was trying to re-educate Henry in English. My mother was helping him learn. He would run around the apartment saying things in German like "Heine liebt Eier" ("Henry loves eggs") and other expressions, which everyone would translate until he finally began to learn English.

My mother told me Dad paid little attention to her in those days, and when the Bermans eventually left Kansas City and moved to New York, she was heartbroken.

But just like a Hollywood movie, fate intervened, and Mom and Dad met again in Los Angeles in 1927. Mom was twenty years old and had developed into a stunning young woman. She had delicate features, beautiful blue eyes, and a captivating smile that everyone loved. Dad was no longer ignoring her, and a serious romance began to blossom.

Mom had moved to Los Angeles because Grandpa Frank had lost his theater in Kansas City and had gone bankrupt. He got a job as an usher for one of the theaters in the 20th Century Fox chain. He moved up quickly in the organization, making a strong impression on the Skouras brothers, who owned the theaters. After a couple of years managing a Fox theater in Hollywood, Grandpa Frank was promoted to a huge job as head of the Northwest Division. He and Grandma Fannie were moved to Seattle to run the Fox Northwest Circuit, which encompassed a large number of theaters in Washington,

Oregon, Idaho, and Montana. Grandpa had made a great impression on Spyros and Charlie Skouras, and they eventually rewarded him for his hard work.

Mom had always lived with her parents, and it made her sad that they were moving so far away—especially her mother, to whom she was extremely close. But by then she and Dad were engaged, so she stayed in Los Angeles to be with him. She told me what an exciting time it was. She'd had crushes on a few boys in the past, but this time, she knew she was truly in love.

A few months later, Mom and Dad went to San Francisco to get married, followed by a brief honeymoon—just a couple of days in the Bay Area. Dad didn't have much time for romance; he was about to become acting Head of Production at RKO Studios, and there were too many things demanding his attention.

FRED AND GINGER

A year before I was born, my father produced what is probably the most memorable of the Astaire/Rogers dance movies—and one of the most successful. *Top Hat* received an Oscar nomination for Best Picture. It featured Irving Berlin's finest score to date, with songs like "Isn't It a Lovely Day?," "Top Hat," White Tie and Tails," and the movie's biggest hit, "Cheek to Cheek," which was nominated for Best Song.

Audiences came in droves to see *Top Hat* in both North America and Europe, and it earned a net profit of $1,325,000 in worldwide distribution. That was an impressive figure in 1935, when RKO was still struggling through Great Depression.

"Cheek to Cheek" had a powerful effect on my mother. She sang that song as she danced around the nursery with me when I was a baby, holding me close to her cheek. I was too young to remember it, but someone had followed us around with a camera. When I was around seven or eight years old, Mom opened a desk drawer and showed me several photographs of one of our dances. The heavenly look on her face in the photos made me smile, but the bewildered look on my face made me laugh. I was just a year old, and I clearly didn't understand what was going on.

My mother loved that song. She was always singing it around the house. She used to say it encouraged people to dance close together like Fred and Ginger. Mom was an incurable romantic and a terrific dancer—light and feathery on her feet—but Dad was not. He always looked uncomfortable on the dance floor.

The Astaire/Rogers musicals were enormously popular. They had an incredible run of ten pictures, which were still being made when I was four or five years old. Composers were in and out of our house, playing new songs for Dad on the baby grand in the living room, and many times Hermes Pan, the brilliant choreographer, would be there as well.

He was also the rehearsal pianist at the studio, playing for Fred and Ginger on set and making minor adjustments to the piano score when the dancing got out of sync with the music. The composers would then add the changes into the final score. Hermes Pan played beautifully, and I loved to listen to him. At the age of five, I decided I was going to become a great piano player—just like Hermes. Later, however, when my parents agreed to give me lessons, I learned it wasn't my cup of tea. I was only about seven, and I didn't like the woman sitting beside me on the piano bench trying to teach me to read music. After a few months, my parents realized it too and cancelled the lessons. But I still loved music—and the dance movies.

Strangely enough, it took Fred Astaire a long time to become a hit with movie audiences. It was Ginger they initially came to see. That always puzzled me, because Fred was clearly the better dancer. Dad said it wasn't until the fourth or fifth film that Fred truly came into his own with fans. He explained that most people tend to watch the woman in a couple's dance. Ginger was also an excellent dancer—

and quite beautiful—so it took time before audiences began to see them as a true partnership and to appreciate Fred's masterful footwork.

I also believe the music was every bit as compelling as the dancing. You couldn't go wrong seeing any of those films. We ran them in our home in the 1940s after they had been transferred from nitrate to safety film. There were usually lots of guests for those screenings, and everyone was always exhilarated when the lights came on after a screening.

The plots were classic Hollywood formula: boy meets girl, they fall in love, boy loses girl, boy gets girl back for a happy ending. It didn't really matter—no one was paying close attention to the story. They were there to see the dancing and hear the beautiful music.

As much as I loved those movies, Ginger was not my favorite of Fred's dance partners. In my opinion, Eleanor Powell was a better tap dancer, and if you saw her solo performances in *Born to Dance* and *Lady Be Good*, you'd agree with me. She moved in complete synchronization with Fred—as though two people were dancing in one body. They performed together in *Broadway Melody of 1940*, and they were the greatest dance pair I ever saw on screen.

Unfortunately, my father didn't agree. We had many arguments about it. He was one of Ginger's biggest fans and refused to recognize anyone else as her equal. I never won that argument, but I always knew I was right—and many people shared my view.

I've seen exciting footage of couples dancing in tango bars in Buenos Aires, but I haven't managed to travel there yet. Those dancers look extraordinary on screen, but it must be spectacular to witness them in person. Visiting a tango bar in Argentina is high on my bucket list. I hope to go there someday with a woman I'm madly in love with—and dance until we drop. *Comme c'est romantique.*

MOUNTAIN DRIVE—MY HAPPIEST MEMORIES

The year I was born, my father produced the classic film *Winterset*. It was a hit Broadway play by Maxwell Anderson, with glowing reviews from the New York theater critics. They synopsized the film as follows: *An Italian immigrant with a reputation as a radical is falsely convicted and executed for a payroll robbery and murder. Years later, his son sets out to find the truth of the crime and to bring to account the gangster responsible.*

This movie elevated the career of the talented Broadway actor Burgess Meredith. The cast included Margo, a Broadway actress and niece of the famous bandleader Xavier Cugat. She often appeared as a specialty dancer with his band, exuding her Latin charm and sex appeal. The film also featured the intriguing and somewhat frightening John Carradine in a sympathetic performance early in his career. In time, studios began casting him in horror films, which eventually defined him as an actor.

My dad kept a small, framed version of the movie poster hanging in his office, so I know he considered *Winterset* to be one of his finer efforts. I used to study that miniature poster when I visited him there, and I was fascinated by it. The movie was nominated for two Oscars and was one of the New York Film Critics' ten best movies of 1936. Early in his career, Dad had become known as a producer of comedies and musicals—he produced nine of the ten Astaire/Rogers dance films—but pictures like *Winterset*, *Of Human Bondage*, and *Mary of Scotland* proved that he was capable of making serious films as well.

That same year, my father and mother built an incredible house on Mountain Drive at the top of a hill, north of Sunset Boulevard in the most exclusive area of Beverly Hills. The view from the hilltop was commanding. I used to look out my bathroom window and gaze at the colorful marble dome on the City Hall tower. It was the tallest building in the business district for many years, until developers pressured the city into lifting the height restrictions.

Our lot measured about three-quarters of an acre, and the house was enormous for those days—10,600 square feet, with a pool and a greenhouse on the lowest level of the garden. Eventually, the greenhouse was replaced by a lighted tennis court.

The house was a thing of beauty. It was designed by the famous architect Roland Coate, and the month it was completed, it appeared on the cover of *Architectural Digest*. There were five large bedroom suites with full bathrooms and walk-in closets upstairs, which afforded all of us ample privacy. I got the first one, and there was a bedroom suite waiting for each of my sisters as they arrived. Sue was born four and a half years after me, and Cindy joined us eighteen months after Sue.

Mountain Drive was a magnet for celebrities. After we built our house and moved in, the neighborhood began to fill up with some of Hollywood's most prominent citizens. Dean Martin built a large house and moved in across the street. The gifted actor Ray Milland lived two doors down, and his son Danny used to come over and swim in our pool with me and my sisters.

Next door to us was Max Firestein, who was part of the Max

Factor family and an officer in the company that supplied Hollywood and much of the world with makeup.

Down the street, west of us, was a large house with iron gates inhabited by the Lovelace family. The father was president of Decca Records, and his daughters Linda and Cynthia were occasional visitors. Next door to them was Harry Joe Brown, an early Hollywood producer married to the popular redheaded actress Sally Eilers. Their son, Coco, and I became great friends. We used to wrestle all the time, but he was bigger and stronger. He would pin me down and force me to say "Unconditional Surrender" before he would release me.

Harry Joe eventually moved and sold his house to Nunnally Johnson, one of Hollywood's greatest talents. Nunnally wrote, produced, and directed *The Three Faces of Eve*, in which Joanne Woodward won an Oscar and a Golden Globe for her performance as a woman plagued with multiple personality disorder. We ran that picture at home, and we were all fascinated by it. It was a movie dealing with psychiatry and mental illness, decades ahead of its time.

Across the street from Nunnally was William Perlberg who, along with his writing and directing partner George Seaton, produced some unforgettable films, including *The Song of Bernadette*, *Miracle on 34th Street*, and *The Country Girl* with Bing Crosby and William Holden. Grace Kelly received an Oscar for Best Actress for her performance in that movie.

Next door to Perlberg, on the corner of Mountain Drive and Sunset Boulevard, was the noted costume designer Charles LeMaire, who was nominated for a dozen Oscars and won three for his costumes in *All About Eve*, *The Robe*, and *Love Is a Many-Splendored Thing*.

Around the corner on Loma Vista Drive was David Loew, the son and heir of Marcus Loew, founder of Loew's Incorporated, the large theater chain and parent company of MGM Studios.

A later addition to Loma Vista was the producer Irwin Winkler, who produced all the *Rocky* films with Sylvester Stallone and occupied an office on the second floor of the Thalberg Building at MGM Studios, down the hall from my dad.

Schuyler Road, which intersects Mountain Drive and goes north into the hills, contained some beautiful homes as well, and one of them belonged to Betty Grable and her trumpet-playing husband Harry James. Across from them on Foothill Road was Nat Goldstone, a prominent Hollywood agent. Down the street, hidden behind a high wall and thick foliage, was the home of Lou Wasserman, the president of MCA and later MCA-Universal Studios.

It was a glittering neighborhood, and we were right in the middle of it. Tour buses parked outside our house daily, loudspeakers blaring as drivers narrated which star lived where. Tourists craned their necks and leaned out of the windows hoping for a glimpse of Hollywood royalty. Sometimes two or three buses would line up, bumper to bumper, blocking the street at all hours of the day. It got to be a bit much—but what could we do?

We were living in the epicenter of movie magic.

THE MUSIC MY FATHER GAVE ME

The inside of our home was spacious and elegant, with a beautiful dining room that overlooked the garden, and a cozy paneled library filled with hundreds of books. Nestled in the bay window was an antique card table that offered a perfect view of the sloping back lawn. That library became a sanctuary for my father and me—a quiet place where we read, listened to classical music, and shared some of our most meaningful conversations.

My father was an avid reader, and he encouraged my love of literature just as his mother had encouraged him in her farewell letter. He took genuine delight in my discoveries, and he viewed reading as a form of higher education—the kind he'd missed out on by not going to college. Still, he read voraciously and absorbed the great works, often quoting them in conversation. His literary self-education enabled him to hold his own in any intellectual crowd.

He also passed along his love of classical music—a gift for which I'll always be grateful. I'd be lost in *The Adventures of Tom Sawyer* or Edgar Allan Poe, and he'd grin and say, "You have no idea how lucky you are, getting to read all this good literature. I have to read these lousy scripts they keep sending me."

That library wasn't just a room; it was a haven. I felt safe, seen, and loved there. My father would recommend books—some he hadn't yet read himself but kept in the hope that one day he would. His passion for classical music was born from his own childhood—nights spent with his father, listening to the radio. It was a tradition he longed to pass on. When Grandpa Harry died at the young age of 43, Dad was only 17 and about to graduate from high school. Their bond, formed over music, left a lasting imprint.

Once I was old enough, Dad began taking my mother and me to hear the Los Angeles Philharmonic at the Biltmore Bowl. In the summer, we'd attend performances at the Greek Theater and the Hollywood Bowl. I was exposed to everything—from orchestras to ballet, which my mother adored. Those outings planted seeds of culture that grew strong roots.

My mother also shared her passions with me. She had impeccable taste, especially when it came to clothes. On shopping trips, she picked out stylish outfits with perfect color coordination—I never argued. I trusted her flair.

But our best times were spent in museums and galleries. Mom was a devoted art collector. She first introduced me to painting and sculpture when I was around nine or ten. I still remember how her voice would drop to a whisper when she saw a piece that moved her —as if the information was a secret meant only for me. It made every exhibit feel personal and profound. Her excitement was contagious, and before long, I was just as captivated by art as she was. She filled the house with art books and always bought exhibit catalogues from museum gift shops so we could relive the experience together.

Thanks to both of my parents, I developed deep cultural interests that have brought me joy throughout my life. I've tried, not always successfully, to pass those passions on to my grandchildren—though their interests lean more toward cell phones and social media. A different world, I suppose.

My father was clever about cultivating my musical taste. He must've worried I'd resist classical music, so when I was four, he gave me a 78 RPM record player and a copy of Prokofiev's *Peter and the Wolf*. It had narration, which helped me follow the story. The bassoon's deep growl as the wolf entered gave me chills—but I loved it. I was riveted, rooting for Peter even after dozens of listens.

Soon after, Dad gave me *Alice in Orchestralia*, a whimsical fantasy set to music. In it, a girl named Alice tumbles into an imaginary world through the bell of a tuba and is introduced to each orchestral instrument. The bass viol served as her guide. It was a brilliant way to humanize the instruments—suddenly, the orchestra was a cast of characters. My imagination was hooked.

But nothing enchanted me more than Rimsky-Korsakov's *Scheherazade*. I listened to it nightly, curled up in bed, imagining I was the Kalendar Prince sailing stormy seas in search of my princess. The music was stirring, adventurous, unforgettable. I memorized every melody. Most nights, I'd drift off before the end, and Mom would quietly lift the needle from the record. To this day, *Scheherazade* still moves me—and I now better appreciate the genius of its orchestration. Rimsky-Korsakov, after all, taught orchestration to the Russian greats, including Tchaikovsky.

By the age of eight or nine, I was reading regularly with Dad in the library—weekend after weekend—while Tchaikovsky, Rachmaninoff, and Chopin filled the air. We slowly graduated to more complex pieces. These were the years before television, long before computers or smartphones, when reading was still a favored pastime for young people. It was a quieter, more reflective world.

PANDRO S. BERMAN

NOT YOUR AVERAGE "HOME" MOVIES

Just off the library was our enormous living room—large enough to hold a baby grand piano, a wet bar, and believe it or not, a full 35 mm projection setup. Behind the back wall was a fireproof booth housing arc light projectors like the ones used in movie theaters. At the opposite end, a CinemaScope screen would glide down from the ceiling, and powerful speakers hidden in wooden cabinets provided rich stereophonic sound.

On Tuesday and Friday nights, projectionists from the studio would arrive to run films—sometimes a double feature—complete with newsreels, cartoons, and Pete Smith Specialties. It was just like going to the movies, minus the popcorn. My mother banned it—no kernels grinding into her expensive carpet.

Friday nights were always my favorite. One day, my sister Sue and I were reminiscing about those evenings, trying to tally up just how many films we must have watched over the years. After some mental math and a few laughs, we figured it had to be at least 700 or 800 pictures across an 18-year span. And we weren't watching them alone—we'd invited hundreds of guests over that time, including some of Hollywood's most creative and accomplished talents.

In the early years, I could remember every title. The stories, the actors, the endings—they all stuck in my memory. But as the years passed and the reels kept spinning, they began to blur together like a montage of golden-age glamour. Still, if someone were to name a particular film, we ran 25 or 30 years ago, chances are I could still picture it. I might say, "Oh yes, we ran that one with Deborah Kerr," or "That was the Clark Gable picture," or "Ava Gardner looked incredible in that scene"—and I'd be right.

One of my earliest memories of these movie nights was the evening Elizabeth Taylor came to dinner. She was only 12, accompanied by her mother, and had been invited to watch *National Velvet*. Even at that young age, Elizabeth had the kind of poise and presence that made you take notice. It was the kind of moment that sticks with you.

Often, our movie night guests were people my father was currently working with—actors, directors, writers—and the screenings gave him a chance to talk business in a casual setting. Before dinner, he'd usher them into the library, close the door, pour drinks, and get down to it—always at the card table in the bay window.

But make no mistake: business was never discussed at the dinner table. That wasn't just etiquette—it was strategy. Bringing up deals over the roast beef might have violated a tacit agreement. Many actors, writers, and directors had clear terms—spoken or otherwise—that no business was to be discussed without their agents present. I'm fairly certain that my dad ignored that rule more than once, but he was discreet about it. Closing the library door wasn't just about privacy; it was plausible deniability.

And let's be honest—these weren't make-or-break negotiations. They were usually small matters. Nudges. Ideas. Creative tweaks. Nothing anyone would complain about. But they made the difference. It was in that quiet, wood-paneled room, over a drink and a shared love of film, where many of those "little" decisions turned into something big on screen.

One photo from my fourth birthday party shows us screening a film in the living room. The party had a western theme, and the yard was full of kids dressed in cowboy boots and Stetsons, waving cap guns. An empty lot next door became the perfect frontier for my dad's inspired idea: he brought in ponies from a place called Ponyland. Kids rode ponies at the party, no rink required. Though my father didn't produce westerns, this was a hit. I don't remember the exact film we showed—maybe *Snow White*, but more likely something with Roy Rogers or Hopalong Cassidy to match the theme.

When we got older, my sisters and I were allowed to invite a few friends for screenings, which made us wildly popular. Tuesday nights were mostly reserved for private showings—especially "rushes," or dailies, from the studio. These were prints of scenes shot the day before, reviewed to decide what made the cut. When Dad couldn't attend the studio screenings, he'd have the rushes sent home.

I tried to watch them all, but they could be mind-numbingly repetitive—each take filmed from every angle: master shots, over-the-shoulders, close-ups. What intrigued me most was the candid moments between takes—actors flubbing lines, swearing, laughing, directors chiming in with notes or encouragement. I learned to listen for the phrases: "Cut," "Cut... print," or "Print... pick up," depending on how the scene was shaping up.

Even at six years old, I imagined myself as a director. I practiced calling out "Action!" and "Cut!" with varying tones and styles, trying to sound authoritative enough to lead a crew. Once, while rehearsing in my room, my father overheard me. He poked his head in and asked, "What exactly are you directing?"

Mortified, I froze—but then he smiled. We both laughed. After that, I rehearsed in my walk-in closet, convinced that perfecting my delivery was the only thing standing between me and cinematic greatness.

A BIRTHDAY I'LL NEVER FORGET

One of my earliest and most unforgettable movie memories took place right in our living room, on the occasion of my sixth birthday. I had been told I could invite my entire first-grade class to the party—so I did. I stood up in front of all 23 classmates and made a grand announcement: "Everyone's invited to my birthday party—including Mrs. Kendall!" (She was our teacher.)

Naturally, all the kids showed up. Mrs. Kendall didn't.

But who could resist a party with hot dogs, ice cream, birthday cake, and a private screening of *The Wizard of Oz*? The film had been released just three years earlier, but we'd all been too young at the time to really appreciate it. By now, we'd heard how magical it was—and we were beside ourselves with anticipation.

One of my classmates, Tony Meserve, had a special reason to be excited. His mother was the well-known actress Margaret Hamilton—"Maggie" to her friends. She was managing the formidable task of raising Tony on her own while maintaining a successful acting career. In *The Wizard of Oz*, she famously played a dual role: the strict Kansas schoolteacher and—unbeknownst to Tony—the terrifying Wicked Witch of the West.

Tony knew his mom was in the movie, but apparently, she hadn't told him the full extent of her performance. I was sitting right next to him when his mother zoomed toward the screen on her broomstick, cackling maniacally and cloaked in that eerie green makeup. Every kid in the room froze. We were all terrified including me.

But Tony? He watched calmly... until Judy Garland stood up to the witch and doused her with water. The Wicked Witch screamed, melted, and disappeared into the ground—leaving only a puff of smoke and a crumpled black dress behind.

Tony burst into tears.

"They've killed my mother!" he screamed—and bolted from the room, just as the munchkins broke into "Ding-Dong! The Witch Is Dead."

My mother and I ran after him, hearts pounding. We brought him upstairs and tried to calm him down. He was hysterical. We even called Maggie on the phone so he could hear her voice, but he didn't believe it was really her. He was still crying when she arrived to pick him up. She gathered him in her arms and gently assured him she was alive—that it was all pretend. Eventually, the tears subsided, and she was able to take him home.

Mom and I were still shaken. I felt awful for Tony and wanted to call later to check on him, but Mom advised against it. "Let him settle," she said. She was probably right.

That birthday party became the stuff of Hollywood legend. I've seen the story retold in at least two books—including one written by a classmate who had been at the party: Bill Marx, son of the one and only Harpo Marx. Bill and I have stayed friends ever since. His father's memoir, *Harpo Speaks*, is a wonderful read, and Bill's follow-up, *Son of Harpo Speaks*, contains a vivid retelling of Tony's meltdown during *The Wizard of Oz*.

Despite that traumatic beginning, Tony remained a terrific student and one of the better athletes in our class. We stayed good friends throughout grade school, and eventually I convinced him to return for more movie nights—though I completely understood his initial hesitation.

We lost touch after Tony and his mother moved to New York. Broadway had more to offer Maggie than Hollywood did, and I suspect her unforgettable portrayal of the Wicked Witch, while iconic, may have limited the kinds of roles she was offered afterward. That green makeup left a long shadow.

6

GRANDMA JULIE'S GIFT OF WORDS

At some point in the late 1930s, Dad was able to fulfill his promise to his mother by bringing her and his younger brother Henry out to California to live. No one in the family remembers the exact date, but it must have been about 15 years after Dad left New York. Henry was entering college, with plans to attend USC Dental School, and Dad was thrilled to provide his little brother with the education he never had the chance to pursue himself.

I don't know exactly where they were living when they first arrived, but Henry eventually moved into a dormitory or fraternity house. My earliest memories are of my grandmother living as a resident on one of the upper floors of the Beverly Wilshire Hotel. Mom and Dad would take me to have dinner with her in the hotel's dining room, and that's when I truly got to know this remarkable woman. She had a contagious laugh and showered me with boundless affection. It was clear how proud she was of Dad, but, after a while, I began to feel that she liked me just as much.

She inspired me, much as her wonderful letter had once inspired my father when he first arrived in California. Sadly, I never saw that letter until after she passed away. If I had, I would've told her how compassionate and selfless it was. I would have thanked her for the wisdom she shared in it—especially her advice to read widely and deeply. That letter helped my father educate himself without formal schooling, and because of her, he passed that love of reading on to me.

When I was about 10 years old, Grandma Julie gave me a small bound booklet containing only the poem *If* by Rudyard Kipling. She told me there was great wisdom in those words, and that they would serve me well throughout my life—if I could remember them. I decided the best way to do that was to memorize the whole thing. It's a long poem, and it took nearly a week to fully commit it to memory, but completing the task gave me an enormous sense of pride. Rather than recite it for my parents, I waited for Sunday night dinner, when Grandma would be visiting. I stood at the table and recited it flawlessly, basking in everyone's attention. They were astonished—especially Grandma. She was delighted that I had taken her advice to heart. Even now, decades later, I can still recite it from memory, and people are always amazed when I do.

Grandma was an avid reader, articulate and insightful, with a deep respect for good writing. She kept up with bestsellers but also appreciated great literature, often quoting from famous authors and philosophers. I admired how intelligently she spoke about what she read. She wasn't a classically beautiful woman, but she was elegant—graceful in her manner, refined in her speech, and impeccable in her taste.

She remains, always, one of the brightest lights in my childhood memories.

PANDRO S. BERMAN

A VERY HOLLYWOOD CHRISTMAS

I have fuzzy memories of the early Christmases at the Mountain Drive house. Mostly, I remember the tree in the bay window of the library, beautifully decorated and glowing with lights. I recall my mother swirling a huge swath of cotton around the middle branches to mimic snow, then placing Santa Claus with his sleigh and reindeer —loaded with tiny gifts—on the snowy perch front and center. But beyond that, my earliest Christmases are a bit of a blur.

My first real recollection of that exciting day was in 1943, when I was seven years old. I vividly remember sitting in the library with Sue, who was just three and absolutely buzzing with excitement over the wrapped presents piled under the tree for Christmas morning. We'd usually tiptoe into the master bedroom and gently wake Mom and Dad, only to hear them groan that it was far too early to get up.

But this was two days before Christmas, and Sue and I were already in the library, inspecting the gifts and trying to guess what was inside each box. Sue kept dancing around the tree, picking up every present and shaking it, hoping to figure out the contents. She was especially enchanted by the little ones and kept asking if she could open just one. I kept saying no and pointed out that not all of them were for her. That didn't stop her from running back and forth asking me which ones were hers.

Eventually, she found a small box with her name on the tag and ran over to confirm it with me. When I told her it was hers, her eyes lit up and she pleaded with me again to let her open it. I kept refusing, telling her we had to wait until Christmas morning—but she was relentless. Finally, just to get her to stop pestering me, I told her it might be okay to open just that little one. Even though I knew she shouldn't, I was tired of arguing with her.

She had just started to tear into the paper when the front door opened. Mom and Dad had returned from Christmas shopping, arms loaded with bags—and there was Sue, right in their line of sight. Mom was furious. She dropped her packages and rushed over, giving

Sue a quick spanking. Sue started wailing that I had given her permission, but I flat-out denied it and claimed she had done it on her own. It was a nasty and cowardly lie, but I wasn't about to take the rap for her indulgence.

At the time, I was certain it was an incident Sue would never forget. But when I reminded her of it, years later, she had no recollection of it whatsoever.

Funny how memories work—the ones we think will stick forever sometimes fade, while others linger with the soft glow of Christmas lights in the back of our minds.

THE LEGENDARY LEO SPITZ

Around the corner from us on Loma Vista Drive was the beautiful home of Leo Spitz, the former chairman of the board of RKO Studios. In 1946, he formed International Pictures with William Goetz, which they later merged with Universal Studios to form Universal-International. He was a great friend of my father's, going back to the old days at RKO, when Leo—the company's top attorney—ran the business end, and Dad was head of movie production. Those were the most productive and profitable years in the studio's history, and the two of them had enormous respect for one another. Even though they were at different studios by then, Dad frequently consulted his old friend on important decisions, because he knew Leo had impeccable business sense.

I remember Leo and his wife, Frankie, at our dinner table in the old days. Leo always smoked a big cigar, and Frankie wore pungent gardenia perfume, which I found intoxicating. My mother disliked both aromas—especially the perfume, which she thought was overpowering. *Gardenia* by Chanel was one of the most expensive perfumes in the world, with a scent that smelled like big money. My mother thought Frankie was probably wearing the cheaper version, *Jungle Gardenia* by Tuvaché, which had become known as "an old drag queen perfume," and Mom considered it to be almost vulgar.

I have a vivid memory of Leo and Frankie having dinner with us around Christmas, when I was five years old. Leo said that Santa Claus had gained too much weight to come down our chimney, so he'd come down the coal chute into our basement and left a gift for me in the woodpile. Without my parents' knowledge, Leo had sneaked down into the basement to leave me a Christmas present. Naturally, I couldn't wait for dinner to be over so I could go down and find it.

It seemed like hours until the last bite of dessert disappeared with the final sip of coffee, and we all went downstairs to the basement. Needless to say, I was quite excited to find a $100 bill folded in half and sticking up between two fire logs. I had never seen a $100 bill before, but I knew it was a lot of money. Dad, of course, wouldn't let me keep it. He handed it back to Leo, saying it was much too extravagant for a five-year-old—and I was terribly disappointed. It was a long time before I got to see another Benjamin Franklin.

Leo and Frankie had a 35mm projection room in their home like we did, and since it was just around the corner, we used to walk over to their house to run movies with them on Sunday nights. I loved their projection room, with its bright red carpet, overstuffed couches, and the most expensive boxes of chocolates on every table in the room. Running movies there on Sunday nights remains one of my fondest childhood memories. I saw my favorite western of all time in that projection room—*Red River*, with John Wayne, Montgomery Clift, and the beautiful Joanne Dru.

HOLLYWOOD HITS THE SLOPES

In the late 1930s, my parents became close friends with Milton Bren, a producer at Hal Roach Studios who would later rise to the position of executive vice president at MGM Studios. He belonged to the elite circle that attended high-level production meetings and regularly met with my father and the other producers two or three times a week. Milton was sharp and charismatic, and he and my dad grew genuinely fond of each other.

Milton, his wife Marion, and their two sons—Donald and Peter—were frequent guests at our home, often joining us on Friday nights for dinner and a movie. Donald went on to become the legendary real estate developer behind the Irvine Company, the man who transformed the Irvine Ranch in Orange County into a sprawling suburban empire. His estimated wealth today hovers around $15.3 billion.

I went to school with his younger brother, Peter—easily the best-looking kid I had ever seen. He had a sparkling personality, inheriting his father's sense of humor, charm, and striking good looks. If Peter had gone into acting, he would have been a star, no question. Instead, he followed Donald into real estate and was highly successful in his own right, managing financial investments for wealthy clients. He became president and chairman of KSB Realty Advisors and KSB Capital Management, both nationally respected wealth management firms.

In 1939, our two families traveled together to attend the grand opening of the Sun Valley ski resort in Idaho. The resort had become the destination of choice for Hollywood celebrities and high-powered business leaders from across the country.

Among the opening-week guests was W. Averell Harriman, the railroad and banking magnate, who arrived in style aboard his private Union Pacific railcar. He stayed for a couple of days, mingled at the parties, and seemed to enjoy the company of the Hollywood crowd.

Then, just as casually as he had arrived, he boarded his private train and headed back to New York—with Marion Bren.

To this day, I don't know whether she even said goodbye to her family or simply phoned them from a stop along the way to let them know she had defected. But one thing was certain: she was gone—vanished from their lives without warning.

Milton and his sons were devastated. My parents were stunned. No one imagined something so outrageous could happen. At three and a half, I was blissfully unaware of the emotional wreckage left in her wake. But Peter, who was around five, and Donald, who was older still, surely carried the weight of that loss for years to come.

SUMMER EVENINGS WITH SPENCER AND KATE

For several years during the 1930s and early 1940s, Mom and Dad rented a house on the beach in Santa Monica each summer. I have only fragmented memory flashes of walking on the beach and swimming in the ocean with my dad, but I can't recall anything about the house itself.

We had dinner guests and special weekend visitors almost every week, including celebrities who enjoyed sitting in the warm sun and feeling the cool ocean breeze. Katharine Hepburn and her boyfriend, Spencer Tracy, used to come for dinner and often brought lovely gifts. My sister Cindy still has one of them sitting on her kitchen counter—a large, hand-painted Mexican wooden salad bowl supported by three wooden legs. Although some of the paint has worn off over the years, it remains a real treasure and a special keepsake from one of Hollywood's grandest couples.

Tracy was married but separated from his wife. As a devout Catholic, divorce wasn't an option, so he felt it was inappropriate for him and Hepburn to appear together in public. But they did attend private dinner parties like the ones Mom and Dad hosted, and the two of them often stayed for the movies after dinner. They were the most elegant couple I had ever met, and their visits left a lasting impression on me

HOLLYWOOD LOSES SOME HEAVYWEIGHTS

I was just a year old when *Shall We Dance* was released, and Mom and Dad threw yet another spectacular party to celebrate. It was the seventh film in the Astaire-Rogers musical cycle, and once again, a big hit. This one featured a phenomenal score by George and Ira Gershwin, with songs like "They All Laughed (at Christopher Columbus)," "Let's Call the Whole Thing Off," and "They Can't Take That Away from Me"—arguably the most beautiful song Fred Astaire ever sang. It was nominated for the Academy Award for Best Song in 1937, and Fred's recording soared in record sales.

Naturally, George and Ira Gershwin were at the party, along with Ginger and Fred, Hermes Pan—the brilliant choreographer—and Mark Sandrich, who directed the picture and several of Dad's other RKO films.

My mother once admitted to me that she had developed a real crush on George Gershwin over the years. What woman hadn't, back then? She was devastated when he passed away just a few months later, at the age of 38, from an inoperable brain tumor. His death was a tremendous loss—not just to the music world, but to the whole country.

Another untimely Hollywood death had rocked the town just ten months earlier: Irving Thalberg. He'd battled rheumatic fever since childhood, and doctors had warned he wouldn't live much past 30. Sadly, they weren't far off. He died of a heart attack at age 37.

Dad had rekindled his friendship with Thalberg during those

years. Their old high school bond evolved into a professional one as well. Dad often borrowed contract players from MGM's enormous talent roster—which Mayer had entrusted to Thalberg—and the two were in regular contact. Thalberg, respecting Dad's standing in the business, had even encouraged him to leave RKO and join MGM, the biggest and best studio in Hollywood. But at the time, Dad was at the helm of RKO and wasn't ready to take orders from anyone.

Thalberg's funeral drew everyone who was anyone in Hollywood. He was deeply admired and widely loved. Both of Louis Mayer's daughters—Edith and Irene—had once shown interest in Thalberg, but Mayer had declared him "off limits" due to his poor health.

Mom and Dad attended the funeral, and she later told me it was the first time she ever saw my father cry—not just misty-eyed, but sobbing, his face buried in a handkerchief. "It felt like losing a member of my family," he told her. He remembered, as a boy, watching his friend struggle to breathe on the playground. More than once, Dad had run to fetch the school nurse and oxygen after watching Thalberg turn blue, gasping for air.

These weren't just industry colleagues—they were friendships, rivalries, heartbreaks, and histories bound together by the flickering light of Hollywood's golden era.

7

1939—HOLLYWOOD'S GREATEST YEAR

In 1939, Hollywood released 365 films—more than any other year before or since. Moviegoers bought 80 million tickets per week, flocking to theaters to see what has come to be known as the most creatively fertile year in cinematic history.

Many critics and film buffs agree that it wasn't just the most productive year in Hollywood—it was the best. The crown jewel of that glittering lineup was *Gone with the Wind*, which, for decades, held the record as the highest-grossing movie of all time—at just 25 cents a ticket. While inflation and modern pricing eventually knocked it off that pedestal, it's likely that *Gone with the Wind* has still been seen by more people in theaters and on television than any other movie ever made.

The Wizard of Oz also debuted that same year and quickly became the most beloved film to watch with a child. These two blockbusters topped the box office charts, but 1939's top ten list was crowded with other smash hits—an astonishing show of creative firepower.

One of the biggest box office successes of the year was my father's most expensive film to date, *Gunga Din*. It became an American classic, landed a nomination for Best Picture, and placed second on the New York Film Critics' Top Ten list. (Katharine Hepburn was also nominated for Best Actress that year.)

Director George Stevens had already worked with Dad on *A Damsel in Distress*, starring Fred Astaire, Joan Fontaine, George Burns, and Gracie Allen. That film earned an Oscar for Best Dance Direction thanks to Hermes Pan, Astaire's longtime collaborator. Stevens also directed *Swing Time*, one of the most celebrated Astaire/Rogers musicals, featuring the lush Jerome Kern–Dorothy Fields score that included "Pick Yourself Up," "Never Gonna Dance," and the Oscar-winning "The Way You Look Tonight." That last one has always been my personal favorite. Dorothy Fields' lyrics were so tender, so endearing—she deserves just as much credit as Kern for that song's enduring charm.

Stevens was a meticulous craftsman with a brilliant eye for composition—unsurprising, since he'd started as a cameraman. He had a rare sensitivity with actors, which is why performers like Hepburn always wanted to work with him.

Gunga Din was a war story of heroic proportions. Set in 19th-century India, it follows three British soldiers and a native water bearer trying to stop the secret return of the murderous Thuggee cult before it can launch a deadly uprising. Cary Grant, Victor McLaglen, and Douglas Fairbanks Jr. delivered standout performances as the soldiers, while Sam Jaffe gave a moving, masterful performance in the title role of Gunga Din, the Indian water bearer.

The film included light comedic moments that helped soften the undertones of British imperialism still present in the story—more so in Kipling's *Barrack-Room Ballads*, on which the movie was based. Before I was allowed to watch the film, my father insisted I read Kipling's poems, and he was absolutely right. I gained far more insight into the film's historical backdrop and understood what

British colonial rule in India actually meant beyond the spectacle of the silver screen.

It wasn't the first time one of Dad's films had gone over budget. *Bringing Up Baby* (1938)—a wild comedy starring Cary Grant, Katharine Hepburn, and a pet leopard—had drawn in solid crowds, but Howard Hawks' indulgent directing style pushed it well over budget, and it ultimately lost money.

But this time, Stevens' gamble paid off. *Gunga Din* became one of the top-grossing films of 1939, and all was forgiven. Years later, the Library of Congress would designate it as a "classic film" and select it for preservation in the National Film Registry—a well-deserved honor for a film that helped define Hollywood's greatest year.

· * · ★ · ★ · · ★ · ·

HOWARD HUGHES, A MAN OF QUESTIONABLE HABITS

My parents threw a huge party for the release of *Gunga Din*, and Howard Hughes—a serious investor in RKO stock—was invited, though my father considered him a bit unhinged and wanted nothing to do with him. Hughes wouldn't gain full control of the company until 1947, but even then, rumors about his plans to purchase the studio were already swirling.

According to my mother, Hughes arrived at the party in a tuxedo... and a pair of white tennis shoes with white cotton socks. Because of a long-standing phobia about his feet, Hughes only wore brand-new cotton socks, never reusing them—not even after laundering. He believed they'd somehow contaminate his skin. He reportedly owned hundreds of pairs, wearing each only once before discarding them.

He was an odd man with certain obnoxious habits, and he horrified my mother by extinguishing a cigarette on the library carpet, grinding it out with his tennis shoe. Mom thought he may have done it on purpose—furious that Dad was leaving RKO just as Hughes had bought part-ownership in the company. At the time, Dad was considered RKO's greatest creative asset, and his departure could've impacted Hughes' sizable investment.

There might be truth to her theory, but I never agreed. Dad said he thought Hughes had aimed for the marble hearth of the fireplace when he tossed his cigarette, and when it rolled back onto the carpet, Hughes stamped it out quickly to avoid starting a fire.

We'll never know. Whatever the reason, it left a burn mark that couldn't be removed. Luckily, it was at the corner of the fireplace and not in the middle of the room.

I was just three years old at the time and have no recollection of that party or the guests. But my mother told me I had come to the top of the stairs in my pajamas and slippers and peered through the banister to see what was going on. When Dad spotted me, he came upstairs, scooped me up, and brought me down to the party. He introduced me to everyone and gave me something to eat and drink.

It was a memorable night, and *Gunga Din* went on to become a true classic. Years later, I was told I'd been the life of the party—of course, I was the only child there: a little boy in pajamas with a cute smile. My sisters hadn't yet been born, and I was just a few months shy of my third birthday. I don't remember any of it, but there's a photo of me in my pajamas, peeking through the banister of the front hall stairs. It might've been from that very night—or another party entirely. My parents threw a lot of parties back then... and took a lot of pictures.

DAD AND DISNEY

Walt Disney came to my dad in late 1939. He had made a full-length cartoon feature called *Fantasia*, which was designed to resurrect

Mickey Mouse, whose popularity had somewhat diminished in recent years. Disney Studios, at that time, was not distributing its own movies, so they had to make deals with other studios to get their films into theaters. None of the studios in Hollywood were interested in releasing *Fantasia*. The film consists of eight animated segments set to pieces of classical music conducted by Leopold Stokowski. Among other historic compositions, the music included Beethoven's *Pastoral Symphony*, *Toccata and Fugue* by Bach, and the memorable *Sorcerer's Apprentice* by Paul Dukas.

Disney had incurred what he feared were unrecoverable production expenses in the making of the film, and he needed to release this version to recoup some of the costs. The problem was that none of the studios wanted to release a full-length cartoon feature set to highbrow music. They were sure it would play to empty theaters—which, on the surface, looked like a good bet.

However, Dad came up with a strategy to roadshow the movie in thirteen American cities, publicizing its new multi-level soundtrack, which they called "Fantasound." At the same time, they encouraged the orchestras in those cities to give special *Music of Fantasia* concerts, where they could promote the movie by handing out color brochures featuring the animation. The people who attended those concerts would, hopefully, be interested in taking their children to see the movie. Disney was sure that any child who saw it would enjoy it—and that word of mouth would bring more and more people into the theaters.

To a certain extent, Dad's strategy worked, and Disney got enough money to embellish the Mickey Mouse cartoons with more elaborate animation in future releases.

Over time, *Fantasia* has done very well indeed. As of 2012, the cartoon feature had grossed $76.4 million in domestic revenue, and it is currently the 22nd highest-grossing film of all time in the U.S. when adjusted for inflation.

Walt Disney showed his gratitude to my dad for getting him that distribution deal. To thank him for his faith in the movie and for all his help, Disney sent an original cel from *Snow White and the Seven Dwarfs*, beautifully matted and framed and signed: "To Mickey Berman from Walt Disney." It's a shot of Dopey stirring the stew pot, and it's still hanging in my office at home after all these years. It has always been one of my most prized possessions.

8

DAD LEAVES RKO

In 1939, my dad made a monumental decision to leave RKO. The trade papers reported that he was upset when an internal power play conspired to diminish his authority over the kinds of pictures he wanted to make. That wasn't entirely true—but it was widely believed that Howard Hughes was planning to buy a major stake in the studio, and Dad didn't want to work for someone he considered to be crazy. That part wasn't entirely true either, but once word got out, speculation swept through Hollywood about what Dad would do next.

The truth behind his departure didn't come to light until years later, when Mike Steen interviewed my father for *The Oral History of Pandro S. Berman*, published by the American Film Institute in 1972. In that interview, Dad discussed his frustrations with RKO chairman George Schaefer, who had revived the "unit production" concept first introduced during the Selznick era—this time with expanded use. The model allowed RKO to contract with independent producers to complete films that RKO would then distribute. Dad wasn't opposed to the concept itself, but Schaefer began negotiating deals with producers without once consulting him.

From the interview:

> "I was always resentful of the fact that he [Schaefer] did not discuss any of his deals with me. I felt I had a lot to say about an awful lot of people he was hiring whom I wouldn't have hired. So, this really started me on my way out of RKO. I began to get burned up about it, and I resigned as a result."

On March 1, 1939, still masking his true frustration, Dad sent the following resignation letter to George Schaefer:

> "I will not bore you by going into the details of how long I have been attempting to accomplish this deed, and for what various reasons of loyalty and friendship I have restrained myself, but I simply want to state, that regardless of any circumstances whatsoever, I do not wish to continue my employment in the motion picture business as of the expiration of my contract in March 1940. I am going to take off a considerable amount of time and travel around the world for my health, which my doctors have advised me will not stand many more years of the strain and responsibilities I have been going through for the last ten years... I know the only way to get peace of mind will be by severing all connections with the industry until I am in a position to return."

Mike Steen characterized the letter this way:

> "Even though Pandro claims, later in his letter, that he is not unhappy with the company or with George Schaefer as president, and that there are no ulterior motives in his decision, there was apparently more politeness than veracity in his words. In truth, Pandro was distinctly annoyed by George Schaefer's performance. Schaefer was insisting on final say in all production decisions."

Dad had two layers of camouflage for his departure. When I once asked him directly whether it was really about Hughes or Schaefer, he told me there was some truth to both. Either way, leaving RKO turned out to be the best decision he could have made. His departure marked the beginning of a steep decline at the studio—one it never truly recovered from.

George Schaefer resigned in 1942. Howard Hughes, who had already been a major investor, took over as head of production in 1947. Eventually, he sold the failing studio to the General Tire and Rubber Company in 1955, where it became RKO General. But the company was already "dead on arrival," and RKO officially shut down in 1957. Truth be told, the slide had already begun when Dad submitted his resignation in 1939.

Once word leaked that he was leaving RKO, the phones started ringing off the hook. Every major player in the industry wanted to know what he'd do next. Irving Thalberg was gone, and David O. Selznick had already broken away from MGM to start Selznick International Pictures on a backlot in Culver City. He'd formed a partnership with John Hay "Jock" Whitney—whom we always called "Uncle Jock."

Uncle Jock had made a shrewd early investment in Technicolor, just as the company was perfecting its revolutionary three-strip imbibition process. The color quality was unlike anything seen before, and Technicolor quickly became the industry standard. Whitney's 15% stake in the company made headlines on Wall Street.

He also invested nearly $1 million in Selznick International Pictures and became chairman of the board. Whitney helped finance the purchase of the film rights to *Gone with the Wind*, raising half the money needed to acquire them from Margaret Mitchell.

Louis B. Mayer, Selznick's father-in-law, never forgave him for taking business outside "the family"—and he didn't just mean the immediate one. Mayer meant the Jewish moguls who ran Hollywood. Whitney, after all, was one of the most prominent and wealthy gentiles in America.

Now Mayer had lost two of the industry's three "boy wonders." The only one left was my father.

At the time, Dad was toying with the idea of launching his own production company. But Louis B. Mayer made a private overture—an offer too tempting to refuse.

To avoid being spotted by the Paparazzi, who could write damaging stories in the trade papers about the meeting of two studio heads, they arranged a secret meeting in the basement barber shop of the Hollywood Roosevelt Hotel. Mayer sent two of his men ahead to give the barbers a generous bribe—$200 each, a small fortune in 1939—to close the shop for the day.

Mayer arrived first. When Dad walked in, they locked the door, unplugged the phones, and put up a CLOSED sign. Then they both sat in the barber chairs and talked business. Two hours later, they shook hands—and a new chapter began.

* * * * * * * *

A NEW ERA BEGINS

Dad came out of that meeting walking on air. Mayer had offered to create an elite production unit for him—one as generous as those given to Thalberg and Selznick—and granted him total creative autonomy over his pictures. It was as though Dad had opened his own studio. He had all the freedom of an independent producer but with the full backing of the biggest studio in the world: MGM. It had its own film lab right there on the lot, a vast publicity department, and its own releasing and distribution arm.

On top of that, he was making more money than he'd ever dreamed of—and he was entering the innermost chamber of Hollywood's elite. It was known as "The College of Cardinals," and Louis B. Mayer was the Pope.

The College of Cardinals was composed of the studio's most important producers and executives. These included Hunt Stromberg, Lawrence Weingarten, Arthur Freed, Sidney Franklin,

Harry Rapf, and one or two others. Some became personal friends who came to our house to watch movies—especially those who didn't have their own projection rooms.

Only two of the original Cardinals were studio executives, both powerful figures just one rung below Mayer himself.

Eddie Mannix was vice president and studio manager. He oversaw every department at MGM and handled the frequent labor disputes that flared up. MGM's parent company, Loew's Incorporated —owner of an enormous theater chain—was run by Nicholas Schenck, who despised Mayer. The feeling was mutual. Mayer referred to Schenck as "Skunk," and when Schenck got wind of it, he started calling Mayer "Merde"—an unattractive French word for feces.

Before MGM, Mannix had worked for the Schenck brothers, Nicholas and Joseph, who owned the Palisades Amusement Park in New Jersey. Although his official title was "treasurer," Mannix was really the park's general manager—and its unofficial bouncer. Rumors swirled that he had mafia ties. The Schenck brothers used their influence on Loew's board to force Mannix into the high-powered job of MGM studio manager—over Mayer's objections. In doing so, they increased their grip on Hollywood's biggest studio and planted a spy who could report back on Mayer's every move.

Mannix was deeply involved in the day-to-day running of the studio and ruled with an iron fist. Though Mayer knew he was being watched, he couldn't deny Mannix's effectiveness. Eventually, they developed a cordial working relationship. Mayer even invited Mannix into the College of Cardinals. It turned out to be a wise decision.

Mannix took charge of union disputes, which were heating up across the industry. He managed to settle most of them out of court— but when negotiations broke down, Eddie had his own ways of "resolving" things.

In the late 1930s, a famous incident occurred on a soundstage where Erich von Stroheim was directing a film starring Marlene Dietrich. The two clashed over how a scene should be played, shouting at each other until the crew began to take sides. A burly cameraman sided with Dietrich and began intimidating the rest of the team into joining him.

Mannix was called to the set. He assessed the situation, walked up to the cameraman, and knocked him out cold with a single punch. Then he grabbed the electric bullhorn and barked:

"Awright everybody, back to woik."

That kind of resolution wouldn't fly today—but back then, it worked like a charm.

Mannix worked closely with Howard Strickling, MGM's head of publicity, to keep scandals out of the papers and patch up messes—especially when it came to the studio's stars. He treated celebrities no differently than anyone else and kept a sign on his desk that read:

"The only star at MGM is Leo the Lion."

Some in Hollywood saw Mannix as nothing more than a gangster. But he was far more complex than that. His persona was fictionalized in the Coen Brothers' 2016 movie *Hail, Caesar!* And, in real life, his name surfaced in the mysterious shooting death of actor George Reeves—TV's Superman. It was rumored that Mannix's wife, Toni, was having an affair with Reeves, and that Eddie used his mob ties to "resolve" it. But those rumors were ultimately disproved. The police ruled Reeves' death a suicide, and no charges were ever filed.

Despite his reputation, Mannix had a softer, almost comical side that few ever saw. If he liked you, there was nothing he wouldn't do for you. My parents adored him, and I remember Eddie and Toni being frequent guests. Toni Lanier, a former Ziegfeld Follies dancer, was an absolute knockout—tall, sexy, with a smile that could melt steel. She used to catch me staring and would flash me that smile, sending butterflies through my stomach every time.

The other executive in the College of Cardinals was Benny Thau. He and his wife, Betty, often came over for dinner and movie nights. Benny was nicknamed "The Quiet Man"—a playful nod to the John Wayne movie. He had the softest voice I'd ever heard. Even in a quiet room, you had to strain to catch what he said. My father believed

PANDRO S. BERMAN

Benny deliberately kept his voice low to make people lean in and listen. And he was probably right. I've tried it myself—lower your voice in a noisy room, and suddenly everyone's straining to hear you.

Benny was vice president in charge of studio contracts. His gentle nature and quiet charm earned him deep respect from the studio's contract players. Many actors said MGM was the only place they felt treated kindly during auditions, and they all had good things to say about Benny.

Judy Garland and several young actresses saw him as a father figure. Elizabeth Taylor, who couldn't stand Mayer, said Benny was the only executive at MGM she trusted. Rosalind Russell described him as "the soul of understanding."

Before marrying Betty, Benny dated singer-actress Frances Langford and was also romantically linked to Greer Garson when she arrived from England to replace Greta Garbo on MGM's roster.

At our dinner table, Benny impressed me with his deep knowledge of the film business. He knew what was happening not just at MGM, but at every major studio—and he was generous in sharing that intel. I'm sure that's one of the reasons my dad remained close to him for so many years. Benny Thau was a fountain of information.

Looking back, it wasn't just the power or prestige that mattered—it was the people. And for a while, it really did feel like the College of Cardinals had found its own kind of Hollywood heaven.

9

THE PHILADELPHIA STORY

Shortly after Dad arrived at MGM in 1940, he began preparing to produce the musical *Ziegfeld Girl*, but Louis Mayer asked him to postpone it for a most special and important assignment. MGM had agreed to produce *The Philadelphia Story*, Philip Barry's hit Broadway play, to which the studio had recently acquired the rights. Mayer had purchased those rights from Joseph Mankiewicz, who had obtained them directly from the playwright. Mankiewicz refused to write the screenplay or direct the film—he was already heavily involved with other projects outside MGM. However, he insisted on being credited as the producer, a condition guaranteed in writing as part of the sale.

Mayer knew Mankiewicz would have little or nothing to do with the picture once the deal was done, so he asked my dad to produce it —quietly and without credit. Dad loved the play and knew it would make a terrific movie. He also felt indebted to Mayer for giving him such a fantastic deal at MGM, so he threw himself into the project, working tirelessly on the script with screenwriters Donald Ogden Stewart and Waldo Salt. Together, they crafted a screenplay that some—including Mayer—believed was as good as, if not better than, the original play.

Dad convinced his friend George Cukor to direct, knowing Cukor would guarantee a spectacular performance from Katharine Hepburn, who loved working with him. At the time, however, theater owners considered Hepburn box office poison. Dad and Mayer convinced A-list stars Cary Grant and James Stewart to sign on in the roles originally played on Broadway by Van Heflin and Joseph Cotten. Dad was betting that the powerhouse trio of Grant, Stewart, and Hepburn would bring audiences back—and he was right.

The picture was a smash hit, nominated for six Oscars and winning two. Hepburn earned a Best Actress nomination, and the film completely turned her fortunes around. She was now a legitimate movie star with a powerful box office following. The Best Picture nomination went to Mankiewicz, but it should have gone to my dad—he was the one who'd done the heavy lifting to get the film on screen.

Even so, the success of *The Philadelphia Story* validated Mayer's decision to bring the third and final "boy wonder" to MGM. From then on, Mayer leaned heavily on Dad to develop strong scripts, showcase the studio's actors, and deliver the kinds of films that kept audiences pouring into theaters.

Louis Mayer was a workaholic, but aside from the occasional duck hunting weekend, he allowed himself just one true distraction: horse racing. We'd often see him at Hollywood Park on Saturdays. Mayer owned a stable of racehorses, and two of them—Honeymoon and Butcher—were frequent winners. They were usually odds-on favorites, sometimes going off at 1 to 10, meaning that if you bet two dollars, you'd get two dollars and ten cents back—not even worth the risk. After all, a horse could fall or break a leg mid-race. Mayer's horses were so predictably dominant that they were often booed as they came down the stretch—audiences who had bet against them were bored to death watching them win.

Mayer kept his horses at a private ranch in Perris, California, out near Riverside, and one weekend he invited my father and me to join him and his grandson, Danny Selznick, for a stay at the ranch.

He arrived at our house in his gleaming new Chrysler Town and Country station wagon. He was sitting in the back with Danny and motioned for Dad to join them. I got to sit up front with the chauffeur. A special table had been mounted on the back of the front seat, which could be pulled down and adjusted—either for writing or for eating—but Dad and Mayer used it to play cards on the long drive to Perris while I chatted with Danny.

The ranch sat in a cozy green valley surrounded by hills and was completely private. Neither Danny nor I had seen the place before, and we were both dazzled. We were shown to one of the outbuildings and told we'd be bunking with the stable hands. The building looked like an army barracks, with double-decker bunks and a huge bathroom full of sinks and shower stalls—just like in the military. We unpacked and each put our clothes in an empty locker with a padlock. We were given keys on leather thongs to wear around our necks and told not to take them off—not even in the shower.

Some of the stable hands had worked on famous horse farms in Kentucky and had taken horses to the Derby, the Preakness, and other major races. Their stories were fascinating—some slightly inappropriate for ten-year-old boys like Danny and me—but we loved every second of it.

At dinnertime, we walked up to another building next to the main house that looked more like a mess hall. We were joined by my dad, Louis, and a man introduced to us as the trainer. When everyone was seated, the cook came out of the kitchen with a huge tray of beef and a gravy boat, setting it in the center of the table alongside mashed potatoes and vegetables. The cook looked like he'd just stepped off a cattle drive—long beard, weathered face, full cowboy aura. But man, could he cook. We went to bed that night well-fed and very happy.

We were up at the crack of dawn—that's when they run the horses. As I brushed my teeth, I noticed that the stableman beside me had left his razor on the sink. I decided that my hairless face needed a shave, so I ran the razor down my soft cheeks, just as I'd seen my father do countless times. Eventually, I nicked myself just below my left earlobe, and it started to bleed. I blotted it with toilet paper as best I could and managed to stop the bleeding—for a while. But it started trickling again at breakfast, and someone brought me a bandage.

My father said, "What the hell did you do to yourself?"

When I explained that I'd cut myself shaving, the whole table erupted in laughter—including Dad and Louis Mayer.

That morning, I also had my very first cup of coffee. Someone poured it for me, and I took sneaky little sips when my father wasn't looking. It was delicious, and I couldn't wait to be old enough to drink it openly at the dinner table back home.

I noticed several teenagers at the breakfast table that I hadn't seen before. They were the jockeys who would ride the horses during their workouts. All of them were short and skinny—about the same size as the professionals who would ride those same horses at Hollywood Park. They knew how to handle racehorses, which is why they'd been handpicked for the job. They didn't live at the ranch but came in early on Saturday mornings for breakfast before heading out to the track for the time trials.

After breakfast, we walked over to watch the runs. Danny and I had each been given a pair of binoculars so we could see the horses on the backstretch. We climbed up onto the rail, feeling like a couple of seasoned racetrack touts. The trainer stood next to us, stopwatch in hand, timing each horse and giving a subtle shake of his head—yes or no—depending on the performance. It was all new, thrilling, and unforgettable. Danny and I were in heaven.

After the workouts, the stable hands saddled up a couple of horses for us to ride. They were a pair of old nags that didn't look even remotely like racehorses. Danny complained, "I thought we were supposed to be riding Honeymoon and Butcher," which earned a good laugh from the stablemen. One of them replied, "Those horses are high-strung—they'd toss you boys to the ground in two seconds."

We mounted up and set off on a two-hour ride around the ranch, accompanied by one of the stable hands just in case anything went sideways. It turned out to be one of the best horseback rides I've ever had. The ranch was lush and green, and when we reached the top of one of the hills, we had a breathtaking view of the valley below and the city of Riverside in the distance.

In the 1940s, the Southern California sky was bright blue with puffy white clouds. It reminded me of those pristine Ansel Adams black-and-white photographs—sharp and luminous, thanks to the red filters he used in the 1920s. This was long before smog, pollution, or freeways. There was hardly any traffic. I haven't seen a California sky like that since.

After the ride, we helped put away the horses. Danny and I got to wipe them down, curry their coats with brushes, and feed them apples and carrots. There's nothing like being close to nature with horses. It was a weekend we would never forget.

Later, I walked up to the main house to find Dad, but he and Mayer were in the den, deep in conversation. As I suspected, it had turned into a working weekend for Dad after all.

That night, we piled into the Town and Country, and the chauffeur drove us to the movies in Riverside. I can't remember what picture we saw, but it didn't matter—Danny and I were having such a good time, the movie was almost beside the point.

We headed back to Beverly Hills after Sunday brunch. Dad and Louis talked business the entire ride home, and Danny and I listened intently, soaking it all in. When we were alone, we'd mimic their Hollywood slang, pretending we were producing the movies they'd discussed—and inventing brand-new ones, just for fun.

When we pulled up to our house, Mayer got out and gave my dad a big hug.

"You are truly a boy wonder, just like my poor Irving," he said, referring to Irving Thalberg, who had died far too young. "He built me a stable of stars. But you—you're making big hits with them. God bless you, Pandro."

He never mentioned Danny's father, David Selznick, who had also been one of Hollywood's original boy wonders. But Mayer, his father-in-law, now considered him a traitor for having left MGM to start his own studio—and thus, an unmentionable. I was grateful that Danny had stayed in the car and hadn't heard his grandfather. He would have been hurt to hear that his father had been left out of a conversation about Hollywood's legends.

10

THE PURPLE DREAM BEGINS TO FADE

I can't remember exactly when it started, but I think I was around seven or eight years old when I began noticing tension building between Mom and Dad at the dinner table.

We had dinner every night in the big dining room, meals prepared by the cook, and my mother always made sure there was nothing on the table my father didn't like. For example, Dad couldn't tolerate garlic—just the smell of it cooking was offensive to him—so I didn't even know garlic existed until I was in my late teens. Dad was a highly respected figure in the movie industry, and my mother was careful to create a peaceful, proper setting.

She felt it was important that we all eat dinner together, in the quiet of that beautiful dining room. Back then, she didn't use terms like family bonding, but that's exactly what she wanted. Mom also knew Dad liked to eat as soon as he got home—he usually had scripts to read in the evenings and didn't want to waste time waiting.

She would have my sisters and me all scrubbed up and dressed in nice clothes, hurrying us to the table the moment he walked through the door. My sisters wore little pinafores. Mom used to dress me in wide-collared white shirts, short pants, and a child-sized blue blazer with no lapels. At the time, I didn't realize she had me looking like Little Lord Fauntleroy, but years later, those old pictures gave me a good laugh.

Mom was a strict disciplinarian. She believed it was her duty to monitor our behavior and dole out punishments she felt were fitting. In truth, we rarely committed any real crimes—just small misdemeanors—but whatever we did wrong, we paid for.

She never said, "Wait until your father gets home." Mom administered justice on the spot. But she'd always bring it up again during dinner, and that's when things got tense.

The punishments were usually banishments of some sort: dinner alone in our rooms for a week, missing the Friday night movie, or no visiting with friends.

No matter what we'd done, Dad always thought the penalty was too harsh.

"They shouldn't be forced to do that," he'd say. "It'll make them feel like outcasts."

Maybe he believed that. Maybe he just didn't want to suffer through our punishments with us.

Mom would argue her side. Then Dad would raise his voice.

"For Christ sakes, Vi, this is the only chance I get to be with the children. I have to go right back to work after dinner!"

The look on my mother's face said it all. She hated having her authority undermined in front of us. And I could tell that resentment was quietly building.

Of course, my sisters and I loved having our punishments rescinded. But even as a kid, I wasn't happy about the tension it created.

What I didn't realize then was just how damaging those dinner table episodes really were. None of us liked hearing Dad raise his voice—it was frightening, disruptive. We also felt guilty, deep down, that our behavior had sparked the conflict... though we couldn't have articulated that at the time.

Years later, sitting in a psychiatrist's office, I started to understand just how dysfunctional those moments were. When parents have unresolved arguments in front of their kids, the kids start to play sides—to manipulate things to get what they want.

I never did that. But Sue learned how. I knew better. There were always consequences for that kind of behavior, and I was determined I would never subject my own children to what we went through.

What really bothered me was how the tension kept growing. I was old enough to understand the logic in what Dad was saying—but sometimes, I agreed with Mom, even if it meant we'd be punished.

I began to wonder if Dad's feelings for Mom were changing. My earliest memories were so different—soft voices, loving glances, the warmth between them palpable when I was three or four.

Now, there was raised tension at nearly every meal. The idea that they might not love each other anymore... it was too painful to think about. So, I buried it.

Later, therapists told me I should have said something. That I should have voiced my fears, asked my parents directly. They said Mom and Dad would have reassured me—and maybe, just maybe, it might've made them realize how much damage they were doing.

At the age of eight, I decided that when I grew up and had children of my own, my wife and I would discuss every disciplinary issue in private and agree together on what kind of punishment was appropriate. Then we would explain it quietly to our child, showing that we were completely united—and doing it because we loved him.

That was the ideal. But when I became a father, I learned that ideal circumstances for that kind of calm, thoughtful parenting weren't always available.

My sister Sue used to get upset about these dinner table confrontations and would talk to me about them. I tried to reassure her, telling her it wasn't anything serious, but it didn't always help.

My mother used to say that Dad's bark was worse than his bite, and I repeated those words to Sue, hoping she'd believe them.

Even though I was concerned about what was happening, I wanted to protect her. I didn't think she was ready to handle the truth, so I downplayed the tension. But the truth is, none of us really understood what was happening. We just knew we didn't like it.

Of the three of us, Cindy was probably affected the most. She was the youngest, and she managed to conceal her anger for a long time. But eventually, it became clear that something deeper was going on.

Cindy felt that I received more privileges because I was the oldest and a boy, and that made her resentful. Sue was clearly Dad's favorite—something he never tried to hide—and Cindy, being the least noticed, began to feel left out.

I could see how hurt she was. I even spoke to Mom about it. But she wouldn't take any responsibility.

"She's very angry," Mom said. "And she brings it all on herself."

I didn't agree with that. I tried to assure Cindy that she was just as loved as Sue and I were, but those dinner table tensions were taking a toll.

Years later, I vividly remember driving both my sisters to the drug store to pick out Father's Day cards. Sue and I found cards we liked, but Cindy couldn't find one she felt expressed how she truly felt. I tried showing her a few, but she rejected every one of them.

"There's nothing in any of these cards that says how I feel about him," she told me.

She refused to buy one. I could see how hurt and angry she was, and I didn't know what to do about it. None of us did. We didn't have the tools to handle those emotions—so we didn't. There was enough selfishness in each of us to avoid dealing with it, even as the damage slowly accumulated.

I was always careful to avoid my father's wrath at the dinner table. But one misstep of mine, in particular, infuriated him and I was terrified.

It happened sometime in the early 1940s, before we built our swimming pool. There was a giant pepper tree in the middle of our sloping backyard, and it had to be removed for construction. I hated to see it go.

That tree was enclosed in a two-foot circular fieldstone wall. It was the centerpiece of the backyard—visible from my second-floor bedroom window—and it gave me a sense of calm. The yard itself was wide and lush, framed by flower beds on either side and bordered in the back by tall bushes and chain-link fencing to keep everything tidy and private.

When I was about eight years old, my parents built a treehouse in the sprawling branches of that pepper tree. It had a sturdy ladder, a window, and a small arched door.

It became my Saturday morning refuge.

I furnished it with a sleeping bag, old blankets, a flashlight, comic books, and magazines. My prized possession was one of the earliest, battery operated, transistor radios, a birthday gift.

Each Saturday, I'd pack a peanut butter and jelly or tuna sandwich, a banana, and a couple of cookies. I'd fill my Cub Scout thermos with ice-cold Coke, head out to the treehouse, and pull up the ladder behind me—hanging it on the scoop-shaped hooks on the door.

There was no real reason to do that. No one was coming into our backyard. But pulling up that ladder made me feel safe from the world, tucked away with my radio and my comics.

For a while, I was quite happy in my little hideaway, but eventually it got a bit boring, and I started thinking of ways to enhance my treehouse adventures.

We were in the middle of World War II, and I'd seen a number of the war movies the studios were turning out. I remembered one in particular—it had a scene with snipers in trees behind enemy lines, and I thought that was incredibly cool. I brought some "sniper gear" down to the treehouse: my father's 12-gauge shotgun and his high-powered binoculars.

I would peer through the binoculars like the soldiers in the movie, scanning every inch of the garden for intruders. If a bird landed in another tree, I'd lift the shotgun, get it in my sights, and fire. Of course, there were no shells in the weapon—but it was great fun. I did the same with butterflies, lizards, squirrels... anything that dared interrupt the sanctity of my imaginary battlefield.

For some reason, I could lie still for hours in that treehouse, trying not to be spotted by the enemy.

My Welsh Springer Spaniel, Penny, used to come to the base of the tree and whine for me to come down and play with her. I'd shoo her away and yell, "Get out of here—this is a war zone!"

I should've returned the shotgun and binoculars to my dad's closet each day, but I figured they were safe enough in the treehouse. I left them up there for a couple of weeks, ready for action whenever I wanted.

That was a serious mistake.

One night at dinner, Dad announced he was going duck hunting with his buddies in Bakersfield—and that one of his shotguns and his binoculars were missing.

I stayed silent as long as I could. But Dad was looking right at me—and the guilt must've been written all over my face.

"Did you take them?" he asked, his voice sharp with suspicion.

I had to admit that I had—and explain what I'd been doing with them.

The look on his face was terrifying.

"Are you out of your mind?" he shouted. "What could have possessed you to do something as imbecilic as that?"

I had never seen him so angry. His eyes were blazing.

I'd never been subjected to physical punishment before—no belt, no slaps—but I was sure that was about to change. I was terrified.

Fortunately, my parents didn't believe in physical punishment. Instead, I was grounded from the treehouse for a month and had to eat dinner alone in my room for a week. But the worst punishment by far was the humiliation.

I had never felt anything like it before—at least not with that intensity. I was ashamed, and it was hard to even look at my father.

The next day, I went to my mother and asked her why Dad was being so mean to me. She told me he wasn't being mean—he was trying to teach me responsibility.

I told her I had never seen him that angry at my sisters. She explained that he expected more of me because I was a boy and the oldest.

That was hard to accept—and it didn't ease my fears.

The memory of those angry eyes has stayed with me all my life. Even now, when I think about it—or about other moments like it—I still get that same uncomfortable feeling.

After a week, I was allowed back at the dinner table, but Dad wouldn't speak to me for some time. His anger had turned to scorn, and I was sure he would never feel the same about me again.

I couldn't imagine how he could just stop loving me.

When I told that to my mother, she was horrified. She assured me it wasn't true—that he would never stop loving me, no matter what.

And of course, she was right. It wasn't true.

But it was how he made me feel.

CHECK YOUR EGOS AT THE BOX OFFICE

By the time my sister Cindy was seven or eight years old, she was beginning to rebel against everything—and my mother wasn't having it. Cindy was constantly confined to her room, being punished for misbehaving, especially for talking back. If she wanted to do something and my mother said no, Cindy would ask why—and get the same answer every time:

"Because I said so."

It was the most maddening, frustrating phrase imaginable—and we all heard it from Mom at one point or another.

My mother was a woman of great charm and warmth. She had a lot of compassion, but this was one of her least attractive traits. She hated being challenged—especially if it came with attitude. She could be liberal with us about a lot of things, but she demanded respect. If you crossed that line, she would turn to stone.

I didn't hear that annoying phrase very often, because I'd learned early not to push her. Instead, I'd get her talking about something she liked—fine art, cooking, movies—and then I'd sneak in a request when the moment felt right. If it wasn't too unreasonable, she usually said yes. And if she said no, it came softly:

"Oh... I don't think so. Maybe another time."

But it was never said in anger.

Cindy never quite figured out how to talk to her. As a result, they rarely had a civil conversation. She also managed to get under my father's skin with her tone.

Cindy was afraid of his temper, so she avoided him when she could. But when he overheard her mouthing off to Mom, he didn't like it—and he let her know.

One morning, I came out of my room, which was next to Cindy's, and saw her standing in the hallway, peeking toward my father's den. The lights were on, and the door was open, which meant he was awake and having his morning coffee. He usually had it in the den or in the large bath and dressing room adjacent to the master bedroom.

I asked Cindy what she was doing, and she said she was trying to work up the courage to go talk to him. There were tears in her eyes.

I asked what was wrong, but she didn't want to talk about it. I told her she should go down and speak to him—he wouldn't bite.

"Yes, he would," she said.

I offered to go with her, to help ease the fear, but she shook her head and closed her door.

I felt awful for Cindy. She was having problems with both of our parents, and neither of them seemed to know what to do.

She felt she was being treated unfairly—but she was so angry and defensive with them that it was hard to blame them entirely for their reactions.

I wanted to talk to her about it, to help in some way—but I didn't know how. I didn't want her to think I was siding with them. But if I criticized her, even gently, I knew she'd shut down or get angry with me too.

So, I said nothing.

Later in life, I realized there were probably a dozen things I could have said that might have helped.

But they didn't occur to me at the time.

I was still just a teenager.

I was also having my own problems at the dinner table. With all the good food, I'd put on some weight—and my dad had not failed to notice it.

When he had something to say, he always waited until I had a big bite of food in my mouth before dropping the bombshell:

"I hope you're enjoying this meal, because I'm not buying you any new clothes. When you bust out of those pants, you'll just have to diet yourself back into them."

He knew it would take me some time to chew and swallow, which gave him enough runway for two or three additional insults before I could even answer.

I finally told him that I was starting to exercise more to lose weight, and he came back with the classic:

"Pushing yourself away from the table is the only exercise that works."

It wasn't said in anger—it was his other form of disdain: cruel humor. It usually got a laugh from everyone at the table.

Everyone except me.

I was too busy trying to pull the stinger out. I wasn't mortally wounded—just a little hurt. And truthfully, I wasn't that upset with him. He was playing the part of the wise and powerful father-figure whose pronouncements were never to be questioned.

He could also turn on the charm when he needed to—and he was convincing. But sometimes he'd try to shame you into changing your ways with jokes at your expense. It was uncomfortable being the punchline, but it was better than when he raised his voice.

Mom, on the other hand, was subtler—but just as cutting in her own way. She knew exactly what to say to demoralize you.

When it came to guilt, my mother was the West Coast distributor.

The two of them were like a tag team in the ring. There was no escape. Together, they were a left hook followed by a right cross.

Years later, I described those dinner table scenes to a psychiatrist, who shook his head in disbelief.

"How could you deal with a situation like that?" he asked.

The real answer was too painful to say out loud, so I gave him the short version: "You check your ego at the box office before coming to the table."

Early on, I learned to use humor as a kind of armor. It helped dull the sting, at least in the moment. But humor is just a Band-Aid over a wound that will keep bleeding if you don't face the pain head-on so healing can take place.

All of us were vulnerable when it came to Dad's dinner table jabs —including Sue, though she probably got the least of it.

One evening, he noticed she wasn't eating much. After two or three nights of picking at her plate, he asked why. Sue said she just didn't have much of an appetite at dinnertime.

Dad told Mom to take her to the doctor.

But Mom suspected the cause wasn't medical—she had a hunch Sue was snacking after school. She asked the cook, who confirmed that Sue had been making herself a bologna sandwich with lettuce and mayonnaise every day at around 4:00 p.m.

That night, with all of us at the table, Mom broke the news. When Dad saw Sue's untouched dinner again, she told him about the sandwiches.

Dad issued an immediate ban: no more bologna in the house.

The next morning, he went into the kitchen, removed all the

bologna from the fridge, stuffed it into his briefcase, and took it to the studio. There, he tossed it onto his secretary, Eleanor's desk and asked if she liked bologna.

Later that day, I called Dad at work, and Eleanor told me with a chuckle, "Your father is such a character—he brought me bologna! He's always full of humorous surprises."

I didn't say it out loud, but I was tempted to tell Eleanor she should try sitting at our dinner table sometime. It wasn't always so humorous.

11

WORLD WAR II COMES TO MOUNTAIN DRIVE

One of my other good friends was David Rosenson. He lived two doors down on Mountain Drive, and his father owned a department store in downtown Los Angeles. Next door to his house was an empty lot, full of tall pine trees and thick underbrush—perfect for hiding out and waging imaginary battles. Like most eight-year-olds growing up in America during World War II, David and I played endless war games, inspired by the propaganda that vilified our enemies. The only thing anyone talked about was the war. We heard horrifying stories, saw newsreels, and watched plenty of war movies—most of which portrayed the Japanese and Germans in deeply demeaning ways.

My grandfather had given me one of those antique portable Zenith radios, made of Bakelite, which were all the rage in the 1940s and '50s. I used to listen to Hitler's speeches on the shortwave band. They were terrifying—but I was fascinated. I practiced imitating his guttural cadence until I had a fairly decent Nazi accent. I would pretend to be the commanding officer of a concentration camp, and

David—always a willing participant—was the captured American soldier. In a harsh, snarling voice, I would interrogate him and describe the tortures he would suffer if he failed to answer my questions.

David loved being the victim. He couldn't stop laughing at my accent, so I would make it even uglier and bark: "Do you think this is funny, Rosenson? Let's not forget—you are a Jew in Nazi Germany... laughing at the Third Reich."

Eventually, the routines got stale, so I shifted gears and started practicing a Japanese accent—easier to imitate, and just as funny to us at the time. I'd narrow my eyes into tiny slits and pretend to be Emperor Hirohito, describing gruesome Japanese tortures, which were, in our young minds, even scarier than the German ones.

We named the empty lot "Bataan Forest," after the infamous Bataan Death March that had shocked the American public. It was thick with pine trees and had several large holes in the ground, which David and I had dug and camouflaged as foxholes. We covered them with dead branches and layered on fresh-cut pine boughs, topped with needles for concealment.

We stocked our hideout with toy guns, mechanical tanks, and little jeeps. We had canteens filled with water and a stash of candy bars to keep us going through long summer afternoons.

I was always the evil captor. David, always the sport, played the perpetual prisoner. I would march him around Bataan Forest at toy gunpoint, pretending we were on the death march. Then I'd order him into a foxhole, where he would beg for his life before I riddled him with imaginary machine gun fire—complete with my own sound effects.

When the war finally ended, we weren't quite sure what to do with ourselves. We had to find new enemies... and new games.

PANDRO S. BERMAN

GABLE AND LOMBARD

In early 1941, following the success of *The Philadelphia Story*, Dad produced his first credited picture under his new MGM contract. It was the big and splashy *Ziegfeld Girl*, featuring a mammoth collection of Metro's top stars, including James Stewart, Judy Garland, Hedy Lamarr, Lana Turner, Tony Martin, Jackie Cooper, Eve Arden, and Dan Dailey.

The musical numbers were directed by the renowned Busby Berkeley, who staged some of the most elaborate dance routines Hollywood had ever seen. Later, he directed some of MGM's less lavish—but still popular—back door musicals starring Judy Garland and Mickey Rooney.

Dad referred to *Ziegfeld Girl* as a musical mixed grill—with something in it for everybody. Mayer used to like packing his pictures full of stars, all of whom were under contract with fixed incomes. That way, it didn't cost him much to feature a roster of box-office attractions. He considered it an insurance policy for creating hits.

My dad got off on the right foot at MGM with *Ziegfeld Girl*, but it was one of the last musicals he would produce. The big, expensive dance numbers with endless chorus girls in fancy costumes were going out of style. Mayer had Arthur Freed—the famous songwriter—transitioning into producing MGM's newer style of musicals. Meanwhile, Mayer wanted Dad to focus on what he called his "bread and butter pictures" with his biggest stars—the ones that played to broader audiences. He was counting on Dad, just as he had once counted on Thalberg, to make quality films and build up his contract players into stars.

Clark Gable was becoming MGM's biggest male star, and Lana Turner was rising quickly alongside him. In 1942, Dad put them together in a little gem of a movie called *Somewhere I'll Find You*, a romantic comedy with an intriguing wartime storyline. The picture takes place during World War II. Two brothers—played by Clark Gable and Robert Sterling—are rival correspondents at a newspaper.

They're constantly battling their editor over whose stories get published, and they're also competing for the affections of Lana Turner, a journalist who vanishes from the newsroom and later turns up working at an orphanage in China.

Gable, of course, gets the girl—and Louis Mayer chalked up another win on the scoreboard rumored to hang on the big wall in his office. It reportedly read: Mayer 27, Schenck 0. I was in Mayer's office a couple of times with my dad, and I never actually saw the chalkboard—so I think it may have been a figment of Danny Selznick's fertile imagination. Still, it sounds like something Mayer might have done, given his intense hatred of Nick Schenck.

A great tragedy occurred during the filming of that movie. On the morning of January 16, 1942, Dad received a call from someone in the publicity department. A plane carrying Carole Lombard and her mother had crashed in the mountains southeast of Las Vegas, and all twenty-two people on board were killed. Dad was shocked. He knew that Carole Lombard was the great love of Gable's life, and he was certain his star would fall to pieces.

He called Eddie Mannix to accompany him down to the set to break the news, but they waited to tell their star until they had gotten him back to Dad's office. Dad suspected he might need Eddie's physical toughness to help contain Gable, who was a tall and powerful man.

My father's instincts proved accurate—Clark Gable went crazy. He started screaming and burst into tears, and Dad was afraid he might try to jump out of the second-story window. It took all of Dad's strength and all of Eddie's to restrain him. They eventually managed to lock him in a closet and summon a doctor. Gable banged on the closet door, screaming to be let out, but by the time the doctor arrived, he had slumped to the floor and cried himself into hyperventilation.

The following day, my father and Eddie Mannix accompanied Gable on a flight to Las Vegas so he could claim the bodies of his wife and her mother. Production of the movie was suspended for a week to give their big star time to recover, but my dad told me Gable was never quite the same after that. It changed his life forever.

Later that year, my father produced *Honky Tonk*, another movie with Clark Gable and Lana Turner, which audiences loved. Dad refused to start shooting until he was convinced that MGM's biggest star had sufficiently recovered from his loss.

In *Honky Tonk*, we see Gable in a different kind of role—as a conman forced to turn on the charm. When you combine that charm with his striking good looks and just a touch of danger, he appealed to both men and women. The story goes like this: Candy Johnson, a slick crook of the Wild West, is looking for a town where he can become a big boss. He manages to conceal his identity and pretends to be an honest man, leading the fight against the town's corrupt sheriff. But he meets his match in the woman he falls for—played by Lana Turner—who appeals to his better nature and begins to turn him into an honest man.

Every male in the audience imagined himself as that handsome devil Clark Gable portrayed. And every woman imagined herself falling for him.

Also, that year, Dad received a script from the MGM story department that came with a strong recommendation. He usually received about a hundred scripts a year, and many of them weren't even worth reading—let alone producing. But this one showed promise.

The writer was a young man named Thomas Lanier Williams, who worked in the MGM commissary as a busboy and rode a bicycle from Van Nuys all the way to MGM in Culver City—a twenty-mile ride. Dad was developing a story for a movie called *Marriage Is a Private Affair*, starring Lana Turner and John Hodiak, and he thought maybe he could work with this young man to develop a solid script.

Unfortunately, this was a comedy, and young Tom was a more serious writer—but he worked hard and turned out a decent screenplay, even if it wasn't terribly funny. The movie wasn't a hit, although some audiences came just to see Lana Turner.

When the picture was released, Dad called Tom up to his office.

He told him, "I know this script wasn't your cup of tea, but I believe you've got it in you to be an excellent writer." He encouraged Tom to go to New York to recharge his batteries. He said many writers flourished in the excitement of Manhattan and that he'd like to see more of Tom's work in a year or two.

It turned out to be excellent advice—because Tom Lanier went on to write a number of great plays under the name Tennessee Williams, including *The Glass Menagerie*, *A Streetcar Named Desire*, *Cat on a Hot Tin Roof*, and *Sweet Bird of Youth*. My father ended up producing two of them as films—and both were enormous hits.

Looking back, I realize Dad's real gift wasn't just producing hits—it was helping others such as actors, writers and directors— discover their own greatness.

12

THE SEVENTH CROSS

In 1944, my father was finally able to persuade Fred Zinnemann to direct a film for him. It was the frightening and suspenseful war movie *The Seventh Cross*, and he arranged a special screening of the first cut to run in our projection room. It was a couple of weeks after the shotgun incident, and Dad had finally forgiven me for my stupid behavior. There was no discussion about it—he suddenly warmed up and invited me to watch the movie with him, Mom, and the director. I was thrilled. That meant I was finally vindicated, and I was dying to see the film. Dad had been talking about it at the dinner table for weeks, and I could tell he was really excited about it. World War II was still raging, and the story centered on Nazis and their prisoners escaping from death camps—something I was completely fascinated by.

Dad had signed a cast of brilliant actors, including Spencer Tracy in the leading role. Signe Hasso, Hume Cronyn, Jessica Tandy, and Agnes Moorehead also appeared in the film, and they were all eager to be part of it. Hume Cronyn received an Oscar nomination for Best Supporting Actor and later called it one of his finest roles.

What really drew Zinnemann to the project was the powerful script by Helen Deutsch: In Nazi Germany in 1936, seven men escape from the Osthoven Concentration Camp near the Rhine River. The camp commander erects seven crosses, waiting for each escapee to be recaptured. As the Gestapo returns each man, he is executed on one of the crosses in the same manner as Christ was crucified by the Roman soldiers.

That premise was chilling for a young boy to watch—but also exhilarating. The seventh and final cross, however, remains empty as George Heisler (Spencer Tracy) flees toward freedom in Holland, doing everything he can to outwit the Gestapo. When the film reached theaters, audiences were on the edge of their seats, praying he would escape. There wasn't a single slow or wasted moment.

I was only eight years old, but I remember it vividly. I had heard so many horror stories about Hitler and the Nazis that I was mesmerized by the film—I was riveted to my seat. I also remember Zinnemann speaking afterward, offering a few thoughtful suggestions to tighten the picture. Dad agreed completely. Even I, as a kid, could understand what they meant—and how much the changes improved the pacing.

Although *The Seventh Cross* isn't as well remembered today as some of Dad's other pictures, I always thought it was among his best. We ran it again years later, and it was just as compelling—maybe even more so now that I was older and better able to appreciate it.

Fred Zinnemann went on to direct an incredible slate of classics: *The Search*, *The Member of the Wedding*, *High Noon*, *Oklahoma*, *A Hatful of Rain*, *The Nun's Story*, and *The Day of the Jackal*. But perhaps his crowning achievement was *A Man for All Seasons*, which swept the Academy Awards with nine Oscars, including Best Picture and Best Director, and a host of Golden Globes and other accolades.

In my opinion, Zinnemann ranks among the greatest American film directors of all time—up there with William Wyler, George

Stevens, Frank Capra, John Ford, John Huston, George Cukor, and Billy Wilder. You won't get much argument about that from anyone in the industry.

As we left the screening room that evening, Dad patted me on the head. Maybe Mom had told him it was time to forgive me, or maybe he came to it on his own. Either way, I was overjoyed. When I went to bed that night, tears ran down my cheeks, soaking the pillow—tears of pure happiness.

A week or two later, after editing changes were complete, Dad invited Spencer Tracy and Katharine Hepburn to dinner, and we ran the film again. That night, Dad did something rare: he asked Tracy if he had any suggestions for improving the film. Both Tracy and Hepburn were thrilled with the result—especially Spencer's performance, which truly was outstanding. Even at eight, I knew it was something special.

Tracy said he wouldn't change a thing. Hepburn agreed. I couldn't have been prouder of my father in that moment.

Years later, I realized that Dad rarely asked anyone outside the director or editor for input during post-production. That he sought Tracy's opinion showed just how deeply he respected him. Spencer Tracy was, without question, one of the greatest and most versatile actors in American cinema. While he didn't receive an Oscar nomination for *The Seventh Cross*, he had already won Best Actor for *Captains Courageous* (1938) and *Boys Town* (1939), and he was later nominated six more times—for *Inherit the Wind*, *Bad Day at Black Rock*, *The Old Man and the Sea*, *Judgment at Nuremberg*, and *Guess Who's Coming to Dinner*.

He was also nominated for his performance in one of Dad's finest films, *Father of the Bride*—a personal favorite of mine, not just because it was so funny, but because my dad produced it.

Years later, I changed my mind. After watching *Bad Day at Black Rock*, and again after seeing *Guess Who's Coming to Dinner*, I realized those were some of Tracy's best work. But his performance in *The Seventh Cross* will always hold a special place in my memory.

MY FIRST LOVE

That same year, we screened some other wonderful movies and, for the first time in my life, I fell in love.

At the age of eight, who knows what that really meant? I just couldn't stop thinking about that beautiful woman on the screen I had just spent two hours with. It was Gene Tierney in *Laura*—and everyone in the movie, including Dana Andrews and Clifton Webb, fell in love with her right along with me.

Of course, at my age, it wasn't anything physical. I thought she was incredibly beautiful, but it was her innocence and her charm that really got to me—along with David Raksin's hauntingly lovely theme song, which framed her in such a delicate, almost dreamlike way. I didn't understand any of this at the time. I only knew that something powerful had taken hold of me.

When the lights came up, I just sat there in a daze.

My father asked, "Are you dizzy? Feeling sick?"

"I'm in love," I said.

That got a big laugh from everyone in the room.

Dad chuckled and said, "Sorry to disappoint you, kid, but she's already taken. She's married to your mother's favorite clothing designer, Oleg Cassini."

To which my mother quipped, "He's not my favorite—but he's up there." That got an even bigger laugh.

The *Laura* theme had no lyrics in the original movie. Johnny Mercer hadn't even seen the film when he wrote the now-famous words: *"Laura... is the face in the misty light..."* The melody was so captivating that Darryl Zanuck demanded lyrics be written immediately. It became a smash hit, and nearly every major singer of the era jumped to record it.

A year or so later, we screened *Pinky*, and I fell in love again—this time with Jeanne Crain. She played a beautiful Black woman who passes for white and is pursued by several men. There were also unforgettable performances by Ethel Waters as her mother and the great Ethel Barrymore as the aging woman she cares for. Pinky is an accomplished nurse and caregiver who rejects romance to honor her duty and extend the life of her patient. In the end, she is rewarded with a substantial inheritance.

I think I fell in love with her strength and courage, as well as her beauty. But this time, I didn't say a word to my father. I was sure he'd tease me for being fickle—falling head over heels for the next beauty to appear on screen.

When I was thirteen, I had a short-lived crush on Gloria DeHaven after seeing her in *Summer Stock* and *Three Little Words*. She wasn't quite as glamorous, but she was cute, and I was beginning to discover my sexuality. She was... interesting to me. But that phase passed quickly.

Then we ran *I'll Cry Tomorrow*, and I was completely smitten with Susan Hayward. When she looked into the camera, I felt as though she was looking directly at me. I thought if I could just lie next to her for a couple of hours and stare into her eyes, that would be heaven—and that memory alone would be enough to sustain me for a lifetime.

But the most beautiful of all those women—and my true favorite—was someone I met in person before I ever saw her on the screen.

One Friday night, I came home late, and everyone was already seated at the dinner table. Our guests included an attorney named Ed Lasker, who dabbled in film production, and his wife—Jane Greer.

She turned toward me as we were introduced and smiled, and I felt my stomach drop to the floor. I just smiled back, too nervous to speak for fear my voice would shoot up two octaves. She was the most beautiful woman I had ever seen. I prayed we were running one of her movies that night, just so I could stare at her on the screen.

We weren't. And I can't for the life of me remember what movie we watched. But I never forgot that smile.

A FIVE-DOLLAR BET THAT WENT MY WAY

In 1945, I attended my very first Academy Awards. I was eight years old, and my mother bought me a tiny tuxedo and a pair of patent leather shoes with bows on the instep. She came into my room while I was getting dressed and tied my bow tie for me.

"You look so handsome," she said, beaming. "Go show your father."

I went into his dressing room and watched him putting on cologne. He looked at me, gave a low whistle, and then spritzed a little cologne on me too, which made me laugh.

I asked him who he thought would win Best Picture. He was sure it would be *Double Indemnity*, that murder thriller with Fred MacMurray, Barbara Stanwyck, and Edward G. Robinson—a classic shot in rich black and white. I had seen *Going My Way* starring Bing Crosby and Barry Fitzgerald and told him I was sure it would win. Dad bet me five bucks that it wouldn't—but I didn't even have five bucks to pay him if I lost.

He grinned. "Musicals never win," he said. "Serious dramas get the Oscars."

A limousine picked us up and drove us to the theater, and I was practically levitating with excitement. There's no feeling quite like stepping out of a limo onto the red carpet, with flashbulbs popping and a crowd cheering on all sides.

Dad saw the look on my face and smirked, "That applause isn't for you, kid. It's for Rita Hayworth."

She and her husband, Orson Welles, were just ahead of us entering the theater.

An usher led us to our seats—way down front. I glanced around and spotted my friend Danny Selznick a few rows away, waving excitedly. He and his brother Jeffrey were dressed in tuxedos too, seated with their famous parents. I wanted to go over and say hi, but Dad held me back.

"If the lights go down while you're over there, you won't be able to find your way back," he said.

Going My Way swept the night, winning seven Oscars including Best Picture. It also won three Golden Globes and the New York Film Critics Circle Award.

Dad gave me a look and said, "Out of the mouths of babes comes wisdom."

When the show ended, the Selznicks slipped out quickly. I tried to catch up with them, but the crowd in the aisles made that impossible.

When we got home, Dad pulled a five-dollar bill out of his money clip and tucked it into the handkerchief pocket of my tuxedo jacket.

"Don't spend it all in one place," he said.

That was the first time I ever heard him use that expression—but certainly not the last. It always made me laugh, though I suspect he meant it in earnest.

Years later, when I finally watched *Double Indemnity* again, I had to admit—my dad was right. It should have won. It really was the better picture. But what did I know back then?

I was just an eight-year-old kid who liked listening to Bing Crosby sing and was completely captivated by Barry Fitzgerald's Irish brogue.

13

A MOST MEMORABLE HOLLYWOOD PARTY

Over the years, Danny Selznick came to many screenings at our house, and I got to see him all the time. But after his parents divorced, he moved to New York with his mother, and there were long stretches when we didn't see each other. To fully describe the nature of our great friendship, I have to momentarily, jump forward to our college days. We were twenty-three years old and brimming with ideas—how we would enter the Hollywood mainstream as accomplished producers and executives, setting the town on fire just like our fathers had.

When Danny came out to California to visit his father—usually in the summer or over the holidays—he always called me ahead of time and said, "Bring your tennis racket, your bathing suit, and a tie and jacket for the dinner table." In the Selznick household, dinner was a major production, and everyone dressed for it—every night.

David Selznick was now married to the beautiful and talented Jennifer Jones, a major star who appeared in many of his notable films, including *Duel in the Sun* and the hauntingly poetic *Portrait of*

Jennie. Joseph Cotten co-starred with Jennifer in that film and several others, and they became a popular on-screen duo who could fill a theater.

I first saw Jennifer as the innocent young nun in *The Song of Bernadette*, for which she won the Oscar for Best Actress. That was 1944—a competitive year, especially for a new actress. She was up against some of Hollywood's most formidable leading ladies: Ingrid Bergman, Greer Garson, and Joan Fontaine. For Jennifer to win that year, early in her career, was remarkable. These other actresses had already won the hearts of Academy members in earlier roles. I was only eight years old when I saw it, but I was stunned by Jennifer's ethereal beauty and moved by her performance. She was childlike in her portrayal, and I could relate—because I still was a child. The amazing thing is, Jennifer was actually, twenty-four years old, playing a fourteen-year-old girl.

My father was a big fan of hers, too. In 1949, he cast her in the title role of one of his finest films, *Madame Bovary*. It featured a powerhouse cast: James Mason, Van Heflin, Louis Jourdan, Gene Lockhart, Gladys Cooper, and Harry Morgan. The film resonated with audiences and earned an Academy Award nomination for Best Art Direction and Set Decoration. The musical score, by composer Miklós Rózsa, later received the International Film Music Critics award—and he went on to become a dear friend of mine when I first entered the business.

The Selznicks lived in a beautiful home on Tower Grove Road, high in the hills above the city. It was a secluded area surrounded by eucalyptus trees, which—during certain hours—cast shade over the pool and tennis court. Jennifer had two sons from her first marriage to the popular actor Robert Walker, and both boys lived in a guest house on the property. With David Selznick, she also had a beautiful daughter named Mary Jennifer. When I drove up, the two of them were on the front lawn having a Tai Chi lesson—way ahead of their time, practicing that graceful fusion of dance and self defense. Back then, almost no one outside Asia had even heard of Tai Chi.

Jennifer's sons were both handsome young men, well-tanned from hours on the tennis court. They were much better players than Danny and me, so we split up for a game of doubles. I was paired with Michael Walker, who looked just like his mother, Jennifer. Danny played with Robert Walker Jr., who was the spitting image of his father. Bobby had trained at the Actors Studio in New York and was following in his dad's footsteps. Michael also became an actor, but sadly, he died in 2007 from an overdose of propofol—the same drug that would later take Michael Jackson's life.

After tennis, we cooled off in the pool. Danny brought me up to speed on what he'd been doing in New York and Cambridge—he had just finished his sophomore year at Harvard. We hadn't seen each other in months, and he wanted to catch up while we had the chance, knowing we wouldn't get a word in once dinner started—not with the illustrious company that would be seated around that table.

Dinner at the Selznicks' was always an event, but this one was even more lavish than any I'd attended before. It wasn't my first invitation, so I knew what to expect—but this surpassed everything.

After our swim, Danny and I went upstairs to change into ties and jackets. As we descended the stairs, I heard a booming, unmistakable voice. It belonged to none other than Joseph Cotten. I was thrilled to meet him—he was one of my favorite actors. His film performances were always first-rate, but more than that, he carried the mystique of "Old Hollywood," that elusive magic which once defined movie stardom. It's a quality that has largely vanished.

That's not to say today's actors take a back seat to them—they're incredibly talented and command their own enormous followings. But the era of mystery, of carefully curated public personas and untouchable glamour, is gone. The stars of the 1930s and '40s lived behind a kind of veil that only added to their allure. Today's celebrities are far more accessible, their private lives often laid bare. The mystique is different—or perhaps it simply doesn't exist anymore.

You'd have to be at least sixty to truly understand what I mean. Sure, you can catch glimpses of that era in the old films on television

—but to really *feel* it? You had to be there. You had to be growing up in Hollywood, like Danny and I did, to experience the full impact. Back then, a star sighting didn't just turn heads—it stopped time.

STAR POWER AND SEATING PLANS

Standing next to Cotten was the beautiful Patricia Medina, also an actress and Jennifer's closest friend. When Joe's wife, Lenore, passed away, Jennifer couldn't wait to pair him up with Patricia—and it turned out to be an excellent match. They eventually married, and while both had successful film careers, his, of course, was far more celebrated.

The doorbell rang again, and in came the unmistakable, hulking frame of Orson Welles—preceded only by the orange glow of his enormous cigar. He was another one of those rare, larger-than-life characters who radiated that old-Hollywood mystique I keep talking about.

Orson and my father were well acquainted, even though Welles never worked at RKO during the time Dad was head of production. I had never met him before, though I certainly admired his work. When we were introduced, he pulled the cigar from his mouth, pumped my hand, and said, "Your father has made an enormous splash in this town."

I didn't know how to respond. And instead of just nodding or smiling like a sane person, I blurted out, "Thank you." The moment the words left my mouth, I knew it was the dumbest possible reply. Later, I thought of a dozen better responses such as *"That's very kind of you to say,"* or *"That's a great compliment coming from you."* but of course the moment had passed. Naturally, Danny never let me live it down. And he was right to tease me. If the roles had been reversed, I would have done the same.

There were a small number of other guests that evening, though the years have dimmed my memory of exactly who they were. I do remember William Dieterle, the German director of such notable films as *The Devil and Daniel Webster* and *The Life of Emile Zola*. He also directed one of my father's classics, *The Hunchback of Notre Dame*, which starred the beautiful nineteen-year-old Maureen O'Hara, whose career was launched by that role. Of course, the true star of that film was Charles Laughton, whose Oscar-worthy performance as the unforgettable Quasimodo still lingers in the hearts of movie lovers. The film remains one of the great masterpieces of Hollywood cinema.

The dining room table was set for twelve, dressed in English bone China and dazzling crystal that glittered under an enormous chandelier. After a long and lively cocktail hour, during which some of the guests were already on their third martini, the butler entered the living room to announce that dinner was served.

With beautifully handwritten place cards, David Selznick had arranged the seating to encourage lively conversation. Danny and I were placed at the far end of the table, seated across from each other near David, who occupied the foot of the table. It was no accident—he wanted to keep an eye on us and make sure we didn't pester his esteemed guests.

I'll admit, it felt a little insulting to be seated like children. It was one thing when we were too young for adult conversation, but we were both in college now. It reminded me of when my mother used to say, "Children should be seen and not heard." My sisters and I hated hearing that, and sitting at the foot of the table under David's watchful eye gave me that same unwelcome feeling.

When everyone had taken their seats, I noticed Jennifer's boys weren't there—and neither was Mary Jennifer. Later, Danny explained that the boys were probably out with their girlfriends, and Mary Jennifer was still too young to join such a formal dinner.

Jennifer herself hadn't made an appearance yet either. But that was typical. She never descended until all the guests were seated.

Upstairs, she was being attended to by a studio hairdresser and a professional makeup artist.

· * · ★ · ★ · ★ ★ · · ★ * ·

THE GREATEST SHOW OFF-SCREEN

The timing of her entrance was impeccably staged. Jennifer whirled into the dining room in a high-shouldered formal gown, reminiscent of Loretta Young's famous entrances on her 1950s television show. Hers was just as dramatic—and she was even more beautiful. Gliding through the room, she lit up each guest with that radiant smile, personally welcoming everyone to her table.

The moment she took her seat at the head of the table, champagne was uncorked, as though the party were celebrating her arrival. Later, I suggested to Danny that the coordination between Jennifer's entrance and the pop of the bottles had been blocked out and rehearsed like a scene in a movie. At first, he took slight offense —but then he smirked, and we both burst out laughing.

After dessert, Jennifer quietly slipped away while the rest of us were ushered into the living room for after-dinner drinks and coffee. I noticed the CinemaScope screen had been lowered and the projector ports opened. The projectionist stood behind the glass, awaiting instructions.

About twenty minutes later, Jennifer returned—less dramatic this time, but no less striking. She now wore a red and black Chinese silk pajama set with matching slippers and pale makeup to complement the look. Her formal updo had been replaced by a looser, more relaxed style—perfect for movie-watching comfort, and still utterly chic.

With a flourish, she raised her hand and made a circular motion in the air—her signal to the projectionist that the show could begin. Everything she did had a touch of theater. She reminded me of Gloria

Swanson in *Sunset Boulevard*, making the same gesture to her projectionist and former director, von Stroheim, before declaring that iconic line: *"All right... I'm ready for my close-up, Mr. DeMille."*

Unlike screenings at our house, the Selznicks didn't run newsreels or cartoons. Instead, they showed home movies—lavishly produced family films, many of which became legendary within the Hollywood community.

That night, the first film was Danny's sixth birthday party, shot at the Beverly Hills estate of his grandfather, Louis B. Mayer. It was captured in black-and-white 35mm by a studio cameraman and edited by an MGM professional. Technicolor might've been deemed too extravagant for kids, but this was still the most elaborate home movie I've ever seen. Honestly, I wouldn't have been surprised if Mayer screened it privately for Hedda Hopper in hopes of a glowing review in her column.

Danny and I had seen the film before, but it had been years, and I was excited to watch it again. The party centerpiece was an enormous custom-built playhouse with a full garage and multiple foot-pedal toy cars. Studio carpenters had constructed a rear ramp to launch the cars through the garage at speed, giving the illusion of a driveway packed with mini-Cadillacs.

Behind the house, servants and uniformed nannies acted as a loading crew—pushing kids up the ramp and releasing them one by one on the cameraman's signal. Among the young guests were some of Hollywood's most famous children: Warner LeRoy, the grandson of Harry Warner and son of director Mervyn LeRoy; Linda LeRoy, now the wife of famed attorney Morton Janklow; Susan and Jean Stein, daughters of MCA president Jules Stein; and Danny's cousin Barbara Goetz, daughter of William Goetz, head of Universal Pictures.

It might have been the most over-the-top gathering of spoiled children in Hollywood history.

Some kids loved it, squealing with delight. Others—like Danny and me—looked terrified as we shot past the camera at a dangerous speed. We were only six, and it felt like a roller coaster. One crash could have been disastrous. Still, it was surreal to see ourselves that young again, and Jennifer kept giggling and pointing at the screen, insisting how adorable we all were.

The home movie was followed by a far more grown-up selection: *The Third Man*—one of my favorite films. No doubt chosen in honor of guests Orson Welles and Joseph Cotten, the film showcased their finest work. Written by Graham Greene, directed by Sir Carol Reed, and produced by David Selznick and Alexander Korda, it's a thriller set in post-war Vienna, full of intrigue, shadowy streets, and unforgettable moments.

The scenes of Welles running through the Vienna sewers under gunfire are iconic, as is the dizzying Ferris wheel sequence where Cotten and Welles share a tense exchange. A camera was bolted to the wheel itself, capturing the movement in real time—still one of the most inventive shots in film history. Even a decade after its 1949 release, the movie held up brilliantly. It still does.

That party remains one of the most vivid evenings of my life. My parents hosted some remarkable gatherings—many of which I'll describe later—but this night at the Selznicks' stands apart.

Over the years, Danny and I have revisited that evening countless times, reminiscing not only about the glamour but also about the kids in that playhouse driveway. Sadly, many of them paid a heavy price for growing up in Hollywood. Some ended up in psychiatric hospitals, some became addicts. One or two went to prison. Too many died young.

Hollywood is no easy place to raise a child. Between career pressures, long hours, and relentless public scrutiny, many parents—however loving—simply weren't present enough in their children's lives when they were young to give them proper guidance. In recent years, certain celebrities have chosen to raise their kids elsewhere. Julia Roberts, for example, moved to Colorado in search of a saner, healthier life for her children.

Danny, I believe, found a healthier atmosphere in New York, immersed in culture and education. I, too, benefited from going away to school and being exposed to different lifestyles. It opened my eyes to the world beyond the Hollywood bubble. It made me realize how sheltered my sisters and I had been—though, in fairness, the world felt safer back then.

Still, there were shadows. After the Lindbergh kidnapping in 1932, my father transformed our house into a fortress—wrought-iron gates on every window and door, decorative yet unmistakably secure. We even had a night watchman stationed in the garage every evening.

Those are the memories I carry. Some make me smile. Others haunt me. But they're all part of the legacy of growing up in the golden age of Hollywood.

14

REEL TROUBLE AND A RISING STAR: MY NIGHT WITH ELIZABETH TAYLOR

Mayer was always inviting my dad to special events, including screenings of MGM movies he was proud of. My mother usually accompanied him, but sometimes Dad would take me instead—and that was always exciting.

I remember one particular night going to a special showing of *Lassie Come Home* in Mayer's private screening room in the basement of the Thalberg Building at MGM. Everyone knows the classic story of Lassie, and the MGM publicity department released the following synopsis to the newspapers when the picture opened nationally:

> *After her destitute family is forced to sell her, a collie named Lassie escapes from her new owner and begins the long trek from Scotland, where she has been taken, to her home in Yorkshire. She travels many miles over green hills and fields, faces many perils, but finds her way back to the waiting arms of her family—and the little girl Priscilla*

(Elizabeth Taylor)—all of whom have been grief-stricken since her departure.

It was exactly the kind of heartstring-tugging movie that Louis B. Mayer loved. His lifelong dream was to bring wholesome family entertainment to America and the world.

Elizabeth Taylor was his new child star, and he was absolutely over the moon about her. Throughout the movie, he kept leaning over to whisper into my dad's ear—which I could hear, because I was sitting right next to him. Louis wanted Dad to cast Elizabeth in a film he was developing called *National Velvet*, which is why he'd invited him to the screening in the first place. I could tell my father liked the idea. Elizabeth was innocent and beautiful, and she gave a wonderful performance in *Lassie*.

Then something unforgettable happened—something I'm willing to bet has never happened before or since.

The projectionist missed a changeover from one reel to the next. That in itself wasn't unusual. In the old days, projectionists watched for two sets of cue marks—tiny circles that flash in the upper right corner of the screen during the last twelve feet of a reel. At the first set, they'd start the second projector. When the second set hit, they'd switch over. If they missed by a beat, the screen would briefly go black before the movie continued. It didn't happen often, but it was common enough that most audiences had gotten used to it.

This time, though, the second projector never started. The film ran out entirely. The screen exploded in bright white light, momentarily blinding the audience.

Mayer hit the intercom, barking, "What the hell's going on?" But there was no response. Furious, he stormed into the projection booth —only to find the projectionist passed out cold on the floor. An ambulance was called. After a quick exam, the paramedics determined the man was drunk.

Louis was livid.

He stormed into the next booth over, where another movie was being screened, and ordered that projectionist to immediately stop their film and finish screening the last two reels of *Lassie* for us. I've often wondered about the people sitting in that other screening room—how stunned they must've been when their movie cut out mid-scene, the house lights snapped on, and a voice over the PA said the screening was suspended due to a studio emergency.

As for the drunken projectionist? He'd certainly run his last reel at MGM—maybe anywhere in Hollywood.

All the way home, Dad couldn't stop talking about Elizabeth Taylor. He was sure she'd be perfect in *National Velvet*. It was a solid twenty-five-minute drive from Culver City back to our house in Beverly Hills—and he never once stopped singing her praises.

NATIONAL VELVET

In 1944, as World War II neared its end, my father produced *National Velvet*—one of his greatest triumphs, and a film that would touch all our lives in extraordinary ways. It launched 12-year-old Elizabeth Taylor into international stardom, with unforgettable performances by Mickey Rooney, Angela Lansbury, Donald Crisp, and Anne Revere. Audiences everywhere fell in love with Elizabeth, and the movie was a resounding hit.

Anne Revere won the Academy Award for Best Supporting Actress, and Clarence Brown earned a nomination for Best Director. The film also took home Oscars for Best Cinematography and Best Film Editing and received a nomination for Best Art Direction. Everything about *National Velvet* was magical—especially for a nine-year-old boy like me, who adored horses and, like the rest of the world, had a serious crush on Elizabeth Taylor. Watching her ride her horse, Pie, to victory in the Grand National Steeplechase was pure movie magic.

After the film was completed and ready for release, Dad took the whole family on an extended vacation—six months in New York followed by three months in Florida, with a side trip to Havana. He said he was thinking about retiring and wanted to explore the idea of producing a Broadway play. In New York, he spent time scouting theater properties and possible productions.

We stayed in the elegant Savoy-Plaza Hotel, right across from Central Park at Fifth Avenue and 59th Street—next door to the Sherry-Netherland. It was a beautiful old hotel, eventually torn down in 1965 to make way for the General Motors Building. From my bedroom window, I could see the glowing red neon sign of Reuben's Delicatessen across the street—our favorite go-to spot, just steps away.

Shortly after we arrived, *National Velvet* opened at Radio City Music Hall in Rockefeller Center. I was dazzled by the Art Deco design, especially when lit up at night. The buzz was electric, and crowds were lined up around the entire city block just to get in. The first people in line must've been waiting for hours.

The theater manager came out to greet my father personally and escorted us to a roped-off section in the back row, elevated on a platform for the best possible view. Though I had already seen the film once, I was thrilled to experience it again on that massive screen with Radio City's state-of-the-art sound system. It was a joyful night. MGM's New York team was there congratulating Dad, and Eddie Mannix had flown in for the premiere. That evening left an indelible mark on my memory.

Looking back, it's remarkable that my father was even there at all.

Just two years earlier, in 1942, the War Department contacted him. He was being inducted into the Army—offered the commission of Brigadier General in the Signal Corps, where he would have overseen the production of military training films. It was a prestigious assignment, but it would have taken him away from everything.

Fortunately for us—and for MGM—Louis B. Mayer stepped in. Using his powerful Washington connections, Mayer argued that my father was essential to the studio's operations and that releasing him would cause undue hardship. The request was approved, and my father remained a civilian. Thanks to that intervention, *National Velvet* became the landmark film it was—and I got to experience one of the most thrilling nights of my childhood, watching my dad's movie light up Radio City.

UNCLE HENRY'S ARMY ASSIGNMENT

My Uncle Henry wasn't quite as fortunate as my father when it came to avoiding military service. Thanks to his Hollywood experience, he was conscripted into the army and commissioned as a captain. He was stationed at the Signal Corps Motion Picture Center in Fort Monmouth, New Jersey—just a few miles outside of New York City. At the time, Henry was married to a lovely woman named Rosemary, and they were expecting their first child.

Henry was assigned to an administrative role as assistant to Colonel Emmanuel Cohn, commander of the Fort Monmouth motion picture unit. Colonel Cohn—better known in Hollywood as Manny Cohn—had once led a special film division at Paramount and was considered a top-tier studio executive.

Fort Monmouth was stacked with heavyweight talent from the Hollywood elite. Frank Capra was there, brimming with energy. George Cukor, the iconic director, was in the mix. William Saroyan, the Pulitzer Prize-winning writer, was also part of the team—along with other big names too numerous to mention. Together, they were tasked with writing, directing, and producing training films for the army.

It was, frankly, a bit of overkill—like using an elephant gun to kill a flea. These creative giants were making short films on riveting subjects like how to fold a blanket or make a bed with hospital corners.

With not much to do beyond editing—which Henry could have done in his sleep—Colonel Cohn invented a more specialized assignment for him. Since the Colonel had no love for army food, Henry's daily duty became this: check out a jeep and a driver from the motor pool, drive into Manhattan, and head straight to Reuben's Delicatessen. There, he would pick up a hot corned beef sandwich for the Colonel's lunch and a hand-picked entrée from the dinner menu to bring back later.

Thanks to this gourmet military operation, we got to see Henry almost every day. While the deli man was preparing the sandwich, Henry would cross the street and visit us at the hotel. I thought Uncle Henry looked terrific in his uniform—and back then, I couldn't wait for the day I'd wear one too. Of course, when I eventually did join the army, my only dream was to get discharged as fast as possible. Looking good in the uniform was the last thing on my mind.

Over the years, I've told people about Henry's unusual daily assignment. Some could hardly believe it. It certainly wasn't the most efficient use of taxpayer dollars—but having served myself, I can tell you: I've seen far worse.

AUTUMN IN NEW YORK

My sister Sue was with us in New York, but she was only two years old and needed constant attention. Cindy was still a baby—barely a year old—so she had stayed home in California with a governess and housekeeper. I, on the other hand, was old enough to need activity but too young to be left to my own devices. With no backyard, no playground, and no plan for what to do with me after school, I found myself sitting around the hotel suite, bored out of my mind.

My mother came up with a solution: she arranged for Henry's wife, Rosemary, to take me out in the afternoons. Rosemary, pregnant with their first child, wasn't living on the post with Henry but had an apartment uptown—just minutes away by subway. She'd join us for lunch in the suite, then sweep me off to explore the wonders of New York City.

We visited the Metropolitan Museum, the Bronx Zoo, and my absolute favorite: the American Museum of Natural History on 79th Street. I made a beeline every time for the Hall of African Mammals to stare in awe at the lions and tigers posed in their natural habitats. They were taxidermy, sure—but so lifelike that it felt as thrilling as the zoo, minus the subway transfer.

We also went to the movies. I don't remember what films we saw, but I vividly remember one show where Frank Sinatra appeared during intermission, singing with the Tommy Dorsey Orchestra. When he walked onstage, the bobby-soxers in the audience—high school girls in slim skirts, white ankle socks, and saddle shoes—absolutely lost their minds. The screaming was deafening. I had never experienced anything like it.

Everything in New York felt brand new, and I loved it. Well, almost everything. I wasn't exactly thrilled about wearing a shirt and tie to school every day, which was a requirement in the New York public schools at the time. I attended P.S. 186, where some of the kids were rough around the edges and made me uneasy at first. But I adjusted, and I took my studies seriously. My father assured me it was nothing compared to what he and Selznick and Thalberg endured at DeWitt Clinton High School back in their day.

For Thanksgiving, Mom invited Rosemary to stay at the hotel with Sue for the weekend while we took the train to Pittsburgh to have dinner with some of Dad's relatives—people I had never met. The visit was a long time coming. Dad's Aunt Loretta, his mother's sister, had been close to him during his childhood in New York. But they hadn't seen each other in years—not since he'd moved west and she'd relocated to Pittsburgh.

When we arrived, Aunt Loretta came to the door and immediately wrapped my father in a flood of hugs and kisses. She greeted my mother warmly, complimented her beauty, and gave me a beaming smile and kiss on the cheek. We settled into the living room, chatting for hours before dinner as she eagerly caught up with my father.

Her husband, Louis, was a soft-spoken, pipe-smoking gentleman with a bald head and a mustache. He owned a coal mine in western Pennsylvania and was clearly doing well. He asked me lots of questions, listened with great attention, and laughed generously at my stories. I was flattered to have his full attention.

Their son, Robert—ten years younger than my father—had graduated with honors from the University of Pennsylvania. It was said that he rarely cracked a book but still managed stellar grades. He had a photographic memory and a brilliant mind, which he put to profitable use not in business but at the bridge table. Instead of joining his father in the family coal business, Robert made a living winning tournament prize money as one of the country's top bridge players.

I had met Robert before—he came to the Los Angeles Bridge Tournament at the Ambassador Hotel each year and often joined us for dinner. He was a showman with card tricks and had a way of making magic feel real. One night, he fanned out a deck on our library table, studied it for ten seconds, then flipped it face down. "Remind me after dinner," he said with a smile, "and I'll show you a trick."

Sure enough, over an hour later, I brought it up. Robert had me pick a card—without showing it to him—and then named it perfectly. He continued through the entire deck, naming every single card in order, without making a single mistake. My sisters and I were wide-eyed with disbelief.

Robert went on to become a Life Master in bridge—a title requiring 300 master points earned through consistent high placement at sanctioned tournaments. By his late twenties, he had surpassed 5,000 points, achieving the rare status of Diamond Life Master. It was a dazzling achievement in the world of contract bridge, and I remember thinking how much I wished I had a memory like his.

Just then, the cook came out to announce that dinner was ready. We all moved into the dining room and had just started eating when the doorbell rang. Louis excused himself and went to answer it.

From my seat, I had a clear view of the hallway. When he opened the door, two Marines stood on the front step, in full dress uniform. I turned to my father. "There are soldiers at the door," I said.

He looked up, and I saw the color drain from his face. My mother's expression turned solemn.

One of the Marines handed Louis a telegram. He stepped back and saluted.

The message was from the War Department. Their son, Richard —another of Dad's cousins—had been killed in action in the south of France.

FROM GRIEF TO HAVANA NIGHTS

We were all plunged into grief as we watched Louis and Robert rush to embrace Loretta. She was hysterical, rocking back and forth in her chair like a Holy Roller, tears streaming down her face. It's a moment I'll never forget—and one I hope never to witness again.

We quietly called a cab and returned to our hotel so the family could grieve in private. The painful memory stayed with me for days. I couldn't stop thinking about Aunt Loretta, or what it must be like to lose a child. And then I thought about Robert. What would it feel like to lose a sibling? I couldn't imagine the pain of losing Sue or Cindy. I started to cry in the cab on the way back to the hotel. We left for New York early the next morning.

About a week later, Dad returned to Pittsburgh for Richard's funeral. I asked if I could go with him. He had flown in Grandma

Julie to comfort her sister, Loretta, and I wanted to be there too. But Dad looked at me and gently shook his head.

"I don't want you to go," he said. "It's just too sad."

The look in his eyes told me he was right. Still, I felt heartbroken for Aunt Loretta.

We ended up staying in New York for six months, which seems incredible now, because the time flew by. Dad never managed to get his Broadway play off the ground, so we packed up and headed to sunny Florida.

That was more like a vacation. We stayed at the beautiful Versailles Hotel, right on the beach in Miami. We went swimming every day. My sister Sue got stung by a Portuguese Man o' War, and her foot swelled up like a balloon. A doctor came to the hotel and gave her shots, but the swelling didn't go down for days.

I had my own mishap—I kneeled down inside of a hotel closet and landed on a rusty carpet tack. It left a small scratch just below my left knee. My mother patched me up with iodine and bandages, then wrapped it in plastic to keep sand out. That turned out to be a mistake. The lack of air caused an infection, and the doctor had to come back again—this time for me.

But the real highlight of that Florida trip was our side trip to Cuba. Eddie Mannix flew down to join us, and we boarded a boat to Havana. I had never seen anything like it—tropical fruit, spicy food, warm ocean breezes. The sound of Spanish fascinated me. I hadn't heard much of it before, and while most people also spoke English, I was captivated by the rhythm of the language.

Eddie's arrival was no coincidence. Mayer had sent him to talk my father out of retiring. Dad was Mayer's right-hand man, and Mayer wasn't about to let him slip away quietly to Broadway or Florida beaches.

We were in Havana for the Cuban premiere of *National Velvet*. I was excited to see it again, even though I'd already watched it at the New York preview. When we got to the theater, a huge crowd had gathered—some in line, others staring up at a strange metal structure on a long pole outside the entrance.

A booming announcement came over the loudspeaker in Spanish, followed by fireworks. A group of mariachis began to play, and the top of the structure lit up. We watched in awe as it began to "write" across the sky in brilliant sparks:

Nacional Velveta... Una Producción de Pandro S. Berman.

The crowd erupted in cheers. I looked up at the Havana night sky, watching my father's name explode in light. I'll never forget the expression on Eddie Mannix's face—cigar clenched between his teeth, watching it all with a smile on his face.

The only letdown? The film had been dubbed into Spanish. I would've preferred subtitles—I wanted to hear Elizabeth Taylor's real voice, not a different pitched female voice

out of sync with Elizabeth. It ruined the picture for me.

That night we went to the famous Tropicana Club to see Meyer Lansky's spectacular revue. It was dazzling. The showgirls—fifteen or twenty of them—were dressed like Carmen Miranda, with elaborate costumes, sky-high platform heels, and fruit-laden sombreros. I had seen Carmen dance on screen in front of bands led by the legendary Latino conductor José Iturbi—but seeing a live performance like this was on a whole other level. It was all hips, glitter, and spectacle.

After the show, Mom and I were bundled into a cab and sent back to the hotel. My little sister Cindy had flown out to Florida with the nanny, freeing Mom to enjoy an occasional night out. But as we pulled away from the club, I saw the look on my mother's face—and I knew she wasn't happy. Dad and Eddie hadn't come with us. She didn't like the idea of them roaming the streets of Havana at night.

There was a quiet tension at breakfast the next morning. Dad explained that he and Eddie had gone out for a couple of drinks and a talk about studio business.

But even as a kid, I knew there was more to that story.

15

FORCED LABOR

Shortly before my twelfth birthday, I was given my first bicycle and told I could now ride to school and back instead of being driven. I could also ride to the drug store, one of the markets in Beverly Hills, the library—or wherever else I wanted to go.

The problem was that the bike was a heavy balloon-tire clunker, a hand-me-down from one of my mother's cousins, and I didn't have the strength to ride it up the steep hill to our house on Mountain Drive. Halfway up, I had to get off and walk it the rest of the way home. After a while, that got tiresome and annoying—a waste of time and energy.

My friend Stan King had been given a beautiful new Schwinn racer that was light as a feather. I'd seen one just like it in the window of the Hans Ohrt bicycle shop in Beverly Hills, and I seriously coveted that bike. To make matters worse, Stan was getting an allowance of ten dollars a week, which was a fortune for a twelve-year-old. He told me his older brother Bob was getting twenty. I was getting three dollars and fifty cents, and I'd requested a raise to five for my birthday—but it was still under consideration.

It all felt terribly unfair.

At dinner one night, I announced that I could no longer ride my bike up the hill. It was exhausting, and I was getting pains in the back of my legs. I described Stan's bicycle to my dad and told him I really wanted one. He said he couldn't afford it, and if I wanted a new bike, I'd have to get a job and pay for it myself.

I told him I didn't believe that.

He said, "It costs a fortune to run this house, and money doesn't grow on trees. If you want a new bicycle, you'll have to earn the money to buy it."

End of conversation.

I complained to my mother and told her I knew he could afford it —he was just being mean. She told me he was trying to teach me the value of money and how hard it was to come by.

"If you want to earn his respect," she said, "you'll go out and get yourself a job. If you do that, he might help you pay for the bike."

I did just that.

All the paper routes in Beverly Hills were taken, and I didn't know where else to apply. There weren't many jobs available for a twelve-year-old—unless you went someplace like China or South America, where they don't observe child labor laws.

Eventually I landed a job at a bakery inside McDaniel's Market in Beverly Hills. I worked for a couple of hours after school and all-day Saturday, which was their busiest day.

The job consisted of scraping down baking pans with a metal tool to remove the cement-like dough stuck from previous batches. Then I'd rub them with gunny sacks to get rid of the smaller sticky bits and brush them with cooking oil for the next round. I also washed dishes, ran trays of fresh bread and desserts out to the counter girls, and cleaned the toilet every night before I left.

When I described the job at dinner, my dad asked if that offended my sensibilities.

I told him it wasn't the highlight of my day, but I'd gotten used to it.

It was my first real job, and I was earning $1.75 an hour—with tax withheld. It took a while to earn the $180 I needed for that bike. The work was repetitive and boring, but I stuck it out. I worked the entire summer, able to log a full eight-hour day during the week.

On the last day of summer, I left my balloon-tire monster in the garage and asked Mom to drive me to work. At lunch, I walked to the bank and withdrew the cash I'd saved. Then I headed to the bike shop and bought the shiny red Schwinn with the snap rack behind the seat—the one in the window I'd been dreaming about. I also bought a chain and a lock, things I'd never needed before. Nobody was going to steal the old clunker.

I rode back to work with my head in the clouds and chained my gorgeous new bike to a street sign outside the market. After work, I rode it home—painlessly—shifting into low gear and gliding all the way up the hill to our house.

Mom and Dad were so proud of me.

Dad wrote me a check for the entire amount I'd paid for the bicycle. "I know you thought I was being mean," he said, "but I really wasn't. I wanted you to get a taste of real life while you're still young—and you did."

He told me one day I'd appreciate the experience.

I'm still waiting for that day to come.

That was one way to teach a young person the value of a dollar—but I can think of other methods that would've been less dramatic and worked just as well. Still, I have to admit, I felt a real sense of pride riding that beautiful bicycle home.

I imagine it was the same feeling Prince Charles had when he drove his first Bentley through the gates of Buckingham Palace.

I'm quite sure though, that he never had to scrape pans in the palace bakery to pay for it.

GOOD ADVICE

After giving it a great deal of thought, my dad took Eddie Mannix's sage advice and abandoned the idea of retiring from the motion picture business. He cast Katharine Hepburn in a World War II drama called *Dragon Seed*, alongside Walter Huston, Agnes Moorehead, and Akim Tamiroff. The film told an inspiring story about a young Chinese woman who leads her fellow villagers in an uprising against Japanese invaders during World War II.

Hepburn gave another outstanding performance in a quality picture, and once again re-established her stardom and box office potential. I remember my dad taking me to the set one Saturday—back in the days when studio employees worked six days a week. The makeup department had given Hepburn "Chinese eyes," and she was barely recognizable, but she came right up and patted me on the head. Back then white actors played characters of different ethnicities. That has evolved over the years, and the Hollywood of today is so different in so many ways, especially when it comes to a character's ethnicity.

I loved going to the studio with my dad, but Saturdays were the only days I could watch filming—except during the summer, of course.

Working six days a week was standard for most studio employees back then, and if you were a top producer at MGM, you worked all seven. Louis B. Mayer hosted a brunch at his beach house every Sunday, and if you were part of his "College of Cardinals," attendance was not optional. Brunch began promptly at 11:00 a.m., and you were expected to be in your seat before the Pope—Mayer himself—descended the stairs to take his place at the head of the table. Business was discussed seriously until 2:30 or 3:00 p.m., when Mayer would rise and say, "Goodbye, boys—have a nice weekend."

Even though my mother enjoyed attending those brunches and mingling with the other wives, my father hated them. One day, he finally told Mayer he'd had enough—he wasn't coming anymore. He said he needed at least one day of rest a week to avoid total exhaustion.

He fully expected a blow-up—maybe even to be fired—but Mayer simply nodded. Sometimes in life, you must take a stand, whatever the risk.

I also remember going to screenings at Mayer's beach house with Danny Selznick when we were kids. We watched *Show Boat* with Howard Keel and Ava Gardner in Mayer's private screening room at a Fourth of July party. The music by Jerome Kern was lush—songs like "Ol' Man River" and "Can't Help Lovin' Dat Man" filled the room—and I couldn't take my eyes off Kathryn Grayson, who I thought was just as beautiful as Ava Gardner.

I was also captivated by Howard Keel's booming voice, but I liked him even better in *Annie Get Your Gun*, which Mayer also ran for us that summer. Keel was never more charming than when he and Betty Hutton faced off in Irving Berlin's "Anything You Can Do I Can Do Better."

DREAMS OF GLORY

By the time we were twelve, Danny Selznick and I were making grand plans for our future—legendary plans. Sprawled out under the big oak tree off the patio of our house on Mountain Drive, we concocted one of our most elaborate fantasies yet: a hostile takeover of Hollywood itself.

Our vision? We would merge all seven major studios into one enormous empire, operated from the MGM lot in Culver City. The only sticking point was the name. We'd draw straws to decide between METRO-SELZNICK-BERMAN INTERNATIONAL or METRO-BERMAN-SELZNICK INTERNATIONAL. Either way, it sounded impressive—maybe even Oscar-worthy.

Naturally, we'd need to expand Louis B. Mayer's office. Our version would be twice the size, with two towering mahogany desks mounted on platforms high enough to let us look down at our employees like Elizabethan judges—minus the white wigs, of course. The drama, the power, the perfectly waxed floors...

We made a list of people we'd fire. First on mine? Darryl Zanuck. Not for any business reason, but because his son Richard once held my head underwater at our old Santa Monica beach house, and I nearly drowned. If my mother hadn't been watching from the window, I wouldn't be here writing this chapter. Hollywood may forgive, but twelve-year-old boys do not forget.

We also started staffing our mega-studio with the most qualified people we knew: our birthday party friends.

Jill Schary, daughter of Dore Schary, got the top spot in the story department. Why? She had exquisite handwriting and drew her own pencil illustrations. Plus, her dad was the new head of production at MGM and a seasoned writer himself, with *Sunrise at Campobello* and *The Battle of Gettysburg* under his belt. We figured he could help Jill whip up some award-winning scripts.

Warner LeRoy, son of director Mervyn LeRoy and Doris Warner (yes, that Warner), was tapped to run our New York office and oversee all the theaters. But unlike Mayer's setup with the Schenck brothers, Warner would be taking orders from us. Later in life, he proved us right—he became a superstar restaurateur with places like Maxwell's Plum, Tavern on the Green, and The Russian Tea Room in New York City. (The Potomac in D.C. didn't do so well, but even moguls strike out occasionally.)

As for publicity, that job went to George Lemaire, son of veteran producer Rufus Lemaire. George was suave, sharply dressed, and had the kind of polish that just screamed "Hollywood spin doctor." Every empire needs its charm offensive.

We never got around to writing all this down, but I still remember how certain we were that it would all happen... eventually.

Alan Reed Jr. was slated to become one of our leading men. He was good-looking and determined to follow in his father's footsteps. Alan Reed Sr. starred in the radio show *Life with Luigi* and had a respectable film career, but he'd eventually become most famous as the voice of Fred Flintstone. We figured Junior would get a proper education in acting at home—and with a little help from us, he'd be on his way to stardom.

Brooke and Bridget Hayward, close friends of Danny's, were two undeniable beauties and perfect casting material. Their parents—Broadway producer Leland Hayward and legendary actress Margaret Sullavan—made them Hollywood royalty. We imagined pairing the Hayward girls with Bobby and Michael Walker, the handsome sons of actress Jennifer Jones. They were aiming for acting careers, and we were happy to offer them contracts. Between those four, we'd have the beginnings of a golden-age Hollywood dream team.

For head of Special Effects, we chose George Pal Jr., son of the famed animator and producer. George Jr. was in my fifth-grade class at Hawthorne and had a deep love of pyrotechnics. He nearly burned down his house with his ChemCraft set, which made him the perfect guy for blowing up model spaceships and orchestrating alien invasions. Risk-taker? Absolutely. Which is just what we needed.

Now, about Barbara Goetz—Danny's cousin. Her inclusion was... complicated. Her mother, Aunt Edith, was not someone you wanted to cross, and her father, William Goetz, ran Universal Studios. Political casting was part of the business, after all. We considered adding Barbara to our roster of contract players, but ultimately decided she wasn't quite leading lady material. Instead, we thought we might tuck her into the story department alongside Jill Schary... assuming they could get along.

As you can see, Danny and I put a tremendous amount of serious, strategic thought into this wildly ambitious merger. We had the players, the power, the plans—and the passion. And yet, somehow, it all slipped through our fingers.

We never got our two-throne office. No fanfare. No ticker-tape parade through the backlot. Just the quiet heartbreak of two would-be moguls whose Hollywood dreams were, apparently, shattered.

We thought it was terribly unfair. But there was no one to appeal to—except maybe the man upstairs. And somehow, I had the feeling he wouldn't greenlight a prayer like that.

16

A TERRIBLE DAY IN MY YOUNG LIFE

After playing baseball one afternoon with a friend, I was invited to stay for dinner at his house. I wasn't usually allowed to do that on a school night, but my mother gave me permission, since it was summer and still light out by the time I'd be riding home on my bicycle. I got home around 8:00 p.m. and walked into something I had never seen before.

My mother had locked herself in the bedroom, and I could hear her crying. My father was banging on the door, demanding to be let in, clearly upset. When I asked him what was wrong, he told me one of their close friends had opened his mouth and told some lies about him to my mother, and now she was very unhappy. I asked what had been said, and he told me it was a private matter between him and Mom—none of my business.

As I walked down the hall to my room, I heard his angry tone shift to pleading, which was very unlike my father. I could tell this was something serious. He was proclaiming his innocence and swearing the accusations were false—but the more he pleaded, the more guilty he sounded.

I closed my bedroom door, but I could still hear the muffled arguments, and it was deeply unsettling. I didn't know what it was all about, but I had a sinking feeling it involved infidelity—and that terrified me. A few of my friends were going through divorces in their families, and the thought of that happening to mine was overwhelming. I felt awful for my mother... and, if I'm being honest, I started to feel resentment toward my dad. My sisters were too young to understand what was happening, but they'd feel the ripple effects, too.

The next day I asked my mother what was wrong and told her I'd heard her crying. I said I was really worried about her.

"Oh, I just got over-emotional about something between me and your father," she said. "It's nothing... it's not even worth discussing."

At first, I felt instantly relieved. And unfortunately, I was naïve enough to believe her. I accepted what she said at face value. I don't know whether it was because she was such a convincing liar—or because I just desperately wanted to believe her. Probably a little of both.

It wasn't until years later that I learned what had really happened—and even then, I didn't want to believe it.

Sam Briskin, co-executive at Columbia Studios under Harry Cohn, told my mother that my father and Lucille Ball had been having an affair for years. He said she shouldn't tolerate it. His reason, supposedly, was that he thought Mom and Dad were a wonderful couple and wanted to see them patch things up. He believed that giving her this information would somehow be helpful.

I couldn't believe that he'd do something so insensitive and cowardly. Sam and his wife, Sarah Briskin, were among my parents' closest friends. If Sam felt compelled to get involved, why hadn't he gone to my father directly? He could've warned him that his indiscretions might eventually become fodder for nasty gossip and potential public scandal and urged him to end the affair and salvage his marriage. That would've been the decent thing to do. But Dad likely would've blown up—and the friendship would've been over anyway.

Of course, the friendship did end. My mother was furious with Sam for opening his mouth. Years later, she told me she would rather not have known the truth than endure the pain of confronting it.

I never saw the Briskins at our dinner table again after that. However, Sam's wife Sarah remained one of my mother's closest friends and supporters. She lived well into her nineties, and she and my mother were constant companions. I remember Sarah as a wonderful woman of great character who brought cheer into my mother's life during their declining years.

Both Sarah and my mother were well thought of by Hollywood's elite. When they went out to their favorite restaurants, they'd often run into friends who would send drinks to their table or special desserts. Lew Wasserman, the head of MCA/Universal, was very fond of them both. Whenever he and his wife Edie were in the same restaurant, he would discreetly instruct the waiter to bring him their check and pay it without their knowledge.

Dad's infidelity really damaged all of us. To me, he had been Jupiter—King of the Universe—my great hero, even if he was overbearing at times. Now, he felt like a fallen statue. Trust had been painfully shattered, and I found myself standing on shaky ground around him. It was deeply troubling, and something I couldn't reconcile for a long time.

Adjacent to the master bedroom—and adjoining my father's bath and dressing room—was a beautiful upstairs den. The couch and armchairs were covered in a rich navy tartan plaid, with tiny yellow and green vertical stripes and red horizontal ones. It was striking to the eye. The furniture, all mahogany, included a large antique desk, a high-back chair, and a magnificent daybed with high-gloss mahogany head and footboards, set into a wall niche designed especially for it by the architect.

My mother had a hand in furnishing that room, and it was a stunning showcase of decor. I thought it was the most beautiful room in the house—though the wood-paneled library downstairs, filled with antique treasures, was a close contender. To sit in that room, reading while listening to fine music, was pure serenity. I remember Dad once brought home a collection of Chopin piano works recorded by the Polish virtuoso Witold Małcużyński. His playing was so brilliant it distracted me from reading. I especially loved the longer works—the ballades and scherzos—and I would stop reading, close my eyes, and let the music overtake me.

Upstairs in the den, there was no music, but it was also a wonderful place to read. In the evenings, Dad and I would read together there when serious concentration was needed. I'd curl into one of the armchairs with my English Lit assignments. Somehow, reading was more fun in that room than in my bedroom. Dad would prop himself up on the daybed with a pile of fluffy pillows, reading scripts or marking up the racing form in preparation for Hollywood Park on Saturday. I remember him deep in thought, puffing on his pipe, breaking the silence now and then with a grumble:

"Why do they keep sending me these lousy scripts?" or "This moron has no idea how to write."

He always used that room on weekends. It opened onto a small upstairs patio he jokingly referred to as "The Palm Springs Corner." Sheltered from the wind, it caught the full sun. You could get a real desert tan in under an hour, which is why he gave it that name.

Around the same time as the altercation with my mother, I noticed Dad had started sleeping in the den at night. I was afraid she might never forgive him. When I finally got up the nerve to ask her about it, she said, "Oh, your father reads scripts late into the night. The light keeps me awake, so he moved into the den so I could sleep."

It sounded logical, so I accepted it. I was naïve—but also, I wanted to believe her. In retrospect, though, if the accusations were true, then he deserved to be thrown out of her bed. I hated seeing them apart and held onto hope that things would eventually get better. It was too painful to think otherwise.

Years later, I finally found the courage to talk to my father about his affair with Lucille Ball. Enough time had passed that I could face it—and accept that my father wasn't perfect. He was no longer Jupiter, King of the Universe. He was just a man, flawed and human like everyone else. That was a big step for me.

Over time, I began to weigh his virtues against his faults. I found his virtues far outmatched them. He wasn't a serial womanizer, a drunk, or a gambler who put our family at risk. He had long since ended the affair with Lucy, and there was no evidence of any other indiscretions. He treated Mom with more respect and remained the compulsive worker who had given us all a wonderful life. I began to feel it was time for me to forgive—or at least set his mistakes aside—even if my mother could not.

By then, Sam Briskin had been gone for years. But Dad still hadn't forgiven what he had done. Sam had been an RKO executive in the old days and one of Dad's good friends. He had run the business and sales division of RKO alongside Ned Depinet, while Leo Spitz served as senior attorney and eventually chairman of the board.

They'd all worked tirelessly to make movies—often without much financial backing. Sam had wanted badly to return to producing, as he had at Columbia. But Ben Kahane, then chairman of the company, worried that Sam and Dad might clash if both were in production. Being cautious, Kahane kept Sam in business affairs. He made no secret of his desire to replace David Selznick as head of production—but Dad was given the job instead. That must have stung. He never let on, but it couldn't have sat well with him.

Dad told me Sam must've known about the affair for ten or fifteen years before he chose to tell my mother. If he had been so upset about being passed over for the job, why didn't he expose Dad back then—rather than keep their friendship intact and pretend everything was fine?

I couldn't begin to fathom the fickleness of people. And why people do what the things they do, such as covering up an illicit affair only to expose it later.

17

HOLLYWOOD EMBRACES THE ART WORLD

Other than Sarah Briskin, my mother's other best friend of many years was Mildred Jaffe. She was a bright and sensitive woman whose husband, Sam Jaffe, was the high-powered Hollywood talent agent who also produced *The Fighting Sullivans*. He was often confused with the famous actor of the same name, who played the Indian water bearer in *Gunga Din*.

The Jaffe Agency was one of the largest and most powerful in Hollywood. Sam represented many of the top stars and directors of his era, including Humphrey Bogart, Lauren Bacall, Fritz Lang, Raoul Walsh, Stanley Kubrick, David Niven, Zero Mostel, Richard Burton, Mary Astor, Barbara Stanwyck, Jennifer Jones, and Lee J. Cobb, among others. You can imagine the kind of income a client list like that generated.

Mildred Jaffe was the sister of another Hollywood heavyweight, talent agent Phil Gersh, whose own client list rivaled her husband's. Her cousin was the well-known screenwriter, playwright, and lyricist Leonard Gersh, who wrote the 1957 smash-hit musical *Funny Face*. He also penned the play *Butterflies Are Free*, which had a successful run both on Broadway and in Hollywood at the old Huntington Hartford Theatre. It remains one of the best plays I've seen.

Sam Jaffe's sister, Adeline, was married to B. P. Schulberg, head of production at Paramount Studios in the late 1920s. She later founded the Ad Schulberg Agency in 1933 and became a prominent theatrical agent in her own right, with offices in Hollywood, New York, and London. Her clients included Marlene Dietrich, Fredric March, Herbert Marshall, and others. She was the mother of Budd Schulberg, the screenwriter behind *A Face in the Crowd*, *The Harder They Fall*, *What Makes Sammy Run*, and his greatest film, *On the Waterfront*.

The Jaffe–Gersh–Schulberg clan was, to put it mildly, a Hollywood dynasty—remarkably talented and exceptionally well connected.

Sam and Mildred also had exquisite taste in fine art, and they invested wisely. They discovered artists early in their careers and purchased their work at rock-bottom prices. Their home was filled with early pieces by French Impressionists and modernists, including Georges Braque, Juan Gris, Raoul Dufy, Edgar Degas, Henri Rousseau, Giorgio Morandi, and German Expressionist painters Ernst Kirchner and Alexej von Jawlensky.

There was also a large Alexander Calder mobile hanging in the stairwell that fascinated me. In their master bedroom hung a stunning portrait of Mildred painted by the renowned Mexican artist Rufino Tamayo. Sam had commissioned Tamayo to paint his wife, and it was one of the most beautiful portraits I've ever seen.

The Jaffes' home was a cultural oasis, and my mother and I were often invited for meals. My father and Sam weren't particularly fond of each other, so—to my great delight—I became my mother's frequent escort. I would wander through the house studying the paintings, and I could feel them elevating my spirit. My mother would gaze at them for long stretches, pointing out the brushstrokes and details that made them so special. Mildred, with her exceptional taste and eye for art, would share insights that had never occurred to me. I was only twelve or thirteen when we began these visits, and I was receiving a rare and wonderful education in fine art.

We were often invited to accompany Sam and Mildred to galleries and museums in search of new painters, along with other cultural events—all of which I loved. It was brain food, education, and family bonding all at once. The warmth and inspiration it gave me made me want to pursue it forever.

Two well-known actors—also avid art collectors—occasionally joined us at galleries: the silver-toned Vincent Price and Hollywood's favorite gangster, Edward G. Robinson. Like the Jaffes, Robinson had purchased numerous paintings by little-known French Impressionists early in their careers, holding on to them as their value skyrocketed. When he passed, he left his collection to his daughter—it's now worth millions.

In real life, Robinson was nothing like the tough guy he played on screen. He was charming, witty, and fascinating to listen to, especially when discussing his art. Vincent Price's collection wasn't as large as Robinson's, but it was certainly equal in quality. The two men were unquestionably in a quiet competition for who had the more sophisticated eye. There was a subtle tension between them at times, but it only made those gallery visits more intriguing.

The most knowledgeable person in that group was an art dealer named Frank Perls, who owned an important gallery in Beverly Hills. He was fond of my mother—an occasional customer and friend—and we often had fascinating conversations with him. I had never known anyone so deeply informed about painting and sculpture until years later, when I met Mumsey Nemiroff.

Mumsey, a highly respected professor of art at UCLA, had traveled extensively around the world, lecturing in museums to groups who followed her from one cultural destination to the next. I was with her in the city of Arles when she gave a lecture on Rodin. Her talk was so captivating that people outside of our group—those who had rented recorded cassettes to guide them through the exhibit turned them off to listen to Mumsy instead. I often wished she had been part of that early art circle with my mother, me, and the Jaffes. Even Frank Perls could have learned a great deal from her.

I was blessed to have parents with broad cultural interests who passed them on to me and enriched my life immeasurably. As I've mentioned before, my father introduced me to literature and classical music, while my mother gifted me with a love and appreciation for fine art. I remain deeply grateful to them both, and I've always tried to pass those gifts along to the younger members of our family.

When I attended UCLA, I majored in English Literature and minored in Art Appreciation. I had a distinct edge in both subjects thanks to the head start my parents had given me. At one point, I considered enrolling in UCLA's renowned film school, hoping to eventually enter the movie business—but my dad talked me out of it. He insisted that film schools were always behind the curve technologically, and that I'd end up having to relearn everything once I started working in the studios.

In addition to being a fine actor, Vincent Price was incredibly knowledgeable about painting and sculpture, and he regularly gave lectures on college campuses. One particularly memorable event took place at Royce Hall on the UCLA campus, where my mother and I joined the Jaffes and Frank Perls for two evenings that were nothing short of magical. Price delivered dramatic readings of Vincent van Gogh's letters to his brother Theo, who had represented him as an art dealer in Paris before the turn of the 20th century.

Price's voice was rich and resonant. He lowered it dramatically during the more sensitive passages, and the subtle shifts in lighting mirrored the intensity of his performance. It was acting at its finest, and those evenings left me with cherished memories—unforgettable moments I shared with my mother that were rarely, if ever, replicated.

PANDRO S. BERMAN

ART AT HOME: A LEGACY OF AESTHETIC INFLUENCE

Mom and I were both so taken with the Jaffe art collection, and we were learning so much about the art world, that it inspired her to begin adding more artwork to our own home.

Mom loved Matisse, and we had two Matisse lithographs—one was a minimalist portrait of a woman with flowing hair, resembling a pencil sketch. That piece now hangs in my sister Cindy's home, on the south wall of the den. We also had a Marc Chagall lithograph—primitive in style, with the appearance of something a child might have painted. My sister Sue even suspected that it had been painted by a child, but it was, in fact, a genuine Chagall.

A large Joan Miró color lithograph hung over the fireplace in our living room. It was printed on non-textured canvas and had been enhanced with oil paint by the artist before it was sold. It was a true masterpiece, full of brilliant color and some of Miró's most interesting and inventive figures. It eventually sold for thousands of dollars.

Jean Negulesco—the Romanian American film director—was also an accomplished artist. He directed the psychological drama *Johnny Belinda* starring Jane Wyman as a deaf-mute, and the musical comedy *How to Marry a Millionaire* with Marilyn Monroe, Betty Grable, and Lauren Bacall. But in Hollywood circles, he was just as well known for his artwork.

Negulesco used to make continuous line drawings using red or black magic markers. Once he began a drawing, the felt tip wouldn't leave the paper until it was done. When he went to people's homes for dinner, he often drew right on the dining room table and left the artwork behind as a gift. Many members of Hollywood's elite had one of his signature drawings—though they were so common, they never became especially valuable. Still, they made for striking wall art. He once drew a wonderful likeness of my mother in our own dining room. We also had one of his lithographs featuring nude women in various poses, and it now hangs in the entryway of Cindy's home.

We also had two beautiful oil paintings by the Italian neo-realist artist Ubaldo Magnavacca, which my father had purchased in Italy. I was particularly impressed with one that showed a scrubwoman cleaning a marble floor in a public building. She used a whisk broom and had poured a puddle of water across the tiles. The water looked so real I thought it might feel wet to the touch. I loved that painting and thought both were wonderful acquisitions—especially for the price—but my mother never really cared for them.

Another unique touch in our home was a series of small ivory cameos of women's faces, each mounted on black or plum-colored velvet and framed in oval dark wood frames. When grouped together on a light-colored wall, they were stunning. We also had several rare and beautifully preserved Currier and Ives prints displayed in the upstairs den.

My mother had exquisite taste—not only in art, but in fashion and interior design. Those days we spent with Sam and Mildred Jaffe were among the most joyful of my childhood. I cherish the memories of sharing them with her. That time together gave me a strong sense of belonging and helped soften the emotional blows from some of the more difficult moments I had with my father.

Dad, too, had a great eye for art—and the paintings in his office came with a story of their own. He had invited playwright Clifford Odets to his office to discuss a potential screenplay for a project he was developing.

Odets had made his mark in the early 1930s with *Waiting for Lefty*, a play that put him on the Broadway map almost overnight. Critics declared that he had picked up the mantle from Eugene O'Neill, who was then in his twilight years. That assessment was confirmed when Odets followed up with *Awake and Sing*, which opened to rave reviews and box-office success.

Dad had worked with Odets at RKO on several projects and loved his writing. Now, years later, Odets had gone on to write *The Big Knife*—starring Jack Palance and Ida Lupino—and the unforgettable *Sweet*

Smell of Success, featuring brilliant performances by Burt Lancaster and Tony Curtis.

Clifford Odets was also an avid art collector with a deep love for German Expressionist painters. He had acquired their works early in their careers, back when prices were still modest. Among his collection were pieces by Paul Klee, Emil Nolde, Franz Marc, Gabriele Münter, Wassily Kandinsky, Otto Dix, Max Beckmann, and others—artists whose paintings had now become quite valuable.

One afternoon, Odets noticed the long, narrow closet in Dad's office—the very one where Dad and Eddie Mannix had once locked Clark Gable to prevent him from harming himself. It was empty now, and Odets asked Dad if he was using it. When Dad said no, Odets explained that he was heading to Europe and always worried about the safety of his collection when he traveled. He asked if he could store his paintings in that closet while he was away.

Dad was happy to oblige, and Odets was thrilled to have such a secure location. A few days later, movers arrived with 25 valuable paintings, which were carefully transferred into the deep closet and locked up. At that time, the combined value of the collection was likely several million dollars—and that was in the 1950s.

When Odets returned from Europe, he was enormously grateful. As a token of his appreciation, he gifted Dad four Paul Klee paintings. My father initially refused—he didn't want to accept something so extravagant—but Odets insisted. He still had several Klee canvases, had acquired new work abroad, and was out of wall space. He genuinely wanted Dad to have them.

Dad hung all four paintings in his office, where they would be safe. The MGM lot was secure at night, and studio security patrolled the Thalberg Building hourly.

I spent as much time as I could in that office, studying the paintings. My favorite was one of a cat and a bird who had become friends. I also loved a vibrant red house set against an orange sunset. Paul Klee was a remarkable artist, though not a strict Expressionist—his work incorporated elements of Cubism and Surrealism, too. Because of the education I'd absorbed from Mom and the Jaffes, I was able to recognize those influences and appreciate the subtle complexities of Klee's work.

My father loved the paintings too—though he never quite admitted that to me. He'd only say they were "interesting" and that he wasn't sure he fully understood them. But when I shared my own impressions, I could tell he was impressed. I think, in that moment, he started to see the paintings differently, maybe even to enjoy them more.

He asked if all my insights had come from my mother. I told him that some had—but that I'd also learned a lot from Frank Perls, from my gallery visits with the Jaffes, and from reading *I Like What I Know*, Vincent Price's thoughtful book on modern art. Dad gave me a smile and said, "You're starting to sound like an art critic... just don't become an intellectual snob."

That was my father. He always saw the glass as half empty, while I saw it as half full. At one point, he told my mother he thought I was too naïve—too vulnerable to the disappointments of life. That stung. But in hindsight, I think that's why he was always throwing me into the deep end. He wasn't trying to be harsh. He was just trying to prepare me—for the real world.

18

A GREAT DIRECTOR MISSED HIS MARK

In 1949, my dad adapted the popular novel *The Sea of Grass* into a movie starring both Spencer Tracy and Katharine Hepburn. Hepburn, playing a headstrong New York woman, marries Tracy, a rugged New Mexico cattleman, only to discover that he's a tyrant. He uses brute force to keep homesteaders off the government land he's been grazing his cattle on—land that stretches like a vast, windswept "sea of grass." Hepburn's sympathies lie with the homesteaders, who have just as much legal right to the land as her husband, and she stands up for them with a powerful, compelling performance.

Elia Kazan, the brilliant Broadway director, had somehow gotten hold of an advance copy of the script. He was so taken with it that he was ready to abandon—or at least postpone—all of his stage commitments in order to direct the picture. At that time, Kazan was still primarily known as a theater man. He had only one film credit to his name: *A Tree Grows in Brooklyn*, which had been nominated for Best Screenplay and won an Oscar for James Dunn as Best Supporting Actor.

Dad was thrilled to have a director of Kazan's caliber interested in the project, and he brought him on board immediately. Still, he wasn't entirely confident in Kazan's understanding of the camera, so he hired Harry Stradling Sr.—one of the greatest cinematographers in Hollywood—to design the shots. The camera moves were elaborate and stunning.

Kazan worked incredibly well with Tracy and Hepburn and drew marvelous performances from both. And Harry Stradling's imaginative cinematography beautifully captured the wide-open prairie lands of New Mexico—though, in truth, the film was shot in Nebraska using process screens and stock footage originally filmed in New Mexico. The process work was seamless, the screenplay was a strong adaptation of the novel, and everything should have worked.

But it didn't.

Something essential was missing. Kazan, for all his brilliance, failed to capture the emotional heart of Conrad Richter's powerful novel. Whatever it was that made the book so gripping just didn't make it onto the screen. The film left audiences cold and critics unmoved. Reviews were disappointing, and word-of-mouth was even worse. It didn't perform well at the box office. Rumors circulated that Kazan himself was so disappointed with the final cut that he was privately telling friends not to see it.

My dad fell into a depression the likes of which I'd never seen before. My mother did everything she could think of to lift his spirits. She told me later that in all their years together, she had never seen him so low—and she had no idea what to do. Finally, she decided to host a dinner party with some of his favorite people: Cedric Gibbons and his wife Hazel, Tracy and Hepburn, and, of course, Sam and Mildred Jaffe. She hoped the gathering might offer him some comfort. Tracy and Hepburn, both magnetic and wonderfully down-to-earth, were as good a couple in real life as they were on the screen. To me, they were the grandest pair in Hollywood.

I remember that dinner party vividly. There were ten or twelve guests, and the dining table was fully extended, all the extra chairs pulled in from around the dining room walls. Tracy and Hepburn were so fascinating, you could hear a pin drop whenever either of them spoke. They had everyone's full attention—yet not once did they mention the movie.

The only other guests I clearly recall were the Jaffes, though I know there were at least two more couples at the table. After dinner, we screened a movie that Sam Jaffe had produced three years earlier but that none of us had seen yet: *The Fighting Sullivans*. It was the first picture he ever made.

The film tells the tragic, true story of five brothers—sailors in the U.S. Navy—all assigned to the same ship. When the ship was sunk by German forces, all five brothers were lost. It was heartbreaking. The room was silent when the lights came up. Even Tracy and Hepburn were visibly moved and praised Sam for the film. Hepburn called it one of the most touching war films she'd ever seen.

Sam told us that the real-life deaths of the Sullivan brothers had led to a major change in Navy policy. From that point on, brothers—and possibly even fathers and sons or cousins—were no longer allowed to serve on the same ship.

The movie struck a deep chord with everyone in the room, including my father. It helped lift his spirits. When the lights came on, he couldn't stop talking about it. That film, along with a tender hug from Kate Hepburn as she and Spencer were leaving, made all the difference.

I was standing nearby and overheard her say to him, "You're a great man, and you're going to make many more great pictures."

That would be sweet music in anyone's ears—but coming from Kate Hepburn? It was magic. It made me swell with pride, and I lay in bed that night thinking about it, unable to fall asleep.

THEY NAMED NAMES

Years later, something odd happened on another Oscar night that reflected a dark time in Hollywood. I had attended the Academy Awards with my parents in 1957 and, it turned out to be an historic night.

At that time, the Academy still presented separate Oscars for Best Story and Best Screenplay. (Eventually, those categories would be renamed Best Original Screenplay and Best Adaptation from Another Medium.) That night, in the Best Story category, the Oscar went to "Robert Rich" for *The Brave One*—a charming film about a young Mexican boy who tries to save his beloved pet bull from being forced into a deadly fight with a champion matador.

When the name "Robert Rich" was announced, a ripple of gasps passed through the audience. But when no one came forward to accept the award, the room filled with awkward titters and whispers. I leaned over and asked Dad what was going on.

"Everyone knows Dalton Trumbo wrote that story," he said flatly.

Dad had known Trumbo for years, going all the way back to their RKO days. He had tremendous respect for his talent and integrity. Trumbo had written the screenplay for the 1939 film *A Bill of Divorcement*, which my father supervised as head of production. He had worked closely with Trumbo during post-production, and they'd forged a lasting mutual admiration.

But in 1947, everything changed.

Trumbo was one of ten Hollywood writers who refused to testify before the House Un-American Activities Committee (HUAC) during its investigation into alleged communist influence in the film industry. Branded part of "The Hollywood Ten," they were cited for Contempt of Congress. The very next day, the Motion Picture Association of America fired all ten.

I'll never forget my father's fury.

He ranted at the dinner table, slamming his fist against the wood in anger at what he saw as a flagrant violation of the Constitution.

"The government is denying them their First Amendment rights," he growled. "It's disgusting. And I'll tell you something else—I'm going to hire them. We all are. Under fake names, under the table, in cash. And the government bastards can forget about collecting a dime in taxes from the work they blackballed."

He wasn't bluffing. I think if someone had walked in and asked him to join a paramilitary raid on the HUAC offices, he would have signed up on the spot.

"This," he said, jabbing the air for emphasis, "this is exactly why my grandparents left Poland and came to America."

His voice shook with a mix of outrage and principle. And for the first time, I saw my father not just as a producer, but as a true patriot. Passionate, rebellious, unwavering. He believed in the freedom to speak and create—and that night, so did I.

Dad's fury didn't stop with the government. He was equally outraged by what he called the "Hollywood turncoats"—industry insiders who cooperated with the House Un-American Activities Committee, betraying their colleagues to save themselves. He included director Elia Kazan, actor Robert Taylor, and other high-profile figures in this group.

Elia Kazan, who had done a terrible job directing *The Sea of Grass* for my father, in 1949 had been one of the people who'd "named names" to the House Un-American Activities Committee in his testimony in 1952.

Kazan had received a lot of criticism from the industry for his testimony. When he made *On the Waterfront* in 1954, it was considered his attempt at "redeeming himself" to Hollywood and to those he had wronged. Given that he went on to win the Oscar for Best Director, for *On the Waterfront*, in 1955, some people in Hollywood forgave him. Others, including my father did not. His testimony had ruined peoples lives.

But at the time, during the worst of the HUAC hearings, my father was angry and upset. He was especially distressed to hear rumors that his friend Walter Mirisch might have been involved. Whether there was any truth to those whispers remains unclear—but to my father, even the suspicion was painful.

During the HUAC hearings, several witnesses (including Kazan) named names, handing over lists of alleged Communists, and implicating people who had done little more than attend a few left-leaning meetings. Most of those accused weren't politically active or engaged in anything remotely subversive. They were just struggling creatives, attending gatherings in hopes of networking or landing a job. But once their names appeared on Communist Party membership lists—no matter the context—they were branded as enemies of the state and blacklisted from the industry they loved.

Trumbo ended up serving ten months in federal prison for Contempt of Congress—simply for refusing to answer the committee's invasive and unconstitutional questions.

When he was released, he sold his ranch up the coast and quietly moved to Mexico City, hoping to find covert screenwriting work from sympathetic Hollywood producers. He was still radioactive in the eyes of the industry, but Dad didn't turn his back on him.

He stayed in touch, sent him cash through Western Union to help him get by, and did what he could behind the scenes to support him.

In time, Trumbo found his rhythm again. Working under pseudonyms, he wrote more than thirty screenplays from exile—many of which became major films.

Watching my father stand up for him—not just in words but in deeds—gave me a rare glimpse beneath his stoic, "Rock of Gibraltar" exterior. Beneath the unshakable producer and family patriarch was a man who cared deeply about justice, friendship, and doing the right thing... even when no one was watching.

19

FATHER OF THE BRIDE

In 1950, Elizabeth Taylor was just eighteen years old when my dad developed a wonderful project for her called *Father of the Bride*—a comedy with a terrific storyline and a sharp, funny script. It centered on a father overwhelmed by the impending marriage of his daughter: he's heartbroken about "losing" her and spiraling into a full-blown meltdown over the rising costs of the wedding.

With brilliant performances by Spencer Tracy, Joan Bennett, and Elizabeth Taylor, and the sensitive, pitch-perfect direction of Vincente Minnelli, the film became an enormous hit. It was nominated for Best Picture, Best Actor, and Best Screenplay—but, as my dad often said, comedies almost never win Oscars for Best Picture.

We attended the Academy Awards that year hoping for a win, but once again, it wasn't Dad's night. The evening belonged to Darryl Zanuck, who took home the Oscar for Best Picture with the spectacular *All About Eve*. He was also honored with the Irving Thalberg Award for lifetime achievement. My father nodded in quiet agreement—he always believed Zanuck was the greatest of the early pioneer filmmakers.

Spencer Tracy was nominated for Best Actor for *Father of the Bride*, but he lost to José Ferrer, whose electrifying performance as Cyrano de Bergerac would have won in almost any year. Frances Goodrich and Albert Hackett, the husband-and-wife writing team behind the script, didn't win either. Instead, Joe Mankiewicz scored big, winning two Oscars for writing and directing *All About Eve*.

We later screened *All About Eve* at home, and it was, without a doubt, one of the best films I had ever seen.

Though *Father of the Bride* went home empty-handed at the Oscars, it was a runaway success at the box office. As soon as the Hacketts finished the sequel, my dad got it into production. He instructed MGM not to strike any of the essential sets from the first film so they could move quickly into filming *Father's Little Dividend* with the same cast and Minnelli again at the helm.

The sequel picked up right where *Father of the Bride* left off. The young bride announces she's expecting a baby, and now the flustered father must come to grips with the idea of becoming a grandfather—and possibly helping raise another child.

It was a sweet film. Not nearly the cultural touchstone the original had been, but still enjoyable, with another excellent performance from Tracy. Vincente Minnelli even won the Directors Guild of America Award for Best Director that year, which in some small way made up for his earlier Oscar snub.

I remember our whole family going to the preview screening at a little theater in Pasadena, and we all really liked it. Still, it wasn't a franchise. A third installment would've been a step too far—it almost certainly would have lost money.

Nearly forty years later, *Father of the Bride* was remade. Remarkably, Frances Goodrich and Albert Hackett wrote the screenplay for that version as well. Steve Martin stepped into Spencer Tracy's role, and Diane Keaton reprised the mother's part originally played by Joan Bennett. But Kimberly Williams-Paisley, who played the bride, was rather forgettable. Then again, almost any young actress would pale in comparison to Elizabeth Taylor.

IVANHOE AND THE SWASHBUCKLERS

In the late 1940s and early 1950s, my dad produced a series of swashbuckler movies, inspired by the 1938 Errol Flynn version of *The Adventures of Robin Hood*, which had been a smash hit. Louis B. Mayer convinced him to take on a slate of action-adventure features, beginning in 1948 with *The Three Musketeers*, which brought Lana Turner and Gene Kelly together on screen for the first time.

Kelly's athleticism and flair added something entirely new—he brought stylized, dance-like choreography to the sword fights, adding both excitement and humor. I went down to the backlot one Saturday to watch the filming of one of those elaborate scenes, and I was captivated. It looked like great fun—and it made me seriously consider taking fencing lessons.

Gene Kelly personally blocked out every move of the scene, which included spectacular leaps, wild rope swings, and fighting off two swordsmen simultaneously with his back against a wall. It was bold, romantic, and surprisingly balletic.

I had no idea sword fights could be choreographed like dance numbers—but of course, why not? They choreographed all the swimming routines in the Esther Williams movies. It made perfect sense.

Following *The Three Musketeers*, Dad produced five more swashbuckling adventures: *Ivanhoe, The Prisoner of Zenda, Knights of the Round Table, Quentin Durward,* and *All the Brothers Were Valiant.* These films featured an impressive roster of MGM's finest leading men and women, including Robert Taylor, Ava Gardner, Mel Ferrer, Joan Fontaine, Stewart Granger, Deborah Kerr, Van Heflin, Jane Greer, Kay

Kendall, Vincent Price, June Allyson, and Angela Lansbury—just to name a few.

In those days, Stewart Granger and his wife, Jean Simmons, were regular guests at our home. They'd join us for dinner and private movie screenings. Granger was charismatic and funny, while Jean Simmons was strikingly beautiful, with a graceful elegance and an appealing British accent. I found her to be quite enchanting.

One Friday night, we screened *All the Brothers Were Valiant*, and we were all thrilled—not just by the film, but especially by Stewart's performance. Interestingly, his real name was James Stewart, but that name had already been claimed (and carved into Hollywood history), so he adopted the stage name Stewart Granger. Some people still called him Jim, and my dad used to refer to him fondly as "Jimmy Granger."

IVANHOE AND THE OSCARS

The most important of Dad's period action films was *Ivanhoe* (released in 1952), which starred Elizabeth Taylor and Robert Taylor (who ironically had also "named names in his testimony to HUAC in 1947). They were arguably the most dazzling couple ever to appear on screen together. George Sanders gave a brilliant performance as the villainous Sir Brian de Bois-Guilbert, and the film earned three Academy Award nominations, including Best Picture, along with several Golden Globe nods. Director Richard Thorpe won the Directors Guild of America Award for Best Direction and was also nominated for the Golden Lion at the Venice Film Festival.

I went to the Academy Awards ceremony that year with Mom and Dad. All the male nominees, including my father, were required to wear powder blue tuxedo shirts. At the time, television was still broadcast in black and white, and white shirts caused a flare effect on camera—blinding the cameraman and creating a bright flash on home screens if the subject moved even slightly. Powder blue was the fix. Eventually, when color television became standard, everyone switched back to classic white.

That night, I closed my eyes and crossed my fingers as the presenter opened the envelope, praying *Ivanhoe* would win the Oscar. Dad's pictures had been nominated before, but I thought this one really deserved it. *Ivanhoe* had a sweeping story, elegant performances, and was so much more than a typical action-adventure film.

But it wasn't to be.

The 1953 Best Picture Oscar went to *The Greatest Show on Earth*, Cecil B. DeMille's lavish circus extravaganza. It was a spectacle, no question—but I was biased, and in my eyes, Ivanhoe was better. When the winner was announced, I saw the expression on my father's face—one I'll never forget. It said, What the hell do you have to do to win an Oscar? It was the first time I remember truly feeling sad for him. That feeling wouldn't return until many years later, when he was an old man facing illness and the slow decline of age.

That same year, *High Noon*, another nominee, was just as deserving—and perhaps even more impactful. Starring Gary Cooper and Grace Kelly, it would go on to become one of the greatest Westerns of all time. It was produced and directed by Stanley Kramer, a cousin of ours. His grandfather was part of our original Pandrovitz family who immigrated to America at the turn of the century. Stanley built his own legacy in Hollywood—and I'm sure he and my dad went out and got good and drunk together that night, both nursing the sting of their lost Oscars.

Stanley would go on to make many great films, including the powerful and controversial *Guess Who's Coming to Dinner*, starring Spencer Tracy, Katharine Hepburn, and Sidney Poitier. It was Tracy's final film—he passed away just weeks later, in 1967, at his home in Beverly Hills.

THE LIGHT TOUCH IN EUROPE

In 1951, when I was fourteen, I had the thrill of going on my very first trip to Europe with Mom and Dad. My sisters stayed home that summer—they were busy with camps and other activities, and Mom felt they were too young for the kind of travel we had planned, especially since our itinerary included parts of North Africa as well as Europe.

The trip revolved around the location shoot for Dad's movie *The Light Touch*, and I was beyond excited to tag along to Rome, Taormina in Sicily, and Tunis—the capital of Tunisia—to see the film in production.

Richard Brooks had adapted the Broadway play *Crown of Thorns* into a suspenseful new script about an art thief played by Stewart Granger. In the story, he steals a Renaissance painting from a luxury hotel in Sicily, intending to sell it to an underground collector for $100,000. But instead of handing over the stolen artwork, Granger fakes an accident on the boat ride across the Mediterranean. When they dock in Tunis, he claims the painting was lost in a storm, washed overboard.

His real plan? Have six near-perfect copies made and sell each one as the original—keeping the true painting for himself. Once the fakes were out in the world, he'd expose them as forgeries and cash in on the authentic one.

He enlists a woman—played by Pier Angeli—who's both artistically gifted and financially desperate. Though deeply conflicted about forging a masterpiece, she agrees. And of course, she falls in love with him.

Brooks directed the film as well, aiming for a blend of romantic intrigue and action-adventure. While he envisioned it as a suspenseful caper, audiences saw it more as a romantic comedy. Still, with strong performances by Stewart Granger and George Sanders, *The Light Touch* became a modest hit.

· * · ★ * * ★ · · ★ * ·

JEAN SIMMONS, CINECITTÀ, AND A SURPRISE IN ROME

Jean Simmons was also with us on location, but I was surprised to see her spending more time with Richard Brooks than with her husband —who happened to be the leading man in the picture. One evening, after we'd returned to the hotel from dinner, we spotted Brooks and Jean together in the lounge, enjoying drinks and looking quite cozy. I asked my father why she was with Brooks instead of Stewart Granger.

Dad looked at me and said simply, "Brooks is her husband."

I blinked. "What do you mean? She was just at our house for dinner with her husband—Stewart Granger."

"They're divorced," Dad explained. "She's married to Brooks now."

That stopped me cold. I had no idea. It had all happened so quickly—within the space of a year. After that, she came to our house for dinner many times with her new husband, since he was now working with Dad on several upcoming projects.

The Light Touch's interior scenes were filmed at the Cinecittà Studios in Rome, with location shooting in Taormina, Sicily, and Tunis. The Taormina hotel where the opening art theft takes place was breathtaking—easily the most beautiful hotel in Sicily. Originally, the script had the painting stolen from a museum or church, like in the stage version, but no museums would allow filming inside. Therefore, the location was changed to a luxury hotel—problem solved.

When we crossed the Mediterranean to Tunis, high winds kicked up, and I ended up getting a bit seasick. Several scenes were shot in the Souk, a sprawling open-air market owned and run by local Arab vendors. Their long robes and head coverings were fascinating to me—but I'm sure we looked even stranger to them. The sight of an American movie crew setting up lights and cameras in their busy marketplace drew stares and whispers. We must have looked like we'd landed from another planet.

Rome was dazzling. We shopped at elegant boutiques near the Spanish Steps and dined in top-tier restaurants. That's where I discovered real pasta. Until then, my only experience with Italian food had been my mother's spaghetti and meatballs—which I loved, don't get me wrong—but the pasta in Rome? Life-changing. It opened up an entirely new world of flavor and possibility.

Back then, Rome's streets were a sea of motorcycles and scooters, easily outnumbering cars five to one. The roar of engines was constant—so loud, we could hear it clearly from our eighth-floor hotel room, even with all the windows closed. Dad explained that during the war, Italian auto manufacturers had shifted production to jeeps, tanks, and other military vehicles. Post-war, they still hadn't returned to full passenger car production. The result? Streets choked with motorbikes—and a deafening city soundtrack.

When filming wrapped, we flew to London for a short vacation and to take in some theatre. One of the highlights for me was seeing Handel's *Messiah* performed live at Covent Garden. That experience stayed with me for years. I've always believed *The Messiah* sits at the very top tier of liturgical music, right alongside Bach's *Mass in B Minor*. Hearing it in that grand hall was one of the most moving moments of the entire trip—and one I'll never forget.

20

THE LONG, LONG TRAILER

In 1953, my dad produced *The Long, Long Trailer* starring Lucille Ball and Desi Arnaz—one of the funniest comedies he ever made.

Lucy and Desi played a young couple about to get married. Desi wants to buy a house and settle down, but Lucy has other ideas—she wants to buy a trailer and spend their honeymoon driving across the country. The mishaps they run into along the way would have ended most marriages, but somehow, Lucy and Desi's characters stick it out. The film was a major hit, and it boosted their popularity with audiences. It also helped pave the way for their groundbreaking TV show *I Love Lucy* and their eventual studio, Desilu.

You can imagine my surprise when, one Saturday afternoon, Desi and Lucy showed up at our house to have lunch on the patio and run the film. Dad had told Mom that Desi was coming over to do some work and warned her she might feel a little uncomfortable having him there. What he didn't tell her—possibly because he didn't know—was that Lucy was coming, too. Desi may have just assumed they were both invited. After all, inviting one half of Hollywood's most famous couple without the other might have felt awkward.

As a result, Mom went off to Hillcrest to play cards with her friends, not realizing Lucy would be there. She didn't return until dinner. Sue and Cindy were out for the day as well. That left me home—and I was invited to join the lunch and movie screening. It was a surreal afternoon: there I was, sitting on the patio having lunch with Lucy and Desi Arnaz, watching them laugh at themselves onscreen.

At one point during the screening, Dad made a comment about a particular scene he didn't like and said he planned to cut it. Desi and Lucy immediately objected. They loved that scene and begged him not to take it out. I silently agreed—it was one of my favorite moments in the film—but I didn't dare voice my opinion. This was between them.

Dad said that if they both liked it that much, he'd leave it in. But on Monday, he told the editor to cut it anyway.

That day, Desi and Lucy were deep into forming their own production company. They asked Dad to leave MGM and join them. They offered him a generous amount of stock in the company and a percentage of ownership of all their television shows—if he would agree to be their head of production. They saw him as one of the greatest executives in Hollywood and believed he was the strong leader Desilu needed.

In what turned out to be the worst decision of his career, Dad said no.

He couldn't bring himself to leave the greatest movie studio in the world, where he was producing hit films, for a gamble on television—a medium that, at the time, was still considered a step down. As he put it, "You don't leave the big screen to go to the little screen. It works the other way around."

At the time, it seemed like the logical decision, but it turned out to be his worst.

Desilu became a juggernaut. *I Love Lucy* went on to become one of the most successful and enduring television shows in history. And yes—if Dad had accepted their offer, we would have become billionaires on the revenues from that show alone. It's still in reruns more than sixty years later.

NEPOTISM IS ALIVE AND WELL AT MGM

The enormous trailer used in *The Long, Long Trailer* had been loaned to MGM by a company that sold trailers and mobile homes. When the picture wrapped, my father called the company to arrange for its return. But to his surprise, he was told the trailer had been gifted to the studio as a tax write-off—they couldn't take it back.

Dad went to Louis B. Mayer to ask what should be done with it. Mayer already had a plan.

Enter Yetta—Mayer's sister—and her husband, a man burdened with the unfortunate name of Orville Dull. Even worse, he went by "O.O. Dull," and somehow had acquired the nickname "Bunny." Yetta had been pestering her powerful brother for years to give poor Bunny a steady job. Mayer had already given his brother-in-law several jobs, all of which ended poorly. Around the studio, it was common knowledge that Mayer wasn't exactly fond of Bunny and had no idea what to do with him.

Now, though, he saw the perfect opportunity.

The trailer would be loaded with food and liquor and driven to the Pin Tail Duck Club in Bakersfield, where it would become Bunny's new kingdom. His job? To keep the trailer well-stocked with refreshments for the club's members—and for the game wardens, who often hovered nearby. Mayer, once fined in court for exceeding his limit on ducks, saw this as a golden chance to curry favor. If the game wardens were full of tasty food and bourbon during the week, maybe they'd look the other way come Saturday if a hunter—say, hypothetically, Mayer himself—was a little overzealous with his duck bag.

At last, Mayer had found a job even Bunny couldn't bungle.

Mayer's other sister, Ida, had married Nate Cummings, an industrial giant who served as president and CEO of Consolidated Foods, one of America's largest companies. Their son Jack had his sights set on the movie business, so Ida did what any Mayer sibling would—she pestered her brother until he relented.

Jack started as an office boy at MGM in the 1920s, expected to work his way up like everyone else. To his credit, Jack didn't just meet expectations—he exceeded them. By 1934, he was a staff producer in the studio's B-movie unit, and just two years later he produced the extravagant Cole Porter musical *Born to Dance*, starring Eleanor Powell and James Stewart. That film gave Jack real credibility in Hollywood.

He went on to produce some of MGM's most beloved musicals, including *Broadway Melody of 1940*, *Seven Brides for Seven Brothers*—featuring Michael Kidd's groundbreaking choreography—and *Three Little Words*, with Fred Astaire and Red Skelton playing legendary songwriting duo Bert Kalmar and Harry Ruby.

In my opinion, Jack's crowning achievement was *Teahouse of the August Moon*, starring Marlon Brando and Glenn Ford. It racked up six Golden Globe nominations, as well as awards from the Writers Guild, Directors Guild, and festivals around the world. We ran the movie at home with Jack, his wife Margie, and their two daughters. I was young and impressionable, but at the time I thought it was one of the greatest films ever made—and I'm sure I'd still feel the same today.

Jack had a terrific sense of humor, and both Mom and Dad were quite fond of him. Truth be told, I think we all liked him more than his uncle Louis did. For reasons known only to Mayer, he never really embraced Jack, despite his string of hits. He never invited Jack into the so-called "College of Cardinals," the upper echelon of MGM's decision-makers. That must have stung, considering all Jack had accomplished.

But Jack got the last laugh.

When Mayer was ousted by Nick Schenck in 1951, Jack stayed. Schenck kept him on as a producer despite his family ties, a move that spoke volumes. It was a quiet but powerful validation of Jack's talent, professionalism, and value to the studio. He was a fine producer—one whose films rarely lost money—and in the end, that's what mattered most.

21

MY FIRST CAR

When I turned sixteen and finally got my driver's license, I needed a car to get to school. My father, never one to miss a character-building opportunity, told me that if I wanted a car, I'd have to earn the money to pay for it. Another "lesson in the value of a dollar," he said—except this time, it was a whole lot more complicated than the Schwinn racer deal from four years earlier.

There was no chance I could afford a new car. So, my dad made me an offer: I could buy his old 1948 Buick Roadmaster—for a "very good price." The problem? I didn't particularly want the car. It was a hulking gray tank with no power steering, and it was not easy to drive. It was really a family car, not something fun and flashy for a sixteen-year-old to be seen in. But I had no choice in the matter. Dad wouldn't let me buy any other used car—he didn't trust the condition of something from a stranger, and safety came before personal preference.

On top of that, I couldn't take possession of the Buick until I'd paid for at least half of it. Which meant no more swimming team. I'd have to get a job—after school, on weekends, whatever it took. My social life, such as it was, became non-existent Meanwhile, a few of my friends were cruising around in shiny new cars their parents had given them. No part-time job. No sacrifice. Just a full tank of gas and teenage freedom. I was not pleased.

Luckily, a couple of those friends were working at Lew Gonyer's Mobile Service station on Cañon Drive in Beverly Hills. They helped me land a job there, pumping gas and wiping windshields. I made about $2.20 an hour. Gas was 29 cents a gallon—which seemed outrageous to me at the time—and I worked the 4:00 to 8:00 p.m. shift every weekday after school. I was the one who turned off the lights and locked up.

Things usually quieted down after 6:00 p.m., so I'd sit in the office doing homework and waiting for the occasional customer to roll in. I also worked Saturdays until 5:00 p.m., which gave me Saturday night and Sunday off—though with no car, I was still at the mercy of friends who were willing to pick me up.

After closing the station, I'd catch the last bus to Sunset and walk up the hill home. It was usually after 9:00 p.m. by the time I got there. My mother would be waiting up for me, pulling leftovers from the fridge so I could have something for dinner. She wasn't thrilled about the arrangement and finally went to my dad to lodge a complaint. "Didn't you once say that dinner was the only time you could be with the children? Well, your son hasn't been home for dinner in months."

Dad held his ground. "He's old enough to have his own schedule," he told her—and reminded her that after his father died, he'd worked every after-school job he could find in New York and gave all his wages to his mother to help with the bills. Compared to that, he thought I had it easy.

It took months of work, but I finally earned enough to cover half the cost of the car. When Dad finally grew tired of Mom's nightly guilt trips, he relented. He handed me the keys to the Buick.

A few months later, I finished paying off the balance, quit the gas station job—and finally started having a little fun. I even managed to go on a couple of dates... in my very first (very used) car.

MY FIRST LOVE

My first two dates were with girls from my class at school. They were nice enough, but I knew right away I didn't want to take either of them out again.

Date number three, however, was a revelation.

From the very first evening, I couldn't wait to see her again—and I had a pretty strong hunch she felt the same, judging by the way she kissed me goodnight. I was new to dating, still navigating the mystery of girls and their signals, but I had never been kissed like that before.

She was a real beauty—dark hair, dark eyes, elegant and poised. She reminded me of Shakespeare's Dark Lady of the Sonnets, and I was smitten. We shared an appreciation for classical music and fine art, and her father was also a prominent Hollywood producer, just like mine. We had a lot in common, and our connection was immediate.

On our second date, we parked along Mulholland Drive, gazing out at the twinkling lights of Los Angeles while we steamed up the windshield of my immaculately polished Buick. It felt like a scene from one of the black-and-white romances we both loved.

At Beverly High, some girls had labeled her—unfairly—as a "Jewish Princess," but to me, she was simply Ellie. Elegant, refined, and far more thoughtful than people gave her credit for. In time, Ellie and I became very affectionate. We took our passion right to the threshold of the "forbidden"—a place she'd never been, and I'd only visited in dreams.

Still, I didn't push. I figured if it was ever going to happen, it had to be her idea. That way, she wouldn't have regrets, and I couldn't be accused of pressuring her. Besides, I liked her too much to jeopardize anything.

She showed she cared in all kinds of ways. One afternoon, she surprised me with a handmade gift—a giant pair of knitted dice to hang from my rearview mirror. It was the latest craze, and girls were making them for their boyfriends all over Beverly Hills. Mine were navy and white. I hung them proudly.

Her kisses were electric—each one building with anticipation, always stopping just before we crossed the line. Still, each week we edged closer. Some Saturday nights ended in disappointment, but I always left with renewed hope. Until one night, when that hope paid off.

It was Ellie's birthday. I took her to a nice dinner, brought her flowers, and finally—after months of restraint—was rewarded for my patience.

The only downside? The Buick. Big as it was, it wasn't exactly built for comfort. We couldn't go to either of our homes—there were always people around. A motel? Too sleazy. Not even up for debate. I suggested the back seat. She vetoed that. Unladylike and dangerous, she said. Even my idea to set up a sleeping bag or a blanket in our greenhouse—half an acre away from the main house—was met with a hard no.

Then came an unexpected opportunity: Ellie had taken a liking to my friend Artie. They got along well enough for her to introduce him to her best friend, Jane. Soon, the four of us were double dating—drive-in movies, weekend cruising, the whole teenage dream. And since the girls were best friends, they weren't shy about heating things up in the car, even in front of each other.

One night, after dropping them off, I confided in Artie about our... logistical dilemma. "I've been looking for a safe bed for weeks," I told him.

Artie—who always seemed to have an answer—didn't miss a beat. "My folks are out of town next weekend," he said. "Stuart's away at college. You can use my room. Just be out by midnight—I need my beauty sleep."

At first, Ellie was appalled that I had told Artie anything about us. But I could tell—behind the shock—she was intrigued. She valued privacy above all, and the idea of anyone knowing—even Jane—made her hesitate. But Artie was sworn to secrecy. He was trustworthy. We'd been through other top-secret teenage operations before. And besides, he planned to bring Jane back there eventually and didn't want her to know Ellie had already christened the bed.

Ellie needed time to think. She didn't give me her answer right away. I tried not to press. I knew she liked Artie, and I was sure I'd convinced her he could be trusted.

Finally, on Saturday morning, she said yes.

That evening, we went to Webb's Drive-In for burgers. I was so excited I could barely eat. Ellie, on the other hand, was calm and collected, slowly working her way through her meal—burger, fries, Coke—and then she leaned close, smiled, and whispered, "Let's go..."

MY FIRST ENCOUNTER

The key to Artie's house was exactly where he said it would be—under the big rock on the path to the front door. Ellie and I slipped inside and went straight to his room. I reached for the light switch, but she stopped me. "Turn it off," she whispered. "I want it dark."

She disappeared into the bathroom and returned a few minutes later wearing a silky nightgown she'd somehow folded into her purse. I swear, I'd never seen her look more beautiful. She climbed into bed and gazed up, just then noticing the skylight directly overhead. It was a crystal-clear night, stars scattered across the sky, softly lighting the room. The moment couldn't have been more perfect if I'd scripted it myself.

I don't know how long we were there—maybe two hours—but they were the greatest two hours of my young life.

Eventually, Ellie slipped out of bed and went into the bathroom to change. Her parents wanted her home before midnight, and she never missed curfew. Just as she closed the bathroom door, I heard a faint tapping noise. I looked up.

And there, hovering above the skylight, was Artie—grinning like the cat who caught the canary.

He waved.

I nearly fell over. My heart slammed into my ribs as I scrambled to get dressed. I called to Ellie through the bathroom door, trying to sound calm. "We better go. It's getting late."

We locked up the house and returned the key to its hiding place under the rock. I half-expected Artie to jump down and ruin everything, but thankfully, he stayed hidden on the roof. Smart guy. A surprise cameo at that point would've meant disaster—with Ellie, with Jane, with everyone. But somehow, we pulled it off. I got Ellie home before her curfew, and no one was the wiser... at least for the time being.

.·*·★·*·★·★·*··★·*·

CHROME, CAUTION, AND A CURBSIDE ARGUMENT

Every Saturday morning, I had a ritual: wash the car, polish the chrome, and make that Buick shine like it had just rolled off the showroom floor. The grill looked like a shark's mouth full of silver teeth. The whitewall tires took extra work—I'd scrub them with soapy water and steel wool, then brush on a special rubber compound to make the black pop. The contrast was my pride and joy.

Dad sometimes wandered outside while I worked, watching quietly for a while. "This car has never looked so good," he'd say, and I could tell he meant it. But even with all his compliments, I knew he wasn't thrilled about me having the car. He thought I was reckless behind the wheel. In truth, I was cautious—too cautious sometimes—but whenever I drove him somewhere, he acted like I was Mario Andretti on a death wish. Every pothole, every turn, every stop sign was a minefield in his eyes. He was the ultimate backseat driver, and he made me nervous as hell.

One Saturday, right after I finished cleaning the Buick, he asked me to drive him down to the drugstore. He got in, settled himself, and then noticed Ellie's handmade dice hanging from the rearview mirror.

"Where did *those* come from?"

I told him proudly that my girlfriend had made them for me. Knitted from white and silver yarn, they were stretched over stiff cardboard, the silver used just for the dots. They were perfect. Trendy. Cool. All the guys had them.

He didn't see it that way. "They're too big," he grumbled. "They'll block your view."

I insisted I could see just fine. He gave me a look but let it go... for the moment.

Then, about halfway down to the drugstore, I hit a bump a little too fast. The dice started bouncing like crazy, swinging wildly from the mirror.

That was it.

Without a word, Dad reached up, yanked them off, rolled down the window, and hurled them into the street.

I slammed the brakes, jumped out, and sprinted after them. But it was too late. The dice hit the curb, rolled once... and vanished down a sewer grate. Gone.

I was furious. But I didn't dare let it show. Not out loud. Not to him.

When I got back into the car, all I could manage was, "Ellie spent *weeks* making those for me."

He laughed.

That made it worse.

He said they were a hazard, and that he cared too much to let me get in an accident over "some stupid dice." I said nothing. But inside, I was mourning that glittering symbol of teenage love—now floating somewhere in the dark underground rivers of Beverly Hills.

* * * * * * * * *

TROUBLE IN PARADISE

After our big night at Artie's house, Ellie and I became inseparable. We thought we were in love. Our mothers, of course, chalked it up to "puppy love"—as if deep feelings and racing hearts were somehow less real at seventeen. Whatever they called it, we were completely wrapped up in each other.

We hung out after school, did our homework side-by-side in the library of her gorgeous home, and fell deeper into our little world. I got to know her parents rather quickly, and to my surprise, they really seemed to like me. I was invited to dinner often, and by the third week, I felt like part of the family.

Eventually, I even convinced Ellie to forgive my father for the Great Dice Disaster and to come over to my house for Friday night dinner and a movie. She was nervous at first, but my parents took to her immediately. My mom complimented her poise, my dad admired her intelligence, and for one brief, shining moment, I felt like I had it all—love, approval, and harmony between the generations.

For the first couple of months, everything was smooth sailing.

Then Ellie told me she had missed her period.

My blood ran cold. I froze—absolutely paralyzed by the thought that she might be pregnant. Every horror scenario flashed through my head in one awful montage: angry fathers, ruined reputations, whispered scandals, and my entire future crashing down like a badly edited melodrama.

Thankfully, her regular appointment with the gynecologist was already scheduled for the following week. It was close enough to provide answers, but far enough away to leave me a jittering wreck for the next seven days.

I was terrified that her mother might accompany her and find out everything. But Ellie assured me she always went alone after the initial visit. It was their arrangement. Still, I worried her doctor might spill the beans—maybe out of moral obligation, maybe just by accident.

But Ellie said no. He had promised her full confidentiality. It was part of the Hippocratic Oath, she explained. That solemn vow doctors take, swearing to protect their patients' privacy and trust.

I clung to that oath like a life preserver in stormy seas.

One week. That's how long we had to wait. But it felt like forever.

TURNS OUT, LOVE HAS CONSEQUENCES

Ellie *was* pregnant—and I had no idea what to do.

For a couple of days, I just wandered around in a fog, trying to weigh options that all seemed worse than the last. I couldn't talk to my parents. I didn't trust a teacher. And I sure as hell wasn't going to confess to Ellie's father. I needed someone who already knew the backstory—someone I could trust. That guy was Artie.

When I told him, he gave me a tight smile and said, "The only intelligent answer to your problem is Doctor Jimenez... in Tijuana."

I stared at him. "That's not funny."

But he wasn't joking. Dead serious. He told me that a friend of his had gone down there with the same problem. Dr. Jimenez had taken care of it—quickly, cleanly, quietly. No complications. No infections. No lingering effects. And best of all, no one ever found out.

I told Artie he was nuts. "Ellie? In a Tijuana abortion clinic? She's a Beverly Hills girl. A *Jewish* Beverly Hills girl."

Artie just shrugged. "Trust me. She wouldn't be the first."

I shook my head. "There's got to be a better way."

"There's not," he said. "Give her time. She'll see it's the only real option. It's the best thousand bucks you'll ever spend."

That hit a nerve. "I don't *have* a thousand bucks," I said. "I've got maybe six hundred to my name, and the rest is Bar Mitzvah money locked up tighter than Fort Knox. My dad would have to sign off on it, and that's not happening."

Artie, without blinking, said he'd loan me the other four hundred. I could get my old job back at the gas station and pay him back over time.

It still didn't feel like a "good" answer, but the more I thought about it, the more it felt like the *only* answer.

The hardest part was figuring out how to talk to Ellie about it without her blowing up. It took me nearly a week to work up the nerve. And as expected, she was horrified. But not just at the idea—at the fact that I had discussed it with Artie.

She was terrified her parents would find out, terrified of the shame, terrified of what it might mean for her future. But she didn't slam the door shut either. She was *thinking* about it. And that told me something.

A few days later, she came back to me and asked how it would even work. I told her everything I knew—including the part about Artie helping us. That made her furious all over again. But I explained that I was scared and inexperienced and had nowhere else to turn. Artie was the only person I trusted who had any idea how to navigate this kind of thing. He was willing to loan us the money, drive us down, and introduce us to Dr. Jimenez himself. That level of support... it mattered.

Still, it was a lot for Ellie to swallow.

She started talking about telling her mother. She said maybe, just maybe, her mom would know what to do—something better, safer, more dignified.

But I knew what her mother's answer would be: marriage. A

wedding. A baby. Two high school juniors pushed into a life neither of us was ready for. Her parents liked me. We were from similar backgrounds. In their eyes, it would be the "honorable" solution.

I asked Ellie point-blank: "Do you really want to get married right now? Raise a baby at seventeen?"

Of course she didn't.

A few days passed. She came back with more questions—this time, logistical ones. "How would we make this work?"

I told her the only way was to talk to Artie. She didn't want to—too embarrassed, too exposed—but I told her I wouldn't go through with it unless he came with us. We'd need him, not just to get there and back, but to make sure we were safe.

"Artie's a good guy," I said. "He understands. And the awkwardness? It'll pass in a minute. You'll see."

She didn't say yes. But she didn't say no, either.

And I could tell… she was getting there.

22

SOUTH OF THE BORDER...DOWN MEXICO WAY

It took a lot of cajoling, but I was finally able to convince Ellie to meet with Artie and plan our course of action. As I predicted, she got over her embarrassment right away. Artie made her feel comfortable, assuring her he was one hundred percent behind her—and that his lips were sealed. He was also quite concerned about me.

"You don't know Pandro like I do," he said. "If he finds out about this, it'll be all over for your friend and mine."

That gave us all a good laugh and loosened her up a little. Then Artie went on to describe exactly what had happened with his friends the last time they were there. He painted the clinic as bright and clean with all the modern medical equipment you'd expect in a doctor's office in Beverly Hills.

"You mean you'll be going down there with us?" she asked.

"Absolutely. You don't want to do this alone, do you?" he replied.

I could see that she was relieved he'd be there to support us. He was convincing—too convincing—and after a few minutes, she began to agree. We started making plans, talking through every aspect of the trip for more than an hour, and we devised credible cover stories for everything.

We would leave on Friday after school and drive straight to Tijuana, which would take about two and a half hours. We'd tell the border patrol we were going for dinner and dancing and planned to be back by ten o'clock that night. After recrossing the border, we'd head to a restaurant in Hollywood to meet Jane, who would then drive Ellie back to her house, where she'd be spending the night.

Of course, that meant Jane would have to be in on it—something I thought Ellie might object to. But Jane already knew Ellie was pregnant. I should've realized Ellie would've been desperate to confide in someone, and who else would it be but her best friend?

I needed as much cover as Ellie. I would be sleeping at Artie's house that night to avoid violating my own curfew in case it got later than planned. I didn't want to be forced to lie to my parents about where I'd been. I wasn't very good at lying—and I might've blown it.

Fortunately, everything went exactly as planned, and Ellie seemed relieved it was over. On the way home, I sat in the back of Artie's Ford Crestline with my arm around her, trying to comfort her after what must've been a horrible experience. She wasn't feeling well when we left the clinic, but by the time we reached the restaurant, she was already doing better. She kissed me goodbye, hugged Artie, and thanked us both for seeing her through the ordeal.

She and Jane drove off, and Artie and I went back to his house and talked into the night about every detail of the adventure. The next morning, we called Jane's private line, and Ellie told me she was feeling fine—no excessive bleeding during the night. Everything seemed to have gone off without a hitch.

On Sunday, she reminded me that she was leaving for New York with her parents. They always spent a week there at the beginning of summer, visiting relatives and seeing a couple of Broadway shows. I told her I'd miss her terribly and wanted to see her the moment she got home.

She was supposed to be back the following Thursday, but I didn't hear from her on Thursday or Friday. I thought about calling her house but assumed they might have extended their trip by a few days. I decided to wait—let her call me when she returned.

The weekend passed. By Monday evening, I still hadn't heard from Ellie. She was supposed to be home several days ago. I'd been thinking about her constantly—and I was dying to talk to her.

THE BIG FALLOUT

I was sitting in my room just above the motor court when I heard my dad's car pull into the garage—tires squealing. Moments later, he burst into my room and locked the door behind him. When he turned to face me, his eyes were blazing with that quiet fury that always terrified me.

"You have humiliated me in this town—and in my own business," he said, his voice steel-edged.

I blinked at him, confused. "What did I do?"

"What did you do?" he repeated, like a lit match to gasoline. "You knocked up the daughter of one of my oldest friends. I'm embarrassed to go to Producer's Guild meetings, and I may have to resign as President."

He wasn't shouting. His voice was quiet, tight, and full of controlled rage—which somehow made it even more terrifying.

I stood frozen, stunned. I had no idea how he found out. And I knew this wasn't going to go away.

"You are a thoughtless moron," he snapped. "You can't be trusted to do anything right."

The look on his face made my stomach churn. I hadn't seen him this angry since I left his shotgun in the treehouse. Then, with an outstretched hand, he said, "Give me the keys to your car. You won't be driving it anymore."

I stared at him. That car wasn't just transportation—I'd worked for over a year and paid him for it. It felt like a betrayal. But he didn't budge. His hand was still there, waiting.

Too scared to argue, I took the car key off my ring and handed it to him.

"How could you do this to me?"

I wanted to say that I didn't do it *to him*, that he hadn't even entered my mind—but I knew better than to talk back. I kept my mouth shut.

His voice dropped even lower. "You are to discuss this with no one. Do you understand me? Not your sisters. Not even your mother. Although I'm going to have to tell her."

That's when it hit me—why he'd been whispering. He didn't want *anyone* to know. Not even in our own house.

"And you are not to go near that girl. Don't even speak to her at school. Do you understand me?"

"I'm really sorry, Dad," I stammered. "But I don't know how I'm supposed to get to school or work without the car."

"That's your problem," he said flatly. "You're grounded until further notice." Then he shook his head in disgust and walked out.

I called my friend Don Factor, who lived up the street, and told him I needed a ride to school. I couldn't bear to go down to the dinner table that night. I'd never felt so low in my entire life.

Later that night, Mom poked her head into my room. The look on her face was heartbreaking—like someone in the family had died.

"We have to talk about this," she said softly.

"I can't... not right now," I said.

She nodded, saw the look on my face, and gently closed the door.

The next morning, I left early and walked up the hill to Don's house. I needed to be sure I had a ride. Thankfully, he was also in summer school, so we'd be on the same schedule. When I arrived, he was just finishing breakfast, and I sat with him for a cup of coffee.

He asked me why I was grounded.

I told him the truth.

"That it was personal."

And I couldn't talk about it.

THE AFTERMATH

When I got to school, I immediately started looking for Ellie. I had to talk to her—just to find out what had happened—but she hadn't enrolled in summer school. Instead, I found Jane at her locker. She explained that Ellie had broken down under the weight of everything. While in New York, she had burst into tears in the hotel room and confessed everything to her mother.

Jane told me that Ellie was angry—angry with herself for being careless, and angry with me for pushing her into the abortion. She said Ellie didn't want to see me or speak to me again.

I was crushed.

I was convinced I was in love with Ellie. The idea of not seeing her anymore felt unbearable. I begged Jane to give her a message—that I loved her, and I was heartbroken. Jane looked at me with sympathy. "She's heartbroken too," she said. "She told me she's in love with you. But her parents threatened to send her to boarding school if they catch you two talking again."

It was a small comfort, but it hurt all the same.

Thankfully, Artie and a few other friends were also taking summer classes, so I usually managed to catch a ride to my part-time job after school. If not, it was about a twenty-minute walk, which I had to make more than once. Getting home after work was another issue. The buses ran less frequently after 7:00 p.m., so sometimes I wouldn't get home until close to nine, grabbing whatever I could from the fridge for dinner.

It was not a happy time.

The atmosphere at home was just as bleak. I did everything I could to avoid my father, and I was relieved to hear he'd be going on location in Pakistan for a couple of months. Distance was exactly what we both needed.

Eventually, I had that dreaded conversation with my mother. I braced myself for a second round of condemnation—but to my surprise, she was far more forgiving than Dad. Mom had met Ellie. She knew she was a refined girl from a good family, not some reckless flirt trying to trap me into anything. Mom believed Ellie wouldn't have gone to bed with me unless she truly loved me—and that I must have loved her back. In her mind, we were a modern-day Romeo and Juliet, undone by youth and inexperience.

She stayed home during the Pakistan shoot. She didn't want to go—said it would be filthy and depressing—and she didn't want to leave us, especially with all the trouble I'd caused. She had gone to England with Dad when he was shooting *Ivanhoe* and loved that trip. Back then, the house had been closed up, and we kids were sent to stay with relatives. This time, she stayed put. Things between her and Cindy were strained, and although she'd forgiven me for what she called my "illicit romance," she still wasn't thrilled about it. Leaving home didn't feel like an option.

The night before Dad left, I waited in my room, hoping he'd come in to say goodbye. Hoping he'd let me know this wasn't the end of the world. But he never did. That silence cut deeper than any punishment. I honestly thought this was it—that he'd never want anything to do with me again. But Mom reassured me. "He'll come around," she said. "Eventually."

A couple of weeks later, my friend Don started missing school. Whether he was sick or just skipping, I never really found out, but it left me without a ride. If he didn't show up at my place by twenty to eight, I had to go upstairs and wake up Mom. She'd wash her face, throw on a robe, and drive me to school—grumbling all the way. Sometimes she had to pick me up from work too, especially if I missed the last bus. She was getting fed up with it.

After a few weeks of this, she decided she was done sharing my punishment. One night, she found a spare key to my car and handed it to me.

I stared at it, stunned. "What if Dad finds out?"

"I'll clear it with him on the phone before he gets home," she said.

I wasn't sure whether to be grateful... or terrified.

BHOWANI JUNCTION AND FAMILY FIREWORKS

Bhowani Junction had originally been scheduled to shoot in India, but the Indian government began making all sorts of demands—script approval, hefty tax payments up front, bureaucratic delays. So, the studio struck a deal with Pakistan instead, which welcomed the production with open arms. They were happy to have the revenue and the prestige that came with hosting a major Hollywood film.

The story, based on the novel by John Masters, tackled serious social issues, and my dad was eager to bring them to the screen—while still making a big, star-driven movie that would resonate with audiences. It was set in India in 1947, just as the British Empire was being shown the door by factions of the Indian government eager to reclaim their country. Ava Gardner played an Anglo-Indian woman, scorned as a "half-breed" by both the British and Indian communities. She knew life would only get harder when the British left. Stewart Granger played a British Colonel—one of the rare few who sympathized with the Indian people. He and Ava's character fall in love, but she's torn between fleeing with the man she loves or returning to her roots, hoping to be embraced as a native Indian woman once again.

It was one of the best pictures my father ever made. I still don't know how it missed out on an Academy Award nomination. Ava Gardner absolutely deserved one. So did George Cukor for his direction. Stewart Granger, usually known for playing charming rogues, delivered a performance full of quiet strength and compassion. It elevated the film to something truly special. I had read the novel while the picture was in production and knew even then that it was made for the big screen.

That same summer, we spent the Fourth of July at the home of one of my mother's cousins. Grandpa Frank and Grandma Fannie had come down for an unplanned visit and were with us at the dinner party. The mood should've been festive, but Cindy and Mom had been snapping at each other all day, and by the time we sat down to eat, it exploded into a full-blown argument. Cindy—frustrated, rebellious, and emotional—dropped the F-bomb in front of everyone.

Unfortunately, Grandpa Frank witnessed the whole thing.

He was old-school to the core, and I'm sure his first instinct was to drag her out to the metaphorical woodshed. He didn't say anything directly to Cindy, but the way he glowered at her across the table made her squirm. Then, as if to twist the knife, when my other sister Sue arrived a little late to the party, Grandpa greeted her with, "Ah... here's my favorite granddaughter," loud enough for everyone to hear.

It was a brutal blow. Cindy never forgot it.

She was already feeling isolated—struggling for a little understanding and respect from Mom and Dad—and that public humiliation, especially from a grandparent, cut deep.

Dad was away in Pakistan for nearly three months on that shoot. When he finally returned, Mom asked me to pick him up from the airport. I dreaded the car ride—figured it would be tense and awkward—but Mom assured me he wasn't angry anymore. Then she added, with a wry look, that when *he* first arrived in California, he got himself into the same kind of trouble... with a young woman at the studio.

I couldn't help but laugh.

Mom didn't.

"It's not funny," she said firmly. "It was serious. And it nearly ruined him."

A CHAPTER CLOSES

With great trepidation, I went to pick Dad up at the airport. But when he saw me, he smiled and put his arm around me. I sighed with relief. Finally, all was forgiven.

On the drive home, he told me stories about Pakistan and the shoot—funny things, interesting things, the kind of stories I'd always loved hearing from him. I was thrilled. We were talking again. We were good again.

Back at the house, Mom immediately pulled him aside to plead for help with Cindy. She told him how bad things had gotten while he was away—that Cindy's anger had reached a boiling point, and she didn't know what to do. But Dad and Cindy hadn't exactly been getting along before he left. He just threw up his hands and said, "What do you expect me to do about it?"

I probably should have realized then that things between my parents were reaching a breaking point. But I didn't want to see it. I told myself it would pass. I still believed things would somehow return to normal. I was pretty naïve in those days. I tended to see the glass as half full. My father, on the other hand—always half empty.

As summer drew to a close, I started thinking about school again. Seeing Ellie again was inevitable, and I had no idea what I'd say to her. I was still in love with her, but I was also deeply hurt. She hadn't reached out—not even a note or message. And the longer I waited, the harder it was to believe she still loved me, no matter what Jane had said. If it was true, I needed to hear it from Ellie herself.

I watched for her when school started, but she was nowhere to be seen. Eventually, I started waiting by her locker after school, hoping for even a glimpse. After a few tries, she finally showed up. One look at her face and I could tell she was scared to see me.

She said hello—quietly—and didn't have much else to say.

Then she launched into what sounded like a carefully rehearsed explanation. She told me how close she'd always been to her mother. How, after a few days in New York, the guilt overwhelmed her, and she felt she *had* to confess everything. She said she and her mother never kept secrets, and this was tearing her apart.

She apologized again. And again. But as I listened, I felt the anger creeping back in.

When she finished, I said, "Cut... Print... What a performance. Problem is—I don't believe a word of it."

She looked stunned.

"If you wanted to break up," I said, "you should've just told me to my face. But I guess it was easier to do it through your mother."

She insisted that wasn't true. Swore she still loved me. But I didn't want to hear it. I told her that by telling her mother, she knew exactly what would happen—she knew it would end things between us. "And that's what you wanted," I said.

She kept denying it, insisting that she still cared about me. But I turned and walked away.

I felt...vindicated. Like I'd finally said what needed to be said. She was the one who broke our trust. But I also knew I'd said those things to protect myself—to make it easier not to see her again. Deep down, I still loved her. I loved her dearly.

But our parents would never have allowed us to be together again. And maybe we knew that.

After that, we passed each other in the halls without a word. I didn't see her at graduation. I didn't see her parents either. Maybe she was sick. Maybe the guilt was too much. Either way, her absence made it easier—for me, and probably for my family too. Graduation didn't just mark the end of high school. It marked the final page in the broken love story of Ellie and me.

23

DAD GOES INDIE

In the mid-1950s, my father made a bold and life-changing decision: he left the safety of his executive position at MGM to form an independent production company. Instead of earning a fixed salary, his company would co-produce movies with the studio and split the profits fifty-fifty. The move came with substantial tax advantages at the time—benefits that have long since disappeared—but back then, it made good financial sense. One of the biggest advantages was the ability to cross-collateralize: losses from one film could be written off against profits from others, creating a more favorable overall tax situation.

Of course, MGM had some requirements. For the partnership to be approved, Dad had to bring in another established producer to join him in the new company. The studio wanted a broader slate of films to work with—for creative momentum, yes, but also for the accounting department, which needed multiple titles in the hopper to calculate tax liabilities with precision.

Plenty of talented producers were eager to team up with him. But in the end, Dad only considered one man worth the risk: Lawrence Weingarten.

Weingarten's track record was impeccable. He had produced *Broadway Melody of 1929*, *A Day at the Races* with the Marx Brothers, *Adam's Rib* and *Pat and Mike* with Spencer Tracy and Katharine Hepburn, *The Tender Trap* with Sinatra and Debbie Reynolds, and *I'll Cry Tomorrow* starring Susan Hayward. That last one earned Hayward both the Best Actress award at the Cannes Film Festival and a BAFTA. Dad admired Larry for his taste, business savvy, and steady hand.

What he didn't know was that Larry had leukemia. He wouldn't live long enough to see through the slate of films they had planned together. My father ended up producing several of Weingarten's projects alone, without taking producer credit. But they were successful—each one—cementing the viability of the partnership and, importantly, securing long-term royalties from theatrical and television distribution. That mattered a great deal, especially later in life and after my father's passing, when those royalties became part of what we, his children, inherited in partnership with MGM.

The contracts were drawn up by a brilliant attorney named Seymour Bricker, and Dad wasted no time getting to work. His first independent release? A landmark film called *Blackboard Jungle*.

Starring Glenn Ford, Vic Morrow, and a young Sidney Poitier, *Blackboard Jungle*, released in 1955, hit audiences like a punch to the gut. It told the raw, unvarnished story of an inner-city teacher trying to maintain order in a classroom filled with rebellious, violent students. It was provocative, urgent, and timely, shining a glaring light on the crisis in public education and youth culture in postwar America.

And then there was the music.

Rather than commission a new song, Dad sifted through over a hundred rock and roll tracks before landing on "Rock Around the Clock" by Bill Haley and the Comets—a song that had already been a smash hit but had lost some steam. His decision to feature it in the opening credits was genius. The song roared back onto the charts, helping fuel the rise of rock and roll and giving the movie an electric edge that spoke directly to its audience.

But music and message aside, the film owed much of its success to Richard Brooks, who adapted the screenplay and directed with a fearless, kinetic style. His script cut like a knife, and his direction gave the story urgency and depth.

That year, I put on my tuxedo again and joined my parents at the Academy Awards. It felt different this time. There was a quiet sense of inevitability in the air. *Blackboard Jungle* had been nominated for four Oscars, including Best Screenplay for Richard Brooks. Brooks also received nods from the Writers Guild and Directors Guild for his work.

I was seated between Brooks and my dad that night, and I can still remember how tightly I crossed my fingers when they opened the envelope.

But the Oscar for Best Screenplay went to Paddy Chayefsky for *Marty*, which swept the night—winning Best Picture and Best Actor for Ernest Borgnine, among others.

It was a tough loss. *Blackboard Jungle* would likely have fared better in a less competitive year. The field was stacked: *East of Eden*, *Bad Day at Black Rock*, *The Rose Tattoo*, *Rebel Without a Cause*, and *Guys and Dolls*—each a box office success, each of exceptional quality. Any one of them could have taken home gold.

But even without the statue, *Blackboard Jungle* left its mark. It was the kind of movie that started conversations, challenged institutions, and changed perceptions. And that, in the long run, was its greatest reward.

MICHAEL BERMAN

TEA AND SYMPATHY

It was 1956, and Dad was going into production with a movie that would give any producer or director a great sense of satisfaction and accomplishment. *Tea and Sympathy* had been a successful Broadway play, directed by Elia Kazan, which ran for 712 performances at the Ethel Barrymore Theater. It was written by Robert Anderson, the American playwright, screenwriter, and theatrical producer, who later became president of The American Theater Wing—the organization that created the Tony Awards.

I went downstairs to the library, found a copy of the play, and read it in one afternoon—then I read it a second time to make sure it was as good as I thought it was. The New York critics had raved about it, and I thought it was one of the best plays I had ever read. With that work, Robert Anderson had placed himself close to the top tier of American playwrights. In my opinion, that was a group of three: Eugene O'Neill, Arthur Miller, and Tennessee Williams. I'd rank Anderson just a half-step below those luminaries, sharing a rung with Edward Albee.

I placed him in a group with Carson McCullers, author of *The Member of the Wedding* and *The Heart Is a Lonely Hunter*, and Budd Schulberg, who wrote the classic *On the Waterfront*. William Inge also belongs on that level, having written *Picnic*, which won two Academy Awards, and the unforgettable *Bus Stop* with Marilyn Monroe and Don Murray. I'd also include Clifford Odets, with works I've previously described.

I was thrilled to discover that Robert Anderson was a talent of that magnitude, and I went to my father and told him how impressed I was with the play. I asked if I could read the screenplay as soon as it was available, and he provided me with a copy the following day.

John Kerr plays the role of a slightly effeminate, non-athletic prep school student who is accused of being homosexual. The headmaster of his dorm—a hyper-masculine type played by Leif Erickson— makes life very difficult for him. The dorm master prefers hanging out with his male buddies to spending time at home with his beautiful wife, played by Deborah Kerr. She feels rejected by her husband and disturbed by his demeaning treatment of the boy, who is not, in any way, homosexual. She takes pity on him, invites him into her home, offers him tea and a little sympathy—and ends up falling in love with him.

It was a groundbreaking work, and I was so excited about it that I wanted, somehow, to get involved with the production. My dad offered to let me come on the picture as an unpaid apprentice film editor, working with Ferris Webster—one of Hollywood's finest picture editors. I could have some fun and learn something at the same time. I was thrilled. I joked with my dad, telling him I didn't think it was good business to work for no money. He replied, "Sorry, kid—there's no way I can squeeze you into the budget."

Before the picture started shooting, Anderson came out from New York to make some final changes to the script, and he and his wife came to the house for dinner and a Friday night movie. His wife, Phyllis, was in a wheelchair, and I was moved by the loving way he looked after her. We sat in the library before dinner, and I was tremendously impressed by the discussion of the script and what changes were being made. Most of them were minor—accommodations necessary to move it from stage to screen.

At the dinner table, Anderson picked his wife up out of the wheelchair and placed her gently in a dining chair so she could sit at the same level as the rest of us. I was struck by his tenderness with her—something that was sadly missing in the relationship between my parents. The way she looked at him, with such love in her eyes, hit a deep chord in me. I couldn't take my eyes off them during dinner, and I went to sleep thinking how wonderful it would be to have a relationship like that.

I thought that if I were married to a woman in a wheelchair, I would treat her in exactly the same way. I could be a hero in my own home and, more importantly, I could feel proud of myself for doing something noble and wonderful for another human being. It took many years and two divorces, but I finally found a relationship like that. Fortunately, she wasn't in a wheelchair—but our relationship reminded me of Bob and Phyllis Anderson's, and I hoped they were still living that wonderful life.

The next morning, I went to work in the editing room—making labels for film boxes and rounding up empty reels. I couldn't wait to screen the first day's shooting and see Vincent Minnelli's work with the actors on film. It was the same cast that had appeared on Broadway, but with Minnelli replacing Elia Kazan as director.

Critics later praised Minnelli's direction, saying it was the finest non-musical directing job he had ever done. That must have been galling to Kazan, who had wanted desperately to direct the movie. He knew what a great vehicle it was. But Dad remembered what he had done with *Sea of Grass*, and he would never trust Kazan again.

On the first day of shooting, Dad invited me to lunch in the private dining room of the Thalberg Building, which I was really looking forward to. Louis Mayer had built that dining room in the 1940s and hired a famous chef from a restaurant in Paris to operate it. He had been concerned that a number of his producers were going off the lot for long lunches in fancy restaurants, which cost him a loss of precious man-hours and productivity.

He was hoping that the convenience and high quality of this new restaurant—right in the same building as their offices—would encourage his highly paid producers to stay on the lot and devote more time to their work. It also provided another opportunity for "the Pope" to hold court and conduct a working lunch, so that he could stay in the loop with what his "Cardinals" were doing.

I went into the restaurant with my dad and took a seat. Louis Mayer was no longer running the studio, so he wasn't there. Dore Schary was sitting in the Pope's chair at the head of the table, with many of the "Cardinals" seated around him, and some of them were already eating.

I felt quite ill at ease sitting at that table of champions. I sensed that some of them felt uncomfortable talking about their movies in front of me, and I couldn't wait to get out of there. I thanked my father for inviting me but told him I'd be eating in the Commissary from now on.

MGM had a huge commissary capable of seating several hundred people, and there was a smaller sandwich shop adjoining it, where you could grab quick takeout or sit at one of the long tables to eat your lunch. I had filled a tray with lunch items and was walking around the large dining room looking for a place to sit. The commissary was still remarkably busy in those days, with lots of movies shooting on the lot, and I was having trouble finding an empty seat.

I heard a voice from behind me say, "Vy don't you sit vis me?" I turned around to see a man motioning me to join him. He was sitting alone at a table for four, and I thanked him and sat down. He had an Eastern European accent, which I guessed to be Czech or Hungarian, and he introduced himself as Bronislaw Kaper—but he encouraged me to call him Broni, like everyone else in Hollywood.

Broni was actually Polish, and he had written one of my favorite jazz tunes, "Green Dolphin Street," along with a number of movie scores, including *Lili*, which starred the French actress Leslie Caron —and for which he had won an Oscar.

Of course, I was thrilled to meet this talented composer, and when I told him that Pandro was my father, he was happy to meet me as well. He told me he had worked with Dad at RKO and that Dad had recommended him to Louis Mayer, who then brought him over to MGM and gave him huge assignments. Mayer had told Broni that he was making a movie about San Francisco and needed a San Francisco theme for the score.

Broni wrote, "San Francisco...Open your Golden Gate..." which became a classic. I told Broni that my dad had introduced me to classical music, and suddenly we had plenty to talk about. Broni and his friend Miklós Rózsa had both written scores for my dad's movies, and they were very fond of him. I told Broni that I was very lucky to have Pandro for a father, and Broni said that my father was the lucky one —to have such a nice, intelligent boy like me for a son.

It was a wonderful thing for him to say and something I really needed to hear at that time in my life. I remember that hearing those words almost brought me to tears at that lunch table—and I still get emotional at times when I think about it.

Broni was a wonderful man, and after many lunches together, he and I became good friends. He invited me to parties at his home, where I met Miklós Rózsa and other movie composers, including David Raksin, who had been nominated for two Oscars and had written the compelling theme for *The Bad and the Beautiful*, which everyone in Hollywood was humming in the shower.

I also met the tremendously talented Erich Korngold, whose Oscar-winning score for *The Adventures of Robin Hood* contains one of the most haunting violin passages ever written. It is the beautiful love theme of Robin and Maid Marian. Korngold stands at the top of a distinguished group of Hollywood composers. In my opinion, his violin concerto is among the very best, comparable to those of Tchaikovsky, Brahms, and Max Bruch. He also composed the score for the movie *Of Human Bondage*. It was not the version my father produced in 1934 with Bette Davis and Leslie Howard; it was the Warner Bros. 1946 production with Paul Henried, Eleanor Parker, and Alexis Smith—and his music was first-rate.

I spoke to Korngold at length one evening, and he told me that he had left Vienna in 1938 after Hitler's invasion of Austria, which put all Jews at risk. Hollywood's most prolific composer, John Williams, has said that Korngold's music was his inspiration in scoring the *Star Wars* series. John Williams is Hollywood's most successful composer of all time, with fifty Oscar nominations and twenty-three Grammy Awards. However, I never met him at any of those parties—I met him years later when I was working at 20th Century Fox.

Miklós Rózsa and I had many discussions about classical music. He told me that it was wonderful that my father had given me such a foundation in good music, but that we were listening to what Rózsa considered to be lightweight composers. If I really wanted to learn something about great music, he said, I should listen carefully to all nine of Beethoven's symphonies. That, he promised, would teach me all I needed to know about the great music of the Romantic Era. I took his advice and listened to them all, over and over, and I began to get a real sense of what they were all about. But there was something that puzzled me—something I was hoping Rózsa could explain.

I knew that Beethoven's first two symphonies were a nod back to the 18th-century music of Haydn and Mozart. The 3rd Symphony, the *Eroica*, was revolutionary and changed the face of classical music forever. Beethoven continued to develop that new style in all the rest of his symphonies—except for the 4th, which seemed very similar to his first two. I didn't understand why he would have taken a step backward after the phenomenal success of his 3rd Symphony.

Rózsa explained that Beethoven's 4th Symphony was commissioned and paid for by Count Oppersdorff, a wealthy member of the Viennese aristocracy. His taste in music was conservative, so Beethoven composed it in the style of Haydn and Mozart to please his benefactor.

In those days, I had many conversations with Miklós Rózsa and Bronislaw Kaper, and I got a real education in classical music. I told my dad about it, and he was very impressed with the cultural level of those conversations.

He said, "Why don't you get me an invitation to one of Broni's parties?"

I knew he was kidding, so I said, "Oh no... those are only for serious musicians and insiders like me."

My dad and I were at our best together when we were bantering like that with humor. He had a great sense of humor—often a bit fatalistic—and I tried hard to emulate that. I had been told more than once by the women in my life that I was taking myself too seriously, so I was always looking for ways to lighten up.

Working on *Tea and Sympathy*, I had to haul film back and forth to the projection rooms, and I was running any number of errands. But I also learned some wonderful things about pace and timing in editing just from standing behind Ferris Webster and watching the screen on his editing machine. I got a real feeling for when to let things play and when to end them—something that's not easy to learn. You begin to acquire a feeling for it as you work with the film. Ferris had a natural instinct for creating pace, and I got a valuable education just watching him work.

24

MY GREATEST FEAR BECOMES A REALITY

In the spring of the following year, my parents separated. My father came home one night and told my mother he was leaving. Then he came to me and explained that he couldn't stand the arguing anymore—that he needed some peace in his life. I was seriously taken back by the news. I knew there was plenty of trouble in their marriage, but after they'd survived the affair with Lucy, I didn't think he would ever actually leave us.

Dad must have read the expression on my face, because he said, "Don't worry... nothing is going to change... I'm divorcing your mother, not you."

My sister Sue came home just as Dad was coming down the stairs with two suitcases. She begged him not to leave, but there was no stopping him. She ran upstairs to see Mom, but the bedroom door was locked. She could hear that Mom was crying and wouldn't open the door. Sue came to me in tears and demanded to know why I hadn't told her. I said I'd just found out a few minutes ago, and that honestly, I wasn't surprised. Mom and Dad hadn't been happy for years.

Sue thought I was cold and callous for saying that, but it was the truth. Her whole world fell apart at that moment. She couldn't believe Dad would do this to the family. Unfortunately, I don't think she ever really got over it. She blamed the divorce for some of her own behavioral changes—and for a few unreasonable fears she developed in the years that followed.

Cindy was the last to find out. She came home from a party and walked up the front stairs past my mother's bedroom. She noticed all the doors were closed, including the entrance from her dressing room. Sensing that something was wrong, she knocked on one of the doors and tried to open it—but it was locked. My mother opened the door just long enough to say, "Your father has left us," and immediately closed and locked it again.

Cindy was only thirteen years old, and I thought she'd be the one most affected by the separation—but I was wrong. She was so angry at both Mom and Dad that it probably didn't make much difference to her whether Dad lived at home or somewhere else. She might even have been relieved that he wouldn't be around anymore.

I thought she might come to my room to talk about it, but she went to her own room and got ready for bed. Later, when I did talk to her about it, she told me she believed Dad had left for another woman. That happened to be true—but I didn't know it at the time, and neither did Sue.

I went to my mother and asked if it was true, and she told me that it was. Dad had told her he was exhausted from years of demanding work and from all the tension between the two of them. He said he needed help—and that Kathryn was going to be his associate producer and take some of the burden of his job off his shoulders.

I didn't really believe his departure was due to exhaustion or the need for assistance at work, and I'm sure my mother didn't believe it either. In spite of everything they had gone through, she was still very much in love with him, and this was completely unexpected. It left her devastated, and I felt so sad for her.

There was doom and gloom in our house that summer, so my mother booked a cruise and took both Sue and Cindy to Hawaii. When they got back, a decision was made to put Cindy in the hands of a psychiatrist to try to find the answer to her troubles.

After a few visits, the psychiatrist called my mother and told her that Cindy was feeling like an outcast within the family—and that something had to be done to change that. Among other things, Cindy had complained that she resented having to share a car with Sue, who had been taking advantage of her and monopolizing it. Cindy also told the psychiatrist that Mom always sided with Sue on that and other issues. It was an inequitable situation that, in the doctor's opinion, needed to be reversed.

Mom didn't know what to do, so the psychiatrist suggested she buy Cindy a car of her own—something she could feel comfortable driving to school and around Beverly Hills. Cindy and Sue had been sharing a 1957 Thunderbird, but Cindy wanted a new Corvette like several of her friends at Beverly High were driving. The parking lot at Beverly Hills High School was filled with the most expensive cars imaginable, and Cindy didn't want to feel like a pauper in some hand-me-down.

Mom did by her a fancy new car—but not the Corvette she was craving. Instead, it was a Mercedes Benz 190SL convertible, which was more expensive than the Corvette and a much classier car.

Of course, that offended Sue, who thought it was unfair that Cindy got a Mercedes while she had to drive the Thunderbird.

That one even got to me. Both my sisters were given fancy cars, and I'd had to drive that used Buick tanker when I was in high school —and I had to work for months to pay for half of it before I could even get behind the wheel. I would have loved to have been given the Thunderbird that Sue was driving. As far as I was concerned, she had nothing to complain about.

Honestly, I thought the Mercedes Benz was much too extravagant for Cindy. But she had been so unhappy with both our parents for so long that something had to be done. I was hoping this might bring her back into the family—but that was wishful thinking.

NEW EXPERIENCES

I'd enrolled in Harvard University to take a few light classes and spent the summer in Eliot House with my friend Danny Selznick, who was also taking extra courses to lighten his load for the fall semester.

It was a breath of fresh air to get away from home and the ugliness and despair of the separation, and I was happy to reunite with my good friend Danny. I took an art appreciation class on the German Expressionist painters, which was one of the most interesting classes I've ever taken. I also enrolled in a music appreciation course taught by Henry Clark, a Harvard professor who occasionally composed serious music. The class focused on the Russian composers, and I fell in love with the piano compositions of Alexander Scriabin and the symphonies of Vasily Kalinnikov.

I had previously been unfamiliar with both composers, and I was delighted to make their acquaintance and add their work to my music library. I also played some of their music for Dad when I spent time with him at the end of the summer. Listening to good music together was always a bonding experience for us.

Professor Clark was being inducted into the American Institute of Arts and Letters, and his wife hosted a reception for him at their home in Cambridge one afternoon. All his students were invited, as well as some of the faculty. She served wine and little tea sandwiches. I was moved by her pride in her husband and by their devotion to one another, and once again, it made me think about my parents. If they had grown together and built a relationship like the Clarks', our lives would have been so different.

After a couple of weeks in Cambridge, I got a call from my father asking if I knew a composer named Walter Piston, who was teaching in the music department at Harvard. I told him that I was taking a music class just across the hall from where Piston was conducting his master class in composition.

Dad asked if I had met him, because Dore Schary wanted to contact Piston about writing a film score. Dad thought I might be able to pass the message along.

I told him I hadn't met the man and that I would feel extremely uncomfortable approaching him with a request like that. Dad explained that Dore was looking for an American composer to score *The Battle of Gettysburg*—someone prestigious, like Aaron Copland or Ferde Grofé, whose name would lend gravitas to the project. He was certain, however, that Copland wouldn't take the assignment.

I agreed. And I suggested Dore's office should reach out directly to Piston through the music department. But I also predicted he'd turn it down. Classical composers, with some exceptions, generally avoid writing motion picture scores—mostly because they don't want the world to think they've "gone commercial."

A day or so later, a teaching assistant in Walter Piston's office answered a call from MGM Studios.

"This is the office of Mr. Dore Schary of MGM Studios. Mr. Schary would like to speak to Mr. Piston right away."

The assistant replied that Mr. Piston was in the middle of teaching his master class and was not available. The secretary on the other end insisted that it was an urgent call and requested that Mr. Piston be asked to leave the class and come to the phone.

Piston's assistant was stunned. "I wouldn't interrupt his class if the President was calling. Mr. Piston will return your call at his convenience," she said—and promptly hung up.

The influence of MGM Studios was felt in many places around

the world in those days, but not in the music department at Harvard University.

I was familiar with Piston's work and particularly fond of his five string quartets and his piano quintet. He was an important American composer.

As I suspected, Walter Piston turned down the job. The final score for the film was made up of traditional American songs by composers like Stephen Foster, with additional music by Conrad Salinger, a composer of movie scores. It was a wonderful film, and it received two Academy Award nominations. But it was only a thirty-minute documentary, and people didn't exactly rush to the theaters to see it.

A couple of weeks later, I got another call from my father. He was going to New York to see an actor in a play and invited me to join him for the weekend. The actor was Ben Gazzara, and the play was *A Hatful of Rain*, which was becoming a major Broadway hit.

I took a shuttle flight from Boston and landed at LaGuardia Airport at 3:15 p.m. on Friday. I waited for my dad, whose flight was due to arrive at 4:00. I hadn't seen him for some time, and I found myself wondering which version of him would show up—the amusing one, or the scary one.

When I met him at the gate, he gave me a hug, and I knew it was going to be a great weekend. We took a cab into Manhattan, checked into the hotel, and had an early dinner in the dining room before heading to the theater. *A Hatful of Rain* was playing at the Plymouth Theater on 45th Street. It was only about ten blocks from our hotel, but we were buried in a sea of cabs on Fifth Avenue and barely made it before the curtain went up.

It was a heart-wrenching play by Michael Vincent Gazzo.

The playbill synopsis read: *A war veteran returns home to New York City and repeatedly falls victim to drugs, nearly destroying his relationships with his wife and brother as he struggles to break the habit.*

Ben Gazzara played the addicted war veteran. Shelley Winters played his wife. Tony Franciosa played his brother Polo. All three gave brilliant performances. The supporting cast included Broadway veteran Frank Silvera as Gazzara's father and the ominous Henry Silva, who delivered a chilling performance as the drug dealer. The entire cast was outstanding, and my dad was tremendously impressed with Gazzara. He was ready to cast him in the lead of his next picture—if he could find the right vehicle.

It was one of the most memorable nights I've ever spent in a Broadway theater, and there have been many. What a perfect start to our weekend in New York.

Don Murray eventually replaced Ben Gazzara as the lead in the movie version, and Eva Marie Saint replaced Shelley Winters. But Tony Franciosa and Henry Silva kept their original roles, and the film cast was every bit as good as the actors onstage.

MY DINNER WITH AUDREY

The next day, Dad and I went to a Dodgers game in Brooklyn, followed by dinner at Romeo Salta's on 56th Street with two wonderful actors—Audrey Hepburn and George Peppard.

They were so charming together I thought they might be a couple, but they were just friends. Audrey was married to actor-director Mel Ferrer, and George Peppard was single and highly sought after by most women. It was hard to take my eyes off Audrey Hepburn. She was slim, pristine, cultured—and impossibly beautiful.

Dad had purchased an option to produce *Green Mansions*, a novel by the celebrated British author William Henry Hudson. It told the story of a wealthy young man who fights in a revolution in Venezuela and nearly loses his life. He flees to the Guyana forest, where he meets and falls in love with a forest nymph named Rima, the Bird Girl. Rima has special powers—she can talk to the birds and sing like them.

Dad was convinced Audrey Hepburn would be a smash as Rima,

and he gave her his best pitch over dinner. I was fascinated watching him work—calm, charming, weaving an irresistible web. And I could see Audrey was buying it. That was one of Dad's great strengths: convincing people to commit to his projects.

George Peppard looked like he was interested as well, but he was much too old for the male lead. I was watching both of them closely while enjoying the light and slightly spicy Northern Italian cuisine—especially my green risotto, something wonderful I'd never tasted before.

As we left the restaurant, Dad said, "That was easier than I thought it would be… I wish I had brought a contract for her to sign."

But things didn't stay that simple for long. During the more serious negotiations, a major problem arose: Audrey wanted her husband, Mel Ferrer, to direct the film. That was a problem for my father, who didn't think highly of Ferrer's talent behind the camera.

MGM, however, wanted Audrey in the picture—at any cost. So, they bought the option from Dad, paying him an exorbitant price, and handed the project to producer Edmund Grainger with Ferrer as director.

Dad was bitterly disappointed. He had envisioned Vincent Minnelli directing, convinced he could get a brilliant performance from Audrey. She had already won both an Oscar and a Tony for *Roman Holiday*, and she was luminous in *Sabrina* with Bogart and William Holden. But in *Green Mansions*, her performance was dulled by a questionable script and uninspired direction. What could have been a magical film fell flat.

WHO'S ON FIRST?

On Sunday, we had breakfast in the hotel dining room and slowly made our way through every section of *The New York Times*. Then we walked over to the Museum of Modern Art and took our time going through each floor, pausing for coffee and soft drinks. I was excited to introduce Dad to some of the modern painters he hadn't encountered before. He complimented me on how much I knew, and I thanked him—reassuring him there was no danger of me turning into the "intellectual snob" he once joked I might become. That got a good laugh out of him. He remembered saying it.

Dinner that night was another memorable experience. We went to Dinty Moore's on West 46th Street, a well-known haunt for Broadway stars and sports legends. As we stepped out of the cab, we were greeted by the doorman, who had an uncanny memory. Though my father hadn't been there in at least a decade, the man said, "Good evening, Mr. Berman... Welcome to Dinty Moore's."

We were both impressed.

The restaurant was packed. People were standing shoulder to shoulder in the entry, waiting for a table. Dad figured we didn't stand a chance—we hadn't made a reservation—but just then, the maître d' approached us and pointed to a table at the back of the room. A man was frantically waving for Dad to come join him.

When we reached the table, I did a double take.

It was the Yankee Clipper himself—Joe DiMaggio—having dinner with his friend, Lou Costello. Costello, of course, was half of the famous comedy duo Abbott and Costello. They'd made a string of successful films together, including *Rio Rita*, which Dad had co-produced. And who could forget their iconic baseball bit, "Who's on First?"

I had met Lou Costello years ago, at a dinner in Arrowhead Springs, when I was a child. One night, in the hotel dining room, he gave me a New York Yankees baseball cap that he said had been given to him by Joe DiMaggio. I was a wide-eyed boy—starstruck, and over the moon.

But when I brought the cap home and showed it to a friend, he took one look at it and said it was too big for DiMaggio's head—and I began to wonder... Had Joe really given that cap to Lou? Or was it just part of Costello's comedy routine?

I was tempted to ask DiMaggio right then and there if the story was true—but with Lou sitting across the table, it was probably best to keep that question to myself.

DiMaggio had been retired from the Yankees for seven years, and he had recently been married to Marilyn Monroe. Although they were now separated, he was still in love with her and looking out for her best interests. He was determined to get her signed with MGM and no other studio, and he begged my dad to use his influence to bring her into what he considered the best studio in the world.

Joe was worried she'd end up at Fox—which was the last thing he wanted. He was certain that if Louis B. Mayer were still in charge, Marilyn would've already been gobbled up and signed to a multi-year contract. But Mayer was gone, replaced by Dore Schary. DiMaggio wasn't impressed. He called Schary "highbrow" and didn't believe he'd produce the kinds of films that would be good for Marilyn. Still, he hoped she would land at MGM.

Dad promised DiMaggio he'd do his absolute best to get Marilyn under contract. He told Joe he had become friendly with Schary and that we'd been invited to his home for Passover dinners over the past few years. He was confident he could convince Schary to sign her.

We finished our steaks and went back to the hotel to pack. It was one of the most memorable weekends of my life—and some of the best days I ever spent with my dad. I truly felt like we were back on track, and that our time together was better than ever.

I was also having a great summer with Danny Selznick at Harvard. We dated girls from Wellesley and took them to movies at the Brattle Theater in Cambridge. I went out with the beautiful Johanna Mankiewicz, daughter of Herman Mankiewicz—who wrote the screenplay for *Citizen Kane*—and niece of the great Joe Mankiewicz. She was at Wellesley that summer with her best friend, Judy Jaffe—Sam and Mildred's youngest daughter. Danny and I had known both Johanna and Judy since we were kids; they used to come to our birthday parties.

We went to Boston Pops concerts on the Esplanade along the Charles River and had Sunday brunches at Jack and Marion's, the famous Brookline deli just outside the city. I grew to love Boston, and revisiting New York had been equally thrilling, bringing back memories of the six months I'd lived there as a child. The four of us had some truly great times together that summer.

Danny's mother lived in New York City, but she also had a charming house upstate in Bedford Village, just across the Connecticut border. She could take a commuter train from Manhattan and be there in just over an hour. The property included a tiny lake—which, in true East Coast fashion, was referred to as a "pond." She called her home IMSPOND, a clever play on her name: Irene Mayer Selznick.

One weekend late that summer Irene was hosting a special dinner party. Danny and I were invited, and we planned to stay overnight. That Saturday, we spent the afternoon studying for Monday exams. Then we packed our jackets and ties for dinner and jumped into Danny's convertible for the drive to Bedford Village.

It was a little less than a two-hour drive over mostly quiet country roads, and along the way, Danny briefed me on his mother's particular ideas about etiquette—especially at the dinner table. I don't remember most of them now, but one stood out above all: there would be *no yawning* at the table, no matter how late it was or how exhausted we might be from the trip.

Danny warned me that if his mother saw me yawn, she'd be furious—and might even ask me to leave the table. That would have been mortifying in front of the other guests, most of whom were celebrities. That Saturday night, she'd invited the entire cast of the popular game show *What's My Line?* The guest list included Dorothy Kilgallen—the syndicated Broadway columnist; Bennett Cerf—the publisher and founder of Random House; Betsy Palmer—a well-credited actress in film and television; Arlene Francis—a seasoned actress and TV personality; and her husband, Martin Gabel—actor and producer, best known for his portrayal of James Dean in a powerful documentary.

It was an illustrious group, to be sure, and most of them were occupying the guest bedrooms in the house. Danny and I were shown to the guest house to shower and dress for dinner. That same guest house had once been home to the playwright Tennessee Williams (Tom Lanier), who had taken my dad's advice and moved to New York to write.

My father had read an early work of his, titled *The Gentleman Caller*, which was later rewritten into the powerful play *The Glass Menagerie*. The play went on to win the Drama Critics' Circle Award in 1945 and established Williams as one of America's great playwrights.

Irene Selznick, recognizing both Tennessee's enormous talent and his fragility, purchased the rights to the new play and moved him into her guest house at IMSPOND—where Danny and I were now staying.

Tennessee wrote the play on an old Royal typewriter, which still sat on the desk in the guest house. Danny told me that Irene hovered over Tennessee like a mother hen. Each morning, when she heard the typewriter clacking away, she would walk out to the guest house and go straight to the wastebasket, which was usually overflowing with crumpled pages that Tennessee had ripped from the typewriter and discarded. He called them his "false starts"—words abandoned before he found his writing rhythm for the day.

Even though Tennessee had relegated those pages to the trash, Irene would uncrumple and inspect them. Occasionally, she'd encourage him to reconsider a line or two and put them back in the script. Danny said Tennessee had even tossed away what would become the most famous line in *A Streetcar Named Desire*, only to reinstate it at Irene's insistence.

It was Vivien Leigh's tragically naïve line near the end of the play, as she's being carted away to a mental institution: "I've always relied on the kindness of strangers." It remains one of the most iconic lines in the history of Broadway theater.

The dinner party was more spectacular than I had ever imagined. All those glib, quick-witted guests kept topping each other with humorous anecdotes, and the laughter went on for hours. During the cocktail hour, Bennett Cerf approached me and said, "Your father is my favorite producer in Hollywood... I love all of his movies."

This time, I was ready with the proper response. "That's very kind of you to say, Mr. Cerf."

"Call me Ben... and sit down here with me for a while. I've got a lot of questions for you."

I don't remember what was served for dinner, but there were quite a few courses, and it was nearly ten-thirty by the time dessert arrived. I was starting to fade, but I remembered what Danny had told me in the car—yawning would not be tolerated. I had no desire to incur his mother's wrath, especially not in front of all those guests, so I kept taking deep breaths and holding them at intervals, hoping to stave off the urge to yawn.

I glanced across the table at Danny to see how he was holding up. He looked tired too and kept raising his fist to his mouth. It looked like he was stifling a cough, but later he told me he was suppressing yawns. I asked why he hadn't excused himself and gone to the powder room to splash cold water on his face. His response? "I wish I had thought of that."

The summer away had been good for all of us—including my mother and sisters, who were baking away their troubles under the Honolulu sun. We all had to cope with the separation and divorce, and it was better to do it in different surroundings, away from the daily reminders of Dad's absence.

A couple of weeks after I got home from Boston, Dad called and asked me to come to Projection Room A in the MGM Thalberg Building. All the top brass at the studio had assembled to view a test reel that had been shot with Marilyn Monroe, along with one of her scenes from *The Asphalt Jungle*. Everyone who saw that film had raved about Marilyn's performance, and now the moment had come to decide whether to offer her a contract.

We ran the film. When the lights came up, the room buzzed with excitement. A star had just been born in that projection room, and we all knew it. Howard Strickling, normally a reserved man, couldn't contain himself. Neither could Benny Thau or my father, who were visibly animated and full of enthusiasm. Dad looked over at Dore Schary, who held the ultimate decision, and said, "How can we not sign her?"

Dore was equally energized. "Of course, we're going to sign her... We really have to."

But sadly, MGM never did.

It was inconceivable to everyone at the studio how Dore Schary could have let her get away, but Marilyn signed with Darryl Zanuck at Fox and began making blockbuster after blockbuster—*How to Marry a Millionaire, Gentlemen Prefer Blondes, The Seven Year Itch*... just to name a few.

25

DAD'S INDIE FLAG FLIES HIGH

It was 1958, and my dad had acquired the rights to produce *The Reluctant Debutante*, a smash-hit play in London that had also been well-received on Broadway. It was a comedy Dad knew would work beautifully on screen—especially after replacing the theater actors with stars. He had already secured Rex Harrison for the lead.

Rex played an Englishman who had been married to an American woman, with whom he had a daughter. Now divorced, he is remarried to an elegant Englishwoman, played by Kay Kendall. The daughter, portrayed by Sandra Dee, comes to visit her father and stepmother, and they decide she should be "presented" as a debutante. That is, they place her on the marriage block to be claimed by one of the eligible English bachelors. But of course, she wants none of it—she's fallen for Johnny Saxon, an American drummer who plays in the orchestra at the "coming-out" balls.

It was a clever and amusing comedy, and Dad wanted to capitalize on the real-life romance between Rex Harrison and Kay Kendall, which was the talk of the season. Much like the buzz surrounding Taylor and Burton had drawn audiences to *Cleopatra*, this romance was poised to do the same for *The Reluctant Debutante*.

Strangely enough, the film had to be shot in Paris because Rex Harrison was facing serious tax troubles in both the U.S. and the U.K. He couldn't set foot in either country without his earnings being frozen by the government to satisfy his debts.

By the late 1950s, the era of the big Hollywood musical had begun to fade. Gene Kelly, who had dazzled in *"An American in Paris"* and *"Singing in the Rain"* just a few years earlier, now struggled to find work as a dancer—either in Hollywood or on Broadway. Theater audiences had grown weary of musicals and were gravitating toward serious dramas from playwrights like Arthur Miller, Tennessee Williams, Edward Albee, and others. Hollywood, always quick to follow trends, began to shift its focus.

Dad and Larry Weingarten acquired the rights to Tennessee Williams' *Cat on a Hot Tin Roof*, which had enjoyed an enormously successful run on Broadway. Although it was originally part of Weingarten's contractual obligations to MGM, he was gravely ill at the time. So, my father produced the film, along with several other of Weingarten's properties, for which Larry still received producer credit. This arrangement served to satisfy Weingarten's contractual commitments to the studio and to navigate the complex tax implications of independent film production in those days.

The original Broadway cast featured Ben Gazzara as Brick, Barbara Bel Geddes as Maggie the Cat, Burl Ives as Big Daddy, and Madeleine Sherwood as Mae, the greedy daughter-in-law.

As talented as they all were, Dad envisioned bigger names for the film. He cast Paul Newman as Brick and Elizabeth Taylor as Maggie, while retaining Burl Ives and Madeleine Sherwood from the original cast. He added the brilliant Australian actress Dame Judith Anderson as Big Momma. Richard Brooks directed the picture, which became a critical and commercial success—and a landmark in Elizabeth Taylor's meteoric career.

Besides being a huge hit, *Cat on a Hot Tin Roof* was one of my father's most penetrating and provocative films. It was nominated for six Academy Awards, including Best Picture, with both Elizabeth Taylor and Paul Newman receiving nods for Best Actress and Best Actor. Richard Brooks was nominated for Best Director and shared a Best Screenplay nomination with James Poe.

The Golden Globes also recognized the film, nominating it for Best Picture and Best Director. It received dozens of other honors—from the New York Film Critics Circle, BAFTA, the Writers Guild, the Directors Guild, and from film festivals around the world. It was a major triumph for everyone connected with the picture.

But it didn't win a single Oscar.

The big winners that year were *Gigi* and *Separate Tables*, and once again, Dad and Richard Brooks went home disappointed. Personally, I believe *Cat* stands among the very best of my father's films—a remarkable achievement in a career that spanned fifty years and included 113 movies. Although he never spoke a word about his disappointment, he must have, on some level, felt there was a strange sort of conspiracy preventing him from receiving the recognition he deserved for so many wonderful films.

But there wasn't.

Years later, after I'd outgrown my own youthful frustrations, I went back and looked at all the films that won Best Picture in the years when Dad's movies were nominated. And in each case, it was a true clash of titans. The nominated films were all exceptional, and while a strong case could be made for my father's films to win, there were equally compelling reasons for the winners to take the prize. Except on rare occasions, the voting is close, and in the end, it comes down to personal taste. A few more votes one way or another doesn't negate the quality of the other contenders. When you're standing in front of a buffet with five exquisite dishes, how do you pick just one? It's subjective—there is no wrong choice.

Even if Dad understood that—and I'm sure he did—he still must have felt crushed each time he walked away empty-handed. Yet, deep down, he had to know how proud he could be of what he'd accomplished. By that point in his career, he had produced more quality films than almost anyone in Hollywood—and most of them were box-office successes.

He used to tell me he felt a real responsibility to the stockholders of Metro-Goldwyn-Mayer. He knew that some of that stock was held by widows raising young children, and he never wanted a film to lose money and jeopardize their futures. I always thought that was incredibly noble. Certainly, one of his finer traits—and not something I've ever heard from another top executive in any business, especially not the movie industry.

Dore Schary lasted only five years as head of production at MGM. He was temporarily replaced by my father, and then by Sol C. Siegel, who came over from 20th Century Fox to take charge. It's unclear whether Dore lost his job because he failed to sign Marilyn Monroe, but it certainly didn't help. That misstep cost MGM millions in lost box office revenue—and gave 20th Century Fox a major boost back into the black.

My dad was immediately chosen to step in as Schary's temporary replacement. He was already in the middle of producing another film, so the added responsibility was a heavy burden. But Nicholas Schenck told him there was no one else capable of handling the job—or at least no one they trusted—so Dad agreed to take it on for a limited time.

He had to supervise a slate of pictures in various stages of production, the most high-profile being *Raintree County*, a big-budget film starring Elizabeth Taylor and Montgomery Clift—who, together, were absolute magic on screen. But the picture came with plenty of challenges that Dad had to tackle head-on.

The most important move he made was hiring Edward Dmytryk to direct. Dad had worked with Dmytryk back in the old RKO days and had always respected his talent. He knew Dmytryk was the kind of director who could handle tough situations—and that's exactly what *Raintree County* needed.

Dmytryk was one of the so-called "Hollywood Ten"—filmmakers who were blacklisted and imprisoned for Contempt of Congress during the McCarthy era. He'd gone to prison alongside Dalton Trumbo and the others. After his release, Stanley Kramer was the first to hire him, bringing him on to direct *The Caine Mutiny*, starring Humphrey Bogart and Fred MacMurray. That film became the second-highest grossing picture of 1955 and earned an Oscar nomination for Best Picture.

It was a triumphant comeback, and Dad was thrilled that Dmytryk was now available for *Raintree County*. He had always believed that Dmytryk had been unjustly imprisoned, and he was eager to help revive his career in any way he could.

Dmytryk used to come to our house for dinner and to run the dailies with Dad—footage they didn't have time to watch during the day at the studio. I was fascinated by him. He was sharp and articulate, and he had a keen instinct for filmmaking. Watching him and Dad work together in our home projection room was a real education. I was soaking it all in—learning a great deal more about how movies were truly made.

ELVIS AND THE ARMY

Following the release of *Raintree County* and the remaining four or five of Dore Schary's unfinished projects, Dad began pre-production on a most unlikely movie. He was encouraged by his friend Hal Wallis to make a film with Elvis Presley, who had become hotter than Tabasco. Elvis's first movie, *Love Me Tender*, was an enormous hit, so Dad signed him for *Jailhouse Rock*.

It turned out to be one of my father's biggest hits—and it also gave me a great opportunity, many years later. I was in my last year at UCLA when Dad called and said he had a special job for me. He wanted me to take Elvis Presley around the studio and show him everything: the sound stages, the music department, the editing rooms—even the back lot, if he wanted to see it. Dad was conducting meetings with Elvis's manager, Colonel Parker, and the Colonel didn't want Elvis to be in on those negotiations.

I only had classes on Tuesday and Thursday mornings that semester, so I had plenty of time for the job. I was fascinated to meet the man with more hit records than anyone in the history of the music industry. I was pleasantly surprised to find him open and friendly—and quite happy to be touring the studio with me. He told me all kinds of stories: how he started at Sun Records, where his music had taken him, and how much he loved his treasured Ford pickup truck back in Nashville, which he'd had painted six times to get it the exact shade of the water in the Gulf of Mexico—his favorite blue.

He was a private person and didn't say much about his personal life, except to tell me what a wonderful person his mother was.

When the movie started shooting, Dad assigned me, once again, to the editing room as an unpaid apprentice. I could help the editors and keep learning about the business I wanted to be part of. It was a fantastic opportunity, and I picked up skills that would later help me land my first job. Editing musicals requires a specific set of techniques, and I learned a lot working with Bill Saracino—one of the best music editors in Hollywood.

Elvis turned out to be a perfectionist. If something wasn't exactly right, he would keep doing it over until he was satisfied—even if it took all night. When they filmed the big title song inside the jail, Elvis liked parts of three different takes, and he wanted to keep shooting until one take had everything just right. But it was late in the evening, and the studio shut down production. They were incurring serious costs, and another crew had an early call the next morning on another stage.

Elvis complained to my dad, who told the editors to work on the scene and show him a cut he could approve. Then it could be handed off to the music department. Bill Saracino would lay in the prerecorded music track and sync it to the edited picture.

The following day, Saracino worked from morning into the night using segments from the three takes Elvis had liked. The next day, Dad booked a screening room and called Elvis up from the set to view the edited musical number with the synced soundtrack.

Elvis was ecstatic. Everything was in perfect sync. He came down to the commissary, where Saracino, Ferris Webster—the picture editor—and I were having lunch. He put his hand on Bill's shoulder and said, "This man's a genius."

Elvis was so thrilled with Bill's work that, when the picture wrapped, he bought him a brand-new Cadillac convertible as a parting gift. It was a beautiful car—cream-colored with a tan convertible top. Bill insisted on taking us for a ride in it, and I could see how much he loved it.

I was deeply impressed by Elvis. His work ethic was incredible, and so was his generosity. He was a wonderful human being.

The end of the picture coincided with my graduation from UCLA, and as it happened, both Elvis and I were off to join the Army. Elvis was sent to Germany, while I joined a National Guard unit and was sent to Fort Ord, California, for basic training. After that, I was stationed at Fort Sam Houston in Texas, at the Brooke Army Hospital in San Antonio.

Now that I had graduated, I was vulnerable to being drafted—and I didn't want to spend two years in the infantry in some foreign country, where war could break out at any moment. My goal in joining the hospital unit was to avoid front-line combat, but we still participated in some hair-raising combat maneuvers right on base, including parachuting out of airplanes and operating the field hospital under simulated combat conditions.

Among other duties, I was responsible for sterilizing medical instruments in an autoclave—a nightmare of a job. There was no way to operate that boiling-hot machine without burning your fingers. We also had to pack up the entire field hospital into helicopters, fly to remote landing zones, and set up from scratch in under an hour. It was a grueling six months—and it felt more like six years before it was finally over.

26

MY FIRST PAYING JOB IN THE FILM INDUSTRY

When I returned home from active duty in the Army, a brand-new Volkswagen Beetle was waiting for me in the garage. I had sent money home for a down payment and asked Mom to arrange delivery.

I needed the new car to look for a job. In addition to reaching out to friends like other things I did when I got back home from my stint in the army was to apply for membership at the Motion Picture Editors Guild, hoping that would also lead to a job.

But there was a catch.

The Guild operated under a strict seniority system—you couldn't be hired unless you were already a member, and you couldn't become a member unless there were no Guild editors currently out of work. The studios had signed this agreement with all the Hollywood Unions under the IATSE (International Alliance of Theatrical Stage Employees), which made it nearly impossible for newcomers to break in.

Frustrated but determined, I started looking for work with independent companies that weren't signatory to the IATSE contracts. The pay wasn't as good, and these jobs often came without medical insurance, but I was burning through my savings and needed to start somewhere.

After a couple of weeks of knocking on doors, I got a call from my Uncle Henry. He told me that ABC Television was hiring apprentice editors at their Hollywood film distribution center near Vermont and Sunset—and for once, there was no one on the Guild roster out of work. That meant I could take the job *and* be inducted into the Editors Guild immediately.

I was ecstatic.

I threw on a coat and tie, rushed over for the interview, and got hired on the spot to start the following Monday.

In those pre-videotape days, everything was still done on film. For each network TV show, the lab would create three 35mm prints—one for New York, one for Chicago, and one for Los Angeles. Those prints would feed a web of stations within the broadcast range of each major city. But since the network wasn't yet fully national, the rest of the country had to be handled differently.

For stations in remote or rural locations, the lab struck 25 to 30 additional 16mm prints and sent them directly to those affiliates with early air dates. Smaller stations with later airings had to wait until an existing print was returned to the distribution center—at which point it would be re-edited with updated commercials and shipped out again.

REALITY, REELS, AND RESENTMENT

My initial job as an apprentice editor was far from glamorous. I was tasked with rewinding the film reels returned from outlying stations and inspecting them for damage. Once cleared, I'd hand them off to one of the editors, who would replace the old commercials with new ones delivered by the advertising agencies. The new spots arrived clipped together with paper clips, and it was my job to hot splice them into the print.

After each splice, I had to apply a swipe of black "blooping" ink over each edit to nullify a loud popping noise when the splice hit the projector's sound head. The process was slow, tedious, and painfully uncreative. This wasn't exactly the thrilling entry into Hollywood I had envisioned.

To make matters worse, the pay was just as dull as the work—$86.50 per week. Even back then, that wasn't much. I was dating a southern girl at the time, and when I told her my salary, she didn't miss a beat.

"Darlin'," she said, in her southern drawl, "we just *can't* make it *on* $86.50."

A couple of weeks later, I had lunch with Dad in the men's grill at Hillcrest. I told him how little I was making and mentioned I was thinking about picking up a second job in the evenings.

He laughed. "Now you're beginning to understand what the real world is like."

I didn't find it funny. In fact, it made me angry.

How could he be so understanding and supportive sometimes and so flippant and dismissive other times? I left that lunch with a bad taste in my mouth—and not from the food. His comment stirred up a familiar ache, one I had tried hard to ignore.

As I thought back on our many interactions, I realized I'd been quietly collecting these kinds of remarks for years—filing them away, sweeping them under the emotional rug. I rarely said anything at the time. I just let them build up inside, assuming that's what sons were supposed to do. But later in life, I came to understand what a toll that kind of emotional storage can take.

THE MARX FAMILY

One of the first people I looked up after I got home from the army was my friend Bill Marx. Harpo had sent him to Juilliard for a proper musical education, and when I found him in his small apartment on Genesee Avenue in West Hollywood, he was writing music and playing beautiful piano. I could tell he was destined for a great future in the music business, but at that moment, he was still struggling.

I happened to be there one day when he got a phone call from his uncle Groucho in Las Vegas.

"Hello... Is this Billy Marx, the great lover? There's a girl sitting next to me pining her heart away for you. Why don't you get on the next plane to Las Vegas?"

Bill, used to these kinds of calls from Groucho, replied, "Thanks, Grouch. I don't need a girl just now. What I need is a job."

Groucho didn't have an answer for that one—but knowing him, he probably could've helped Bill find a job if he'd really wanted to.

Groucho was one of the funniest men I've ever known, but much of his humor was rooted in human suffering. He'd insult people with a smile, often asking, "Can I buy back my introduction to you?"—and sometimes, I think he genuinely meant it. One of his more infamous zingers? "I never forget a face, but in your case, I'll make an exception." He once said that to the doorman at Hillcrest Country Club who had his hand out for a tip.

Hillcrest was the country club for prominent (and mostly Jewish) families in Los Angeles. My grandfather Frank—my mother's father—was a charter member, and my dad joined shortly after it opened. I grew up there: taking tennis lessons, occasionally playing golf with my father in my early teens, and hanging out with Bill Marx and Norman Siegel, the son of legendary producer Sol C. Siegel. Hillcrest provided a quiet, close-knit social life for all of us.

Sunday brunch in the main dining room was a major highlight. It was a buffet to rival the best spreads in Las Vegas—only more delicious—and it offered something for everyone, even the pickiest eaters.

There was also a posh men's grill and card room with a bar, where the men would lunch after golf, smoke cigars, and play cards. No women allowed. On the other side of the main dining room was the women's card room, where they'd go after lunch. My mother used to play canasta with her friends there—and she was a shrewd, strategic card player.

It seemed like every third person at Hillcrest was a celebrity. Frank Sinatra, Milton Berle, Dean Martin, Jerry Lewis, Jack Benny, George Burns, Gracie Allen, Johnny Carson—icons like that were constantly around. As were top movie producers and powerful industrialists. It wasn't just a country club—it was a glittering social hub of Hollywood's elite.

To even qualify for membership, you had to be both prominent and charitable. I remember my father donating as much as $10,000 a year to the United Jewish Appeal and other meaningful causes, which was part of the unspoken price of admission.

In the men's grill, tucked into a corner, there was a famous round table reserved for George Burns and his circle. It was "by invitation only." The regulars would discuss potential new members for the table, and if you got the nod, you were in—you could sit there anytime.

On any given Saturday, you'd spot a comedy Mount Rushmore gathered around: Harpo and Groucho Marx, George Burns, Milton Berle, and other legendary names. My dad was a regular, which meant I sometimes had the privilege of joining him. Occasionally, Harpo would bring his son Bill Marx over, and the two of us would sit among giants, soaking in their stories, their wit, their incredible timing.

There were also brilliant minds like producers Fred Kohlmar and Jerry Wald, and screenwriters like Irving Brecher—who not only contributed uncredited lines to *Gone with the Wind* but also wrote a couple of the Marx Brothers films. The banter around that table was rapid-fire, insightful, and often hysterically funny. Business was also on the menu. More than once, I saw deals being sketched out between jokes and gin rummy hands.

Guests were welcome—on occasion. I remember one lunch where I sat with Henry Kissinger. Another time, it was Herman Hahn, president of Union Bank. You never knew who might turn up. One day, someone brought a builder who was developing post offices under a handshake agreement with the U.S. Postal Service. He'd raise capital, build a post office, and the government would lease it back—typically for ninety-nine years. My dad invested and received not only a stake in the property but regular rent checks from the government. It was a shrewd and very profitable arrangement... for a time.

Years later, in the early 1980s, I happened to be at the round table during a particularly memorable lunch. A top executive from Lehman Brothers had joined us, and he was discreetly floating the idea that a private investor group could take over Disney Studios. Walt Disney had passed away, and the company, under the leadership of his son-in-law Ron Miller, was floundering. Movie production was slowing, and most of the studio's income was coming from its theme parks in Anaheim and Orlando.

But there was gold in Disney's vaults—films like *Snow White and the Seven Dwarfs*, *Peter Pan*, *Cinderella*, and others. The studio had a savvy strategy for re-releasing these classics every generation or so, bringing in new waves of revenue from theatrical runs before eventually licensing them for television. Sometimes, they'd add fresh animation or enhance the soundtracks to make the old new again. It was like a time-release fortune, just waiting for the right moment to be unlocked.

The Lehman Brothers plan was bold—some would say brazen. Their strategy was to gather a small group of wealthy investors, buy enough stock to gain control of Disney Studios, and immediately release the classic films locked away in the vault—before the Disney family could mount a legal counterattack.

Of course, the Wall Street sharks were circling too. Everyone could smell the opportunity. Lehman figured the investors would make millions in just the first few months, siphoning off profits from film rentals before any lawsuits or boardroom battles could oust them. If the Disney heirs won back control, or if another corporate titan forced them out—it wouldn't matter. The money would already be made. The vault would be raided, the treasure spent.

My dad's eyes nearly popped out of his head hearing all this. I told him I wanted in. He was ready to bet the farm. But like many brilliant schemes, this one never got off the ground. In 1984, Michael Eisner left Paramount to take the reins at Disney—and everything changed. He stabilized the company and turned it into a juggernaut. That tiny window of vulnerability was slammed shut and sealed tight.

Eisner didn't have to plunder the vault. He built Disney into a media empire. I don't know how much of his billion-dollar net worth came from that period—but I imagine it was a hefty slice.

The whole idea of the round table at Hillcrest had roots in New York, at the legendary Algonquin Hotel. Back in the 1920s and '30s, the Algonquin Round Table was the beating heart of Broadway's golden age—home to the sharpest minds and wittiest tongues in theater and literature. Harpo Marx was a charter member of that table, and later, a founding member of the Hillcrest version. That same irreverent, intellectual spirit crossed the country with him.

The Algonquin's roster was stacked with legends: Charles MacArthur, playwright, and husband of Helen Hayes. Robert Benchley, the sly humorist and actor. Dorothy Parker—sharp-tongued, brilliant, and biting. George S. Kaufman, Broadway's master wordsmith. Noël Coward. Alexander Woollcott. The table was a who's who of America's literary elite.

Being invited to that table was a badge of honor. So was getting a seat at Hillcrest's round table. I was proud that my father had earned his spot among the greats—and, truth be told, thrilled when I got to sit beside him.

There was one thing Hillcrest lacked: Otto. A beloved German waiter at the Algonquin, Otto was something of a New York icon, once even caricatured in *The New Yorker*. His thick accent and deadpan delivery made him a walking punchline—and everyone adored him.

Someone—maybe Harpo—got the idea that Otto should escape the harsh New York winters and come west. They collected money from everyone at the round table, and they paid for his plane ticket, covered his moving costs, rented him an apartment. They even paid the rent for a full year. Otto came to Hillcrest and brought a slice of old New York with him.

When Bill Marx and I went to the club for tennis or a few swings on the practice tee at the golf course, we'd always head to the men's grill afterward and try to sit in Otto's section. His accent was music to our ears, and we'd imitate him as soon as he walked away, cracking each other up.

But the memory I hold dearest is one lunch in the mid-1950s. My father and I were sitting in the main dining room—rather than the round table—because Johnny Hyde, vice president of the William Morris Agency, was bringing a guest. And women weren't allowed in the men's grill.

That guest? A girl named Norma Jeane Mortenson. You might know her better as Marilyn Monroe.

The moment she walked in, I was smitten. She wasn't just beautiful—she radiated sweetness, a kind of open-hearted vulnerability you couldn't fake. She made you feel like you already knew her.

I didn't yet understand what "vulnerability" meant in the context of acting, so my father explained: A vulnerable actress makes you feel like you're having a personal relationship with her while watching her perform. Every emotion reads on her face. She invites you in—shares something intimate with you—and as a result, wins your heart. That combination of beauty and vulnerability was more than rare. The only female star who possessed this magic combination of qualities was Elizabeth Taylor. In Hollywood history I can only think of one other female that could qualify... Greta Garbo.

But Marilyn had everything they had and something more. I couldn't take my eyes off her. She had an indescribable inner glow that commanded your attention. She had a little giggle that seemed to make Johnny Hyde melt. He'd smile and pat her hand every time she laughed.

Johnny, who was deeply devoted to Marilyn, was doing everything he could to get her signed at MGM. Like Joe DiMaggio before him, he came to my father, hoping he could pull some strings. But it didn't work. MGM passed—and 20th Century Fox signed her instead.

The rest, as they say, is Hollywood history.

27

FAMILY CONFLICTS AND HEARTBREAKING GOODBYES

One day I was driving with my mother through Beverly Hills when we spotted Cindy in her new Mercedes. Mom had something she wanted to tell her, so she asked me to catch up and flag her down. I tried my best, but Cindy was driving fast. I made a few quick maneuvers, but I just couldn't catch her.

Mom was horrified by how Cindy was driving. As soon as we got home, she called Dad and told him Cindy was driving like a maniac —and that she was selling the Mercedes.

When Cindy got home, Mom said, "I talked to your father, and he told me we have to sell your car."

Cindy lit up in anger. "That wasn't Dad's decision—it was yours," she said. "You don't have to take away the car just because I was speeding."

Mom replied, "No... it was your father's decision."

But Cindy wasn't buying it. "Your name's on the pink slip. So, it's your decision," she snapped, before storming off to her room.

Mother never should've lied to her—because from that moment

on, Cindy never trusted her again. She accused Mom of lying in every confrontation after that. Taking the car away completely undermined whatever Mom was trying to accomplish. I realized there were better ways to handle the situation than buying her an expensive car in the first place, and I blamed that psychiatrist for suggesting it. I also blamed my mother for handling it in such an imperious manner—it sent Cindy straight back to square one. It was a terrible time for her, and I felt deeply sorry.

I wanted to talk to Dad, to see if there was a better solution, but he'd flown to New York on business. By the time he got back, Mom would likely have already sold the car.

But something else happened that took my mind off the situation and plunged me into grief.

Grandma Julie, who had moved from her apartment at the Gaylord Hotel into Henry and Rosemary's house in her later years, had suddenly passed away. I got a call from Henry—he was in tears. He told me Dad would be flying home the next day and asked if I could pick him up from the airport and bring Henry along.

When Dad arrived, he and his brother embraced—and both burst into tears. They got in the back of my car and cried most of the ride home, remembering how wonderful she'd been. I felt the urge to cry with them—but I'd cried most of the night before, and I was pretty much cried out.

Grandma Julie's death was an enormous loss. It would take time for all of us to heal.

They talked about the beautiful marriage she had with Grandpa Harry, and how strong she'd been when he passed away at forty-three. They spoke about the tragic loss of their baby brother Maxie and began to cry all over again. In my entire life, I'd never seen my father cry. Watching him sob alongside his brother was both deeply moving and incredibly unsettling.

Dad was deeply affected by his mother's death, and while I felt sad for him, I was also moved to see how much love and compassion he carried. It reminded me that he loved me—and all of us—and it gave me a renewed sense of security.

I never forgot his quiet, sorrowful words to Uncle Henry in the back seat of my car. I think of them every time we lose someone we love: "It's just the two of us now... you and me. We're all that's left of the old family."

FACING THE PAST, ONE FRAME AT A TIME

A psychiatrist once told me that if you don't process your pain, it simmers inside you until it hardens into something worse—an emotional scar you carry for years. He said you have to allow yourself to feel the hurt fully and then find a way to cut it off at the source. At the time, I wasn't ready to do that. I had spent most of my life turning away from pain, pushing it aside instead of facing it head-on. It would take time—and experience—before I could even begin to change that pattern.

One memory that stayed with me was what happened with my cousin, Stanley Kramer. He had just graduated from Yale and came out to California, full of energy and ambition. He asked my dad to give him a job—as a producer.

Dad shut that down fast.

He told Stanley that no one gets a producing job straight out of college. You have to earn it, pay your dues, learn the business from the ground up. If he gave Stanley that kind of job, it would reek of nepotism—and in this town, that kind of favor could come back to bite you. He pointed to examples he'd seen firsthand, including the case of Dore Schary's nephew, Joel Freeman. Joel had been working as a producer at MGM but was pushed out by internal politics, and it became a cautionary tale. Dad didn't want that kind of fate for Stanley.

Instead, he offered him an entry-level job as a reader in the MGM story department.

Stanley wasn't impressed.

He turned up his nose, stormed out of the office, and didn't speak to my father for years.

During the Great Depression, Stanley scraped by with odd jobs in the industry. He worked as a set hand moving furniture, then fought his way into the editing room as an assistant editor. Like my dad, he hated editing and couldn't wait to escape the cutting room. Eventually he found work as a synopsis writer and researcher for Columbia and then Republic Pictures, before landing an associate producer role at Loew-Lewin Productions—his long-awaited break.

He had paid his dues, just like Dad said he would have to.

In time, Stanley came to see the truth in what my father had told him. The resentment faded. I remember Stanley and his wife joining us for Friday night screenings at our house, the rift behind them.

Stanley went on to produce and direct some of the most iconic films in Hollywood history: *High Noon, Cyrano de Bergerac, The Champion, Home of the Brave, The Member of the Wedding, The Caine Mutiny, The Defiant Ones, Inherit the Wind,* and *Judgment at Nuremberg*—a remarkable legacy by any measure.

He may have taken the long road, but it was a road paved with integrity, and in the end, it led exactly where he was meant to go.

BEHIND THE SCENES, AND BETWEEN THE LINES

Steven Spielberg once called Stanley Kramer an "incredibly talented visionary" and "one of our great filmmakers, not just for the art and passion he put up on screen, but for the impact he has made on the conscience of the world."

In 1961, Stanley received the Irving Thalberg Memorial Award for career achievement—one of the most prestigious honors in the motion picture industry. Only a handful of producers have ever received it, and two of them came from the original Pandrovitz family: Stanley Kramer and my father.

I had heard the story of Stanley asking my dad for a job more than once, and it was one of the reasons I never asked for one myself when I got out of the service. He might have said yes, but I knew what kind of "yes" it would have been—he'd have planted me in a back room, punching holes in script pages or assembling copies with brass fasteners. Technically, he could say he'd helped, but it would've been more like a test—a challenge. A kind of professional gauntlet he wanted me to run on my own.

Sometimes I wondered if he didn't trust me not to embarrass him. I'll never know for sure. But the truth is, with my father, everything was a challenge. Whether it was a bicycle or a car—or a job—he wanted me to earn it. No shortcuts. No favors. Just grit.

So, when my Uncle Henry called me about a job at ABC, part of me couldn't help but wonder: had Dad pulled some strings quietly, from the shadows? Was this his way of helping without having to admit he was helping? I never asked Henry, and I certainly never asked Dad. Maybe I didn't want to know. Maybe it was enough just to imagine that he might have cared that much, even if he never said it out loud.

28

NEW FRIENDS AND SHENANIGANS

The best part of that job wasn't the film stock or the editing rooms—it was meeting Rob Wollin. We were the same age and immediately clicked. Rob was from Portland and had attended the University of Washington, where he'd made friends with a circle I knew from Seattle summers spent visiting my grandparents. As we traded names and stories, we realized we'd even been at the same party back in the early 1950s. It was a total coincidence—and a surprising discovery.

Rob and I became lifelong friends. We shared the same frustrations and ambitions. Though we were grateful for our jobs at ABC, the work wasn't exactly inspiring. We were apprentice editors hoping to climb the ladder, but advancement in that department had less to do with talent and more to do with time served. Promotions were handed out by seniority—not by spark or drive.

And we had plenty of both.

In our growing boredom—and as an antidote to the mind-numbing tedium—Rob and I cooked up a stunt that would become legendary at ABC. Long after we were gone, people still talked about it in hushed tones of awe and laughter.

Our target was an editor named Don Richards.

Don was a former football player turned film editor—arrogant, egocentric, and the self-appointed king of condescension. He treated us apprentices like we were personal assistants at his beck and call. His favorite pastime was pulling practical jokes on others but always punching down. He could dish it out, but we suspected he wasn't too good at taking it.

Rob and I decided it was time for some poetic justice. We didn't want to hurt him—just rattle his cage a little. Our idea? Classic mischief: sneak a gorilla—or someone in a gorilla suit—into Don's editing room early in the morning, wait for him to arrive, and when he turned on the light—BOOM! Out jumps the gorilla.

It was bold. It was reckless. And it was absolutely perfect.

Step one: acquire a gorilla costume.

Sounds easy enough, right? This was Hollywood, after all—the birthplace of *King Kong*, *Mighty Joe Young*, and every jungle adventure ever filmed. But one by one, the studios and costume houses—Paramount, Universal, even Western Costume—turned us down. Apparently, "We just need it for a few hours to scare a guy senseless" wasn't the kind of demo pitch they were looking for, especially if we wanted them to waive the $150 rental fee.

Then we struck gold at Myers Costume Company.

We spun a tale about working on a children's television pilot and needing to show the suit to our (completely fictional) ABC producer for approval. We even gave the producer a name. Myers bought it. We put the $150 deposit on a credit card, promising to return the suit within three hours, untouched and unscathed. We were *not* to wear it, use it, or breathe too hard on it. Just show and return. Otherwise, bye-bye, deposit.

Now, keep in mind: $150 was a *massive* amount of money for two guys making $86.50 a week. It was nearly our entire combined paychecks. But we figured—naively—*how would they ever know* if we used it?

We picked up the suit the next morning at 7 a.m. sharp, drove to the studio, and immediately hit a snag. Neither Rob nor I was tall enough to fit the thing. It was designed for someone over six feet tall.

Enter Jack Moore.

Jack was an assistant editor, burly and broad-shouldered—a human linebacker with a mischievous streak of his own. He was our guy. He agreed to be the gorilla.

Getting Jack into the suit was an event unto itself. The thing was lined with two-inch-thick sponge rubber padding that clung to him like shrink-wrap. He grunted, twisted, and wedged himself into it. When he finally stood upright, sweaty and breathing hard, he looked like a B-movie beast ready for his close-up.

And that's when the real fun began...

THE DAY THE GORILLA ROAMED THE HALLS

By the time Jack was fully suited up, half the department had shown up for work—and glimpses of a seven-foot gorilla lurking near the editing rooms quickly sparked curiosity. When we let people in on our plan, the reaction was unanimous: pure delight. They couldn't wait for the show to start.

Jack, now fully committed to the role, crouched in the corner of Don Richards' editing room while Rob and I switched off the lights and gently shut the door.

Moments later, Richards arrived. He opened the door, flipped the light switch, and WHAM! our gorilla sprang up with a roar, pounding his chest like King Kong at feeding time.

Richards let out a strangled yelp and flailed backward into the hallway, landing squarely on his backside—right in front of a growing crowd of coworkers, all of whom erupted in riotous laughter. Our plan had worked like a charm. We had scared the bluster right out of him, and for once, the prankster was the punchline.

But the gorilla wasn't done yet.

Flushed with success, Jack started prowling the corridors, still in full character, on the hunt for fresh victims. Rob and I trailed him from a safe distance, savoring every shriek and startled yelp that echoed down the hallway. People jumped, screamed, or burst out laughing at the sight of a wild beast lumbering past the copier or peeking into an edit bay.

Then came Alice.

Alice was the office manager. Stern, cost-conscious, and notoriously humorless, she was not what you'd call beloved among the staff. When Jack approached her door, she was buried in paperwork. He waited in the doorway until she finally looked up.

Roar.

Chest pound.

Scream.

Alice's eyes widened in shock, then rolled back in her head as she collapsed backwards in her chair. We couldn't tell if she fainted from fear or if she'd hit her head on the cabinet behind her, but either way —Alice was out cold.

At that point, the joke wasn't funny anymore—especially not to Jack, who was now sweating buckets inside the sponge-lined suit. He tried to wriggle free but found himself stuck. His clothes were drenched, and the rubber padding had practically vacuum-sealed itself to his skin. It took Rob and me nearly seven minutes to peel the costume off him.

Just as we were freeing Jack from his sweltering prison, we heard the distant wail of a siren.

An ambulance.

And suddenly, it dawned on us: we might have taken things *a little too far*.

Paramedics burst through the building moments later and wheeled Alice out on a stretcher. As far as we could tell, she still hadn't regained consciousness.

Rob and I began to panic.

Simultaneously, ABC got a call from Myers Costume. They had grown suspicious about our youth and the vagueness of our request, and they wanted to verify our story. Myers asked to speak with the producer whose name we'd given them—a name we had completely fabricated. Unfortunately, they got connected to an actual ABC vice president with a similar-sounding name. He informed Myers that there was no such children's pilot in the planning stages, and he said that he would look into the matter.

Meanwhile, our department head, Frank Ralston—the man who'd hired us—was a WWII veteran and a Purple Heart recipient. He had lost one foot in the war and wore a prosthesis fitted inside a regular shoe. Not many people at ABC knew this. Most just noticed that Frank walked with a strange limp, unaware of the reason. The only reason Rob and I knew was because we had witnessed an unfortunate and deeply awkward incident a couple of weeks earlier.

The ABC building had a long exterior flight of iron steps leading down to the employee parking lot. Rob and I were halfway down one evening when we spotted Frank making his way to his car. Somehow, his prosthetic foot got wedged under one of those white wooden parking stanchions—the ones meant to keep cars from rolling. He lurched forward and hit the pavement hard. His prosthetic foot and shoe had become completely detached and were now stuck beneath the wooden stopper.

We froze. Should we go back inside? Call for help? We panicked. Running up the steps would have taken too long, and we knew Frank would have seen us and realized we'd witnessed everything. In the end, we just kept walking—eyes straight ahead—pretending we hadn't seen a thing.

Back in the present chaos: after the ambulance took off with poor Alice, Rob and I stashed the now-soaked gorilla costume in a closet and tried to look busy. That's when Peggy—Frank's tiny, tough-as-nails secretary with a high-pitched munchkin voice—marched down the hallway toward us.

We liked Peggy, but there was no warmth in her tone when she announced, "Frank wants to see you boys in his office... NOW!"

She led us to the outer office and then disappeared on an errand. Rob and I sat there, squirming in our seats, trying to figure out why Frank wanted to see us. It had only been about thirty minutes since Alice was carted off. Surely, he couldn't already know we were the masterminds behind the gorilla stunt. Maybe he wanted to talk about the parking lot incident. Maybe we were about to be guilt-tripped for pretending not to see him lying on the asphalt with his leg detached. But... we were wrong.

Frank opened the door to his office and motioned for us to come in.

"What have you boys done, and what the hell could you have been thinking?"

He'd received a call from the ABC Vice President and now knew everything—including the lies we told to rent the gorilla suit. Rob and I stammered through an explanation while Frank just shook his head.

"You've put yourselves—and ABC—in a position where we might have to defend against a serious lawsuit from Alice. And you're now in jeopardy of being fired. On top of that, you committed a fraudulent rental in the company's name from Myers Costume."

We showed immediate remorse. We told him we truly hadn't imagined our prank would lead to anything this serious.

What bothered Frank the most, he said, was that Rob and I had been two of his best employees—and that both of us were being considered for promotion before this mess. He didn't know if he could save our jobs, but he clearly felt some sympathy in spite of everything.

To protect ourselves—and especially the company—Frank told us to write a letter taking full responsibility, stating clearly that ABC had no knowledge of what we were up to. He also told us to write a sincere apology to Alice, acknowledging the pain and fear we'd caused her, and asking for forgiveness. Lastly, we were to return the gorilla costume immediately and accept whatever consequences came next.

We returned the damp, spongy costume to Myers, lost our $150 deposit to cleaning fees, and were sternly advised never to rent from them again. Dejected, we dragged ourselves back to ABC, dreading the possibility of lawsuits... or unemployment.

To our amazement, ABC accepted our apology. And a few days later, when Alice returned to work, we went to her office to apologize in person. She thanked us for the letter that had been forwarded to her and—amazingly—forgave us. She explained that, as a child, she had been traumatized by a large animal and had feared wild creatures ever since. When she looked up and saw the gorilla, she went into instant shock.

Then came the biggest surprise: our co-workers had taken up a collection and raised more than $150 to reimburse us for the costume rental. After pulling off one of the dumbest stunts imaginable, Rob and I had somehow become the heroes of the day. People told us it was the most entertaining shift they'd ever experienced at ABC.

Thank God we didn't lose our jobs—because that would've confirmed my father's worst suspicions about me. I was certain he believed I'd go through life doing stupid things, incapable of growing up. The gorilla story was already spreading through the industry, and I feared he'd hear about it and never let me live it down. Thankfully, it never reached him.

Eventually, Rob and I both received our long-awaited promotions —but within a year, we each moved on to better opportunities. Rob was hired as a staff editor at CBS and later became supervising editor at their Beverly Boulevard facility. He even received an Academy

Award nomination for a short subject he edited, co-produced, and partially photographed.

As for me, I landed a position at 20th Century Fox doing sound effects and dialogue editing—no help from Dad or Uncle Henry. I also got a raise—$38.50 a week. I was now making $125.

Life, at last, was a little more comfortable.

29

AN UPWARD CAREER MOVE

At 20th Century Fox, I learned how to cut sound effects and synchronize re-recorded dialogue—skills that became part of my daily job. I also worked on the recording stage with actors who needed to redo their lines when unwanted background noise had corrupted the original soundtrack.

One of the first films I worked on was *Let's Make Love*, starring Marilyn Monroe and the French singing idol Yves Montand. I went to the set one day to speak with the script supervisor about a discrepancy in our pages and found myself watching a scene being filmed with Marilyn in a swimming pool. She was still as breathtaking as the day I first saw her years earlier at Hillcrest Country Club—but there was something different now. Her face looked clouded by worry.

After one of the takes, Marilyn broke down in tears and called for her acting coach and confidante, Paula Strasberg. Paula was the wife of Lee Strasberg, founder of the Actors Studio in New York—an institution that had trained the likes of Marlon Brando, Eva Marie Saint, and many others in the art of Method Acting.

Paula ran out of Marilyn's trailer clutching a glass of water and a handful of pills, trying to soothe her. Something was clearly wrong. I was standing beside an assistant director who muttered, "Here comes her nursemaid," with a trace of contempt. Whispers on set blamed her emotional fragility on her recent divorce from Arthur Miller—who, incidentally, had written the screenplay for the movie. I couldn't help but wonder about the pills and what effect they were having. A year later, when she died, the autopsy cited an overdose of barbiturates.

Many of the exterior scenes in *Let's Make Love* were plagued with airplane noise, meaning Marilyn and Montand would have to re-record their lines on a quiet soundstage. Montand, however, refused. Someone from our department had already contacted him, but he flatly declined to re-record any of his dialogue.

Walter Rossi, our department head, was now stuck. Someone had to convince Montand to do it, but Rossi didn't want to bring in producer Jerry Wald or any Fox executives—it would make him look like he couldn't handle a simple issue. I was standing just outside his office when I heard him say, "Let the Berman kid handle it... his old man's got a lot of clout."

It wasn't exactly a vote of confidence in my abilities, but I didn't care. I saw it as a chance. If I could pull it off, it might help my standing at the studio.

I went down to Montand's trailer and knocked. He answered. I laid out the situation plainly—but he was adamant. "It's in my contract," he said. "I don't have to do it."

I explained that the studio couldn't release the film with that level of sound interference, and that if he didn't re-record the dialogue, they would bring in another actor with a similar voice to do it for him.

Montand's eyes widened. "They cannot do that to me!" he exclaimed.

I was surprised by how naïve he seemed. "It wouldn't be the first time," I told him, "And it certainly won't be the last."

Montand was furious. In his thick French accent, he declared, "*Zen I tell zem... fuck yourself!*" Then he stormed back inside and immediately called his agent.

I couldn't stop laughing all the way back to the sound department. But by the time I returned, Rossi had already received a call—from Montand's agent—confirming that he would, in fact, be re-recording his lines.

Rossi clapped me on the back. "Great job, kid."

I knew the truth. It wasn't me—it was the agent who convinced him. But word spread quickly around the lot that *I* was the guy who'd persuaded Yves Montand to cave. And as far as anyone at Fox was concerned, I had pulled off the impossible.

The next morning, Yves Montand showed up at the looping stage, and Walter Rossi assigned me to supervise the recording session. Just like that, I had gained a bit of a persona at 20th Century Fox—and, I must admit, it felt pretty good.

The re-recording process is called *looping* because each line that needs to be fixed is edited into a loop—it plays over and over again on a short piece of film. The actor wears headphones to hear the original take, watches the screen for a visual cue, and repeats the line in sync with the picture until the sound recorder gives us the go-ahead that we've got a clean match. Then it's on to the next line. Rinse and repeat.

Some actors never quite get the hang of the rhythm, and those sessions can drag on forever. But Montand? Montand was a pro. He hit nearly every line in one or two takes. It was clear he'd done this before—probably many times. Like most actors, he just didn't like doing it. I couldn't blame him. Looping isn't glamorous; it's tedious and technical. But he delivered.

That evening, I called my mother and told her the whole story—how I'd had to go toe-to-toe with one of her favorite singers and somehow ended up supervising his session. She was delighted. My birthday was coming up, and she was already planning a dinner party at the house with a full cast of relatives from her side of the family. She said she'd be calling everyone soon—and that she couldn't wait to tell them all about my latest Hollywood escapades.

I asked her to make sure Aunt Rose and Uncle Abe were invited. They were my favorites.

DAD EMBARKS ON HIS NEW LIFE

At some point—before any of us knew—Dad had quietly moved his new lady friend from England to Los Angeles, and the two of them were living in a rented house up in the Hills. The house belonged to actress Dolores Gray, best known for her role in the film *Kismet*. Dolores rarely spent time in Hollywood; she was usually in New York working on Broadway, so her home was listed as a rental.

It was a nice house, with a swimming pool and a spectacular view of the city—but it was modern, cheap construction. No comparison to the Mountain Drive house.

Her name was Kathryn Buchman. She was a former Broadway dancer, well into her fifties—attractive, but not beautiful. Petite with slim legs, she had a figure that looked good in clothes, but she wasn't at all the kind of woman I had pictured. I'd imagined someone younger. Maybe even someone only a few years older than me. Kathryn couldn't hold a candle to my mother, and I'll admit—I was surprised.

She had been born in Connecticut and raised by two maiden aunts after her mother decided she couldn't manage raising a child. According to Dad, he had met Kathryn years earlier when she was dancing on Broadway, and he'd developed something of a crush on her.

Eventually, Kathryn left Broadway and married an American screenwriter named Harold Buchman, who had thirty-six motion picture credits to his name—including *His Greatest Gamble*, which Dad had produced in 1934, starring Richard Dix, one of Hollywood's most dashing leading men. Harold also wrote the screenplay for *Shall We Dance*, the Fred Astaire–Ginger Rogers film my father made in 1937. Dad had known Harold long before Kathryn ever entered the picture.

Many years later, Dad found them living together in a dark and somewhat shabby flat in London. It was up several flights of stairs with no elevator. They had filed for divorce and were waiting for the final papers, and Harold hadn't worked in some time. Apparently, he didn't mind my dad coming by to take Kathryn out to dinner, but my sisters and I found that rather tasteless of both Dad and Kathryn, and none of us were really looking forward to meeting her.

I sat in the living room having drinks with my father, and after almost half an hour, Kathryn appeared and introduced herself to me. She looked nice in slacks, sandals, and an expensive blouse, but there was something peculiar about her that I couldn't quite put my finger on. She was strangely quiet during dinner. I found her to be polite, but she came off as a little cold and not easy to warm up to. I would try to bring her into the conversation by looking away from my dad and addressing her directly.

After listening to me speak, she would say, "Oh, that's interesting..." and when Dad spoke, she would underscore it by saying, "That's right, Pandro." On my way home, I realized how superficial it all had felt. She hadn't really been listening to the conversation, and it made me wonder what she was really thinking about.

My sisters were also introduced to her individually, as I had been, and we all had the same impression. She was not what any of us had expected. Though she was somewhat attractive, she was certainly no match for Mom in terms of beauty and refinement. Dad, of course, was delighted with everything that came out of her mouth. If he had been a dog instead of a human being, Kathryn would have been his prized bone—dug up and taken into his doghouse to enjoy.

Dad was in the doghouse with all of us for some time. We couldn't believe he had left our elegant mother and broken her heart for this woman.

To me, the worst part was that he had made her his associate producer and set her up in the back room of his office at MGM—an office that had once belonged to his longtime assistant, Jane Loring. Kathryn was earning far more than I was for doing little more than reading scripts. I would have loved to have had that job myself. Eventually, I learned that Dad was using her salary to pay some of the income tax on his substantial earnings. He knew that most of his assets might end up with Mom in the divorce, and he was quietly building a nest egg for his eventual retirement. In the end, he was quite fortunate: he went on to make two or three more films that, by themselves, provided him with a handsome cushion for the years ahead.

⁎ ⁎ ⁎ ⁎ ⁎ ⁎ ⁎

BUTTERFIELD 8

In 1958, Dad embarked on a project that almost didn't get off the ground and caused him plenty of grief. It was the famous John O'Hara novel *Butterfield 8*, and he knew that the only actress on the planet who could bring what was needed to the role of Gloria Wandrous was Elizabeth Taylor. All that was required: elegance, fire, beauty, sex appeal, and vulnerability. Neither my father, nor I, nor anyone in "The College of Cardinals" at MGM could name another actress who possessed all those qualities—not even Marilyn.

I thought about her as the innocent little girl in *National Velvet*, who we had all adored. She had since grown up into a torrid beauty —one every man in the world seemed to be lusting after. It was astonishing... a completely unexpected transformation.

By that point, she had already gone through several husbands: Conrad Hilton Jr., Michael Wilding, Mike Todd, and Eddie Fisher—whom she had famously wrested away from Debbie Reynolds and was now discarding. She was beginning to believe she was bigger than the system.

My father called her into his office and offered her the part of Gloria Wandrous. He told her she was the only actress in the world who could bring everything the role required. But she didn't want to do it. He reminded her that it was a major novel by John O'Hara, beloved by millions of readers, and that the role was—excuse the pun—tailor-made for her. It would be a significant addition to a career already on the verge of exploding. But Elizabeth stood firm. She flat-out turned it down, saying she'd already had too much bad publicity and didn't want to play a prostitute.

My dad was more than annoyed. He reminded her that she was under contract and owed MGM one more film before it expired. He promised that MGM would take her to court and prevent her from working anywhere else in the industry until she fulfilled that obligation.

She stormed out of his office and ran down the hall to her beloved Benny Thau—the man she always said had been like a father to her. She knew he was the executive in charge of contracts and would have the final word. She begged him to release her from what she called a terrible burden. But Benny was a company man. He stood with my father and backed up the threat of a lawsuit if she refused to cooperate.

Rounds of phone calls from her agent followed—some pleading, some threatening—but my dad and Benny stood their ground. Eventually, a compromise was reached, and a contract was signed, with a few special provisions.

EDDIE FISHER AND A STAR GONE ROGUE

Eddie Fisher was given the role of the piano player, and his salary helped offset the large alimony checks Elizabeth was writing to him every month. There were other requests—many of which were turned down. After that, she refused to speak to my father or Benny Thau ever again, even though Dad would go on to make more films with her in the following years.

When shooting began on the lot, Elizabeth honored the call sheet and showed up on time—no more arriving an hour or two late, as she had in the past. But if my father walked onto the set, she would immediately escape to her dressing room and refuse to come out until her spies informed her that he had left. If Dad needed to communicate with her, he passed notes through the director, Daniel Mann.

The real trouble began when the production moved to New York. The weather was miserable and caused constant delays in filming the exterior scenes. On top of that, there was a garbage strike. Trash piled up in the streets, and the rat population was exploding. People were afraid to walk outside, as rats scurried boldly along the sidewalks, shoulder to shoulder with pedestrians. Many were lying dead in the streets after being run over by taxi cabs. My dad, who had grown up in New York, said he had never seen anything like it—it was a horror story.

Upon their arrival in New York, Elizabeth did something bold—and completely shocking. She came into my dad's office and handed him a script. When he asked what it was, she told him she had hired a writer and had her entire role rewritten so she would no longer be forced to play a prostitute.

My father looked at her in disbelief, then dropped the script directly into the wastebasket.

Elizabeth became enraged. Kathryn, who was in Dad's office during that meeting, later described the scene to my sister Sue and me when they returned from New York. She said Elizabeth began to bristle and make strange breathing noises. She raised her hands to eye level, curled her fingers into claw-like shapes, and turned them toward my dad. Kathryn said that if she hadn't been in the room, Elizabeth might have lunged at him and clawed up his face.

Dad disagreed. He said that would never have happened—because he would have gotten up and smacked her.

I thought to myself that Elizabeth was still playing the role of Maggie the Cat from the last movie she'd made with Dad—and she had finally taken Maggie over the top, turning her into a vicious character. I wasn't really surprised to hear that story. When two people as volatile as Elizabeth and my father clash over something as major as this, the fur is bound to fly.

Fortunately, audiences liked Lawrence Harvey and Elizabeth on screen together, and they came to the theaters in droves to see them. But I think they were really coming just to see Elizabeth. I'm sure they were also drawn by the popularity of John O'Hara's novel—it had been a bestseller, and millions of people had read it. I read it myself when I found out Dad was going to produce the movie, and I couldn't wait to see it on screen—especially with Elizabeth Taylor in the lead.

To everyone's relief at MGM, the picture was a huge hit, even though it had gone way over budget. Elizabeth was soon off on another high-flying adventure—a movie called *The V.I.P.s*, where she first met Richard Burton.

My sister Cindy reminded me of another incident involving Elizabeth Taylor that happened at a Hollywood cocktail party. According to Cindy, she and Dad had just arrived and were standing together near the front door. Dad was admonishing her in rather loud tones, and Elizabeth had just entered—arriving in time to hear the end of whatever Dad had said before he turned and walked into the party.

Cindy said she hadn't noticed Elizabeth come in, but that Liz came up behind her and tapped her on the shoulder. When Cindy turned around, Elizabeth said, "He treated me exactly the same way when I was your age."

She must have been referring to *Father of the Bride,* because Cindy remembered she was about sixteen when they attended that party—and Liz would have been seventeen or eighteen when she made that film.

30

MY FIRST MARRIAGE

It was the Christmas season of 1960, and my friend Bill Marx had finally landed a decent job. He was playing piano for a group of singers and musical acts at a place called the Cabaret Concert Theater in Hollywood. I used to go down and catch the show from time to time, especially on weekends. The theater was one of the first in L.A. to have stadium seating like the new movie houses, so every seat in the house was a good one. They didn't serve food or liquor, so when the show ended, Bill and I were ready to go out for a drink—and sometimes we'd try to pick up girls.

It was easy to find them when I was with Bill. He had the three characteristics women love most in a man: he was tall, dark, and handsome—and he played beautiful piano. When he walked into a bar, the girls flocked around him.

That night, a tall, beautiful redhead walked on stage and sang like an angel. She had an operatically trained voice and soared into the high registers with ease. I was impressed by her singing and taken with her looks. She had pale skin and greenish-brown eyes that complemented her red hair, and she was stunning in her emerald-green gown. She looked like a true Irish beauty and reminded me of a young Maureen O'Hara.

Her name was Nancy Hall, and Bill had met her through Harpo, with whom she occasionally worked. Harpo used to do an amusing routine in vaudeville—and later in one of his movies—where he'd come on stage while a beautiful soprano was performing a famous aria. He'd notice a loose thread on the hem of her formal gown, pull out a large pair of scissors, and start trimming. As the singer tried not to break character, Harpo would continue obsessively snipping to even things out, cutting and cutting until the dress was completely gone—leaving the singer standing in her undergarments. Audiences loved it. He performed the routine at charity events, bond rallies, state fairs, and other live venues, and Nancy was one of the singers he worked with.

After the show, I asked Bill who she was and told him I wanted to meet her. We got backstage just in time to catch her walking out of the theater. She had taken down her hair and changed into slacks and a blouse. On top of everything else, she had a fantastic figure. We took her out for a drink and a bite to eat, and she warmed up to me right away. Things couldn't have been better.

I was hooked. I started picking her up at the theater every night after the show, and a serious romance developed. Within a few weeks, I talked her into moving into my Westwood apartment, and a month or so later, I introduced her to my parents. By the end of April, we had been together almost six months and were very happy—so I asked her to marry me.

My mother wasn't sure I was making a good decision, but she put her feelings aside and planned a beautiful June wedding in our backyard. All our friends and relatives came, drank champagne, and celebrated with us.

Nancy got pregnant almost immediately, and we had a boy, who we named Frank after my mother's father. The day he was born was the greatest day of my life. Having him was pure joy. I would rush home from work just to be with him, and I took great pleasure in giving him baths in the kitchen sink.

"Our marriage began like a classic Hollywood romance—glamorous, heady, full of promise. But it didn't end that way."

DAD GOES NOIR

In 1960, Dad made a sudden, radical change in his filmmaking style. He produced a movie that was quite unusual and unlike anything he had ever made. It was called *Key Witness*, and none of us believed he would attempt to make this kind of picture, given his age and extensive film experience.

The story follows a man in a phone booth who witnesses a gang murder in East Los Angeles. Although he escapes, the gang spots him and eventually learns his identity. They show up outside his house and terrorize him, threatening to kill his children to prevent him from testifying in court.

We all thought the movie was sensationalist and borderline sleazy, but *Time* Magazine shocked us with a positive review. They called it a "neo-noir" film, describing it as a rebirth of the French *film noir* (dark film) movement of the late 1940s, which was known for its black-and-white cinematography, low-key lighting, unconventional camera angles, and "nouvelle" composition.

Key Witness was shot in black and white and featured low-key lighting, but to me, it felt more like a B-grade murder movie with gang violence and a typical Hollywood ending. There was nothing especially stylized about it that would elevate it to the level of high-class cinema, despite what *Time* Magazine suggested.

I'm sure Dad was just as surprised as I was when he saw that glowing review. He knew exactly what he had with this movie—and it certainly wasn't a pot of gold.

Classic American film noir includes titles like *The Maltese Falcon*, *Cape Fear*, and *The Postman Always Rings Twice*. *Key Witness* wasn't in the same league. I couldn't understand why Dad would make a film like this. The only explanation that made any sense was that he was trying to recapture the massive audiences from *Blackboard Jungle*. But he never admitted that to me. Just as he had tried to remake *Gunga Din* with *Soldiers Three*—which didn't work—and *Father of the Bride* with *Father's Little Dividend*—which didn't quite work either.

In *Key Witness*, Dad cast some seasoned actors to elevate the drama, including Dennis Hopper, Corey Allen, and Johnny Nash—all young and menacing—and he cast Jeffrey Hunter as the terrified witness. He also brought on a young director named Phil Karlson, known for several crime thrillers. After reviewing some of Karlson's previous footage, Dad became convinced he could deliver the gritty look and strong performances the film needed.

Then another shocking review appeared. Writing in *The New York Times*, reviewer Howard Thompson praised the film, stating, "If *Key Witness* could be better, we don't know how." He added, "This little picture is fast, tough, tight, sickeningly real to watch, and wonderfully well put together."

Ironically, *Time* Magazine's glowing review might have hurt the film more than helped it. It made the movie seem like an avant-garde art piece—something mainstream American audiences tend to avoid—and the film ended up losing about half a million dollars in theaters. However, it eventually became profitable through worldwide television distribution.

For the first time, Kathryn's name appeared as producer, while Dad took a lesser credit—executive producer—in smaller print on a separate title card. I told him I thought it was cowardly to let her take the fall by giving her top billing as producer. I knew full well that she was mostly reading scripts and fielding calls for him—hardly the work of a hands-on producer.

That gave him a good laugh. Then he explained the real reason: Kathryn's contract was about to expire, and he wanted to renew it—

doubling her salary—by re-signing her with MGM as a producer. And that was the only part of it that made any sense to me.

· · * · ★ · · · ★ · · · * · ·

SWEET BIRD OF YOUTH

My dad was fortunate in acquiring the rights to another Tennessee Williams play, which he turned into a smash hit movie. It didn't have Elizabeth Taylor to pump up the box office receipts, but it did star Paul Newman, the Oscar-winning and multi-talented Geraldine Page, and Shirley Knight, along with an outstanding supporting cast that included Ed Begley, Rip Torn, and Mildred Dunnock. The film was *Sweet Bird of Youth*, and it garnered a slew of prestigious awards.

Ed Begley won the Oscar for Best Supporting Actor, while Geraldine Page and Shirley Knight were both nominated for their performances. Page also won a Golden Globe for Best Actress, and both Knight and Begley received Golden Globe nominations for their supporting roles. Page was additionally nominated for Best Foreign Actress by BAFTA (the British Academy of Film and Television Arts).

Rip Torn, who received no nominations, gave one of the finest performances in the movie, which told a powerful story: Chance Wayne (Paul Newman) returns to his hometown of St. Cloud, Florida, after several unsuccessful years trying to make it in Hollywood as an actor. He's accompanied by Alexandra del Lago (Geraldine Page), an older Hollywood actress who has promised to help Chance launch his career but has since become a hopeless alcoholic.

Chance, now failed and disillusioned, has come back to reunite with his former girlfriend, Heavenly Finley (Shirley Knight), whose father—Boss Finley (Ed Begley), a wealthy and corrupt politician—had run Chance out of town and warned him of serious consequences if he ever returned.

Chance and Heavenly are secretly seeing each other, as she is still in love with him. One night, he gets drunk and shows up on the front lawn of Boss Finley's mansion, shouting for Heavenly to come out.

Boss Finley arrives with his son, Finley Jr. (Rip Torn), and a gang of toughs from his youth club. They grab Chance, beat him up, and throw him across the hood of a car. Boss then tries to disfigure him with the heavy handle of his cane. Heavenly comes running out of the house and tells her father she's leaving with Chance—and never coming back.

It's a gruesome ending, but far less brutal than the play's original conclusion. In the final scene of the stage version, Chance isn't just beaten—he's violently and inhumanely castrated to make him permanently "useless" to Heavenly. Dad knew the censors would never approve that ending, so he and director Richard Brooks devised an alternative conclusion for the screenplay, which otherwise remained faithful to the play.

Dad arranged a special screening of the movie one night at MGM for a small group of people. Tennessee was invited to fly out and attend, but he couldn't make it. I remember Dad speaking to him on the phone from his office earlier that day. He thanked him for writing such a wonderful play and promised he wouldn't be disappointed in the film.

I thought back to my visit to IMSPOND years ago, when Danny Selznick and I slept in the guest house where Tennessee had written *A Streetcar Named Desire*. We imagined ourselves as the ones who had written that play, basking in the glory of being the "toast" of Broadway. It was just one of the many humorous fantasies we indulged in over the years... back when we were young and still naïve about the movie business.

· * · ★ · * · ★ · · * ·

THE PRIZE

My dad spent over a year trying to develop a strong script from Irving Wallace's best-selling novel *The Prize*. It wasn't easy. Several early drafts had failed to capture the tone and suspense of the book. To fix that, he brought in the legendary screenwriter Ernest Lehman—an Oscar winner known for *North by Northwest* and *Sweet Smell of Success*. Lehman reworked those drafts, and while he brought a lot to the table, ultimately Dad and Lehman found themselves relying more heavily on Wallace's original material.

The two of them collaborated for months, determined to shape something lean, thrilling, and cinematic. They succeeded. What emerged was a taut, intelligent script—now they just needed a director who could bring it to life.

That search proved harder than expected. Many top directors were tied up on other projects, and the ones who *were* available didn't quite match Dad's vision. He had a specific tone in mind—sharp, suspenseful, laced with tension—something reminiscent of Hitchcock. That ruled out a lot of the directors being pushed by the studio.

But Dad was patient. He had two or three directors on a shortlist, and he was willing to wait for the right one—even if it meant losing some of the cast. The only actor he couldn't afford to lose was Paul Newman. Dad believed in Newman completely and was confident that he'd hang on—at least for a little while. But he also knew the clock was ticking. Newman was one of the hottest stars in Hollywood, and the right offer could pull him away at any moment.

Finally, with the studio breathing down his neck, Dad secured a commitment from Mark Robson—a highly respected director whose credits included *Champion* with Kirk Douglas, *The Bridges at Toko-Ri* with William Holden and Grace Kelly, and *The Inn of the Sixth Happiness* with Ingrid Bergman. Robson had a reputation for getting superb performances out of his actors, and once he read the script, he was intrigued.

Dad sat down with Robson and laid out his vision. "I want this shot like a Hitchcock film," he said. "Suspense. Tension. The audience should be leaning forward, not blinking. Gripping their seats."

Robson hesitated. "I'm not sure that's really my style."

Dad didn't blink. "You're the only man in this town who can do it. I have complete faith in you."

That was all it took.

With a cast led by Paul Newman, Elke Sommer, and Edward G. Robinson, Robson threw himself into the project—and delivered. *The Prize* turned out to be a stylish, high-stakes thriller, with Newman playing Andrew Craig, a hard-drinking American novelist who arrives in Stockholm to receive the Nobel Prize in Literature.

But Craig's reputation precedes him. The Nobel Committee, nervous he'll embarrass them with his drinking or antics, assigns Lisa Anderson (Elke Sommer) to keep an eye on him. What begins as a diplomatic babysitting job quickly spirals into a conspiracy involving Cold War espionage, identity swaps, and an assassination plot—all unfolding against the elegant, snow-dusted backdrop of Stockholm.

The Prize had everything—political tension, glamour, action, romance—and Dad had pulled off another winner. It was a testament not just to his persistence, but to his uncanny ability to spot exactly the right people for the right roles, on and off screen.

Craig uncovers a sinister plot orchestrated by the East Germans to kidnap fellow Nobel Laureate Dr. Max Stratman (played by Edward G. Robinson), a brilliant physicist who had defected from behind the Iron Curtain. The stakes are nothing short of global—Stratman's knowledge is seen as essential to the Communist war effort, and they're determined to drag him back across enemy lines by any means necessary.

As Craig digs deeper, what began as a routine awards ceremony spirals into a deadly game of Cold War cat and mouse. Alongside Lisa Anderson, the Nobel Committee escort turned reluctant partner-in-crime-fighting, Craig finds himself swept into a web of deception, danger, and—yes—romance. Their chemistry crackles on screen, even as the danger escalates. Craig risks not only his life, but hers, as he races to stop an international incident from erupting on Swedish soil.

Dad's instincts were razor sharp. His direction to Robson—to channel Hitchcock and dial up the suspense—paid off beautifully. Robson delivered a sleek, gripping thriller that balanced high-stakes intrigue with emotional tension. I remember sitting on the edge of my seat watching it unfold. It was the kind of film that made your pulse race while still letting you admire the craft behind the camera.

The Prize has always reminded me of *North by Northwest*. Not because of plot—those stories couldn't be more different—but because of tone. There's a similar elegance to both, a polished tension. Robson managed to weave that Hitchcockian suspense into the film's DNA, adding a glossy finish that most directors couldn't replicate, even if they tried.

Elke Sommer won a Golden Globe for Most Promising Newcomer, and Diane Baker earned a nomination for Best Supporting Actress. Paul Newman gave a terrific performance as Andrew Craig—charming, flawed, brave—but surprisingly, he received no nominations for the role. Still, it remains one of his more underrated gems, and one of my father's most stylish and sophisticated productions.

THE DIVORCE IS FINAL...FINALLY

An enormous amount of time had passed between Dad leaving home and the beginning of the divorce. Mom didn't want to face it, and Dad was giving her plenty of time to accept it before he filed the papers. One afternoon, I came over and found lawyers in the house meeting with my mother. Because Dad had formed several independent film companies, the accounting was quite complicated, and the lawyers for both sides were fighting like pit bulls over the financial settlement.

Eventually, Dad stepped in and made Mom a very generous offer. I don't know whether he was feeling guilty about leaving her or if he just wanted to stop the escalation of attorney's fees—but it was probably a little of both. In any case, my mother accepted the offer, and the divorce went quickly through the court, which approved the settlement arrangement.

When it was all done, my mother felt guilty about taking so much money. I told her I thought he was feeling guilty about leaving her. She shook her head and suddenly burst into tears. She didn't want any of this. In spite of all the time that had passed, she was still in love with him. I held her in my arms until she stopped shaking. It was a defining moment in our relationship as mother and son, and we both felt it deeply.

She felt better after her cry, so I said goodbye and went home. But I was worried about Mom. I knew it would take a long time for her to get over this, and there wasn't much I could do to help—except to be there for her. She did begin to lean on me a little after that. She couldn't lean on either of my sisters, both of whom were suffering from the divorce just as much as she was.

A BAD BUMP IN THE ROAD

I couldn't understand why, but my relationship with Nancy had suddenly become rocky. We were three and a half years into our marriage before I figured out that my wife had a drinking problem.

She always had a cough drop in her mouth, so I never smelled liquor on her breath. When I asked her why she was using so many cough drops, she said it was to soothe her vocal cords, since she was now singing a lot in the evenings.

She had learned to play the guitar and was working as a folk singer in coffee houses around town. So, I would stay home at night with Frank while she was performing. He was three years old and getting more handsome every day, and I loved being with him.

When I questioned her about her drinking, she got angry and denied that it was excessive. I asked her what she was angry about, and she went silent. I continued to pursue it, and she finally blurted out that she had been hoping that I and/or my father would help build her career—but we had done nothing. She had been hoping my father would give her an acting job.

I told her that he didn't believe in nepotism and that she should hire an agent. She said she already had one. His name was Herb, and he had been getting her gigs in the coffee houses. It surprised me that she hadn't told me about that earlier.

I was worried that this could possibly bring us to the end of our marriage, but I had no idea what to do about it. A short time later, she served me with divorce papers and moved out. We went to court, and she got custody of Frank. I didn't find out until later that she had moved in with her agent, Herb—but at that point, I didn't really care. I was sure he was paying a lot of the bills, because she wasn't hounding me for money, and Frank said he was a nice guy who was treating him well. I was relieved that Frank was doing fine. And when I wasn't spending time with my son, I focused on my career.

31

CLEOPATRA

Spyros Panagiotis Skouras, the son of a Greek sheepherder, came to America with his brothers Charles and George in 1910, where he became a pioneering movie executive. In 1942, he became president of 20th Century Fox and continued to oversee corporate affairs and film production after Darryl Zanuck's retirement and before Zanuck's son, Richard, took over as head of production. I was working at Fox at the time, and things were starting to look a little shaky.

Cleopatra, the notoriously extravagant film starring Elizabeth Taylor and Richard Burton, was in production—and the costs were spiraling out of control. Skouras was beside himself. In all his years at the helm, he had never encountered a situation like this, and he didn't know how to stop the bleeding.

Originally budgeted at $2 million, the film eventually ballooned to $31 million, making it the most expensive movie ever made in Hollywood up to that point.

Shooting began in 1960 in London from a script by Ranald

MacDougall under the direction of Rouben Mamoulian, but production was soon derailed when Elizabeth Taylor became gravely ill and required a tracheotomy to save her life. The damp London weather had been so detrimental to her health that the entire production had to be moved to Rome. This meant tearing down the elaborate sets built in London and reconstructing them in Rome—at enormous expense.

Walter Wanger, a seasoned Hollywood producer, had been hired to oversee the film. He managed to renegotiate the budget to $7 million. New scripts were drafted by Nigel Balchin and later rewritten by Dale Wasserman, but none of those versions made it to the screen.

Mamoulian was eventually replaced by Joseph Mankiewicz, who inherited a project already $5 million over budget—with no usable footage in the can. Mankiewicz began writing his own script as production restarted, but delays meant there was never a complete shooting script at any point during filming.

Peter Finch, originally cast as Julius Caesar, and Stephen Boyd, set to play Mark Antony, both left the project due to other commitments. All their scenes had to be re-shot, with Rex Harrison stepping in as Caesar and Richard Burton joining the cast as Antony.

Elizabeth Taylor was paid a staggering $1 million for her performance—an unprecedented amount and the highest salary ever paid to an actress at the time.

Mankiewicz was fired during the long and chaotic post-production process, but no one else was able to make sense of the existing footage. He was eventually rehired—since he was the only one who understood the story he was trying to tell—and he went to work in the editing room. His first cut ran over six hours, double the length the studio wanted for release.

Mankiewicz's idea was to split the film into two pictures to be released separately: *Caesar and Cleopatra* followed by *Antony and Cleopatra*. That way, he could salvage all of his precious footage—the material he had poured his life's blood into creating. The studio, however, was not on the same wavelength. They forced him to cut two hours from the picture, and after screening the result, he was infuriated. Theaters were unlikely to accept a four-hour film; at three hours, they could squeeze in at least one additional showing per day.

Fox was eager to release the film as soon as possible in order to capitalize on the publicity surrounding Taylor and Burton's illicit romance. The tabloids and trade papers were filled with it, publishing juicy morsels of gossip every day—anything they could uncover or invent.

It all came to a head when Burton's wife, Sybil, came to Rome and confronted Liz. She told her that she had weathered affairs like this before, and that Richard always tired of the fling and came back to her. She turned out to be wrong this time.

Cleopatra won four Oscars, including Best Cinematography, Best Art Direction and Set Decoration, Best Costume Design, and Best Special Visual Effects. It was nominated for five other Academy Awards, including Best Picture, which it lost to *Tom Jones*. It also earned four Golden Globe nominations, including Best Actor for Rex Harrison as Caesar and Best Supporting Actor for Roddy McDowall as Octavian. It won an American Cinema Editors Award for Dorothy Spencer, who probably spent more hours in the *Cleopatra* editing suite than any film editor in Hollywood history. Most editors run a few metaphorical miles in post-production. Dorothy ran a marathon.

Cleopatra was the highest-grossing film of 1963, earning $57 million at the box office—the equivalent of approximately $445 million in 2016. However, due to its astronomical budget and marketing costs, including prints and advertising, it still lost money. It remains the only film in history to top the box office and still operate at a loss. The production nearly bankrupted the studio.

Skouras, desperate for funds, had even skimmed money off the top of television series budgets when the banks refused to continue financing *Cleopatra*. It's no surprise that Spyros Skouras resigned as head of production in late 1962. He told people he had lost his taste for making movies—a sentiment that's entirely understandable after surviving the nightmare that was *Cleopatra*.

As a result of being short of budget money, many of the television shows lacked energy, and some of them were cancelled. Hundreds of people were laid off including me, and the great exodus left Fox studios looking like a ghost town.

At the 1961 Academy Awards, Elizabeth Taylor won an Oscar for her performance in *Butterfield 8*, along with a Golden Globe nomination for Best Actress. She was excellent opposite Lawrence Harvey in that very popular film based on the great John O'Hara novel—but my dad and I felt the Oscar was more of a sympathy vote. Elizabeth had become seriously ill and nearly lost her life while working on *Cleopatra*. The British press reported that she was close to death in the hospital, and one paper even claimed she had passed away.

It wasn't until after Academy voting ended that members learned Elizabeth had recovered. She left the hospital and flew to Hollywood to accept her Oscar, appearing in a low-cut gown that prominently revealed her tracheotomy scar. She walked onstage to a standing ovation, and her speech was filled with heartfelt gratitude for the Academy members who had prayed for her survival.

There were four other actresses nominated that year who also gave outstanding performances—any one of them could have won. They included Greer Garson for *Sunrise at Campobello*, Deborah Kerr for *The Sundowners*, Melina Mercouri for *Never on Sunday*, and Shirley MacLaine for *The Apartment*, which won Best Picture for Billy Wilder. *Elmer Gantry* was also a Best Picture nominee, and Burt Lancaster took home the Oscar for Best Actor in the title role.

All of those films were as good as *Butterfield 8*, maybe even a little better. But Elizabeth went on to stronger roles in more important films. In 1967, she received her second Oscar for *Who's Afraid of Virginia Woolf?* which remains, without question, the finest performance of her career.

32

THE UPS AND DOWNS OF A CAREER IN HOLLYWOOD

A couple of months after I was laid off from Fox, I learned there was a job opening for an assistant editor at MGM. I called to schedule an interview, but I was hesitant to ask my dad for help. I had heard his views on nepotism—especially how he had treated our cousin, Stanley Kramer—and I was hoping to get the job on my own, without involving my father or Uncle Henry. I figured I had earned enough credibility at Fox to be considered for a similar position elsewhere.

My mother was surprised that I felt that way. She was certain Dad would be happy to help and reminded me that he had helped Uncle Henry when he left dental school. She also pointed out that my last name was Berman—and that the first question they'd probably ask in the interview was whether I was related to Pandro.

She was right. Dad had already gotten me onto the MGM lot as an unpaid apprentice on *Tea and Sympathy* and *Jailhouse Rock*, and people still working there would likely remember me. I explained to her that those weren't real jobs—just learning opportunities, more like trade school than employment. I wasn't sure Dad would want to recommend me for a paid position, especially if he hadn't had time to prepare for it. It would put him on the hook.

But Mom was confident. She insisted I'd be more than ready and said Dad would absolutely go to bat for me. Then she insisted I call him immediately—while she was still there. It was a hard call to make, but I did it. When I told him about the interview, his first question was why I had waited so long to let him know.

I told him I had just made the appointment the day before—which was a lie, but it sounded better than admitting I had been too scared to ask for his help.

He said, "I'll do what I can for you."

I thought Dad sounded a little cold over the phone, and I told my mother I didn't think he was going to help—but she assured me that he would.

I was interviewed for the job by Freeman Davies, the head of the editorial department at MGM. He made no mention of my dad, but he told me they had spoken to Walter Rossi at Fox, who gave me a glowing reference.

I got the job.

Freeman said, "I see you're following in your father's footsteps."

I told him I was trying my best.

He replied, "You're in the right place now…"

I was ecstatic that my dad had made the call, and I was thrilled to be at MGM, working with some of the most creative people in Hollywood. I phoned Dad to thank him, and he was gracious—genuinely happy for me.

He repeated his sage advice: "Work hard and keep your mouth shut—until you have a brilliant idea. Something you know everyone will love. Then present it as briefly as possible… and shut your mouth again. Good luck, kid."

I took his words to heart. I worked hard putting in extra hours to learn the craft of picture editing without charging the studio for overtime. I'd punch out, then head back to work for another hour or two in the evenings until I was confident enough not to need the extra time.

I started as an assistant editor on the TV series *Dr. Kildare*, starring Raymond Massey and Richard Chamberlain, and I genuinely enjoyed the work. When the season ended, Freeman Davies called me into his office.

He told me they were more than pleased with my performance and were assigning me something more challenging. A new picture was going into production, and I was to start on Monday.

I was thrilled.

Before going home, I went up to my dad's office to share the news—but he'd already heard. Freeman had called to let him know how pleased they were with me.

"You're on your way, kid," Dad said. "Keep up the good work."

THE SANDPIPER

My new job was much more demanding than my first, and the hours were brutal. It was a major feature called *The Sandpiper*, starring Elizabeth Taylor and Richard Burton. Vincent Minnelli was directing, and thousands of feet of film were arriving daily to be synched and screened in the big projection rooms of the Thalberg Building. Getting everything ready for the producers—Martin Ransohoff and John Calley—by the one o'clock screening deadline was no small feat.

The dailies were screened again at seven in the evening for the director, and Minnelli always had extensive notes on how he wanted the footage edited. We also received notes from the producers, which often conflicted with Minnelli's instructions. Thankfully, the editor, Dave Bretherton, was well-seasoned in the political tightrope walk of big-studio filmmaking and somehow managed to keep everyone happy. Still, it was an incredible workload.

I rarely got home before 9 p.m.—often it was closer to ten or eleven. Dave appreciated my efforts and told me so, and we became good friends. He was married to a beautiful Parisian woman he'd met on location in France. She had a charming accent and used to stop by the cutting room, which was the last one on the street near the commissary. All the guys would glance out the windows to watch her stroll by in her high heels and tight dresses.

The movie was marketed as a mature love story—Taylor and Burton's first on-screen reunion since *Cleopatra*—and they were Hollywood's hottest couple. I could feel it from the very first day we screened dailies. Their chemistry was electric, and audiences were eagerly awaiting the film. Everyone at MGM expected a blockbuster.

The shoot took four months, and Minnelli ended up shooting over half a million feet of film. For comparison, a typical one-hour television show exposes 100,000 feet of film or less for each episode—so this was nearly six hours of un-edited footage eventually to be trimmed to a two-hour theatrical release. By the time we were ready to run the first cut for Minnelli, we were both completely spent and ready for a vacation.

Minnelli was disappointed with the initial cut and gave us hundreds of changes before it could be shown to the producers. That revision process took nearly three weeks. Martin Ransohoff, who had seen all the dailies and envisioned the film in his head, was growing impatient. He wanted Minnelli to step aside and let him see his movie.

When we finally screened it for him, he was unimpressed. He changed numerous things back to the way Dave had originally cut them—and I agreed with nearly every change. I preferred Dave's first version over Minnelli's, and that experience taught me something surprising: Ransohoff's instincts were stronger than Minnelli's. And this was Vincent Minnelli—a man who had directed some of the finest films in Hollywood history.

It took another month to implement all of Ransohoff's changes, which meant more late nights and even deeper exhaustion. We were preparing for a preview and holding special screenings for the publicity department and the distribution executives, who were working hard to secure bookings with the theater chains. Everyone was eager to get the film into cinemas as quickly as possible to capitalize on the ongoing media frenzy around Burton and Taylor's high-profile romance, which had ignited during *Cleopatra* and was still dominating headlines almost daily.

It was cold on the beach at Big Sur during filming, so—as she had done on *Cleopatra*—Liz ordered chili from Chasen's restaurant in Beverly Hills and had it flown up to the location. She also had her luxurious fur coats brought out of storage to stay warm, while the rest of the cast and crew shivered in the coastal chill.

Back in the editorial department, people were curious about the movie and kept asking Dave and me if it was any good. By that point, I had seen the picture so many times, edited in so many different versions, that I had completely lost perspective. I honestly didn't know if it was good or not—and neither did Dave.

We found out at the sneak preview, which turned out to be a minor disaster. Ransohoff made the unusual decision to hold the screening at the Warner Beverly Hills Theatre, right in the heart of Beverly Hills. His plan was to take a group of friends out to an upscale dinner and then walk over to the theater for the 8:30 p.m. showtime. Of course, word quickly got out, and every press agent, trade-paper columnist, and tabloid reporter in town showed up—ready to gossip, judge, and, if the moment presented itself, mock the film right there in the theater.

I went upstairs to the projection booth and located the boxes containing the film. After lining up the reels in the proper order for the projectionist and making sure he was familiar with running double system (separate reels of picture and sound), I watched him thread the first reel, syncing the start marks. Once I was confident that he knew what he was doing, I went back downstairs and noticed the theater was already filling up quickly.

I spoke to one of the publicity guys, who was watching the crowd pour in and take their seats with a worried look on his face. He told me there wasn't a single unfamiliar face in the house.

He added, "This movie's going to be reviewed in every paper in town tomorrow morning. Let's just hope it's good."

He wasn't wrong—bad advance reviews can tank a film's box office before it even has a chance.

Then we hit another snag. The theater manager had been told to reserve an entire row near the back of the house, but he had only saved two seats—one for Dave Bretherton, who was controlling the sound with a fader wired to the theater speakers, and one for me. I had a lighted clipboard and a legal pad and was tasked with taking notes on any technical glitches during the screening so we could fix them later.

I explained to the manager that the rest of the row had been reserved for the producers and their guests and that he'd need to clear it out. But he shook his head and told me it was too late. The people in those seats had been waiting in line for over an hour, and he wasn't about to ask them to move. All the good seats downstairs were already taken.

When Ransohoff and his party arrived, they were ushered to the third row of the balcony—where the best remaining seats could be found. Furious, Ransohoff screamed at the theater manager, but there was nothing anyone could do at that point.

This movie was red meat, and audiences had been waiting nearly a year to see it. Elizabeth Taylor plays Laura, a free spirit living in a beachside cabin in Big Sur, California, where she homeschools her nine-year-old son, Danny, and poses nude for a local artist. Her stuffy neighbors take her to court and influence the judge to remove Danny from her custody. He is ordered to attend an Episcopal boarding school in Monterey, against Laura's wishes.

Richard Burton plays Edward Hewitt, the headmaster of the

school, who visits Laura to convince her that his institution isn't the prison she imagines it to be. He's stunned by Laura's beauty; she's equally drawn to him, and soon they're in the throes of a passionate affair. Edward's wife, Claire (played by Eva Marie Saint), is outraged —and gives a strong performance as the scorned woman.

The preview didn't go as well as we'd hoped. There were several unfortunate laughs, including one in the very first scene between Taylor and Burton. When they meet, she opens the door, leads him into the living room, sits on the couch, and pats the cushion beside her to invite him to sit. The audience roared with laughter. As the chuckling subsided, I could hear Ransohoff's unmistakable voice ring out from the balcony: "What the hell are they laughing at?"

The first move in a seduction scene isn't supposed to be funny— but this one cracked the audience up and primed them for more unintended laughter. In the final scene, Burton stands on a cliff and waves goodbye to Taylor on the beach. It's clear they're parting ways. The audience, realizing they weren't getting a traditional "Hollywood ending," started booing the screen.

Dave turned to me and said, "We are in deep doo-doo."

As I walked up the aisle with the rest of the audience, I overheard all kinds of negative remarks. When we reached the lobby, I spotted Ransohoff storming down the steps from the balcony, visibly furious. A guy behind me shouted up to him, "Hey Marty, I tink you got anudder toikey!"

Everyone in the lobby heard it—and that triggered the biggest laugh of the night, worse than any in the movie. Ransohoff lost it. He stood guard over the preview cards and refused to let anyone see them—especially the publicity department, whose job it was to review them and prepare a detailed report.

He ordered Dave and me to report to his office at nine o'clock the next morning—which was Saturday. Our department head wasn't thrilled, since that meant paying us double time for weekend hours, but there was no choice. Marty was the boss, and he was on the warpath.

The preview cards were, of course, terrible, though only a few reviews appeared in the tabloids. The trade papers didn't run a review, and neither did the *Los Angeles Times*. They were all wary of reprisals from MGM and didn't want to risk losing their screening privileges.

Ransohoff ordered the entire editing suite packed up and trucked to his home in Carmel. That included all the film and trims (the pieces of footage not used in the picture), along with the editing benches and chairs, rewinds, trim bins, film racks, and all twelve reels of edited film. The only thing left behind was the light fixture in the ceiling.

MGM wasn't happy. This was now considered a location job, which meant they had to pay Dave and me per diem—money for meals and lodging—as well as a hefty amount of overtime, since we'd be working weekends.

TURNING A "TOIKEY" INTO A TRIUMPH

I drove up to Carmel with Dave, and we were each given a room in a nearby motel. A great deal of the furniture in Marty's living room was removed to make space for the temporary cutting room, and we went straight to work. Lunch was provided by Marty's cook, and if we got there early enough, she'd make us breakfast as well. Coffee was available around the clock, which helped us work through the day without distractions. We usually went out for dinner—after ten or eleven-hour days, we just wanted to get out of the house.

We worked long hours, six days a week, for three weeks—and one week, we even worked on Sunday. With all that overtime, our paychecks were unbelievable. But we were totally exhausted, walking around like zombies.

A couple of nights a week, and usually on Sundays, Dave and I would drive down the hill to the hot mineral baths that were open to the public. We'd soak for half an hour or so, and it was incredibly refreshing. It gave us the strength to keep going.

One day, I was surprised to see Kim Novak stroll into our editing room with Marty. She lived in a house nearby, and the two had become good friends. Marty let her look over Dave's shoulder while he made changes on the editing machine, and she also came over to my bench to see what I was working on. She was fascinated by the editing process and said, "This is really where it all happens, isn't it?"

I thought that was a rather naïve comment for someone who'd been in the business for as long as she had. Motion picture editors are ultimately responsible for the quality of a film. Sometimes, they need to re-direct it by changing its pace—or even rewrite it entirely by reshaping footage in ways the writer or director never intended. It's the editor's responsibility to make the picture work. That's the bottom line.

In our third week, I began to see that the picture was greatly improved. It was a different movie than the one we had screened at the preview, and Marty was in a much better mood. He even thanked us for all our hard work and said he wanted to hire us for his next picture.

We brought the film back to the studio and ran it for the publicity department and some of the executives. When the lights came up, they were all excited. Those who had seen the earlier version told us the difference was incredible. They wanted to get it into theaters as soon as possible.

Dave Bretherton deserved most of the credit, but I had come up with a few suggestions that Marty liked—and one time, he even came over and patted me on the back.

Every movie has a distinct rhythm, which the editor has to feel while working with the footage. There's the director's pace or rhythm, and sometimes a different one created by the editor. The editor must decide whether the director's pacing is working or if a new rhythm needs to be shaped to captivate the audience. I was beginning to develop a sense for that rhythm on this picture—and it would serve me well throughout the editing phase of my career.

Word got around the studio that *The Sandpiper* was shaping up to be a winner, and I got a call from my dad congratulating me on helping to save the picture. He'd heard all about the disastrous preview and shared a funny story about the one for his smash-hit comedy *Room Service*. That screening was held in Riverside, about sixty miles east of Los Angeles, and the editor had accidentally lined up the reels out of order in the projection booth—then went out for dinner before the preview started.

The projectionist ran reel three followed by reel five—and, for some reason, it worked. My dad had been called out of the preview to take an important phone call, or he would have stopped the screening and straightened it out. The editor was also in the theater, but he must have been asleep in his seat not to have noticed the mistake.

The projectionist then ran reel four, and that also seemed to work. It was a comedy, with one Marx Brothers sketch following another, and there was no major break in the storyline to disrupt the audience.

Eventually, the projectionist realized he had made a mistake, so he ran reel five again in an attempt to restore continuity. If he had simply moved on to reel six, he would have been better off—but instead, he reran footage the audience had seen just ten minutes earlier. They started stamping their feet and howling: "Hey...what's going on? We've already seen this!" Of course, the sneak preview was ruined, and they had to schedule another one. But funny things like that happen all the time in the movie business.

MGM was convinced they had a gold mine in *The Sandpiper*, so they got behind it with a major advertising campaign. With a $5.3 million production budget, they were determined to protect their investment—and it paid off. The film grossed $14 million worldwide, and Dave and I knew we had made a huge contribution to its success.

Johnny Mandel and Paul Francis Webster won an Oscar and

received a Golden Globe nomination for Best Original Song, which became a major hit—"The Shadow of Your Smile." Mandel also won a Grammy for Best Original Score for a Motion Picture.

Dave Bretherton's career got an enormous boost from *The Sandpiper*. Within two years, he had gained a reputation in Hollywood as "the film doctor"—a man who could perform magic on troubled movies that other editors and directors had worked on for weeks or months and eventually given up on. When they couldn't deliver the movie they'd envisioned, Dave was brought in to fix it—and he was paid $1,000 a day to work his magic. That might sound exorbitant, considering that the going rate for a top picture editor at the time was between $3,000 and $4,000 a week—but the industry considered Dave worth every penny. Most of the time, he was able to save the picture and turn it into a box office hit. That could mean the difference of millions of dollars to the studios.

33

PERSONAL LIFE—ACT TWO

Working on *The Sandpiper* turned out to be a blessing for me. Some of the credit that Dave got for turning the film into a big hit rubbed off on me, and my stock rose another notch at MGM. I was welcomed back on *Dr. Kildare* with open arms, and it really felt good. I was getting used to the work, which now seemed much easier. I hadn't been dating much—there was simply no time. I was seeing my son on Wednesday nights and Sundays, and the rest of the week, I would go home after dinner to relax, watch television, or read.

One night, I was having dinner with an old school buddy when an attractive girl with a nice figure came by our table to say hello to him. Her name was Susan, and she had a warm smile. He invited her to join us in our booth, so she sat down to have a drink while waiting for her girlfriend, with whom she had dinner plans. Susan was bright and talkative, and she had a good job as office manager at an insurance agency. When her friend arrived, she got up and moved to another table. My buddy, Marc—who had dated her in the past—told me that her father was a wealthy linen manufacturer. He also said Susan had been invited to join Mensa, the high-IQ society. I asked him why he had stopped dating her, and he admitted her intelligence was a little intimidating.

The next day, I got a call from Marc. He told me that Susan had asked him to give me her number and said she'd like me to call. For a guy who hadn't dated in nearly a year, that was pretty exciting. I called her that night and made dinner plans. She was every bit as bright as she seemed, and I found her intelligence to be a breath of fresh air. It was a long evening—we talked for hours. She wanted to know everything about me. When I walked her to her door, she said, "Please call me again soon," and gave me a passionate goodnight kiss.

Our relationship heated up quickly, and I was enjoying every part of it. I showed her a picture of my son, Frank, and she wanted to meet him right away. She offered to cook a nice dinner for the three of us on a Wednesday night. Frank was now six years old and in kindergarten. I told her I'd ask him if he'd like that, though I thought it might be a little premature. I called my divorce attorney, and he assured me that it was perfectly fine as long as Frank was comfortable with it. Even if his mother objected, I was well within my rights.

SECOND ACTS AND NEW BEGINNINGS

Even though my sisters were still living at home, my mother was feeling lonely. All of us encouraged her to start dating, but she was still in love with Dad and couldn't bring herself to see another man. Unfortunately, many of their friends had backed away from her and gravitated toward my father. It wasn't that they preferred his company —it was that she posed a perceived threat to the women in her social circle.

She was beautiful and elegant, with wonderful taste. You could see it in the way she dressed, in her artwork, and in how she furnished our home. She had a style that people admired, and she was a great conversationalist.

There were quite a few shaky marriages among the Hollywood elite, and those women didn't want their husbands around my mother. She might catch the interest of one of their attractive spouses—someone who could find her irresistible and potentially leave his marriage to be with her. She once admitted to me that many men had approached her over the years, hoping for an affair, but she was never tempted.

When I was in high school, my friends thought she was incredible. They used to say she could have been a movie star. They'd sit and chat with her while waiting for me to get home, and she'd make them snacks and coffee, listening to their stories with genuine interest. Listening was one of her finest qualities. She'd give you her full attention, looking right at you as you spoke, and always offered a thoughtful response.

She stayed busy making dinners for our relatives and the few loyal friends who had stuck by her, including her card-playing lady friends from Hillcrest Country Club. She tried her best to carve out a life for herself. I often brought my son Frank to visit her on Wednesday nights and Sundays, and that really cheered her up—she was absolutely crazy about him.

It was a couple of weeks before Frank said he wanted to meet Susan, and by that time, we were seeing each other every night. Susan was a wonderful cook, and Frank wasn't used to eating such delicious food. Like my mother, Susan was also a great listener. She asked him all kinds of fun and thoughtful questions, and he was happy to answer them. I could tell he was warming up to her.

In the car on the way home, he said, "She's really nice, Dad." I took him back to his mother's place and gave him a big hug. I couldn't wait to get back to Susan and tell her what Frank had said.

DAD AND KATHRYN TIE THE KNOT

Later that year, Dad and Kathryn got married in the judge's chambers at Santa Monica City Hall. Judge Brand, an old friend who had handled Dad's divorce, was happy to perform the ceremony.

None of us really wanted to be there, but Dad would have been angry—or maybe just deeply hurt—if we hadn't shown up. Kathryn had done nothing to ingratiate herself with any of us, which was difficult to understand. If she had made even a small effort to befriend us, we would have responded. It would have been in her best interest—and it would have made Dad a lot happier, too.

The ceremony was brief, and there was no reception afterward, so we all said our goodbyes and went home.

As we walked back to our cars, Sue told me something shocking I had never heard before. She said that Mom and Dad had separated for four months before they got married. I asked how she knew that, and she said Dad had told her after the divorce. She'd been surprised by the revelation and had asked what brought them back together.

Dad had admitted that he slept with Mom during their separation —and because of that, he felt obligated to marry her.

At that point, I was deeply confused by his rather skewed sense of morality. He'd married Mom out of sense of duty and yet carried on an affair with Lucille Ball, which began just a few years into his marriage with Mom.

AN UNUSUAL PROPOSAL

Susan was more than just a pretty girl with a high IQ. As I got to know her better, I found her to be well-centered and full of confidence. I was amazed by how quickly she won over my entire family. Even my mother—who had always been highly critical of the women in my life—told me this relationship was well worth pursuing.

Susan seemed to know exactly what she wanted and how to get it. One night, in the height of passion, she told me she was madly in love with me—and then stole the initiative by asking me to marry her. I was stunned. I had been thinking about proposing to her, but she beat me to it and took the words right out of my mouth.

When I didn't answer immediately, she looked me straight in the eyes and said, "Well?"

I was still in shock, but I said yes.

Even though it was 11:30 p.m., she called her best friend (also named Susan) and said, "We're getting married... Can I please have the wedding at your house?"

ROXBURY PRODUCTIONS

Dad had purchased a house on North Roxbury Drive in Beverly Hills, which had formerly belonged to Rita Hayworth and her live-in boyfriend, Rudy Maté, the well-known cameraman and director. It was a nice house on a huge lot in the northern part of the city, but it was old and needed work. Dad got it at a very good price and named one of his indie companies after it: Roxbury Productions.

I used to take Frank up there on weekends to visit Dad and Kathryn for Sunday brunch. Once Susan and I got engaged, I started bringing her too. Dad was quite taken with her and especially impressed by her intelligence.

Sometimes Cindy would bring her son, Cory, and her daughter, Kerry, and Susan would occasionally bring her daughter, Michele. Dad loved seeing all the grandchildren sitting around the table, and he'd ask them amusing and sometimes embarrassing questions that made them squirm and giggle. He reminded me of Art Linkletter on his 1950s TV show, *Kids Say the Darndest Things*. I have fond memories of those brunches. They were a far cry from the more formal dinners we'd had with him as kids, and I got a real kick out of the way he teased and joked with the grandchildren. They were all mad about him.

Kathryn had a daughter named Gingi, who was in the process of getting a divorce. Gingi had a young daughter named Kate, and she would bring her over on weekends to visit. And so, there was often a large group of adults and children gathered around the breakfast table.

Gingi had been married to Harry Korshak, whose father, Sidney Korshak, was the Chicago Mafia's lawyer in Los Angeles—one of the most powerful men in Hollywood. He was known as "The Fixer" because of his uncanny success in labor consulting and negotiations. His client list included Al Capone, Frank Nitti, and Jimmy Hoffa, and he was deeply involved in West Coast Teamsters operations.

He also represented MGM and Universal Pictures and was famous for preventing Hollywood union strikes, saving the studios millions. This reputation led the FBI to dub him "the most powerful lawyer in the world." They had spent years trying—and failing—to connect him to any criminal activity. They suspected he'd collected massive under-the-table payments from the grateful studios, but they could never prove it.

GET ME TO BEL AIR ON TIME

Susan and I were married on the sunny patio of her friend's beautiful home. Her friend (also named Susan) and her husband Sam lived in the hills of Bel Air. Sam was a prominent Beverly Hills attorney who was doing very well, and they were both incredibly generous in making sure we had a beautiful wedding.

All of my family attended, including Frank, who sat next to my mother. My father showed up briefly—thankfully without Kathryn—and left soon after the ceremony ended. If Kathryn had been there, it would have ruined the occasion for my mother, and my sisters would have been quite upset as well.

At the end of the ceremony, I crushed the traditional wine glass with my foot and kissed the bride. A limo was waiting to take us to the airport for a three-week honeymoon in Europe—six days each in London, Paris, and Rome.

MOM SELLS MOUNTAIN DRIVE

My mother was happy to have a house full of grandchildren on Sunday nights, when we would all come up for dinner, but she was getting tired of rattling around in that big house with no one but a maid to keep her company. She decided to put the house up for sale, and it was soon bought by MCA-Universal as a company property.

It was actually purchased for Jennings Lang, one of Universal's top executives. He and his wife, Monica, would live in the house and hold ownership, but the company shared in the cost and built a guest house next to the pool. That guest house was intended for Universal's New York executives when they came to town for business meetings. Instead of putting them up at the Beverly Hills Hotel—which cost the company a fortune—they would now stay in the guest house at 606 Mountain Drive. They could swim or play tennis on the lighted court and enjoy meals with Jennings and Monica in the beautiful dining room.

My mother bought a much smaller house on Loma Vista Drive in the Trousdale Estates, just a few blocks away. It was a stark, modern structure on one floor, designed by the celebrated architect Richard Neutra. It was a little cold for my taste, but it had a nice pool and a great view of the city. Everything in the house was white, except for the dark wood kitchen cabinets and the wet bar in the living room. It had cool, white terrazzo floors throughout, along with white walls and ceilings—it reminded me of a hospital nursery. Mom tried to warm it up with fancy cushions, flowers, and other colorful accoutrements, but it always looked a little sterile to me.

Mom was crazy about Frank, and I used to take him up to her house, where he could play with his cousins, who were usually there on Sundays. Sue's daughter Michele and Cindy's daughter Kerry often slept over on Saturday nights to keep Mom company. On Sunday mornings, Dad would come up to pick them up—along with Frank and me—and we'd all go down to Cindy's house to get her son, Cory. Then we'd head to Ponyland and Beverly Park next door, which was known as Kiddieland. It had a variety of rides, including a Ferris wheel, which the kids all loved. We usually capped it off with lunch at the Farmers Market.

It was a lot of fun spending Sundays with the kids, but I felt bad for Mom. She would get nicely dressed and spend a lot of time on her hair and makeup, anticipating Dad's arrival. She'd sit at the game table near the front door, waiting for the bell to ring. She was still very much in love with him and was desperately hoping he would have a change of heart and come back to her. But that was never going to happen—and we all knew it. Time was passing, and we encouraged her to start dating again, but she just didn't want to. I felt terrible for her, but there wasn't much I could do except visit her and be supportive.

34

MY CAREER TAKES OFF LIKE A ROCKET

I left MGM for a better job at Universal as a trailer editor. In television, trailers appear at the end of every show to advertise the next week's episode. They are similar to the trailers shown in theaters to promote upcoming films, but in many ways, they are more difficult to produce.

As with feature film trailers, you have to find a way to tell the story—but for a TV trailer, you only have one minute, which is far less time than you're given for theatrical trailers. You have to use snippets of the show's most exciting moments, but without revealing the plot. The editing is critical because the limited time forces you to be clever and creative with the story elements.

I found it a lot of fun and much more challenging than anything I had done previously. I was learning new things all the time, and I felt good about the direction my career was heading. I was also earning $500 per week—double what I was making as an assistant. Needless to say, I was thrilled to land that job.

I spent a season and a half cutting trailers at Universal, including one for a pilot called *Man of Steel*, which became the very successful show *The Six Million Dollar Man*, starring Lee Majors as a man whose body parts had been replaced with bionics, giving him superpowers. The producer of the show was Glen Larson, and he and I got along very well. He liked my editing so much, he got me promoted to picture editor and placed me on his hit show *McCloud*, starring Dennis Weaver.

McCloud was an unusual concept—a sheriff from New Mexico comes to New York on assignment to learn big-city police techniques, only to get materially involved in all kinds of capers. McCloud ends up solving cases that baffle the NYPD, and as a reward, he's allowed to stay on the job even after his training period ends. He even brings his horse with him, and viewers loved seeing him ride up Broadway in heavy traffic or take part in sting operations he cooked up and got approval for.

It was McCloud's country-bumpkin charm that made the show work, and I was very lucky to get on it for my first television series. I was now making $1,200 per week as a television picture editor, while feature editors were earning $2,000 per week and up, depending on the size of the production. In television, there was always lots of overtime and weekend work due to looming air dates that had to be met. For about a decade, I had highly profitable years, earning over $200,000 annually. As a result, I was able to set aside money for leaner times.

When I finished editing my first episode of *McCloud*, I called my whole family and told them to watch it on Sunday night in prime time. My dad was somewhere on location, and I couldn't reach him, but I called my Uncle Henry. He was the man with the Oscar on his mantle, and I was most eager to hear his opinion of my work. He called me the next day and said, "Great job, kid… that was a terrific show."

Of course, I was elated. What a great compliment, especially coming from him—the master film editor. I continued editing *McCloud* until the season ended, and I was having a fantastic time.

The show had a huge audience, and I was beginning to think I was pretty terrific myself... until I saw the rerun of my first episode later that summer.

I was shocked to see how choppy it looked. The rhythm was off, and some of the dialogue sequences felt poorly timed.

I spoke to a friend from MGM—another editor who had also moved to Universal. He told me that kind of roughness was normal for new editors, especially on their first show. He said not to worry and assured me I'd improve with experience. In fact, he told me that being unhappy with work I'd done just four months earlier was a sign I was already growing as an editor.

I was sure that Henry could see what an amateurish editing job it was, but he was too kind to say anything that might hurt my confidence. Henry was a prince.

I loved editing, and I did everything I could to learn the craft and rely more heavily on my creative instincts. The following season, I became the lead editor on the show and was given the added responsibility of directing second unit, which involved capturing background shots in various locations when suitable footage wasn't available in the film library.

At the end of that season, I was hired to edit a two-part episode of *The Senator*, another high-quality TV series, and I won my first Emmy for television editing. That restored my confidence and made me feel like I was truly improving my craft. Dad always told me that confidence is the name of the game—and he was quite right about that.

At the end of the fifth season of *McCloud*, I edited a special two-hour episode that was also slated for release as a feature film in Europe. It was an excellent script, and I knew it would be one of the best episodes in the series. I stayed late in the editing room each night, giving it my all—and I was rewarded with a nomination for an "Eddie" Award for Best Edited Television Show of the Year.

The "Eddie" Awards are presented by the American Cinema Editors, an elite organization made up of the top editors in Hollywood. Being nominated is a prestigious honor; winning one is even more so.

The ceremony takes place each year in the Grand Ballroom of the Beverly Hilton Hotel in Beverly Hills, which is large enough to accommodate hundreds of guests. It's a black-tie affair, hosted by celebrities—just like the Academy Awards—and it's always a sold-out event. That year, Dom DeLuise was the host and he had the room roaring with laughter as he introduced the presenters.

My wife Susan was really excited about attending the awards dinner. I bought extra tickets for her sister Lois and her husband, Stanley. I wanted to bring my son Frank, too, but it was a weeknight, and he was too young to be out that late on a school night.

I put on my tuxedo, and Susan went out and bought a beautiful dress for the occasion. There was a cocktail hour in the foyer of the ballroom before dinner, and I was in a jovial mood—greeting friends from the studios and introducing them to my wife. It was a true gala evening, and I couldn't wait for dinner to be over and the awards ceremony to begin.

The student awards were presented first, followed by the documentary categories. Finally, the television awards came up—and my name was called as the winner. I was ecstatic. I went up to accept the award and thanked Glen Larson and others at Universal for having faith in me. When I walked off the stage, I received a warm round of applause, which told me that my fellow editors, as well as the ACE members who had voted, agreed with the decision.

I returned to our table and passed the statuette around so everyone could read the inscription on the nameplate. Unlike the Oscars, my name was already engraved on the award—but the engraver had been sworn to secrecy to ensure the winner's identity remained confidential until the official announcement.

Since the event wasn't televised, I ran out to the pay phone to call both Mom and Dad and tell them I had won. I didn't need to call Uncle Henry—he and Rosemary were seated just a couple of tables away. They stood up to congratulate me with big smiles and warm hugs.

The following morning, I stopped at the 7-Eleven across from the studio to pick up copies of *Variety* and *The Hollywood Reporter*, both of which had printed lists of the winners of the ACE Awards. I had done the same thing when I won an Emmy for my work on *The Senator*. I wanted to save these publications to show to my grandchildren someday.

The same newsstand clerk who had sold me the trade papers after I won the Emmy came over with a strange request. He asked if I would autograph a copy of that day's *Hollywood Reporter* to send to his father back in India. He told me that his father lived out in the Punjab and was a great fan of movies and television.

I said, "You can't be serious… I'm sure your father has no idea who I am."

"My father would be honored to have your autograph, sir," he replied. He walked over to the magazine rack, picked up a copy of the *Hollywood Reporter*, and handed it to me. I wished his father good health and a long life, signed it, and went off to work. It put a smile on my face to think I might now be famous in some tiny, isolated village in India.

Editing *McCloud*—a quality show with high production values—had been a terrific break for me, and I was eventually invited to join American Cinema Editors. That was a true honor. ACE is an organization of film editors whose work has been judged to be outstanding over a long period of time. In essence, it's a lifetime achievement award. You're voted in by a jury of your peers—all of them seasoned picture editors whose work had been similarly recognized. They were the same people who had voted to give me the "Eddie" award, and many of them were professionals I deeply respected.

Uncle Henry was a member and a former president of ACE, and I'm sure he voted for me, though we never discussed it. When I was inducted, there were only nineteen members out of the six hundred picture editors working in Hollywood. It was, without a doubt, a tremendous honor, and it looked very good on a résumé. It was a giant plus when applying for a job.

My dad called to congratulate me on being voted into ACE. He had seen a few of my shows and was impressed with my work and the direction my career was taking. I was thrilled to finally have his approval. It felt so much better than what I had gotten from him while I was growing up.

I LOVE MY WIFE...THE MOVIE

At the end of the season, I was fortunate enough to land a job on a feature film called *I Love My Wife*, starring Elliot Gould and Brenda Vaccaro. It was a David Wolper production shooting at Universal, and I was hired as a second editor, by the director, Mel Stuart, who had screened some of my work and liked it.

Mel was kind of a crazy man, who ranted and raved at his hand-picked editor, David Saxon, with whom he had worked for many years. However, they were not getting along well at this point, and David was arguing with him about how the picture should be edited. I was getting along extremely well with Mel by not arguing with him and just doing what he asked for with his film. He wanted to take me to Germany to work on his next picture, *Willie Wonka and the Chocolate Factory*, but there was a problem with the German Unions. I wasn't allowed to work there, unless the company hired a full time German editor at full salary to work with me, but that was not in the budget.

I did, however, accompany Mel to New York to hold a special preview of *I Love My Wife*. for the Eastern brass. The New York executives at Universal were anxious to see the picture, so they could decide how to sell it, and they wanted to see it with an audience. So,

Mel and I flew in on the Friday morning red eye and held the preview on Friday night.

The New York office was happy with the movie, and didn't ask for any changes, so Mel flew back to LA on Saturday, but I stayed on for the rest of the weekend, because my dad happened to be in New York at the same time. He went to see a Broadway play on Friday evening, while we were at the preview only blocks away at a movie house on 8th Avenue.

On Saturday, Dad and I went to a Yankee game up in the Bronx, and he took me to dinner at Le Pavillon. The great French Chef, Jacques Pepin, who had made the restaurant famous in the early 1960s was no longer working there, but he happened to be dining in the restaurant a few tables from us. He remembered Dad as being in the restaurant when he was the Chef, and he eventually came over to our table and greeted Dad and me and told us how much he loved Dad's movies. I thought that was quite an honor from the man who was the personal chef to Charles De Gaulle and two other French Prime Ministers.

Dad told him that we loved his cooking, and I raved about the mushroom soup. He told me he had designed that recipe and that his wife, Gloria, loved it more than any other soup. In his charming French accent, he said to me, *"If you love it as my wife does, it will remain in your memory forever."* That whole day and evening will most certainly remain in my memory forever.

TIME FLIES WHEN YOU'RE HAVING FUN

Susan and I were now in our third year of marriage, and we were very happy. We had purchased a house in South Beverly Hills, adjacent to Century City, and we were comfortable there. We had an extra bedroom, and sometimes Frank would sleep over when he asked his mother's permission—if she found it convenient.

Frank always enjoyed being with us, but we were starting to notice that he seemed a little down at times... not like the joyful little boy he had been a year or two earlier. I asked him if everything was okay at home with his mother. He told me it was but mentioned he hadn't seen Herb for some time. That really concerned me. If his mother and Herb had broken up, there was a strong chance she might start drinking again.

When I took Frank home that night, she came to the door—and I could smell the liquor on her breath. I was worried she wasn't taking care of Frank the way she should have been, and I had real misgivings about leaving him there.

A few nights later, I got an alarming call from Frank. His mother was lying on the floor, and she couldn't get up. I asked him if she was speaking to him. He said yes, but he couldn't understand what she was saying. We jumped in the car and rushed over.

At least if she was still conscious, she could tell us what was wrong. Frank let us in, and I could see right away that Nancy was drunk and incoherent. Susan and I got her up and into her bedroom and lifted her onto the bed. I asked Frank how long she'd been like this. He said she'd been acting "funny" some evenings, but nothing like this. I put cold water on her face to revive her, and I told her we were taking Frank home with us. I'd bring him back in the morning when she was feeling better.

She tried to object, but she didn't have the will—and collapsed back onto the bed. Frank was terribly upset. He had never seen his mother in that condition, and he was afraid to leave her. I told him she would sleep it off, and she'd be fine in the morning.

When we got home, Susan called her lawyer friend, Sam, who had given us our

beautiful wedding. He told her that he wanted to get a statement from Frank on a police report, and he suggested we should think about having Frank come to live with us. He thought I had a

good chance to get custody.

Frank was now nine years old and growing up too fast. I wanted to give him his childhood back—and that was a huge task, one that would require two people.

When I spoke to Frank's mother the next morning, she was angry that I had taken

Frank away from her, and she was going to petition the court to double Frank's child support

payments. I called Sam, and he insisted on taking the case. He filed an emergency injunction

asking that I be given temporary custody of Frank while the court investigated the situation in his mother's home.

Both Susan and I testified in front of the judge, and Nancy showed up in court to testify

on her own behalf. But the evidence was damaging, and she was unable to refute our testimony,

and so, I was awarded temporary custody. The judge also ordered regular visits with a court

appointed psychiatrist for Frank's mother, and he scheduled the follow-up hearing in three months.

Susan told me she would be happy to quit her job and become a surrogate mother to

Frank if he were to come to live with us. I was working long hours, and Frank needed daytime

companionship and parental guidance, and he would have the security of two parents living in

the house with him. Susan had once said to me that she was not sure she wanted to have children

of her own, so being with Frank would give her the opportunity to experience motherhood

without having to get pregnant and deliver a baby. I think that was the issue that caused her ambivalence. This way she could have her cake and eat it too.

She handled Frank beautifully, and he responded well to her kindness. He felt much more secure in our home, with the two of us looking after him, and he began to relax and settle in.

At the end of the summer, we went back to court for the final decision. The psychiatrist testified that Nancy had made some progress in her battle with alcohol, but she still had a long way to go.

The judge took Frank into his chambers to speak with him privately. He asked Frank where he would like to live, and Frank was unwavering. He told the judge that he loved his mother, but he felt safer and happier living with Susan and me.

That was it. The judge granted me custody, and Nancy was given weekly visitation—supervised for the first three months. Nancy burst into tears, which was heartbreaking for both of us, and especially for Frank. He leaned over, hugged her, and told her that everything was going to be okay now. That gave me a real lift. It was so adult of him—so strong and comforting—when his mother was so distraught.

When school started in the fall, we enrolled him in El Rodeo, one of the four grade schools in Beverly Hills. Susan gave him snacks when he came home and helped him with his homework, and he earned good grades in his first semester. When I got home in the evenings, we would have dinner together and watch television, or I would have him read aloud to help improve his reading skills. This was the kind of family home life I had always envisioned, and I was happy that both Susan and I could give Frank the stability he needed.

35

THE CONVERSATION OF A LIFETIME

Late one afternoon, just as I was about to leave work, I got a call from my wife, Susan. Her father had passed away. He lived on a boat in the Marina, and friends in the neighboring slip had stopped by that afternoon and found him slumped over his desk. They called for an ambulance, but it was too late. The paramedics determined that he had been dead for two or three hours by the time they arrived. The neighbors called Susan and her sister, Lois, and gave them the bad news.

I got home as fast as I could and found my wife in tears—almost inconsolable. After talking with her for about an hour, I realized what was troubling her the most: all the issues she had with her father were unresolved, and she would now have to carry that for the rest of her life. She had always longed for him to accept her as she was, but now it was too late.

I started thinking about all the unresolved issues I had with my own father—all the pain I'd buried over the years, still quietly haunting me. He was now in his late sixties, and if he died suddenly, I knew I would feel the same regret Susan was experiencing. I called him that night and told him I needed to talk. He said to come to the house on Saturday morning. He asked if something was wrong, and I told him I'd explain it on Saturday.

I spent the next two days rehearsing, digging deep into my memory for all the sarcastic jokes, the criticisms, the subtle traps he'd laid that I'd fallen into. I didn't want to forget anything, and I knew I might only get one shot to say what was really on my mind.

I made a list of everything I wanted to say. It filled an entire page of a yellow legal pad. I ranked my grievances in order of importance, saving the most painful ones for last, hoping that would make more of an impact.

I sat in my car that morning, going over the list twice, after reviewing it a dozen times the night before. When I felt I had everything firmly in my head, I folded the paper and put it in my pocket. Then I walked up to the front door and rang the bell. My dad answered and led me into the den, closing the door behind us.

Before I could say anything, Dad asked me to convey his condolences to Susan and to assure her that he and Kathryn would be at the funeral the following day.

I told him that her father's death was what inspired me to come and talk to him. I explained that she had many unresolved issues with her father, and she was terribly upset that she had never taken the opportunity to speak with him about any of them—to unburden herself (and him) before he died.

I went on to say that I wasn't going to let that happen with us. If I did, it would plague me for the rest of my life, and I was here to get everything off my chest.

My dad didn't say a word, but I could tell by the look on his face that he knew I was about to level the big guns at him. I started with the dinner table conversations that had stayed with me—things he had said or joked about that really hurt me, things I had no defense against as a child.

He didn't like my posture at the table or the way I held my fork, and I heard about it over and over. He also expected me to be informed, at least to some extent, about what was going on in the world. He'd say things like, "How do you expect to get by in this world if you're not aware of what's going on?"

If he had told me to listen to a particular radio station or to read certain newspaper articles, it would have been somewhat understandable. But instead, he just expected me to instinctively know what to do—how to keep myself informed about things like the revolution going on in China or the freezing weather that had destroyed crops in Ireland.

When he tried to defend himself about that, I interrupted him and said, "But I was only nine or ten years old. What did you expect of me?"

My dad suddenly got quiet, and I went on to say that he had humiliated me in front of one of my friends at the dinner table by revealing that I got a D in math on my report card. I told him that was nobody's business outside the family and that I'd been angry about it for a long time. I reminded him that I eventually earned good enough grades to be accepted at UCLA.

He nodded and said, "You're right... I shouldn't have done that... I apologize."

I continued, telling him how angry I was to have to work every night until 8:00 p.m. during the week just to pay for a used car—while my friends were being given brand-new ones by their parents. Most of them went on to become successful lawyers and stockbrokers, and none of them had been subjected to harsh object lessons about money like I was.

My dad countered with that tired old story about how he had to walk five miles to school every day in the snow, saying I had it easy compared to what he went through. I asked him, "Did that make you happy?"

"Hell no..." he replied.

"So then why would you want your son to go through it?"

His answer was quiet and feeble. "I wanted to make a man out of you."

"What about all our soldiers in World War II? Didn't they go to war and risk their lives so their sons wouldn't have to?"

Dad didn't know how to respond to that, so I continued, "Most people fight for success, so their children won't have such a hard life. I would never make my son work like that—no matter what I had to do."

I was shaking with anger by then, so I excused myself and went to the bathroom to splash cold water on my face. I looked at my list to see if I had left out anything important. There was only one thing left —and I was saving it for the end. I stayed in the bathroom for a good five minutes because I wanted to give my words time to sink in.

When I returned to the den, my dad was sitting in his chair with his chin down on his chest, looking miserable. It was obvious that I had gotten to him, and he didn't really know how to deal with it. I sat down and waited until he looked up at me.

I told him that I had been scared to talk to him about a lot of things—and that I was angry with him for making me feel that way. He seemed surprised, and he asked me what I had been afraid to talk to him about.

"I was afraid to ask you to help me get a job, after hearing about what you said to Stanley Kramer, and knowing how you felt about nepotism."

Dad just shook his head. "Stanley wanted me to make him a producer, but he didn't know anything about the business... I offered to get him a job in the story department, but he turned me down."

"And what about Henry?" I added. "He didn't know anything about the business either, but you got him a good job in the editing room."

Dad started to get upset. "Henry was a very confused boy. He should have stayed in dental school. He could have had a much better life."

I cut him off. "But he wanted to go into the movie business, so you broke your cardinal rule about nepotism for Henry. And what about Kathryn? She didn't know a thing about movies, but you made her an associate producer—and eventually, a producer."

Dad was deflated. He lowered his voice in case Kathryn was outside the door. "That's not a career... it's a dead-end job working for me. And I need her help. I'm getting too old to keep doing this over and over again."

I didn't say anything else. I felt that what I had already said was more than enough, and I was exhausted from all the emotion. I had considered telling him that I didn't like the way he treated me when he found out about Ellie's pregnancy, but I thought better of it. Bringing up that past trauma might have triggered him to go back on the attack. *Better to let sleeping dogs lie*, as my mother used to say.

Dad and I just sat there for a few minutes, staring off in different directions. I didn't want to make eye contact with him.

After a while, he spoke up for himself and said what every parent says when confronted by one of their children about why they did what they did: "I did what I thought was best at the time. Apparently, I was wrong, and I apologize."

Any psychiatrist will quote that line verbatim as something every parent eventually says to their child. It's the only way they can justify the way they raised their children—whether it was right or wrong.

Dad got up out of his chair and came toward me, and I got up to leave. With a very sad face, he said, "I had no idea you felt this way, and I wish you had come to me earlier with all of this. I apologize for everything I've ever done to cause you all this anguish. It certainly wasn't my intention. Please forgive me."

He reached over and gave me a big hug, and I hugged him back. It was the first prolonged hug he'd given me since I was about three years old—and it felt so good.

I couldn't say anything because I was fighting back the tears. He walked me to the door and said something remarkable that I'll never forget: "You know... the only thing that's really important in life is that we all love each other."

I got in the car and drove home with tears streaming down my face. I felt like a huge weight had been lifted off my shoulders. I had earned my father's utmost respect—and he never said another demeaning thing to me or made another sarcastic joke. Even if he got angry with me about something, he was always respectful in discussing it.

When I got home, I described the whole thing to Susan, and she was happy that I had been able to do what I did. I think it even helped her deal with some of the issues she had with her own father. I suggested she write him a letter describing all her feelings and telling him that she forgives him for everything.

"Who knows... he might be looking down at you and hearing what you're saying. If not, you'll at least have gotten it all off your chest."

36

SKATEBOARDS, SOUNDTRACKS, AND SECOND CHANCES

That fall, I left *McCloud* to edit Glen Larson's new pilot, *Magnum P.I.* Glen had cast the very masculine and undeniably sexy Tom Selleck to play the lead—a private investigator who lives in the guest house of a wealthy millionaire's estate in Hawaii. I thought Selleck was the best-looking actor in Hollywood, and he exuded charm like Clark Gable.

When the show was finished, I got a videocassette and watched it with my wife and my mom long before its air date. They were bowled over. My mother said Tom Selleck was the best thing to come to television in years, and that the show would run for five to seven seasons—and she was right. Dad predicted Selleck would become the biggest star on television and said he would have made it in old Hollywood, too, starring in feature films.

It was quite fortunate for me to have connected with Glen Larson, because it meant continuous employment. I had edited *McCloud* for five seasons, and now I'd be doing *Magnum P.I.* for another five.

Meanwhile, my son Frank was just entering Beverly Hills High

School and was blossoming into a fine young man. He was very interested in music, and one of his teachers at El Rodeo recommended that I get him guitar lessons. I bought him an electric guitar and arranged a year of lessons—and I watched his self-confidence grow right alongside his enthusiasm for music.

He was very popular, with lots of friends, and he had grown tall and handsome. The girls were interested in him and used to call all the time. It got to the point where Susan and I couldn't get any of our evening calls because Frank was always on the phone. We finally gave him his own line in his room to free up the house phone.

Frank had real joy in his life for the first time in years, and I was so happy for him. When he'd first come to live with us four years earlier, he'd been so depressed I didn't know what to do. But Susan and I worked with him and helped bring him out of the melancholy that had settled over him as he suffered through the pain of my divorce from his mother. I hadn't realized how deeply it had affected him, and I was still trying to find ways to make it up to him.

Helping him improve his reading skills turned out to be one of the best things I could have done. All of his grades improved as a result—and so did his social life.

He had gotten so good on the guitar that he organized a high school band, and they rehearsed in our garage after school. It got a little noisy at times, but we didn't mind—because we knew he was staying out of trouble.

Within a year, he asked for an electronic keyboard, and he taught himself how to play it without lessons. He also learned to read music, and I began to worry that he might skip college for a career as a musician. But that fear turned out to be unwarranted. That boyish enthusiasm I spoke of earlier had matured into confidence, and the bouts of depression he'd suffered while living with his mother were gone for good. I was so happy with the way he was turning out, and I knew I'd done the right thing by getting custody of him at a time when his life could've taken a bad turn.

Two of Frank's friends were on the dance committee, and they asked if his band would perform during one of the intermissions. He was so excited, he raced home from school to tell us about it. I called the school and got permission to bring my dad and Kathryn to the dance to hear him play. I asked my mother too, but she was sick and couldn't go out at night.

Frank put on a real show—we were all stunned at how good it sounded. It was far better than what we were hearing from the garage. I was so proud of him, and so happy to see that he had such a bright future.

Magnum P.I. became the smash hit we all thought it would be, and I was getting a little restless. I was still happy with editing, but I wanted to become a director—and I felt my experience in the cutting room had prepared me in several different ways.

I mentioned it to a friend of mine who had directed quite a few *McCloud* episodes, and he said, "What do you want to do that for? You've got the best job in the studio—sitting here in your editing salon making movies, with no one telling you what to do. And you're getting paid handsomely for it."

I told him that the idea of being handed a script, a cast and crew, and a big budget was a challenge that really appealed to me.

He shook his head. "There's nothing glamorous about it. It's not like the old days when the director was king. *The Suits*—studio execs—come down to the set from their ivory tower and dial up the pressure. They look at their watches, remind you that you've only shot one and three-quarter pages that day, and put the fear of God into you. It's a nightmare."

I said that I didn't care. There was something sexy about directing—and if I didn't like it, I could always go back to editing.

He told me about a directing job he was turning down and said he could recommend me for it if I was really serious about wanting to direct. It was a low-budget industrial film for a skateboard company, and it was ideal for a new director because there were no advertising agencies involved, and I wouldn't have to deal with the Director's Guild either.

I'd get $15,000 for directing it, and there was another $20,000–$25,000 in the budget for post-production, which would be allocated to me for editing, sound re-recording, and lab expenses. If I edited it myself, I could pocket most of that money as well.

I was very excited. My friend called and set up an appointment for me the following day. I went home and told my wife and my son Frank about it at dinner—but I warned them to keep it a secret. I was worried that if anyone at the studio found out about it, I might lose my job.

I arrived at a small storefront in Venice near the beach, with a sign over the door that read *The Wind Wheel Skateboard Company*. The owners were a couple of young guys in their twenties, and they explained to me that they wanted a promotional film—about ten minutes long—to distribute to sporting goods chains.

They showed me a budget that looked way too big for such a small project, and I asked them who had drawn it up. They told me it was the uncle of a friend—someone who was a production manager at Columbia Studios.

I said I'd like to speak with him, but they looked at one another and then said he was too busy and couldn't get involved with their film.

I asked who was producing it, and they said, "We thought you were."

This was beginning to look like a Mickey Mouse operation.

I told them I was directing it—not producing—and explained the difference. They were baffled and didn't know what to do. I pointed out that there was no provision in the budget for a producer, and added that I *could* produce it, but I'd need their help—along with a couple of their friends, if they had anyone willing to work.

They said they would do whatever I needed, and that they had friends who'd be happy to work on the picture as well. I said that was great and asked if they had anyone in mind to ride the skateboards.

"Oh yes," they said. They knew two fourteen-year-old kids who were champion skateboarders and had placed high in competitions—and one of them was a girl.

Then I asked to see the script. They told me there was no script, which was rather surprising. I couldn't imagine how they'd drawn up a budget without a script, but that was alright. This wasn't a story-driven project—it was an action piece—and I was beginning to get a concept of what to do with it. I told them I'd work on my idea for a few days and get back to them.

I thought about two kids racing around on skateboards, challenging each other to dangerous tricks like jumping walls and park benches, and landing smoothly. I couldn't help comparing it in my mind to a car chase.

One of the best chases I'd ever seen was in the movie *Bullitt* with Steve McQueen, shot in the hills of San Francisco. It had been a huge hit and set the standard for car chases years earlier. Other movies and television shows had copied it many times. I imagined this could be a chase too—only with kids on skateboards instead of cars—challenging each other, pulling off spectacular tricks, and passing each other to take the lead in a ten-minute race for glory.

I knew we wouldn't be able to record usable sound with that kind of fast-moving action, so I eliminated the sound man and recording equipment from the budget. We could get background tracks of skateboards on a sidewalk and lay them in later, but the predominant sound would be music.

I shook a few other things out of the budget that we didn't need, and there was plenty of money left to get everything I wanted on film.

I called my director friend and told him about the meeting. I asked if these young guys were good for the money. He assured me that both their parents were quite wealthy—and that they'd be vulnerable to lawsuits if they failed to perform.

So, I went to a motion picture attorney—who was married to an old girlfriend of mine—and asked him to draw up a contract for these young guys to sign, committing themselves to the project and to me as the director. He got it done in a couple of days and charged me $150, which was amazingly cheap, even back then.

I had three local locations in mind for which I didn't need shooting permits, so I made a numbered list of the shots I'd need at each location and estimated the total screen time I'd have once filming was complete. It came out to about six and a half minutes, so I added a few more shots at a couple of different locations, and I was ready to go.

I called the boys and asked them to set up a meeting one night during the week—and told them I wanted the skateboarders to be there. I said I'd be bringing a contract for them to sign, which I would leave with them to review.

When I arrived at the store, the boys had brought their parents to meet me, and I could tell my director friend had given me quite a build-up as an editor making the transition to directing. They also made a big deal about my father, whose movies they were familiar with.

The young skateboarders were good-looking kids—perfect for the film, in my estimation. I wanted to see them in action, so we went out onto the sidewalk in front of the store, and they showed me some of their moves. They looked comfortable on their boards, and I was really impressed with their speed. If I could shoot this movie the way I was seeing it in my head, I thought it could be spectacular.

The boys called me the next night and said they were ready to sign the contract. Their attorney had gone over it and approved it, and they were ready to go.

I went home for dinner and asked my son Frank if he'd like to work on the movie with me and earn some money. He was so excited he almost fell out of his chair. I invited him to come with me after dinner to meet the producers. I was giving the two young owners of the business the title of *producer*, even though there would be no credits on the screen.

We arrived and went into their office to sign the contract. I told them there would be some up-front expenses—such as renting a

Steadicam and a golf cart for the moving shots and purchasing the raw film.

They told me the money was in the bank, in an account titled *Wind Wheels Production Funds*, and we decided they would make me a signatory on the account so I could write checks as needed.

I told them I'd like to shoot on Saturday. As producers, they would be responsible for getting the skateboarders to the locations on time and transferring the equipment between locations—which might involve renting a truck. One of the boys would be responsible for renting the golf cart and driving it during the shoot. The other would position himself behind the camera to keep the path clear for the skateboarders, and my son Frank would help him.

The producers would also be responsible for taking out insurance to cover the day's shooting, and I warned them it wouldn't be cheap. When they bought the insurance policy, I looked it over to make sure everything was covered.

After meeting the boys' families, I was pretty sure that if we ran out of money, their fathers would contribute whatever was needed to complete the project. They had already put up $100,000 for the production budget.

My biggest problem would be finding a good camera operator. I couldn't use anyone from Universal, because I didn't want anyone at the studio to know I was doing this. I called a cameraman I'd known from my MGM days, and he gave me the name of a camera operator he said was excellent—and who needed the work.

I called the camera operator and told him what we were doing, and he promised to keep his mouth shut and keep our secret. I asked him to go with me to Birns and Sawyer in Hollywood to pick out the camera. We also planned to pick up two thousand feet of unexposed 35mm color film from Technicolor—and then we'd be ready.

At 5:00 a.m. on Saturday morning, the entire crew—including the producers—assembled at the bottom of a steep hill in a residential section of Sherman Oaks, near the Sepulveda Tunnel. Dawn was just beginning to break, and we were waiting for the first rays of sunlight to appear behind the hill.

The instant I saw first light, I honked the horn, and the two skateboarders glided over the top of the hill and raced down toward the camera. It was the dramatic opening shot of my movie. I got a second shot—a closer angle on their faces as they came down the hill with big smiles—and a third angle on their feet manipulating the skateboards. Then we were off to our next location: a mall in Studio City with a long row of shops.

I was planning to pan with the kids as they skated past the shop windows, many of which were very colorful. But when we arrived, around 6:00 a.m., there was a major problem: the parking lot was being resurfaced, and it would be a couple of hours before we could enter. That was a huge blow, and I didn't know what to do. I realized I should have planned for an alternate location—but that was part of my inexperience.

My cameraman suggested we go on to our next location at the beach, where we could find shops to replace the ones at the mall. We could shoot along those storefronts in addition to what we'd already planned to film on the boardwalk.

I made some new notes in my shot list on the way to Santa Monica, but I didn't know how to make a smooth transition from our first scene to the beach location. When we got there, the answer came to me: I got a beautiful shot of the ocean from the top of the hill, with billowy morning clouds and still water.

Then we found a whole block of shops on Main Street that weren't open yet, and there were no people on the street to get in the way. It was even better than the Studio City mall. I had the kids stop and peer into a couple of store windows before taking off again.

When the shops began to open, I got some new ideas. I had them skate up to a clothing store, enter, and come out wearing colorful caps. I also panned them into an ice cream shop—and right back out with cones in hand. They were perfectly comfortable on their boards, even eating ice cream while traveling at high speeds.

Traffic was beginning to build up on Main Street, so we skated them across to the boardwalk overlooking the ocean. It's a long strip of walled-in sidewalk with occasional benches for people to sit and enjoy the view. This was what I had in mind for the golf cart: we could drive along the sidewalk ahead of the skateboarders with our camera facing backward, shooting the kids skating toward us. If Frank and our producer were able to clear the way ahead of the golf cart, we wouldn't have to stop and ruin the shot.

We made several passes, shooting the kids from different angles —including one with the golf cart on the grassy area next to the sidewalk, where we ran alongside the kids to get side shots. We also captured special footage of them jumping up over curbs and landing smoothly back on their skateboards. We shot inserts of the skateboard wheels on the pavement, where the logo on the side of the board was clearly visible.

By eleven-thirty that morning, we had gotten all the shots on my list—and a lot more I hadn't planned. We stopped for lunch, and the budget covered pizza and hamburgers for everyone.

While we ate, I started thinking about how I was going to end the movie. I had originally planned to finish at the fountain outside the Studio City mall, but since we couldn't shoot there, I was stuck. Someone mentioned a fountain outside a medical plaza here in Santa Monica and said they knew how to get there.

The fountain was beautiful—large enough to swim in. A circular wall enclosed clear, bubbling water that shimmered in the sunlight. I spoke to the skateboarders and told them what I wanted them to do: we'd start on a tight shot of the water at the base of the fountain. The camera would then pull back to a wide shot as the kids skated into frame, circled three times, and jumped off their skateboards to sit or stand along the wall around the fountain.

At that point, the boy was to move between the girl and the fountain, lean in, and kiss her. That would be the final shot of the film.

We rehearsed the scene a couple of times until I was satisfied that they were skating in on cue, just as the camera pulled back to reveal the sidewalk next to the fountain.

Then, I pulled the girl aside and quietly told her that when the boy leaned in to kiss her, she should push him into the fountain. I wasn't sure she'd go for it—but she *loved* the idea. She timed it perfectly. When she shoved him into the water, the look on his face was priceless. I planned to freeze-frame on his expression and fade to black to close the film.

That was it. We wrapped around 2:30 in the afternoon, returned the camera to Birns and Sawyer, and dropped the film off at Technicolor to be developed and printed. I wrote the camera operator a check—with a little bonus—and told him we'd work together again.

Frank and I drove home, and I told him I'd pay him $200 for the day's work. He was thrilled—and so was I. It was one of our greatest days of bonding, and I assured him there would be more days like this: working together, having fun.

All my life I had wanted to share an experience like that with my father—but we never could. Sharing it now with my son helped satisfy that hunger in me.

On Tuesday morning, I picked up the film on my way to work and took it back to my cutting room, placing it in the rack alongside the *Magnum P.I.* reels. When my assistant left for the day, I began running the rolls of my film on the Moviola—an editing machine that runs film at projection speed and lets you stop on a frame, back up, or move forward.

I didn't do any editing that night. I just screened the footage to make sure everything was there—and I was quite happy with what my camera operator had shot. I put the film back in the cans and headed home.

I planned to edit the next night—when I could bring Frank with me to the cutting room so he could see how film was put together. He was even more excited about watching the editing than he had been during the shooting.

It took me about two and a half hours to cut the whole film and splice it together. When I finished, I ran it straight through for Frank —who decided, right then and there, that he wanted to give up music and become a film editor.

I told him he should never give up his music, and that he was too young to make a career decision like that. I reminded him there were plenty of great things out there in the world he had yet to discover— and that he might change his mind a few times before making a serious commitment to anything.

Over the next two nights, I found sound effects of skateboard wheels rolling on cement in the sound library—along with jumps, landings, and a few other useful sounds—and took them to my cutting room. There, I built a sound reel and synced it with the picture.

On Saturday, I spent most of the day in a rental library listening to music that was out of copyright and within our budget—something I could use as the background for the skateboard race. I finally found some hot Latino big band music, with bongo drums and blaring trumpets, and I knew it would work perfectly. I got copies on 35mm soundtrack for editing.

Laying in the music was a little tricky. I had to create sound dissolves from one track to another, which could only be done on the dubbing stage during the final mix.

I was now ready for the producers to see the film. I got studio passes for them and ran it for them on the Moviola, complete with sound effects. Naturally, they were thrilled. It exceeded their expectations, and they were confident it would help sell their skateboards.

I told them that if they were happy with it, I'd book a dubbing stage and mix the sound. I knew of a couple of sound stages in Hollywood that were far less expensive than the ones at the major studios.

I also called Technicolor and ordered a fade-in to the opening sunrise shot and a fade to black from the fountain—followed by a pop-on at the end that read: *Wind Wheels Skateboards: They Fly Like the Wind*

I photographed the company logo—which was a pair of skateboard wheels with wings—and had it fade up from black for the final shot. Those were the only three optical effects in the film. Once I approved them, I ordered Technicolor to cut the negative and be ready to make a print as soon as they received the optical soundtrack from the recording stage.

These were the major expenses in the budget, but we had spent far less than expected during the shoot, and there was plenty left to finish the film.

I took Frank with me to the dubbing session so he could see how sound was mixed on the recording stage. I also brought him to Technicolor to screen the picture and adjust the color to my liking for the release print. Finally, I ordered a VHS cassette, so the film could be played on any television hooked up to a VHS recorder.

I brought the cassette home and ran it for Susan and Frank—and they thought it was a piece of art. Then I screened it for the boys and their families down at the store, and they had the same reaction. I told them they could order as many VHS cassettes as they wanted from Technicolor, but this one was mine.

Before I left, the boys wrote me a check for $25,000—$15,000 for directing, and $10,000 for editing and dubbing—and I was thrilled with the success of the project.

With some trepidation, I took the cassette up to my dad's house and ran it for him on his VHS recorder. To my delight, he was very impressed when he realized I had written it, directed it, edited it, supervised the sound mix and color correction, and produced it for the skateboard company.

He was genuinely complimentary about the quality of the work—especially my creative instincts. He told me, right then, that I was ready to move on and start directing.

I was thrilled—and overwhelmed by his enthusiasm. It felt like he had just put a heating pad on my aching heart.

I said, "Great... Give me an assignment."

The entire *Wind Wheels* experience was wonderful. I did everything from start to finish on that movie, and everyone was happy...

including me. It gave me the confidence I needed to direct bigger projects, though I knew I'd need more experience working with actors.

I always remembered what Vincente Minnelli once told me when I asked him to name the most important thing about directing: "Make the actors see it through your eyes."

Actors have enormous egos. When they're given a script, they'll rehearse late into the night in front of a mirror, and you never know what they're going to bring to a role. Sometimes it's something wonderful that you never imagined—and sometimes it isn't very good at all.

If you tell them how bad it is, they fall apart. You destroy their self-confidence. You have to be clever in how you handle them.

I used to say things like: "That's a very interesting approach—something I would never have thought of, and I'm definitely going to use it in the picture. But let's also do a more traditional one, just so we have a choice in editing, in case the producer or one of the studio executives has an issue with it."

In Hollywood, if you're smart, you never stop learning—especially if you want to stay standing after the spotlight has dimmed.

37

LITTLE MO

After *Wind Wheels*, I started looking for more directing jobs—which, as a virtually unknown director, were not easy to find. However, just a few weeks later, something came along that combined editing and directing—and I couldn't wait to start work.

I received a call from Jack Webb, who told me he had a partially edited three-hour TV movie that needed a lot of work, and that he wanted someone who could also direct added scenes.

I had known Jack from Universal, where he was producing *Adam-12* and *Dragnet*, but I had never worked on one of his shows. I asked who had recommended me, and he told me that Dick Belding, the editorial supervisor at Universal, had given high praise to my work. He told Jack I had directed a great deal of second unit for Glen Larson on *McCloud* and *Magnum P.I.*, and that he thought I'd be just what Jack needed for this TV movie. I knew Dick and Jack were drinking buddies—and I also knew Jack didn't want to hire an expensive director to shoot the added scenes. So, I was a bargain.

When Jack called to hire me, I sent Dick Belding a bottle of his favorite scotch and a nice thank-you note. He'd always been a good friend, someone who liked my work and had recommended me for many jobs.

Jack's movie was *Little Mo*—the story of the American girl from San Diego who became the first woman to win all four major Grand Slam tennis tournaments in the same calendar year. I was thrilled to work on the project. I asked Jack about the added scenes he wanted me to shoot. He said he needed some women tennis players who could double for Maureen and two of her opponents at Wimbledon. He told me I'd have a better idea of what was needed once I looked at the Wimbledon sequences.

Two senior editors—both of whom I respected—had worked on the show before I took over. But for some reason, Jack wasn't happy with their work. When I started re-editing some of the early tennis matches, I understood why. It was all about timing. The action was just a hair off. I found that by adding a frame or two to the end of certain cuts, the sequences started to flow better.

I ran them for Jack in one of the projection rooms at Goldwyn Studios, where we'd rented editing space. He whacked me on the shoulder and said, "That's what I'm talking about! That's the way I want those tennis games to look." He told me my work was seamless—and that's one of the best compliments a film editor can get.

The dialogue scenes were professionally edited, and there wasn't anything technically wrong with them—except that they were too long and chatty. That wasn't the editors' fault. In a first cut, the editor is required to include all the dialogue that was shot. After the screening, if something doesn't work, it can be trimmed or removed.

I told Jack I wanted to take out some of the dialogue, if he had no objection. I thought it would tighten the pacing. He told me to go ahead. The picture was running slow anyway, and we were going to be over our airtime limit once I cut in the new scenes.

So I went back through the picture, trimming scenes that dragged and cutting superfluous dialogue. When I got to the tennis matches, it became clear where we needed additional angles to enhance the gameplay. Jack had said I'd know better than he would where the new footage was needed—and he was right. Two of the Wimbledon matches felt short and rushed. I made notes about what I needed to shoot.

When I'd made all my changes, I ran the whole picture for Jack and explained what I wanted to do. He agreed with me completely. He assembled a camera and sound crew and called in a script supervisor to meet with me so she could record proper notes based on my shooting plan.

That afternoon, my assistant became ill and went home. I called him later that evening, and he said he felt terrible. He was going to the doctor in the morning and thought he might have caught some kind of Asian flu. He couldn't say when he'd be able to return to work.

I didn't know what I was going to do. It was the height of the TV season, and all the good assistant editors were already working. Then I remembered—my son Frank was just starting Easter vacation from school. He could spend two weeks with me in the cutting room and earn about $1,200.

So that evening, I went into his room and asked him to get off the phone with his girlfriend—I had something important to discuss. After a minute or two, he hung up, though I could tell he was a little annoyed.

When I told him I needed him to come to work with me in the cutting room, he was ecstatic. I explained that we'd need to leave before 7:00 a.m. the next morning—there were things I had to show him.

He'd learned quite a bit during *Wind Wheels*, but now I needed to teach him how to sync the dailies and how to code the reels of picture and sound to keep everything in sync. I showed him how to use the sound head on the sync machine to locate the clapper noise and match it to the exact frame where the clapper closed on screen.

I also had him run all the reels of picture and sound through the synchronizer to get footage measurements and then taught him how to convert those measurements to real time—so we could calculate how much material we needed to gain or lose to complete the film.

He learned fast and took notes for me as I went through the Wimbledon matches, describing the shots I was planning to make. I anticipated he might have a little trouble syncing the dailies, but I'd help him if necessary—and there wouldn't be a massive amount of film.

He turned out to be so helpful that, after the second day, Jack said, "That's a nice boy you've got there." He asked if Frank was planning to go into the business, and I told him that Frank had a number of interests, including music. He was playing guitar and keyboards with his little band, and he wasn't sure yet what he wanted to do in life.

Later that day, Jack called me down to the office to meet the actresses who would be playing Maureen and the women she faced at Wimbledon. They were all accomplished tennis players, and each bore a resemblance to the women they'd be doubling. We'd be shooting them from a great enough distance that they would pass for Maureen's original opponents in the movie.

Jack had already secured permits to shoot on the tennis courts at Poinsettia Park. It was just a few blocks from Goldwyn Studios, and we would only be shooting for one day. I had a list of about twenty shots I wanted to get—including low angles of their legs running to return drop shots, which would match footage already in the film. Mostly, I needed rear angles of Maureen with her opponents across the court. I had to shoot them slightly out of focus so their faces wouldn't be recognizable.

We began shooting Thursday morning, and Frank wanted to be there—but I told him he had to stay in the cutting room, answer the phone, and sign for any deliveries while I was out on set. I could see how disappointed he was, but I couldn't take him with me.

We started shooting around 8:30 a.m., once the cameraman confirmed we had the right light to match the existing footage. The camera was locked down for every shot—any slight movement would have prevented us from superimposing crowd shots to make it look like Wimbledon. We finished before noon, and I went back to the studio and picked Frank up to go to lunch.

His big test would come the next morning, when he'd have to sync his first reel of dailies.

We arrived early and found three cans of film that Technicolor had developed and printed overnight, waiting outside the cutting room door. I asked Frank to go over to the sound department and pick up the soundtracks, while I went inside to get a first look at the picture on the editing machine.

I looked at the first couple of takes, and everything was exactly how I'd hoped. When Frank came back with the sound, I told him I'd sync up the first take and walk him through it again—but he said he was ready to do it himself.

He took the film and the sound and synced the first take with the picture just the way I'd shown him. Then he rolled forward to the second take and did it again, as if he'd done it a hundred times before.

I was genuinely impressed with how quickly he'd caught on.

At eleven o'clock we ran the dailies with Jack and the cameraman, and every take was in synch. It reminded me of the time I synched up my first reel of dailies on Dr. Kildare and I did a perfect job as well. It was a prideful moment for me. We were now three generations of Bermans working in the movie business. If I counted Grandpa Harry we were, actually, four generations, but he was in sales, not production.

I showed Frank how to use the coding machine, and he coded all three reels before taking them back to the cutting room. Then I showed him how to break the film down into rolls for editing and label them with tags showing the beginning and ending code numbers of each shot.

I was pleased to see that his handwriting was excellent—just like mine—and each take was clearly identified. I couldn't wait to begin editing the new footage into the original tennis matches, and Frank stood watching over my shoulder. He was fascinated by the way my footage matched the original, and he complimented me on how well it worked.

We spent most of the day going through stock footage of Wimbledon crowds from various film libraries around town. I finally found three different crowd shots that I thought would work with the new footage and match the look of the original Wimbledon scenes.

I called an optical effects expert at Technicolor I'd worked with many times. If anyone in Hollywood could superimpose those crowd shots over the tennis courts at Poinsettia Park and make it look like Wimbledon, he was the guy.

I sent him the crowd footage along with reprints of the tennis shots I had filmed—delivered by special messenger so he could get started right away. He called me toward the end of the day and said it was tricky to line up the two sets of footage properly, and he wasn't sure if he could make it work—but he'd give it a try. He planned to shoot that night, when the optical effects cameras were free, and have the footage developed and printed before heading home.

The next morning, I was sitting at my editing bench, staring out the window, when I saw the Technicolor delivery truck pull through the main gate and park. A few minutes later, the driver came up the steps to my second-floor office and delivered a can of film.

I loaded it onto the Moviola—and the optical effects were perfect. I searched it frame by frame to check for glitches or camera bumps, but I couldn't find one.

At least twenty or twenty-five cuts of the Wimbledon matches had to be replaced with the new crowd shots, which would take me a couple of hours. I thought about calling Jack to come up and see the shots in the cutting room, but I decided to wait until I had cut them into the picture before showing him. I had a few other changes to make as well, and I was planning to run the full picture for him the next day. So, I went to work.

He called and asked if the stock shots had come back from Technicolor, and I lied—I told him they were having problems and wanted to re-shoot what they'd done the night before.

The next day, we ran the film—with all the new scenes cut in—and surprised Jack. He went crazy with glee and told the projectionist to stop the movie.

"How the hell did you do that?"

I told him he was giving me way too much credit, and that he should send a bottle of champagne to my friend at Technicolor, who had done a magnificent job. But Jack gave most of the credit to me.

"You're the one who composed those shots with a locked-down camera and chose the stock footage that would match."

He also praised me for knowing exactly what to shoot to round out the Wimbledon matches, and he went on and on about the fine editing and how I had saved the picture. He couldn't wait to run it for the network executives, who were calling every day to pressure him into screening the movie.

I was very happy—and I credit much of my success on this project to my Uncle Henry. I had learned so much from him by hanging out in his editing suite at MGM, watching him work, and asking questions. He had many wonderful tricks that he passed on to me.

Another thing working in my favor was the strong cast, which included Glynnis O'Connor as Little Mo, Anne Baxter as her mother, and Michael Learned as Eleanor Tennant, her famous tennis coach. Other cast members included Claude Akins, Martin Milner, Anne Francis, Mark Harmon, and Leslie Nielsen. The American tennis champion Tony Trabert also made a cameo appearance in the movie.

At the end of my second week on *Little Mo*, I took my son to lunch at Musso & Frank's and told him that his grandfather used to eat there all the time when he worked at RKO.

"That was over fifty years ago—and the food's still good."

While we were eating, I came up with a very cute idea. Jack was unhappy with one shot in the movie and wanted to replace it. It was the front door of a posh condominium, but it didn't look classy enough for him. He wanted to re-shoot using his own front door, which was more in keeping with the building shown in the movie. We were planning to shoot it the following day—Saturday.

We finished lunch and drove back to the studio. I sent Frank up to the cutting room, and I went in to see Jack. I told him my idea: to let Frank direct the insert of the front door. Frank would look through the lens and compose the shot. The cameraman would check the framing and give a nod that it was good, then roll the camera. When it was up to speed, the assistant would say, "Speed," just like on a Hollywood soundstage. Frank would then say, "Action," and after about ten seconds, "Cut!"

Jack loved the idea, and we both had a good laugh.

So, I went back to the cutting room and asked Frank if he'd like a chance to direct an added scene in the movie.

His eyes popped out of his head. "Are you kidding?" he asked.

"No, I'm quite serious... you've earned a shot with all your good work."

Before we left that day, we stopped by Jack's office so Frank could say goodbye. Jack handed him a check for $1,200 for his two weeks of work and then added two crisp $100 bills from his money clip as a bonus. I gave Frank a $100 bonus as well, so he walked out with $1,500. It was the most money he'd ever had at one time, and he was happier than I'd ever seen him.

The next day, we went over to Jack's condominium in the Sierra Towers overlooking Beverly Hills, and Frank got his first job as a director. I asked if he wanted to rehearse his lines, and he just laughed. I remembered myself as a child, rehearsing being a director in my room—and how my father had overheard me. I had to laugh at that memory, and I shared the story with Frank after we finished shooting.

It was one of my most memorable moments with my son, and I still get emotional whenever I think about it.

Frank wanted to stay on and finish the picture with me, but that wasn't an option. I told him my regular assistant was feeling better and coming back to work on Monday—and that Frank had to be back in school. The truth is, I would've loved to have him stay on. He was a natural, and I loved working with him.

When we finally ran *Little Mo* for the network executives, they were very happy with it, and Jack heaped a lot of praise on me after the screening. That didn't hurt with the executives in the room—who might one day be my future employers.

Jack kept me on for weeks afterward to supervise the re-recording session with music and sound effects, and to sit at Technicolor and monitor the color correction for the answer print—even though it wasn't in the budget to keep me on payroll that long.

Little Mo aired on a Sunday night in prime time and got enormous ratings—especially in Los Angeles. All of Hollywood wanted to see it, partly because this is a "tennis town," and partly because of the strong cast.

I invited my mother over for dinner that night to watch it with Susan, Frank, and me. I knew she was a fan—and an old friend of Anne Baxter from the early days at MGM—so I knew she'd enjoy the show.

She loved the movie... but all she had to say about Anne Baxter was, "Her eyebrows are too thin."

Frank, meanwhile, was bubbling with enthusiasm as he told his grandmother about working with me, learning how to be an assistant editor, and earning $1,500 in the process.

My dad, who had watched at home, called and raved about the show. He told me I had become a fine filmmaker.

It really lit me up.

I felt like putting on a cap and gown—because I had finally graduated. My father had always seen me as a confused and distracted young man with a questionable—or even hopeless—future. But now, he was heaping praise on me, and I finally felt vindicated.

It was a wonderful feeling... even better than the moment I walked off stage with my "Eddie" Award.

38

THE BOYS IN COMPANY C

As the fifth season of *Magnum P.I.* ended, I was hired to edit a feature film that was shooting on location in the Far East—a huge opportunity for me. *The Boys in Company C* told the story of a group of immature young men drafted into the Marines during the Vietnam conflict, led into battle by a psychotic officer who deliberately risks their lives for battlefield glory.

The director was the highly accomplished Sidney Furie, who had made several excellent films, including *The Ipcress File* with Michael Caine, *The Appaloosa* starring Marlon Brando, and *Lady Sings the Blues*, with Diana Ross playing the iconic Billie Holiday.

It was my first trip to the Far East, and I was thrilled. We were on location in Manila for almost three months, and it turned out to be very hard work. Sidney was shooting an enormous amount of film, and I had only one young Filipino boy to assist me. When you're on location, you're captive to whatever you're asked to do, and my assistant and I had to work nights and weekends just to keep up.

Back at home, the Academy Awards were approaching, and the

Board of Governors of the Academy had announced that my dad would receive the Irving Thalberg Award for lifetime achievement. It's the highest honor the Academy bestows on its most accomplished producers—and it was especially meaningful to Dad because of his lifelong friendship with Irving Thalberg.

He had already received the David O. Selznick Award from the Producers Guild of America—another prestigious lifetime achievement award—but the Thalberg was at the very top.

I had attended at least a dozen Academy Award shows, including several in years when Dad was nominated for Best Picture. As exciting as all those evenings were, I would have given them all up to be there for this one—to watch my father receive such an enormous tribute.

But I was halfway around the world, and it was an eighteen-hour flight each way. I discussed it with my father over the phone and ultimately decided it was just too difficult to make the trip for one night. I was already a little behind and working late into the night trying to catch up. Making that trip could have set me back hopelessly—and possibly jeopardized my job and my relationship with Sidney Furie, who had been gracious enough to hire me in the first place.

I didn't know if I'd be able to see the broadcast in Manila, so I asked some friends to tape it for me so I could watch it when I got home. It was a good thing I made those arrangements—because the show never aired in the Philippines. President Marcos had preempted the time slot and used it for political messaging.

When I got home, my sister Sue described the entire evening to me in great detail, including the Governor's Ball at the Beverly Hilton Hotel, where most of the winners went to celebrate and congratulate one another. Many of them came up to the table to pay their respects to Dad.

I would love to describe the evening myself, but I wasn't there. Those who attended told me it was magnificent. It was one of the great nights of my father's life, and it saddens me that I wasn't able to be there to share it with him.

After returning from Manila, the company rented space at Goldwyn Studios in Hollywood to complete the editing of *The Boys in Company C* and finish post-production. Goldwyn had one of the best dubbing stages in Hollywood, with Oscar-winning sound mixers, so I knew the sound would be terrific.

We were once again working long hours to finish the picture. Raymond Chow, the producer in Hong Kong, had negotiated a distribution deal with Paramount, who wanted to get it into theaters as soon as possible—and the release date was coming up fast. I was coming home late at night, leaving early in the morning, and was still exhausted from the trip to the Far East.

We had a huge complement of sound effects and music editors to help us finish the picture, and we previewed it at the Village Theater in Westwood to a packed house. Michael Eisner, the head of production at Paramount, came to the screening to see what he'd bought.

At three hours and thirty-two minutes, I knew the picture was far too long—but Sidney, like most directors, wanted to keep as much of his footage as possible.

Eisner brought him back to earth.

"Do you think this is an epic? You need to lose a third of this movie. I want to see it again when it's down around two hours."

It was a mammoth job to make all those changes, and it broke Sidney's heart to do it. But the picture was finally released at two hours and five minutes, and the long days and nights were finally over.

I came home to rest for a while before jumping back into work. I still had jet lag from spending three months in the Far East—and I was very tired.

HOME SWEET HOME—NOT SO SWEET

As it turns out, it was not a good time for me to have been away from home. I was unaware of what had been going on between my wife and my son, even though I had been speaking to them regularly on the phone.

Frank had just turned sixteen, and we had given him a new car—so he was out racing around town with his friends and playing small gigs with his band to earn money for gas and entertainment.

He was rebelling, like most teenagers, but he wasn't doing anything stupid or dangerous. He was, however, in conflict with Susan, who was having trouble controlling him—and she didn't know how to handle it. During the three months I was in Manila and Hong Kong, their relationship had deteriorated to the point where she was ready to throw him out of the house.

Frank had done well at Beverly High and had been accepted to several universities, including UCLA, which is where he wanted to go. But Susan was determined to have him go away to college. The situation had escalated so far that I wasn't sure I'd be able to repair the rift between them.

I tried to reason with my wife, telling her that if we forced him to go away to school, he probably wouldn't apply himself—and would eventually drop out. That was the last thing I wanted. I reminded her of all the hard work we had done to get Frank to this point in his life.

Against enormous odds, we had rescued him from his mother and brought him to live with us. We had tutored him every night until his reading skills and academic deficiencies were restored. Most importantly, we had given him love—and turned him into a happy child.

Now she wanted to tear it all down by sending him somewhere he didn't want to go. It made no sense to me.

But Susan was adamant. She wanted him away at college. She had taken care of him for eight years, and she wanted a break.

I suggested a compromise: that he go to school locally but live in a dorm. But that was also unacceptable to her. She didn't want him coming home every weekend to do laundry. She believed it would be better for him to be away from home, living on his own.

A MARRIAGE BEGINS TO ERODE

I started a slow burn. I didn't understand how she could be so callous about my son, who had grown into such a wonderful young man. Everyone in my family was crazy about him—including my father, who believed he had a very bright future. He was my mother's favorite grandchild, and no one could understand why my wife was causing us so much grief.

It was also affecting my relationship with Susan. I had missed her terribly while I was in the Far East, but now that I was home, I found her strangely distant and not at all comforting. I felt like a triumphant warrior returning home—and receiving none of the welcome or adulation I thought I was due.

I tried to arrange romantic dinners and create the perfect mood for lovemaking, but my wife would spend so much time in the bathroom that I'd fall asleep before she came to bed. I told her I was concerned about it, but she denied avoiding me and said it was simply my exhaustion. "You need to catch up on your sleep," she told me. "Then you'll see things differently."

It was true I needed rest—but, for the second time in my life, I was feeling the terrible pain of rejection.

There was something else going on—something I wasn't yet fully aware of. Susan's uncle, who had run the family company for many years, was in the process of selling it. Susan and her sister were about to inherit a lot of money from the sale.

My friend Sam, who had helped me get custody of Frank, pulled me aside one day and said, "Wake up and smell the coffee." He believed Susan was quietly planning a new life for herself—and it didn't include me. I was in denial, unwilling to believe what Sam was telling me. But I should have listened.

Susan had become disingenuous, untruthful, and clearly no longer interested in a life with me or my son. And I was too naïve—or too trusting—to see it.

She and her sister Lois went to New York to sign the papers and receive their checks. They were something in the neighborhood of $5 million apiece. When Susan came back, she was a different person. We had built a great partnership, but it had suddenly turned into a corporation. And she was the Chairman of the Board, President, and Treasurer.

I didn't even know what my role was in this new company.

We finally reached an agreement about school: Frank would go to Chapman College in the City of Orange. It was more than an hour's drive from our house—closer to an hour and a half in rush hour traffic. He wouldn't be running home on the weekends.

It wasn't what I wanted. It wasn't what *Frank* wanted. But at least she agreed to it.

He was heartbroken to leave home, and when we talked about it, there were tears in his eyes. It made me furious. I told my wife that Frank had cried when I explained the arrangement.

She was unmoved.

Amazingly unmoved.

And I could see then—clear as day—that there was a rough trail ahead for all of us.

My sister Sue was horrified by what was going on, and she was more than generous. She told Frank he could come and stay with her in the spare bedroom anytime he wanted. She loved him dearly, and he was very close to his cousin, Michele, who was thrilled that he'd be visiting.

I told Frank he could sleep at Sue's house every weekend if he wanted, and I'd go over and visit him there. I was so proud of him. I promised I'd do everything in my power to transfer him to a local school the following year.

I couldn't believe how much my wife Susan had changed—and I began to realize it was all about the money. She wanted everything her own way, and it didn't matter to her in the least what I wanted. I told her I didn't understand how we had reached such a low point in our marriage—and that I didn't know how we were going to fix it.

She said she didn't either.

"Then what are we doing together?" I asked.

Her answer was shocking—but it shouldn't have been.

"You can move out anytime you want."

That hit me like a truck. I knew things were bad, but I hadn't realized they were *this* bad. And she didn't even want to try. I suggested we go into marital therapy—but she wasn't interested.

Once again, I felt used—the same way I'd felt when Nancy left me. I realized I'd been little more than Susan's meal ticket while she waited for her inheritance. Sam had been right all along. Now that she had her money, she wanted a whole new life—and it didn't include me or my son.

The next day, I went out and rented a furnished apartment in Sherman Oaks, not far from Universal Studios. I tried to get as much rest as I could before starting my new show: *Battlestar Galactica*.

ANOTHER FAMILY TRAGEDY

Dad was becoming more involved with his second family and dealing with a personal tragedy that struck without warning. Kathryn's daughter, Gingi, suffered a brain aneurysm, and several operations were performed to save her life. She was in the middle of a divorce from her husband, Harry Korshak, who was forced to take their daughter, Kate, to live with him in his apartment. But he wasn't really able to care for her properly.

Kate was sent to live with his parents—Bea and Sidney Korshak—in their home in Beverly Hills, where she was in good hands.

After her surgeries, Gingi spent a year and a half in a rehabilitation center in Orange County. She had to re-learn how to speak, how to walk, and how to regain several other critical motor functions.

When she was finally discharged, she could speak well enough and walk slowly with a cane, though it remained challenging for her. She had suffered bleeding from one of the arteries in her brain and was fitted with a cerebral shunt to relieve the pressure. The shunt transferred excess blood from her brain to an artery in her intestines.

At first, the shunt was mounted externally. It was about the size of a vacuum cleaner hose—bulky and awkward—and she was embarrassed to wear it outside the house. Eventually, it was replaced with an internal shunt that wasn't visible, and she felt much more comfortable with her appearance.

She moved in with Dad and Kathryn at their home on Roxbury Drive, taking up residence in what had originally been the maid's room and bath downstairs, just off the kitchen. But Gingi wasn't happy with the accommodations. She told her mother that she should have been given her own apartment with a caretaker to prepare her meals. When Kathryn told her that would be prohibitively expensive, Gingi replied that she knew Pandro could afford it.

She was angry that life had dealt her such a vicious blow, and she took it out on everyone—including her mother, and especially my dad, whom she treated with open disrespect, despite his kindness in allowing her to come live with them.

Gingi had a habit of revealing family secrets just to shock or provoke people. She once told my sister Sue that Kathryn hated her —because Sue was Dad's favorite, and because she had the potential to cause trouble. Apparently, it was true, even though Kathryn denied it vehemently. Whether it was or not, we all believed it. Kathryn had always been somewhat cool toward us, and we suspected she saw us as threats to her position in one way or another.

After witnessing all of this, I made a conscious decision to never get into any personal discussions with Gingi—and I certainly never confided anything sensitive. She was trouble, and I could only hope she wasn't making life too miserable for my father, though I didn't feel it was my place to bring it up with him.

Sue, however, was around more often than I was, and she was able to get more out of Dad. She told me he regretted inviting Gingi to move in, but at that point, there wasn't much he could do about it.

39

BATTLESTAR GALACTICA

Battlestar Galactica was a science fiction odyssey inspired by the original *Star Wars*, which had premiered the same week I returned from the Far East. The first public screening was at noon, and Sidney Furie and I drove up to the Pantages Theatre in Hollywood around 11:00 a.m. to see if there was any buzz. We were stunned to find lines stretching for several blocks down Hollywood Boulevard.

George Lucas had held private screenings for newspaper and trade journalists, under the tacit agreement that no reviews would be published until after opening day.

The big question: what makes people flock to a movie they haven't read about, haven't heard buzz from friends about, and don't even know if they'll even like it?

Advertising helps—but plenty of heavily promoted movies open with a bang and then crash and burn.

I talked about this with my dad many times. His take? "If we knew the answer to that, every movie would be a hit—and we'd all be rich.

The greatest talents in Hollywood and on Broadway have all had flops."

The truth is nobody really knows. Every film is a gamble, even the ones based on bestselling novels or long-running Broadway hits.

Star Wars became one of the biggest box office successes of all time. George Lucas eventually sold the entire franchise—films, rights, and merchandising—to Disney for $4 billion. And that universe will go on making money for years to come.

It was that runaway success that lit the fire for *Battlestar Galactica*—the most challenging show I ever worked on.

Glen Larson created a wildly inventive sci-fi fantasy built around the premise that human civilization had long since left Earth and inhabited a group of planets known as the Twelve Colonies. These colonies had been engaged in a brutal war with a cybernetic race called the Cylons, whose single goal was the annihilation of the human race.

The Cylons were metal beings powered by human-like intelligence, and they became a terrifying force across the galaxy. The humans, on the other hand, were losing. Each episode featured a major space battle—an ambitious visual feat, especially back then. Many of the special effects had to be created by Industrial Light & Magic (ILM), and stitching those elements together was no small feat.

ILM was a company that George Lucas founded to supply *Star Wars* with everything needed to bring its spectacular special effects to life. That included sophisticated models and miniatures, computer graphics, digital matte paintings, animation, optical effects—an entire arsenal of visual magic the likes of which Hollywood had never seen before.

Lucas attracted the most talented people from all over the United States—and beyond. They were the wizards behind the curtain, creating the cinematic magic for all the *Star Wars* films. And they brought that same expertise to *Battlestar Galactica*—at least, the kind of magic a television budget could afford.

Manufacturing that level of visual technology was both expensive and time-consuming. Because of this, our editors had to piece together the action sequences using footage shot that week, stock shots from earlier episodes, and whatever else we could find to complete the space battles. When we had gaps, we'd design additional effects and send them to the optical department, hoping they could build something usable when nothing was available from ILM.

The biggest challenge was time. Each episode had to be delivered to the network just a day or two before its scheduled air date. It was brutal—physically and mentally draining for everyone involved in the production.

At one point, I came up with an idea for a script that didn't include an air battle. It bought some much-needed time. I ran it by Glen, and he liked it. What I didn't know was that he pitched it to ABC right away—and they liked it too. So, Glen came down to my cutting room and told me to get started writing it.

Of course, I wasn't relieved of my editing duties. So, the script would have to be written at night and on weekends... assuming I had a weekend off, which wasn't often. My routine became a grind: come home, make a sandwich, brew a pot of coffee, and start writing. Around 10:00 p.m., I'd pop a Dexedrine, pour another cup of coffee, and keep going until two in the morning. Then, after four and a half hours of sleep, I'd get up at 6:30, shower, and head back to the editing room.

Since I wasn't an experienced television writer, it took me nearly three weeks to write a one-hour episode—and it still needed polish. The professional writers could knock out a script in a week or less, which amazed me. But of course, they were writing during the day, when they were fresh. Not to mention they had loads of experience under their belts.

My episode begins on a distant asteroid, where a small group of people from one of the Twelve Colonies migrate in hopes of building a better life. They bring with them a number of technologically advanced machines designed to dispense the essentials—food, supplies, medicine—everything they will need to survive. The colony consists of just twenty-five people and one doctor responsible for all their medical needs.

As the episode opens, the entire group is standing in line, waiting anxiously for the space shuttle's arrival. It's the shuttle's final trip to this remote outpost, so anyone hoping to leave has to board the shuttle—or be stranded indefinitely. The Cylons have moved into the surrounding region, and future shuttle missions will be far too dangerous to attempt.

While they wait, colonists purchase tickets from a unique all-purpose machine at the shuttle station. This machine doesn't just print shuttle passes—it also performs wedding ceremonies, issues birth and death certificates, and handles a surprising array of bureaucratic needs.

A young couple steps up to be married, inserting five tokens into the machine. Out pops their marriage certificate. Then the machine asks if they'd like flowers. They feed in two more tokens and out comes a large bouquet of red roses. The machine proceeds to ask a few more questions, finally ending with a strange, oddly humorous one: "Would you like your divorce to be processed now?"

The shuttle lands, and the pilot orders everyone to board immediately—they've been spotted by Cylon warships, and an attack is imminent. As the shuttle lifts off, the Cylons begin to arrive. The passengers watch in horror through the windows as their former home explodes into fiery debris. One massive fragment nearly strikes the shuttle as it climbs to safety.

The leader of the group is furious. He demands that the pilot turn back and engage the Cylons. But no one else agrees with him—not even the pilot. While the shuttle is armed with some heavy weaponry, taking on the Cylons directly would be suicidal. They are now in pursuit, and the only hope is to outrun them and make it back to their home planet, where a fleet of warships stands ready to defend them.

The shuttle enters warp speed, but the Cylons remain close enough to fire off a few missiles. One detonates near the shuttle, jolting it violently. Inside, the group's leader is thrown to the floor. Clutching his chest, he suffers a heart attack. The shuttle's doctor has little to offer him beyond a few emergency pills.

Back on the home planet, ground control is alerted to the situation. A medical team is dispatched to meet the shuttle on arrival, and human pilots scramble to their warships, preparing for a potential battle.

As the shuttle nears the colony, the Cylons spot the launch of the human warships. Rather than face the oncoming resistance, they retreat and race for home. The group leader is rushed into surgery—and survives.

I finished the script on a Sunday. Glen read it Monday morning and gave it the thumbs up. That evening, he gathered the team for a meeting with the network, giving everyone the day to review the script.

During the meeting, the critiques came fast and furious and included push back on the *idea of the machine asking the newlyweds if they wanted to process their divorce at the same time as the wedding. They thought that was too cynical for American audiences.*

Glen and I disagreed. We saw it as edgy, tongue-in-cheek humor—a wink at the growing divorce rate in the U.S.—and Glen told them so.

But that wasn't their only gripe. The network had a slew of nitpicky and time-consuming notes. The script would essentially require a page-one rewrite. It didn't matter to them that it was already Monday night, and the episode was scheduled to begin shooting on Thursday. Even the fastest writers at the studio couldn't turn it around that fast—and I wanted no part of the madness.

Glen told me the staff would handle the rewrite, since footage was already piling up in my editing room on another episode, and I needed to get back to it immediately. I was furious.

"Where do these forty-watt junior network clones get off demanding changes like that—and getting the network to back them up?" I asked Glen. It was obvious from the way the network representatives spoke, they didn't know the first thing about filmmaking. None of them had ever been writers or directors—nor would they ever be capable of that kind of creativity.

Glen's answer was predictable.

"Nepotism. These are the unemployable nephews and brothers-in-law of the most powerful people at the networks. They get these jobs because of pressure from their wives and mothers."

Ah, nepotism. I was all too familiar with it—and I was beginning to understand my father's zero-tolerance policy for it. I told Glen I wanted nothing more to do with the episode. I didn't even want to edit it. Luckily, it came up in the rotation of another editor, and I told Glen to take my name off the credits entirely.

When I saw the episode on television, it bore no resemblance to my script—except for the chase scene with the Cylon warships. I swore then and there that I would never write for network television again. (Of course, later in life I changed my mind. But by that time, I was able to do it on my own terms.)

Not long after, I was working on another show with a group of young writers I liked and respected. Over lunch one day at the Universal commissary, they confided they were dealing with the same kind of clueless interference—from yet another group of network morons—and they had no idea what to do.

I shared my *Battlestar Galactica* story. They'd read a copy of my original draft and told me they liked the way I wrote dialogue. Then they made me an offer that was hard to refuse.

From time to time, they wanted me to write a missing act for their show. They'd send over a story outline and whatever scenes had already been written, and I'd deliver the missing act within a couple of days. Depending on the length, they'd pay me $3,000 to $5,000. I could write at home at night, email it over, and they'd send it back with any revisions. Once they were happy with the work, they'd deposit the money straight into my bank account. And best of all: not a soul would ever know it happened.

They would look like heroes to their producers and the network for delivering the episode before deadline, and I could make some quick cash working from home.

Of course, it all had to be kept strictly under wraps. If it got out, they could be expelled from the Writers Guild of America for submitting someone else's work under their own names. But as the saying goes, desperate times call for desperate measures.

· * · ★ · ★ · ★ · · ★ *·

BUCK ROGERS

Battlestar Galactica lasted only two seasons. The special effects drove the budget sky-high, and ABC had no choice but to cancel it. But Glen Larson wasn't finished with outer space adventures. He developed a new TV series around the character of *Buck Rogers*.

I worked on the pilot, which was released as a feature film in North America and surprisingly grossed $21 million. That success convinced NBC to commission a weekly series—this time with fewer elaborate effects and animations. To keep costs down, many of the props and digital matte paintings left over from *Galactica* were reused.

The space battles, however, were just as challenging to edit as they had been on *Galactica*, and I was developing a reputation for being an expert in that kind of editing. It wasn't exactly to my liking. Most television shows were much simpler to cut, and I was spending far too many late nights piecing together laser battles in my cutting room.

By the second season, I told the studio I wanted to move on to another show. But they claimed there was no one else in the Editors Guild with the right experience, and they offered me a substantial raise to stay. So, I stayed—but my social life paid the price.

It had been two years since my divorce from Susan, and I needed to reinvest the money from the sale of our house to avoid a hefty capital gains tax. My sister Cindy, now a real estate broker, found me a great place in Benedict Canyon, near Mulholland Drive. The location was ideal—a quick drive to Universal, and close to other Valley studios like Warner Bros., CBS Television, and Disney. It also wasn't far from the Westside studios like MGM, Fox, and Paramount. Eventually, I became an independent editor and worked at all of them.

The house was dark and dreary when I moved in, but with help from a couple of women I was dating, I managed to redecorate without making any major mistakes I'd regret later. I followed the "less is more" principle when it came to color: I reupholstered the furniture in off-whites with subtle patterns and chose light wood finishes for new pieces. Color came from books in the large bookcases, fresh flowers, and bright cushions on the couches. It worked surprisingly well.

My sister Sue, who inherited our mother's excellent taste, was impressed. She said she could never have done such a lovely job herself—but I was certain she could have done even better.

I was happy with the house once it was finished—but I didn't have anyone to share it with. Since my divorce, I had gone out with dozens of women, but for one reason or another, none of those relationships turned serious. So, I developed a few "specialty relationships" that didn't necessarily involve intimacy.

There was one woman I played tennis with on Sunday mornings, followed by brunch. I enjoyed her company, but I wasn't physically attracted to her. Another companion loved the theater, and we had stimulating conversations about the plays we saw together—but she was a bit neurotic. After a few hours with her, I usually found myself wanting an early exit.

I kept dating, one after another, slowly becoming an expert on the San Fernando Valley's geography. I had taken just about every off-ramp on the Ventura Freeway between Burbank and Woodland Hills to pick up dates. Most of them were "one and done." I could usually tell within fifteen minutes if I wouldn't be seeing someone again—and sometimes, the feeling was mutual.

I wasn't sure what the issue was. Maybe it was my cologne, or my way of speaking. It could've been the car—a late-model black Lincoln—which I didn't think anyone would be embarrassed to ride in. Still, I couldn't seem to find a rhythm or comfort zone with any of them.

I avoided dating actresses or others in the film business—most were focused on their careers, not settling down. But I *was* looking for something real. I wanted to get married again. I wanted another child. But the window for that was closing fast. I was now in my forties, and most of the women I dated were in their late thirties or early forties. If I was going to have another child, I needed to find the right person—and soon.

40

A PATCH OF BLUE

My father was in his twenty-fifth year as a producer at MGM, but there was no cocktail party or dinner to celebrate such an auspicious anniversary. The studio had changed dramatically, and Dad was no longer happy there. He was engaged in a major battle with Dan Melnick, who had replaced the Schenck brothers as Chairman of the Board of Loews Incorporated. Melnick and the New York office were pushing back hard against a film my dad was determined to make, and I was convinced it would never get off the ground. We were all amazed when Dad finally won the fight.

A Patch of Blue was originally a novel by Elizabeth Kata titled *Be Ready with Bells and Drums*, which had been passed over by nearly every literary agent and producer in Hollywood. No one seemed interested in bringing it to the screen.

The book found its way to Dad through Jo Green, the wife of prominent English director Guy Green, with whom Dad had become friendly on one of his many trips to London. Years after its original publication, Jo stumbled across a paperback copy in a drugstore in

Sydney, Australia. She and Guy loved it and sent it to Dad. Guy was eager to direct it—if Dad could get the project moving.

Dad read the book and immediately fell in love with it. He was thrilled that Guy Green shared his passion. Guy had been the cinematographer on *Great Expectations* and had won an Oscar for it in 1948. Since then, he had become a respected director, with credits including *Light in the Piazza*, starring Olivia de Havilland and Rossano Brazzi. Dad considered him a major talent, and attaching Guy to the project would certainly boost its chances of approval. Still, there were significant obstacles ahead.

The story centered on miscegenation—a romantic, mixed-race relationship—and the year was 1965. That same year, violence erupted during the Selma to Montgomery marches in Alabama. On the Edmund Pettus Bridge, police attacked peaceful protestors with nightsticks and tear gas. Seventeen Black Americans were hospitalized with serious injuries. The footage made national headlines.

Emotions were running high, and Loews Inc. felt it was the wrong time to release a film on such a sensitive subject. But when Dad secured Sidney Poitier for the leading role, the conversation shifted dramatically. Poitier was one of the biggest box office stars in America, and Dad's strategy was to lean into the social revolution, not shy away from it. He believed this film could draw both Black and White audiences—each for their own reasons—and that there might be gold at the end of the rainbow.

The story follows a blind white girl, played by newcomer Elizabeth Hartman, who lives with her abusive, prostitute mother (portrayed by Shelley Winters). In a nearby park, she meets a kind Black businessman, played by Sidney Poitier. Unaware of his race, she's drawn to his gentle nature, and he returns each day to see her. As they fall in love, her mother discovers the truth and does everything in her power to tear them apart. But they fight for what they've found, and in the end, love prevails.

Dad and Dan Melnick fought bitterly over this movie, and Dad finally threatened to produce it elsewhere if MGM wouldn't support it. His ten-picture deal with the studio was nearing its end, and he began quietly pitching the project to other companies. Despite the controversy surrounding the film, other studios were starting to show interest.

Melnick was worried the picture wouldn't perform well in the South—a legitimate concern at the time. Ultimately, a different version of the film was released in southern states, with the romantic scenes between Sidney Poitier and Elizabeth Hartman excised so that the film would be allowed to play in Southern theaters.

The deal to make *A Patch of Blue* was verbally agreed to three different times, and Melnick backed out twice. The contracts weren't signed until a special salary arrangement was worked out with Sidney Poitier.

Melnick was convinced the picture would lose money, and the only significant expense was Poitier's salary. As a result, Sidney and my father agreed to something almost unheard of in those days: Sidney would reduce his salary from $750,000 to $200,000, and he and Dad would each receive 10% of the gross box office revenue instead. That way, if the film bombed, the studio wouldn't take as much of a hit—and neither would Dad or Sidney, who'd only profit if the film did.

But *A Patch of Blue* turned out to be a huge success. Dad and Sidney each received $1.45 million for their 10% of the gross. And since Dad's independent production company already owned 50% of the net profits, he was more than satisfied with the outcome. MGM, on the other hand, was left with little or no profit after deducting production costs and expenses for prints and advertising. Melnick was furious. He had made a bad deal and watched the profits walk right out the door with my father and Sidney Poitier.

And that wasn't the only drama during the making of *A Patch of Blue*. Shelley Winters had been causing trouble on set from day one, and complaints were making their way back to my dad.

Hank Moonjean—Dad's right-hand man—was the best assistant director at MGM and worked on most of Dad's pictures. Dad loved him because Hank could handle just about any difficult situation, whether it involved actors, egos, or unexpected issues during production.

Shelley Winters had been living with her boyfriend, Tony Franciosa, and neither of them had worked for some time. They were spending their nights cooking exotic meals, getting drunk, and sleeping in late. As a result, Shelley was late to the set almost every day—and always in a foul mood. If she wasn't in the scene being filmed, she would retreat to her trailer and blast loud music, refusing to turn it down until the second or third complaint.

When she *was* on camera, she frequently forgot her lines, forcing the crew to waste time on extra takes and pickups. Hank had tried to handle the situation diplomatically, doing everything he could to get her back on track—but she wasn't responding to him or to anyone else.

Hank had previously succeeded with difficult stars like Elizabeth Taylor, who was known for arriving one or two hours late each day. During *Cat on a Hot Tin Roof*, he won her over by making her special Turkish coffee and delivering her favorite pastries to her dressing room. She adored Hank—and even invited him to all her parties.

He was well-liked by nearly every actress at MGM, but Shelley Winters was a different story. She was as nasty as she could be to everyone on the production, including Hank and the director, Guy Green.

On the fourth day of shooting, Hank went up to Dad's office and told him about the ongoing problems with Shelley. He explained that he had tried everything he could to get her to cooperate but was getting nowhere. He feared that Dad would have to step in and "drop a bombshell" to finally get her to do her job.

I knew Hank very well, and he told me this story personally. It later appeared in his book *Bring in the Peacocks*, which was published a year or two before he passed away. My dad had his own version of the incident, but Hank's account always struck me as the more realistic one.

After listening to Hank's complaints about Shelley Winters, Dad told him to sit down on the couch—he'd show him how to handle it. He called down to the set and requested Shelley report to his office immediately. When she arrived, Dad made her wait twenty minutes while he and Hank talked business.

Finally, he brought her into the office and told her to sit down on the couch beside Hank.

Dad picked up the phone and pretended to be in the middle of a conversation. After a few moments, he covered the mouthpiece with his hand and said to Shelley, "I've got Eileen Heckart on the line. She's very interested in playing your role in *A Patch of Blue*., I'm considering replacing you after seeing three days of dailies in which you are giving the worst performance of your career.

Then he took his hand off the receiver and said, "I'll call you back in a few minutes, Eileen," and hung up the phone.

He turned back to Shelley and told her, flat out, that he'd been warned—by agents, producers, and others around town—that she was finished. That she wasn't a decent actress anymore. That he never should've cast her in the first place.

Shelley was horrified. She did everything short of getting down on her knees and begging not to be fired. Dad listened to her apologies for a couple of minutes, then told her to get back down to the set, get to work, and stop giving everyone a hard time.

"If I see one more day of that lousy performance... you're through."

She thanked my father over and over, promising him she would do better. Her whole body was shaking as she left the office. Hank was so embarrassed he looked like he wanted to crawl out of his skin. "That was brutal, Pandro," he said.

My dad nodded. "Sometimes you have to be that way to get things done."

Hank never said it, and neither did my dad, but I always imagined the two of them had a good laugh after Shelley walked out.

That little pep talk was just what the doctor ordered. Shelley responded with a terrific performance—one that won her the Oscar for Best Supporting Actress. Elizabeth Hartman, in her first role outside of a college play, was nominated for Best Actress and received the Golden Globe for Most Promising Newcomer.

Tragically, Elizabeth committed suicide twenty-two years later by jumping off the roof of a building.

Sidney Poitier was thrilled that Dad had cast him in the movie. Not only did it earn him a substantial payday, but it also elevated his career in a major way. He was always very fond of Dad and lit up with a big smile whenever my sisters and I ran into him. Dad had truly launched Sidney's film career with *Blackboard Jungle*, and Sidney remained eternally grateful. He often credited my father with giving him his start.

MY CLEVER FATHER

A year later, when Kathryn's contract expired, Dan Melnick sent my father a memo informing him that her contract would not be renewed. He clearly thought this would get under Dad's skin and serve as payback for outsmarting him—and for collecting all that money from *A Patch of Blue*.

But Dad got the last laugh. Kathryn's contract was tied to Dad's independent production company, and when Melnick refused to resign her, Dad's own contract as an independent producer was nullified as well. That contract still had two unproduced pictures Dad technically owed MGM, but now he was released from that obligation entirely.

When his lawyer told him the news, Dad was jubilant. He had grown to hate MGM for the treatment he'd received from the New York office, and he couldn't wait to send Melnick his letter of resignation. He had several other movies he wanted to produce and didn't want to battle for approval on every project the way he had with *A Patch of Blue*. Dad quickly signed a new deal with 20th Century Fox, and Dick Zanuck welcomed him with open arms.

When Nicholas Schenck heard that Melnick had failed to re-sign my father, he called and tried to persuade Dad to stay. He promised that Melnick wouldn't interfere with him going forward. But Dad was ready to move on. He had two new projects that Fox was eager to produce, and he was looking forward to a fresh start—hopefully in greener pastures.

Fox had two special bungalows with multiple offices on the lot—large, elaborate spaces reserved for their top-tier producers. One had belonged to Jerry Wald and had been vacant since his death in 1962. The other was lavishly redecorated and given to Dad and Kathryn. Dick Zanuck was rolling out the red carpet.

It reminded me of the way Louis B. Mayer had treated Dad when he first arrived at MGM. And I was happy to see it. My father was a Hollywood icon. He had earned that respect through decades of great filmmaking.

In the last few years, Fox had begun to recover from the *Cleopatra* disaster. The studio's financial healing had really started a little earlier, thanks to a string of successful Marilyn Monroe films and major hits like *The Longest Day*—a highly accurate account of the Allied invasion of Normandy with a massive international cast. It was released a year before *Cleopatra* and gave the studio an early financial boost.

Planet of the Apes, starring Charlton Heston, also brought in big money. And *The Sound of Music* was a blockbuster, becoming one of the studio's highest-grossing films of all time.

Activity was once again bustling on the Fox lot, and Dad was thrilled to see it—especially after the quiet, depressing days at MGM, where there had been little to no production. The MGM lot had started to feel like a ghost town, with barely anyone walking the streets and empty sound stages casting long shadows in the late afternoon sun. It marked the beginning of the end for MGM. The studio was eventually sold to Sony Pictures, and much of its legendary film library was sold off to Turner Entertainment.

For over a year, Dad had been working on a massive project. He had acquired the rights to *The Alexandria Quartet*, a series of four novels by the acclaimed English author Lawrence Durrell. The tetralogy—*Justine*, *Balthazar*, *Mountolive*, and *Clea*—was described by Durrell as "an investigation of modern love."

The story is set in Alexandria, Egypt, before and during World War II. The first three books explore the same characters and events from three different perspectives. The fourth, *Clea*, takes place six years later and reflects on the earlier events, attempting to untangle what really happened and show how time has reshaped the narrative.

The Alexandria Quartet was both a critical and financial success, though it was a complex and sometimes challenging read. I read all four books, but it was time-consuming. I often found myself flipping back to earlier volumes to compare perspectives and track the differences in how events were portrayed.

As you might imagine, condensing four novels into a single two-hour screenplay posed enormous challenges. Dad brought in George Cukor early on to collaborate with him and screenwriter Larry Marcus, and it took them over a year to craft a version they believed would work. When they submitted it to Dick Zanuck and other executives at Fox, the response was lukewarm—the script was still considered somewhat confusing. So, Dad and Cukor went back to work with Marcus for several more months and eventually produced a version the studio accepted as a shooting script.

Most of the film was shot on location in Tunisia, with certain interior scenes filmed on the Fox lot. Tunisia proved to be a difficult location logistically. Some of the cast and crew fell ill from food and water contamination, forcing delays and extending the shooting schedule. As a result, the production experienced significant cost overruns.

The cast featured Anouk Aimée, Dirk Bogarde, and Robert Forster—all of whom delivered strong performances under Cukor's direction. Having read all four books and the initial draft of the screenplay, I was curious to see how the story would come together after so many revisions. Still, I chose not to read the final draft. I knew there would be many changes during filming and editing, and I preferred to wait and experience the finished picture.

Toward the end of the shoot in Tunisia, a major problem arose. Anouk Aimée abruptly announced she was leaving the production because she could no longer bear being apart from her lover—and future husband—Albert Finney. Everyone, including my dad, Cukor, and several others, tried to talk her out of it.

Cukor persuaded his friend Omar Sharif to travel from Egypt to the location in Tunisia to help convince Anouk Aimée to stay. He warned her that abandoning the production would have dire consequences for her career. But Sharif failed to sway her, so Dad tried another approach—he reached out to Albert Finney and asked if he could come stay with her on location. Unfortunately, Finney was tied up filming on another shoot and couldn't leave. Still, he managed to speak to Anouk by phone and finally convinced her to remain and finish the picture. If she hadn't, Fox would've faced serious legal and financial complications, as they wouldn't have been able to release the film, and lawsuits would have been inevitable.

When my dad returned from Tunisia, he was utterly spent—physically and emotionally. I had never seen him like that, and I was truly concerned. Fortunately, he was able to stay home and rest for several weeks while the editors assembled the first cut. Unfortunately, decisions that should have been made during production were now being hashed out in post, and it made the process far more difficult.

Dad was not at all happy with the initial cut. It took two months of revisions before the film was considered ready for release.

For me, the movie worked—aside from a few minor issues. But I could see how it might be confusing for audiences unfamiliar with the books and characters. It didn't fare well at the sneak preview, which sent Dad and the editors back into the cutting room for another month. When I saw the final version upon release, I honestly couldn't tell whether the extra editing had helped. It looked very much like what I'd seen earlier. The plot was still confusing, and audiences just didn't connect with it.

After all that time, effort, and ambition, *The Alexandria Quartet* was a commercial failure. Dad had poured his heart and soul into it, and the disappointment hit him hard.

Dad was getting desperate to find a project he actually wanted to produce, and the clock on his contract was ticking. Many of the best writers had migrated to television, which offered steadier work—and in some cases, better pay—especially if they created a show that ran for several seasons.

Fox, meanwhile, had a vast library of older films they were eager to remake. Since they already owned the rights, it was cheaper and more convenient than buying new material. Dad spent countless hours screening those old movies and reading through their scripts, but nothing grabbed him.

He brought in some new projects he'd discovered, but the studio rejected most of them. One night over dinner, he confided in me that he wasn't particularly excited about any of the scripts he'd been offered. Still, he said, if he could get the studio to approve even one of them, he'd bring in strong writers to rework it into something better.

What he couldn't understand—and what was really eating at him—was why the Fox executives kept turning down all his projects, effectively preventing him from fulfilling the very contract they had signed.

41

AIRWOLF

NBC canceled *Buck Rogers* after its second season, and I moved on to a new show created by Don Bellisario, a former partner of Glen Larson, with whom I'd previously worked on *Magnum P.I.* The new series featured a high-tech military helicopter code-named *Airwolf*. Jan-Michael Vincent starred as the pilot, with Ernest Borgnine as his co-pilot. The show became an instant hit once it hit the airwaves.

The helicopter—a heavily modified Bell 222—was outfitted with cutting-edge weaponry, including missiles and heat-shield rockets designed to deflect incoming attacks by drawing enemy missiles toward the heat source.

Airwolf was portrayed as a top-secret CIA weapon, hidden in a natural cave known as "The Lair," located in a remote area called the Valley of the Gods—designed to resemble Monument Valley in Utah. The helicopter and its crew operated under the CIA's command and were dispatched on covert missions both overseas and within U.S. cities. Because of its incredible speed and maneuverability, few people ever got a good look at it. It was deployed during Cold War military ops and even in urban crime scenarios—whenever local police or the National Guard needed backup. On the ground, *Airwolf* looked like something from outer space, capable of outrunning and outmaneuvering jet fighters.

That speed and agility were a big part of the show's appeal—and much of it was achieved through clever optical effects in the editing room.

Jan-Michael Vincent, the dashing lead, was a heartthrob who drew younger viewers. Ernest Borgnine, an Oscar-winning fan favorite, appealed to older audiences.

But *Airwolf* was no picnic for the editors. Every episode was packed with aerial battles, high-speed chases, and air-to-ground combat sequences. It was just as complex and time-consuming to edit as *Battlestar Galactica* and *Buck Rogers*. The difference? The scripts leaned on real-world geopolitics rather than science fiction, which gave it a different tone—but didn't make it any easier to cut.

Airwolf lasted four seasons before CBS pulled the plug. After that, I decided I was officially done with shows that had elaborate flying sequences.

．·＊·★．＊．★．．＊＊·

ELECTRONIC EDITING—AN ENORMOUS CHALLENGE

As the second season of *Airwolf* ended, I got a call from a producer named Edgar Scherick. He offered me a job on a two-hour TV movie called *The Stepford Children*, a sequel to his 1975 hit *The Stepford Wives*, which had starred Katharine Ross. The original film was about a group of women in a small Connecticut town who were turned into robots.

Since I had never met Scherick, I asked how he'd heard of me. He told me no one had recommended me—he was simply impressed by my credits, had seen some of my work, and liked it. Once he learned I was a member of the American Cinema Editors, he was convinced I was the right person for the job.

Filming was set to begin within a week. He told me to report to a facility in Burbank called Laser Edit, where postproduction would take place. He also asked for my home address and said he'd send a messenger with the final shooting script within the hour.

The name Edgar Scherick rang a bell—I vaguely remembered my dad mentioning him. I was pretty sure he was a member of the Producers Guild, so I called my father and asked if he'd recommended me. He swore he hadn't. "I haven't spoken to him in quite a while," he said.

When the script arrived, I read it immediately. It was solid science fiction—very much in the vein of the original movie, except this time it included the Stepford children, who were also robotic, just like their mothers.

The next morning, I headed to Burbank and arrived at Laser Edit at 9:30 a.m. I was taken straight to the office of the company's president, Bill Breshears—a white-haired, boot-wearing Texan who spoke with such a thick accent, I had to fight the urge to laugh. He wore a Stetson and a huge silver belt buckle inlaid with turquoise stones to hold up his jeans.

Bill took me down to one of the editing rooms—referred to as "bays"—and I had never seen anything like it. It looked like the cockpit of a B-29 bomber: an enormous panel loaded with buttons, switches, levers, thumbwheels, and flashing lights. The editor sat in front of this console and typed instructions into a built-in keyboard that triggered electronic edits from material stored on laserdiscs sourced from eight different machines. The edited images were recorded onto 3/4-inch videotape and displayed on two color monitors stacked on top of the panel.

It was a sight to behold—like something dreamed up by an electronic megalomaniac.

I asked Bill where the film was edited, and he threw back his head and laughed.

"We don't use no *feelm* here."

I told him he'd better find a computer expert, because I'd never edited anything but film—and there was no way I could operate one of those machines.

"I don't need no computer expert," he said with a grin. "Ah need a good *feelm* editor."

He told me he'd seen my work and, like Scherick, believed I was the right man for the job.

I pointed out that shooting was starting in less than a week, and it would take me *months* to learn how to use that monster of a machine. He assured me his best guy would teach me how to edit with optical discs—and that I'd be up to speed in no time.

My first lesson would begin after lunch in one of the empty editing bays. I was dumbfounded. Still, I decided to give it a shot—because I'm the kind of guy who likes to tackle a challenge. That said, I was pretty sure this one would be too much. I'd just bought my first IBM personal computer and barely knew how to use *that* thing—never mind a futuristic console like this.

The editor assigned to train me was a terrific teacher named Tucker Fredrickson. There was a lot to learn and very little time, but he broke it into manageable segments. He'd show me a basic technique, then have me repeat exactly what he'd done. Once I was comfortable, we'd move on to the next technique, and so on. The challenge was that there was *so* much to remember—I'd forget earlier steps as we progressed.

So, I stayed late—until ten or eleven most nights—practicing and jotting down notes on everything I forgot. Then I'd crawl into bed, only to be up and out the door by 7:00 a.m. to start again. I worked full days on Saturday and Sunday too, and slowly, it started to click.

By Monday afternoon, Tucker told me I was ready. I didn't believe him. The other editors were speed-typing on their keyboards while I was still hunting and pecking, painstakingly laying down each edit and carefully modulating the soundboard as I went.

On Tuesday morning, I got my first day's footage—and it scared the hell out of me. Tucker came in to watch as I laid down the first dozen edits. When I played them back on the color monitor, they actually looked like I'd cut them on film. Tucker patted me on the back and said, "I knew you were ready."

I kept going—still at a snail's pace—but things were working, and I was finally starting to feel good about myself. I was a film guy—trained on 35mm and a Moviola—and here I was, editing on a space-age digital console.

Then, that afternoon, Bill Breshears threw me a curveball. He walked into my editing bay with four sharply dressed Japanese gentlemen—there to watch me work. Exactly what I *didn't* need. My nerves flared up with them all standing behind me, but I forced myself to focus. Somehow, I managed to cut together a full scene that, even though it took a while, looked solid to me.

One of the men stepped forward and looked over my shoulder while I was working. He told Bill that what I was doing looked very difficult.

Bill said, "Difficult...? Hell no. This boy learnt it in five days."

As they were leaving, he pounded me on the back and added, "Ah *knew* you was the right man for this job."

Later, he told me those men were preparing to invest big money in his company. I asked why he didn't take them to watch one of his seasoned editors instead of me—on my *first* day. He said, "Those boys are going too fast. My investors wouldn't understand what they were doing."

After the first week, I began to pick up speed. Before long, I could edit a full day's shooting in one day and pretty much stay up to camera—something that was nearly impossible with film. The only person I knew who could manage that was my Uncle Henry. He was head and shoulders above most editors in Hollywood.

During the third week, I brought my dad in to see what I was doing, and he was floored by the new technology. He said he wished those machines had been around when *he* was editing. He couldn't get over how fast and clean it was—no trims to roll up, no dusty bins of film to sift through trying to find the right pieces. We went out for lunch, and he thanked me. Said he'd had a great time and wanted to see the movie once it was finished.

I told him I'd make him a cassette so he could watch it at home with Kathryn.

Two days after *The Stepford Children* finished shooting, I ran the first cut for Edgar Scherick and his line producer, Gary Hoffman, in my editing bay. They'd been worried about their star, Barbara Eden—who could sometimes go a little "over the top" in her performances. But they were relieved to see that, with careful editing, I'd gotten the best out of her. They were very happy with the movie.

Before they left, they told me they had another picture starting in a month or so—and they wanted me to be their editor. This time, they were planning to try a different editing system called "Montage." They said it looked easier to learn than the one I had just mastered—and they wanted me to start learning it right away.

42

FRANK FINDS HAPPINESS AT CHAPMAN COLLEGE

My son Frank—who had wanted nothing to do with Chapman College in the beginning—ended up really liking it. He was doing well in school, getting As and Bs, and decided to stay and continue his education there rather than transfer to a local college. I was a little disappointed by his decision not to come home. I was living alone, and I'd furnished a nice bedroom for him in my house. He also had a standing invitation to live with my sister, Sue. We all missed him—including my ex-wife, Susan, who suddenly decided she wanted his company again.

Whenever I had free time, I'd drive out to the college to spend the day with him and take him out to dinner. He would also come in from time to time and stay with me in the room I'd set up for him.

Susan and I had belonged to a beach club in Santa Monica, and there were a lot of nice couples our age who were also members. After we separated, I stopped going, but she remained a regular on weekends. It was a good place to meet eligible divorcees—and she managed to find one pretty quickly. He was a Beverly Hills radiologist named Marvin Kolpack, a very nice man. I thought he was perfect for Susan because he never argued with her about anything. He seemed amenable to whatever she wanted to do, which was exactly the kind of man Susan had always been looking for.

Before long, they were married and purchased a lovely home with a swimming pool in an exclusive area of Beverly Hills off Coldwater Canyon. I'd run into them now and then because we belonged to the same temple. I'd occasionally go there on Friday nights, often hoping to meet someone to date. I actually did date a few of the women I met there, but nothing serious ever developed.

Susan eventually decided she wanted Frank back in her life—which I found ironic, considering how hard she'd fought to send him away to college in the first place. I thought maybe she was feeling guilty and trying to make amends, but that didn't seem to be the case. Frank was a handsome kid with a great sense of humor, and she was proud of him. She invited him to her wedding and introduced him to all of Marvin's friends as her son, clearly implying that she was his birth mother.

I wasn't happy when I heard about that, and I told Susan I'd object to Frank visiting her if she didn't stop giving people that impression. Of course, she denied having said anything, but I could always tell when she was lying. I told her Frank wouldn't have made it up—and that I wouldn't tolerate it. I threatened to expose her real nature to him and tell him how she'd treated me after receiving her inheritance. I'd never said anything negative about her to Frank because I didn't want to burden him—but this was crossing the line, and I had to put a stop to it.

Part of the reason Frank wanted to stay at Chapman College was the campus itself—it felt more like a small town than a massive university like UCLA. That made it easier to make friends, including girls. He met a girl named Kelly—a real beauty with a sparkling personality—and it was obvious he was crazy about her. I liked her too. Against my better judgment, I let him bring her to the house and sleep in his newly decorated bedroom. She was nineteen, so no laws were being broken, and they couldn't spend the night together at school since they both had roommates.

Since I didn't have a significant other in my life at the time, I started looking forward to their visits. I'd cook them dinner on Friday or Saturday night and make breakfast on Sunday morning before they headed back to school. I really enjoyed hanging out with them. It had now been over two years since Susan and I had split, and I still hadn't found anyone I really connected with.

MOM'S HEALTH BEGINS TO FAIL

One afternoon, my sister Sue called me at the studio to tell me that Mom had been taken to the hospital by ambulance—she was having serious trouble breathing. She'd already been diagnosed with both acute and chronic bronchitis, but now tests showed she had emphysema as well.

The doctors at Cedars-Sinai Hospital said she needed to be put on a ventilator. It was a life-support machine, and we were worried she might not be able to come off of it, even if her breathing improved. But the doctors warned that without it, she might die from lack of oxygen.

In the first couple of weeks, Mom recovered somewhat, but it was still difficult for her—even with the ventilator. She was using prescription inhalers to help her breathe, and she was on strong antibiotics to fight the infection in her lungs.

All three of us—my sisters and I—were at the hospital every day. Sue was there for fifteen to sixteen hours straight, from eight or nine in the morning until midnight. Being there so long each day really took its toll on her. I would come in the evenings after work, and Sue and her husband Walter would then go downstairs to have dinner in the hospital commissary. Cindy, who had opened a clothing store in

Beverly Hills, would stop in and out, while her husband Sy stayed alone in the store to cover for her.

It put a terrible strain on all of us—especially Sue, who turned out to be the Florence Nightingale of our family. She was desperate for relief and asked me to come during the daytime so she could go home and rest. I understood what she needed, and I sympathized, but there was no way I could leave the studio during the day. *Airwolf* was a demanding show, and I was going in at six-thirty or seven every morning just so I could leave in time to get to the hospital by seven in the evening.

Sue developed a deep resentment toward Cindy, feeling that she could have spent more time with Mom. It did substantial damage to their relationship, which had already been less than ideal to begin with.

After several weeks of slight improvement, Mom's condition began to deteriorate. Sue and I were with her on a Saturday morning when she appeared to be unresponsive. We called the doctor, and I asked him if she was slipping into a coma. He said it was entirely possible. We were shocked. We all thought she was getting better and weren't expecting this kind of news.

My son, Frank—who had been coming in on weekends to visit his grandmother—was terribly upset. He stayed with my sister Sue to keep her company and accompanied her to the hospital. He would sit beside Mom, hold her hand, and speak to her softly, trying to coax her out of the coma.

At one point, the hospital proposed transferring her to a rehab facility miles away, and we fought it tooth and nail, even threatening a lawsuit. Eventually, they agreed not to move her. But we couldn't help feeling that once she slipped into the coma, her level of care declined significantly.

That same week, a gala tribute was being held for George Stevens at the Academy of Motion Picture Arts and Sciences Theater in Beverly Hills. My dad and I dressed in tuxedos and arrived during cocktail hour in the lobby, where we watched in amazement as one

Hollywood legend after another walked through the glass doors. It was a grand evening—more special, I thought, than the Academy Awards, which happened every year. This was a once-in-a-lifetime event, and everyone who was anyone in Hollywood had been invited to fill the thousand-seat auditorium.

From the oldest motion picture pioneers to the new young titans, everyone was there to honor George Stevens. Dad and I sat in front of Hal Roach, who was ninety-five years old, with white hair and a pink face. He was famous for his short films like *The Little Rascals* and *The Dead-End Kids*. When his name was called, he stood up and cheered, and the crowd responded with a warm round of applause.

Mervyn LeRoy, the great director, sat to Dad's left. They had been friends for about fifty years but had a falling out when Mervyn failed to honor his commitment to direct *National Velvet*. They didn't speak for years, but eventually, Dad forgave him, and they became friends again.

All the great young filmmakers were there, including Steven Spielberg and his DreamWorks partners, Jeffrey Katzenberg and David Geffen, along with George Lucas, the creator of *Star Wars*, and the legendary Francis Ford Coppola. They were the new wave of boy wonders, arriving about thirty years after Dad, Thalberg, and Selznick—and there really haven't been any new boy wonders since.

Many prominent actors were also in attendance, including Warren Beatty and Annette Bening. Warren was one of several speakers who introduced the film by honoring the audience's distinguished guests. At one point, he asked my dad to stand and then praised him to the skies—an enormous surprise for both of us. Neither of us had any idea what Warren planned to say. He told the audience that my father had encouraged him not to sign another contract with MGM but instead to go independent so he could initiate his own projects and work with any studio or production company. Warren was the first actor to take that leap, and it changed the business dramatically for both actors and directors. The audience gave my father a standing ovation—an unforgettable thrill for us both.

We were there to watch the premiere of *A Filmmaker's Journey*, a biographical portrait of George Stevens written, produced, and directed by his son, George Stevens Jr. The documentary included clips from many of Stevens Sr.'s films, with commentary by the actors who had starred in them.

Those actors included Jean Arthur, Fred Astaire, Montgomery Clift, James Dean, Douglas Fairbanks Jr., Cary Grant, Katharine Hepburn, Rock Hudson, Alan Ladd, Fred MacMurray, Sam Jaffe, Joel McCrea, Jack Palance, Millie Perkins, Ginger Rogers, Elizabeth Taylor, Spencer Tracy, Warren Beatty, and Shelley Winters. Most of these stars were still alive and in attendance at the screening.

There was also commentary from noted directors such as Frank Capra, John Huston, Rouben Mamoulian, Fred Zinnemann, Alan Pakula, and Joseph Mankiewicz—each expressing their deep respect for George Stevens' immense talent.

Dad had always been a great friend and champion of George Stevens' career, producing several of the films he directed, including *Alice Adams*, *Swing Time*, *A Damsel in Distress*, *Vivacious Lady*, and *Gunga Din*. All that conflict and tension on the set of *Gunga Din* between Dad and Stevens when the movie had gone over budget, was a lifetime ago. After so many years, it became a small blip in the incredible careers of two Hollywood giants.

It was entirely fitting that Dad was there to honor him. He even had a cameo appearance in the documentary—a detail he hadn't shared with me because he wanted it to be a surprise. And what a surprise it was. For me, it was more than that—it was a wonderful shock. I was now in my late forties, and this film offered a glamorous and comprehensive look at the industry in which both my father and I had grown up. Seeing him up on the screen at such a prestigious event was both fascinating and deeply moving.

The film also included reels of George Stevens' private war footage, which had only been discovered after his death. During

World War II, Eisenhower had tasked Stevens with filming the war in Europe. Stevens seized the opportunity to create the only color footage ever shot during the war. The film included stunning scenes from D-Day and its aftermath, the Allied march through Paris, and harrowing footage from the liberation of Dachau. Americans had grown accustomed to seeing the war through black-and-white newsreels—but in color, the reality was far more visceral and terrifying.

George Stevens Jr. had created a powerful memorial. It was a bit jarring to return to the hospital after such an extraordinary evening, but Sue needed a break, and I was happy to relieve her. As I sat quietly by Mom's side, I reflected on all the glitter and significance of the evening. George Jr. had made a beautiful tribute to his father—one that left a lasting impression. It was a night I'll never forget. I knew Mom would have loved it, and I wished she had been awake and alert so I could have told her all about it.

At the end of a sixteen-week vigil, Mom passed away on a Saturday morning. I was on my way to the hospital but arrived a little too late. Sue couldn't bear sitting in the room with her after she had passed, and that was completely understandable—especially considering how Mom looked. Her skin had taken on a sickly white hue, and she was staring blankly at the ceiling. It was deeply unsettling to see her like that, so I gently closed her eyelids and then her mouth.

I sat there for a while, just looking at her, slowly realizing that we had lost the central core of our family. Dad, in some small way, had become a deserter—though none of us honestly thought of him like that. He had always been there for us, but he was now part of a new family and no longer attended the family gatherings that had always revolved around Mom.

As I sat there in the quiet of that hospital room, I began to fully understand how much she had meant to me—more than I had ever realized. She had defended me when she believed Dad was too harsh, and she had lifted my spirits when I was feeling low. We shared a deep intellectual connection—a love of art and beauty, and the joy of spending time with people like Mildred and Sam Jaffe and their circle of friends. I thought back to the time I spent with her after Dad left, trying to lift her spirits the way she had lifted mine so many times during my childhood.

I already missed her terribly, and I knew that pain would linger. To me, she had been something like Mother Nature—providing emotional nourishment, constant support, and enduring companionship. Her loss was profound, and I knew there would be no easy way to fully absorb it.

When we called Dad and told him that Mom had died, he came straight to the hospital and then took all of us to lunch. He was grieving with us, and I got the distinct impression that he still had feelings for her. Sue later told me she had spoken to him about his relationship with Kathryn. He admitted that things had been good for about a year, but then they began to sour. He said he felt like God was punishing him for leaving Mom.

I thought that was terribly sad. Mom had been grieving since the day Dad walked out. She would have given anything to have had him back. And now Dad was stuck in an unhappy marriage, full of regret and convinced that he was being punished for leaving her.

People have tried to tell me that relationships are all written in the stars—that certain astrological signs just aren't compatible. Mom was a Taurus (the bull), and Dad was an Aries (the ram), and according to some, the two should never have gotten together. But I've never put much stock in astrology. I believe they could have made it work if they'd really wanted to. But they were both incredibly stubborn. A lot of damage piled up over the years, and nothing was ever truly resolved. Their expectations of one another became too high, too inflexible, and eventually their relationship broke beyond repair.

I had learned something important about expectations during my first visit to a psychiatrist back when I was in college. I was venting about Dad—how he treated me, how unfair it all felt—and I said, "I think I deserve better than that."

The psychiatrist looked at me and said, "You deserve shit."

I blinked. "What?"

"You heard me," he said. "There's no such word as *deserve* in psychiatry. You get out of life exactly what you put into it."

I was stunned. "But what my dad is doing isn't fair."

He smiled. "There's no such word as *fair*, either. If there's something you want, you have to fight for it. That's just the way it is."

It took years for me to realize how right that psychiatrist had been. When I finally confronted my dad, I was in my early forties. I was fighting for my self-respect, trying to reclaim some dignity—and somehow, I managed to do it. But I had to fight. If Mom had stood up for herself—had really fought for what she needed from Dad—I don't think they ever would have split up. She might have shamed him into controlling his temper. And we all would have had a better life. Including him.

THE NEXT GENERATION

My son had come in from college for his grandmother's funeral, and he was the saddest boy I'd ever seen. My mother had adored him—she'd given him love, encouragement, and constant inspiration. He used to call her from school and talk to her for forty minutes or even an hour. Long-distance calls were expensive back then, so I had warned Frank not to call her collect. I told him I'd cover the phone bill, but I wanted him to present himself to her more like a man than a dependent child.

Mom had been impressed. She told me later that she had encouraged him to call collect, knowing how costly it was—but he never did.

Part of the reason Frank chose to stay at Chapman instead of transferring to UCLA was that he'd found a job he absolutely loved. It was an evening position at an Australian-themed dance club in Santa Ana called *Twain's Down Under*. He convinced the management to hire him as the disc jockey and publicity director. It was the perfect setup—he worked nights and attended his classes during the day.

The club had a loyal mailing list of about two hundred regulars who showed up every weekend, paid a cover charge, and danced to Frank's playlists. One of his jobs was to create ads and flyers for upcoming events and email them to everyone on the list. He also made sure to grow that list by addressing new patrons from the DJ booth between dances, encouraging them to sign up. Within just a few months, he added fifty or sixty new names.

I was a little concerned that the job might take too much focus away from his studies, but he still managed to maintain a solid B average during his second year at Chapman.

Saturday nights at Twain's featured dance contests, with free admission to the next event as the prize. Frank decided to up the ante by launching a sponsorship program—and it turned out to be a hit. He approached nearby businesses like beauty salons, tanning studios, photography shops, and nail parlors, and convinced them to sponsor the contests.

Each business contributed a $100 prize for the winning couple, plus a bonus offering—like a free hairstyle, manicure, or photo session. It was smart marketing: the businesses got new clients, the kids got cool prizes, and the contests drew bigger crowds. Everybody won—including Frank.

Holding that mailing list was like sitting on a gold mine. He leveraged it by offering his services to other dance clubs around Orange County and Riverside County. He pitched them on hosting dance contests on slow nights—like Wednesdays—that wouldn't conflict with his Saturday gig at Twain's. In return, he asked the other club owners for access to their mailing lists. Over time, his list ballooned to over six hundred names.

The club owners had been skeptical at first, and they asked Frank how much it would cost them for his services. None of them wanted to share any of the bar receipts, and they already had their own disc jockeys. But Frank told them he wasn't planning to spin records, and he wasn't asking for a cut of the bar. All he needed was a cash register and a stool at the front entrance.

He charged twenty dollars admission for the guys and nothing for the girls—which encouraged plenty of single women to show up, along with the guys who wanted to meet them. He accepted cash only, a detail clearly noted on the email flyers, and he deposited the money at the bank the following day.

I was amazed at how enterprising he was, but it hadn't really occurred to me just how much money he was earning. I should have figured it out when he told me he was buying a new car. I asked if he needed me to co-sign the loan, but he said that wouldn't be necessary. I found out later that he had paid cash for it.

On Labor Day, Dad invited us all to a barbecue, and I arrived just in time to see Frank pulling in from school—driving his brand-new, bright red Datsun 240ZX. We were all impressed. Dad couldn't wait to talk to him about his job—or, I should say, his *enterprise*.

He said to Frank, "I don't understand how you can make money from people dancing in a nightclub. I used to make money with dancers in movies, but I can't figure how you do it, if you don't own the club."

Frank explained everything in detail—the mailing lists, the sponsors, the dance prizes—and Dad just sat there, stunned. When Frank finished, he excused himself to grab a drink.

The look on my father's face said it all. He turned to me and said, "That boy is the Great White Hope of this family." He was beaming with pride.

It was a positive statement, to be sure—but for me, it carried a little sting. After all the praise he'd been heaping on me, I thought *I* was the "Great White Hope." For a moment, I felt like greatness had skipped a generation—passed straight from my father to my son.

Some of my old paranoia crept back in to haunt me. But after I thought about it for a while, I realized there was plenty of room for both Frank and me up there—in the sunshine.

43

MISSED KISSES, SECOND CHANCES, AND A WOMAN WORTH WAITING FOR

It had been quite a while since I'd been on a promising date, and I was beginning to think I might never find another woman who was truly right for me. The thought occurred to me—maybe I was meant to stay single for the rest of my life. I tried dating younger women, divorcées, even older, more settled types—but I lost interest in all of them after just a few dates.

There was only one woman I was genuinely attracted to, but she was married and had grown children.

Her name was Beverly, and she was a stockbroker at Morgan Stanley, where I had my brokerage account. I'd originally been a client of her boss, who had come to me through one of my father's friends at Hillcrest Country Club. But since he only handled multi-million-dollar portfolios, he'd passed me down to his assistant. I'd been working with Beverly for about three or four years, mostly over the phone, though we met in person a couple of times a year to review my investments.

Beverly was a stunning little blonde with soft brown eyes and a beautiful smile. She had a sharp mind for the market and a deep knowledge of investments. Instead of meeting in her office, we often had lunch together. Somewhere along the way, I developed a real crush on her.

It made it hard to stay focused on business. We'd usually take care of the portfolio talk in the first thirty minutes, then spend the rest of the time chatting about our lives. I was seriously attracted to her, and I was pretty sure she felt the same way. There were little signs—lingering smiles, quick glances, the way she held eye contact. Still, I never acted on it. She was married, and I didn't think it was right to pursue someone in that position.

After one of our lunches, I drove her back to her office and pulled up near the elevator in the underground garage of her building in Century City. I opened the car door to let her out, and the scent of her perfume hit me like a wave. It was intoxicating. It took everything I had not to lean in and kiss her. She hesitated for just a moment—I got the feeling she was giving me the chance—and I think she would have kissed me back.

But the moment passed.

I drove back to work thinking about her the whole way, fantasizing that maybe, just maybe, we could make music together.

A few months later, she called to tell me she was leaving her job. She'd accepted a new position as assistant to a wealthy Beverly Hills entrepreneur, which meant she would no longer be handling my portfolio. I wasn't expecting that—and I didn't welcome the news.

We talked for a bit, and she asked what was going on in my life and whether I had a girlfriend. I told her I didn't—and added, "You know you're my only girlfriend."

There was a long pause.

Then she said she was planning to leave her husband, and she didn't want to lose contact with me. My heart nearly jumped out of my chest.

She told me she'd wanted to leave two years earlier, but he had begged her to stay and give him a chance to redeem himself. She'd felt she owed him that much. But the marriage had continued to unravel, and it had become unbearable.

All I could think was—*I should have kissed her at that elevator.*

Before we hung up, she said she'd call me with her new number once she got settled into her new job—probably within the week.

That turned out to be the longest week of my life.

When she finally called me, it was pure joy—a dream come true. I couldn't wait to see her. But she was still living at home with her husband and two of her three children, and it was going to take time for her to extricate herself from the situation.

I told her we could meet during the day on Saturdays, but she was hesitant. She said it didn't feel right to see me until she had officially moved out. I knew that would take at least a month—maybe longer—and I was disappointed, to say the least.

Fortunately, she had a change of heart. About a week later, she called and suggested we meet at a restaurant in the Culver City Mall, where it was unlikely she'd run into anyone she knew. I asked her what made her change her mind.

She said simply, "I really want to see you."

I arrived twenty minutes early and got a table with a clear view of the entrance.

Our designated meeting time passed, then ten minutes ticked by, then twenty, then thirty. I was worried she'd gotten cold feet. This was the early 1980s and cell phones were a new invention. They were big, clunky devices installed in cars, and neither of us had one. I had no way to reach her and vice versa. No smart phones. No texting. Just waiting and wondering.

Just when I'd given up and thought she would be a no-show she walked through the door.

A wave of relief washed over me when I saw her. She looked so lovely, she took my breath away.

It turns out, the reason she was late was because she'd had an argument with her husband whom she was in the process of leaving.

We had lunch and talked for over an hour—about everything. She told me she'd arranged to move into an apartment with her friend Patti, who was an assistant to another stockbroker at a different firm. She planned to move in about two weeks.

Before we left the restaurant, she surprised me. She got very brave and asked, "Why didn't you kiss me that day at the elevator?"

I told her I'd wanted to—desperately—but I thought it would have been inappropriate.

She smiled and said, "It would've been. But I wouldn't have turned away."

I laughed and said, "Well, I certainly won't be making that mistake again."

As moving day approached, her plans hit a snag. Patti changed her mind and told Beverly that her daughter was coming home from college in a few weeks and would be reclaiming the spare bedroom.

The truth was, Patti had been looking for a playmate—someone to go out to bars with and meet men. When she realized Beverly would be spending most of her time with me, she no longer wanted her as a roommate.

Beverly went into shock. She hadn't planned on, nor budgeted for the cost of getting her own place and buying furniture. That meant she'd have to save up. It would take her longer to move out of the home she'd shared with her husband.

I had the perfect solution to her dilemma. She could move in with me. I figured she might be uncomfortable sharing my bed (at first). Understandable, given that we'd only just started "dating" and hadn't yet been intimate. So, I suggested she could sleep in one of the other bedrooms. I offered to install a second phone line with an answering machine, giving her more privacy to communicate with her children. And they, in turn, would hopefully feel more comfortable knowing they could call her directly without worrying about someone else answering the phone. I also suggested she could still tell her family that she was living with Patti and introduce me to them later, under more respectable circumstances. She thought about it for a while and eventually agreed, although she had some reservations. After a week or two, she got comfortable and decided she'd made the right decision.

But her children weren't fooled by the "temporary" ruse. She had two grown sons and a daughter who was in college. Her oldest son, David, and her daughter, Michelle, lived in Los Angeles, while her middle son, Kenny, was married and living in Phoenix. When they found out their mother was living with me, they were horrified. I became the evil black knight who had stolen their mother away, and they were not at all pleased to meet me. It became a significant issue that took a great deal of time and tension to resolve.

One evening, we'd invited David and Michelle to dinner. Beverly had prepared their favorite meal. But it did not go well. They were rude and disrespectful. I felt like I was walking on eggshells around them. It would take time before they realized their mother would have a much better life with me than she ever had with their father. Eventually, they did grow to accept me, but it took a lot of effort on both sides.

Beverly and I had been together a few weeks when I began helping her find a lawyer for the divorce. I wasn't quite ready to introduce her to my family, but I told them I was dating someone and that they would meet her soon.

One night, Dad called and invited me over for dinner. He said he wanted to talk about some investments I might be interested in. I asked if I could bring my new girlfriend. He was thrilled that I finally had someone in my life again. When he answered the door and saw Beverly, he lit up like a Christmas tree.

"Oh... come right in, dear," he said with a big smile. Dad was always a sucker for a pretty face—and hers was beautiful. He said she reminded him of Carole Lombard and couldn't wait to hear everything about her.

Beverly told him she'd seen his name on the big screen for years and was thrilled to meet him. I had rarely seen Dad so animated, and it was amusing.

As Beverly told him about herself, he kept flashing me looks of approval. Eventually, the conversation turned to the stock market, and Dad was even more impressed with Beverly's knowledge. Later in the evening, he asked her opinion about the investments he wanted to discuss with me. She told him she thought they were a little risky, especially with interest rates beginning to rise.

The next day, I called to thank Dad for dinner, and he couldn't stop talking about Beverly. He was delighted she was in my life. And he'd taken her sound financial advice and opted out of the investment proposal. "She's not going to let you make stupid decisions about money," he said. "Which means I might not turn over in my grave after I'm gone."

Needless to say, I was thrilled that Dad liked Beverly. I had thought it would be better for Dad to meet her before the rest of the family. I knew he'd like her—and if he said nice things to my sisters, it would pave the way for their approval. Of course, I wasn't telling anyone that Beverly and I were already living together.

Cindy and Sue still weren't speaking after their battles during Mom's time in the hospital, so I made separate dinner plans with each of them. Sue was surprised to meet Beverly—pleasantly so. She'd spoken with her before, back when Beverly had handled her investments, but they'd never met in person. I thought it would be fun to let Sue discover that connection during dinner, and it added a light, humorous touch to the evening. I was glad to see that Sue and her husband, Walter, really hit it off with Beverly.

Cindy and her husband, Sy, were also pleased to meet her. They invited us to dinner at their home, along with Cory and Kerry, Cindy's son and daughter from her first marriage. Things were starting to feel a bit more normal for all of us. But we all missed Mom deeply. I was especially sad that Beverly never had the chance to meet her—Mom would have adored her, not only for her sweet nature but also for her intelligence and accomplishments.

I wasn't rushing to introduce Frank to Beverly. I wasn't sure how he'd react to the fact that we were living together. He was busy at school and with his dance club business. I figured the best time for them to meet would be when he came home at the end of the semester. Then he could spend some quality time with her since they'd be living under the same roof. I was confident he'd like her. Everyone did.

MOVE

After months of reading terrible scripts, Dad finally found a project he wanted to produce—and, miraculously, Fox gave its approval. They purchased the novel *Move* by a young writer named Joel Lieber and hired him to write the screenplay. It was a clever comedy about a young playwright, seriously afflicted with writer's block, who moonlights writing porno novels to break through the creative jam. He and his wife live in Manhattan and are trying to move from one apartment to another as their lease is about to expire. But they can't get any mover to commit before the deadline.

Elliott Gould plays the beleaguered writer with obsessive-compulsive tendencies, and Paula Prentiss plays his anxiety-ridden wife. They're very funny together, especially as Gould's character retreats into increasingly surreal fantasy sequences under pressure.

I thought the movie was edgy and humorous, with some genuinely strong scenes, sensitively directed by Stuart Rosenberg—best known for *Cool Hand Luke* and, later in his career, *The Pope of Greenwich Village*.

Move offered irreverent commentary on modern marriage—painfully true at times but delivered with cleverness and plenty of laughs. The problem was the ending. It was weak and unsatisfying—one of the seven deadly sins of moviemaking in Hollywood. Unfortunately, the picture lost money, making it two flops in a row for Dad. Not the best start for his tenure at 20th Century Fox.

He berated himself for the film's failure, saying he hadn't listened to his inner voice. He recalled that many years earlier, the unhappy ending of *Mary of Scotland* had caused an otherwise good movie to tank—and now he'd made the same mistake again.

A NEW "DIRECTION"

I was still looking for directing jobs, which were proving to be very elusive. It had been my dream to direct film since I was a little boy, so I decided to hire an agent to help me find work. But it wasn't easy. Aside from some second unit directing for television, a few small theater productions, and the industrial film I'd previously mentioned, I didn't have enough credits. I was offered a few more industrial and corporate jobs, but the scripts were dull, and none of them inspired me.

Then I found a documentary project on early childhood education that really appealed to me. I met the teacher behind the original concept, a man named Jim Crowley. He had pitched the idea to a friend at the National Education Association. His friend liked it and brought it to the NEA's top executives, who were enthusiastic about the concept. The friend came back and told Jim that if he could deliver a script they liked as much as the idea, the NEA would finance the documentary.

Jim and I started working on the script, and after a few weeks we came up with something we were both proud of. He took it back to his contact at the NEA. A week later, he got the green light—the NEA agreed to fund the project. We were excited and ready to go.

I knew there wasn't much money in it for me, but it was the kind of film I could use as a springboard—something that might open doors to bigger jobs and a more substantive directing career, which was all I wanted.

I broke down the script, created an extensive shot list, and put together a simple storyboard. Jim and I went over everything multiple times. When I finally felt we were ready to shoot, I called my cameraman friend from *Wind Wheels* and assembled a small crew—mostly friends from the studio who were glad to pick up a few weeks of work before the summer television hiatus ended.

Jim arranged for us to begin shooting at the private school in Bel Air where he was teaching a summer class. The school was happy to participate in the project—they saw the documentary as a terrific opportunity to showcase their campus and use it as a recruitment tool.

On Saturday night, Beverly and I had dinner with Jim, and I gave him a copy of the final revised shooting script along with my notes and shot list to review on Sunday. Jim was the principal narrator and on-camera talent, and he already knew all the students who would be appearing in the film. Although he wasn't a trained actor, I felt confident he could handle himself in front of the camera. He was comfortable speaking with children, and his paternal relationship with them would help put them at ease—meaning I wouldn't have to coax performances out of nervous kids.

We stayed out late and had a few drinks, celebrating in advance of production starting Monday.

I had hoped my son Frank could work on the movie with me. I knew how thrilled he'd be—but I hadn't told him about the project yet because I wanted to be certain it was a done deal. I'd planned to call him in the morning and offer him a spot as my assistant.

But when I woke up Sunday, I had second thoughts. I worried he might want to stay on for the entire shoot, which could interfere with his semester at Chapman College. As much as I wanted him there, I didn't think working with me was worth derailing his education. His disappointment would be temporary—but losing momentum at school could take a long time to recover from.

In the end, it didn't matter. Late Sunday afternoon, Jim called with devastating news: the NEA had changed their mind. They were pulling their funding and going with another project.

I couldn't believe it. All the planning and effort we'd put in, had been a complete waste of our time and resources. I was angry, frustrated, and deeply disappointed.

I wanted to call my father. He was on a *Love Boat* cruise at the time, running clips of his films in the ship's theater and telling Hollywood stories to a captive audience of tourists. I needed his support and wanted to share the news, but I thought better of it. He had been just as excited about the documentary as I was, and I didn't want to ruin his vacation. Even though I missed him, I was happy he was enjoying himself on the cruise.

It had been many years since I'd expressed my feelings to him on that emotionally painful but pivotal Saturday morning. It had been tough for both of us, but it had been something that I needed to confront, not just for myself, but for both of us. And over time, our relationship was the better for it.

Even so, I sensed that he'd kept a certain emotional distance since then. It felt like the wound from that confrontation had never fully healed—which was understandable. Perhaps if I'd brought it up again, I could have helped the healing process along. After all, we'd both changed and grown over the years.

Still, I was genuinely happy he'd gone on the cruise. He could focus on the highlights of his life and share those memories with an eager audience, all while enjoying the sunshine and sea breezes of the Caribbean. I knew the trip would be a cleansing experience for him—and for Kathryn, too. I was even hoping they might be able to rekindle the buoyant romance they'd once shared, although I suspected that was more wishful thinking than reality. They were both reaching an age when the patterns of life rarely changed and began to slow down.

THE HOMECOMING

As I had hoped, the Caribbean cruise had been a wonderful rest for Dad and Kathryn. They both returned looking tanned and healthy. Dad said the people on the ship loved watching the old movies and listening to his stories. Even the younger passengers—many of whom had never seen his films—gave him their full attention. He received a big round of applause at the end of each screening. He had a certain kind of charm that captivated strangers, along with a quick wit and a warm sense of humor.

Back at their bungalow on the Fox lot, Dad and Kathryn resumed their search for new projects—but good material was hard to find. They collected piles of scripts from agents all over town and spent their days reading...and then kept reading into the night. Dad admitted the outlook wasn't bright. He said he was growing tired of chasing the dream, but he didn't know how to stop. He hated being idle, and there wasn't much else for him to do besides keep looking for something worth producing.

I gently suggested that he might consider retiring. I reminded him that he'd already enjoyed a phenomenal career spanning nearly fifty years. He had produced more than a hundred films and run two of the biggest studios in Hollywood—including MGM, the most legendary of them all. He'd received every major industry honor: five Oscar nominations for Best Picture, and lifetime achievement awards from both the Academy and the Producers Guild. What more did he have to prove?

He agreed that he had nothing left to prove—but said he'd go crazy being idle. He just couldn't picture a life without work.

But within a few months, a tragic event would force him to reconsider—and ultimately, it led to his retirement.

44

CHIARO SCURO

Kathryn woke up one Saturday morning with darkened, blurred vision. After splashing cold water on her face, she discovered that her sight was also distorted—she was seeing things at skewed, acute angles instead of a normal view. Terrified, she told Dad what was happening, and he immediately called the Jules Stein Eye Institute, known for having some of the best ophthalmologists in the country. Unfortunately, it was the weekend, and the clinic—along with all other doctors' offices—was closed.

Dad rushed her to the emergency room at Cedars-Sinai Hospital, but the resident doctors there couldn't treat her properly without specialized medications administered by physicians trained specifically in that area—and none of those doctors were available. Kathryn would have to wait until Monday.

By Saturday evening, her vision had deteriorated further. By Sunday morning, she could see nothing at all—only blackness. When she finally saw a doctor on Monday, she was diagnosed with temporal arteritis, a condition in which the arteries that supply blood to the head and eyes become inflamed.

Doctors administered high doses of medication to stimulate blood flow, but her temporal arteries had already been inactive for forty-eight hours and didn't respond to treatment. They explained that even if she had been treated on Saturday, her eyesight likely wouldn't have been saved—her case was unusually aggressive. Typically, there are early warning signs, and most patients don't lose their vision for weeks after symptoms first appear.

Dad was devastated. For nearly two weeks, he wouldn't let any of us visit. When he finally allowed us to come to the house, what we saw was heartbreaking. Kathryn was disoriented and terrified to take even a single step—even with help. Navigating stairs was a nightmare. Dad was on edge, nervous, and irritable. I could tell he was slipping into a deep depression.

He admitted he felt lost at the studio without Kathryn by his side. Within a week, he announced his retirement. Fox Studios gave him a nice retirement party—though I was working and unable to attend.

Back at home, he devoted himself to caring for Kathryn, but it quickly became clear how difficult and challenging it was. She began experiencing vivid nightmares or hallucinations. If she nodded off while sitting in a chair, she'd often wake up screaming, convinced that something terrible had happened. She couldn't distinguish between dreams and reality, and she repeatedly insisted that her nightmares were real events.

After a while, we began to wonder if Kathryn had lost her mind along with her eyesight. One day, when Sue and I were visiting, she told us she didn't believe she was in her own home. She said she had been taken to some unfamiliar place where nothing felt right. Sue and I gently asked if she remembered the big white colonial pillars by the front door. She said she didn't. We described them in detail, along with the ivy-lined brick walkway out front. Finally, Kathryn said she did remember the pillars.

We took her outside, placed her hands around one of the

columns, and encouraged her to feel the shape and texture. After some coaxing, she admitted that maybe she was home after all. But later, she reverted—insisting she was still in a strange, cold, and dreary place that she didn't like.

Dad's longtime cook, Cora, finally retired, but Eunita, the other housekeeper, stayed on to do the cooking. Dad realized they needed even more help, so he hired two Filipino sisters, Ching and Anastasia. They helped clean the house and took turns assisting Kathryn whenever she needed to move from one room to another—or up and down the stairs, which was a huge ordeal. It usually took her six or seven minutes to go up or down, with both women assisting her. One of them always had to accompany her in the shower to make sure she didn't slip and injure herself.

This was a difficult adjustment for Dad. He wasn't comfortable in retirement. He used to keep busy by going to Hillcrest Country Club for lunch with his friends at the round table. He also continued spending time with the grandchildren, taking them to Ponyland and other amusement spots, followed by lunch at The Farmer's Market and other favorite haunts.

He began reading voraciously, and was finally enjoying good literature, rather than the mediocre scripts he'd been forced to read most of his life. He also liked to attend screenings at the Academy of Motion Picture Arts and Sciences Theater on Wilshire Boulevard, and one of us would always accompany him, since he was no longer driving.

Fortunately, around this time, Dad was contacted by a young associate professor at USC named Richard Jewell, who was working on his doctoral degree. Richard wanted to write about RKO, and specifically about Dad's early days there. Dad was thrilled. Richard began coming to the house to interview him two, sometimes three, days a week. It gave Dad the opportunity to relive the old days and share stories about the films he made in the 1930s and '40s—years he always said were his favorite in the movie business.

He used to say that the most fun he ever had was the journey to the top. He enjoyed being there once he arrived, of course—but getting there had been even more exciting.

It turned out to be a wonderful association for Dad, because Rick Jewell wrote his doctoral thesis about him—and succeeded in getting him hired to teach the master cinema class at USC. Dad taught the course for a couple of years after his retirement and genuinely enjoyed pontificating on the art and science of filmmaking, punctuating his lectures with personal stories about the stars and directors he'd worked with. The students were enthralled to hear those old Hollywood tales, which Dad loved to tell, and his name on the faculty became a real draw for every new crop of film students.

I was happy to see Dad finally adjusting to retirement. He seemed much happier than he had been during his tenure at 20th Century Fox. When Beverly and I would come over for dinner, he positively sparkled, and it was fun to be around him—though he was indulging a little too freely in his favorite Scotch. My sister Sue was concerned about his drinking, but I felt he had earned the right to enjoy himself in his twilight years. If it ever became excessive, we could step in and encourage him to cut back or seek help.

Beverly and I had been invited to Dad's house for dinner one Friday night, and I was pleased to hear him talk enthusiastically about teaching at USC's film school. His new sense of purpose was obvious.

He told me how much he enjoyed the students, calling them "wonderful," and how eager they were to learn about the old days at RKO. He shared stories about how movies were made back then and how much fun the work had been. He told the class he considered the 1930s the most enjoyable decade of his career. He also admitted he had once thought about retiring at forty—but had changed his mind and gone on to do some of his best work after that.

I'd heard most of those stories before, of course, but Beverly was fascinated. She loved being around my dad and hearing his vivid recollections of old Hollywood.

After dinner, Kathryn was helped upstairs to bed. Her blindness had robbed her not only of her sight but of her energy as well. She was nearly asleep at the table by the time her caretakers got her to her feet. We worried that she was losing her grip on reality. But Dad seemed more content with her now than he had been before she'd lost her vision. I think he was beginning to embrace his role as her protector. And in her vulnerable state, she had become far less combative—and in some ways, for my father, it had become a more positive relationship.

THE LOVE OF MY LIFE

Beverly and I were deeply in love. My feelings for her were more intense than anything I had ever felt for another woman, and I asked her to marry me. She had two weeks of vacation coming up, and I suggested she take an additional week—unpaid—so we could enjoy a proper honeymoon. I knew her new boss was pleased with her performance. She'd only been there a few weeks when he told her she was the brightest assistant he had ever had, and that he was thrilled she'd joined the company. She was confident he'd approve the extra time off for our honeymoon—and he did. In fact, he went a step further and paid her for that additional week, which told me just how much he valued her.

We got married aboard a cruise ship in Miami and traveled to several islands in the Caribbean, where we bought watches and swam on beautiful beaches. We indulged in delicious food and all the comforts of a luxury liner. The cruise ship even made us a complimentary wedding cake, and there was enough left to share with our dinner companions every night for a week. It was the first time either of us had been on a ship that size, and we had a wonderful time.

After the cruise, we flew to New York for three nights, where I took her to the theater and several fine restaurants.

MICHAEL BERMAN

ANOTHER WAVE OF SORROW

When we returned home, I learned that my Uncle Henry had been diagnosed with cirrhosis of the liver, and his prognosis was grim. The doctors said he had only a few months to live. Once again, my father was plunged into grief. He visited his brother every day, and I went with him as often as I could, usually in the evenings. Henry was one of the kindest people I'd ever known, and my father adored him. He had looked after Henry all his life, and now he was doing everything he could to support him. He brought food several times a week so Rosemary wouldn't have to cook, and he brought flowers to brighten the house. He sat with Henry through the afternoons and into the evenings during his visits.

I was moved by his devotion, but it was painful to witness his sorrow. I vividly remembered the day Henry and I picked up Dad at the airport after Grandma Julie died—how they'd cried together. My father's words echoed in my mind with fresh sadness. Years ago, he had said to Henry, *"You and I are all that's left of the old family now."*

They also cried again over their little brother Maxie, who had died at the age of three. It had been overwhelming for them both. I used to ask my dad to tell me about Maxie, but he never really wanted to talk about him. Henry had spent more time with Maxie than my father had—he was very young at the time and not yet in school, too little to grasp the meaning of death. When Maxie died, Dad was twelve and just starting junior high. He once told me that Maxie was the happiest child he had ever known—always smiling—and that Henry was constantly at his side.

Henry had been a big help to Grandma Julie, who was raising two young boys alone in New York City after Grandpa Harry passed away. Henry told me how much he missed my father after Dad made the move to the west coast and how happy he was to be reunited with him when he and Grandma Julie moved to California.

He also told me about the struggle he faced when deciding to leave dental school. His heart simply wasn't in it. He didn't want to spend his life with his hands in people's mouths—even though it would have been a lucrative and stable career. Like my father, he had a fire inside him to make movies. He was lucky that Dad was in a position to help him, but the truth is, Henry was extremely talented, and I have no doubt he could have made it on his own.

He shared much of this with me while he was on his deathbed. It was painful to hear, but also deeply heartwarming. Henry was opening up to me, sharing his most personal thoughts—things I don't think he'd shared with anyone else, except maybe his wife and children. I was honored that he confided in me. I often thought about the legacy he and my father were leaving me—and how I might live up to it. Dad and Uncle Henry were the last of an extraordinary breed of men who faced life head-on with confidence and conviction. I wanted to be just like them.

When Henry passed away, Sue and Walt brought my dad to the funeral at Holy Cross Cemetery in Culver City, just a few blocks from Hillside, where my mother is buried. We helped Dad into a seat in the back row. He was hopelessly depressed and inconsolable. I have a vivid memory of sitting beside him with my arm around his shoulders, trying to comfort him as he cried. He leaned forward, his hands folded on top of his cane, his chin resting on his hands, and he sobbed—loud, wrenching sobs, tears soaking the sleeves of his jacket.

Even though the organ filled the chapel with music, people turned around to see where the crying was coming from. Eventually, we had to take him outside and back to the car. We parked next to the gravesite early, so Dad could watch Henry's interment from inside the car, windows rolled up. It was a terrible day for all of us—one I will never forget.

In the year or two that followed, I worked on several television movies and had to keep adapting to new editing systems with each assignment. Hollywood had moved on from film editing, and digital technology was growing increasingly complex. I worked on several newer systems, including Ediflex, Avid Media Composer, BHP Touch Vision, Lightworks, and a Canadian system called E=MC2. Each one presented its own set of technical challenges—and most of them are now obsolete, as digital technology continues to march forward.

45

GUESS WHO'S COMING TO DINNER...

It was about a year after Kathryn lost her eyesight, and she had begun acting more and more peculiar. My father described a special dinner party he was hosting for Armand Hammer and his wife, who were close friends and longtime business partners. They had heard about Kathryn's blindness and wanted to visit her and offer their support.

Hammer, the CEO of Occidental Petroleum, and Dad had been close friends for years. Dad had invited him to the studio numerous times for private screenings of his films and had invited him to lunch at the round table at Hillcrest, where Hammer met countless celebrities.

In return, Hammer had shown his gratitude by bringing Dad in as a partner on some of his "sweetheart" oil deals—exclusive investment opportunities that only Hammer and his closest friends were allowed to join. These ventures were virtually foolproof. At the start of the year, each handpicked investor would contribute $25,000 to finance drilling in a field Hammer had personally selected—one he already knew, through company research, was rich in oil and practically guaranteed to yield major profits. By year's end, that $25,000 investment typically returned $100,000, and the profits were heavily sheltered through tax loopholes uncovered by Occidental Petroleum attorneys. Investors paid little or no taxes—and could invest in multiples, up to $150,000, which would return a whopping $600,000.

It all sounded wonderful to me, and I told Dad I'd love to invest $50,000 right away. But he shut me down immediately. He said he would never ask his good friend to let me into one of those deals. Hammer's investment group, he explained, was strictly limited to close friends—people who had done meaningful favors for him over the years. There was no way I could qualify for membership in that elite club.

On the evening of the dinner party, Hammer and his wife arrived with a wildly extravagant gift for Kathryn. Most guests might bring a bottle of expensive wine or Champagne. The Hammers brought a gleaming pair of one-carat diamond stud earrings. Dad instructed Kathryn's caretaker, Anastasia, to place them in Kathryn's pierced ears right away.

But Kathryn was disoriented and had no idea what was happening. As Anastasia began inserting the first earring, Kathryn suddenly turned her head, and the sharp post pierced a part of her earlobe that wasn't pierced. She screamed in pain, "You're hurting me! What are you doing?" Blood spurted onto the pristine white linen napkin, and the dinner party was nearly derailed.

Hammer and his wife were horrified. They stood up, ready to leave immediately, but Dad talked them into staying. Kathryn, however, remained upset and refused to be fed. She kept insisting Anastasia leave her alone, and the whole scene left the Hammers visibly uncomfortable.

At that point, Dad realized that Kathryn's condition and mental state had deteriorated to such an extent that inviting friends over for dinner or attending social events would have to be seriously curtailed. She had lost a significant amount of weight by refusing to eat, and she was beginning to look like a scarecrow. Dad was worried she might be developing anorexia and feared she could meet the same fate as Karen Carpenter.

He told Ching and Anastasia that Kathryn was not to leave the table until she had finished everything on her plate. Sometimes they would sit with her for an hour or mor after the meal had ended, coaxing her to take just a few more bites.

Kathryn had lost her taste for most foods. All she wanted to eat were canned peaches and cottage cheese, but Dad insisted she eat some form of protein at dinner. After sitting with her for long periods, her caregivers would eventually leave her alone at the table, to attend to other chores, and return every so often to encourage her to take a few more bites. Sometimes they would settle her into her wheelchair and take her outside for a walk—hoping the fresh air might stimulate her appetite.

One day, while I was visiting, I saw her sitting alone at the end of the table. She was calling out softly to someone, but I couldn't quite make out what she was saying.

After listening for a while, I realized she was whispering *Aunt Coodie*—the name of one of her maiden aunts who had raised her in Connecticut more than fifty years ago. It was clear her mind was playing tricks on her, pulling her back to childhood.

I went to my dad and told him I thought she was losing her sanity. He nodded and said this had been happening for some time. A psychiatrist who had examined her told him it wasn't as serious as it seemed.

One day, several months before the Hammer dinner party, I asked Kathryn to tell me about a big Hollywood event Dad had taken her to the night before. He'd wheeled her around the party, and many people had stopped to chat with her and compliment her on how good she looked. Dad said he'd been very pleased with how she'd behaved at that gathering.

When I asked Kathryn if she had enjoyed her outing, she leaned over and began whispering, "We never got to the party. Your father pulled over to the curb, came into the back of the van, and beat me with his cane. Then he took me up to that horrible room above the garage and locked me in for the night."

I said, "You can't be serious."

"Oh yes, I am," she replied. "Your father has turned into a monster."

I was now certain that her condition was far worse than the psychiatrist had led us to believe. Her entire story was a fantasy on steroids. There *was* no "horrible room" above the garage—and no van, either. They had sold Kathryn's Mercedes, and all that remained was Dad's Volvo. There were no bruises or abrasions on her body. And the idea of my father beating her with a cane was absurd. He only ever used a cane during severe gout attacks, and he hadn't had one of those in years.

I couldn't believe that Kathryn's mind was capable of inventing such vivid and disturbing delusions—and I didn't understand why. Most people who lose their eyesight become depressed, yes, but they don't typically lose their grip on reality.

I felt terrible for her—and even more so for Dad. I didn't know how much more of this he could endure. I was convinced that Kathryn needed to be institutionalized. But her daughter, Gingi, was still living in the house, and there was nowhere else for her to go. Gingi and Dad didn't get along at all, and if her mother were sent away, it would create a huge problem.

AND THEN EVERYTHING GOT WORSE

I didn't anticipate just how bad Dad's living situation could get. One day I went over to the house, and he didn't seem to recognize me. I didn't make an issue of it, but I told Sue he should be examined by his doctor. His internist, Dr. Mel Brody, suspected he might be suffering from some form of dementia.

Sue said she wanted another opinion but, for some reason, felt too embarrassed to bring it up with Dr. Brody. He had been our family doctor for many years, and she didn't want to insult him or hurt his feelings. So, she asked me to call and request that Dad's medical records be forwarded to another doctor.

I agreed, although I thought it was a little absurd for Sue to be afraid of asking for a second opinion. When Dr. Brody got on the phone, I explained the situation, and he was more than willing to comply. He asked me where to send the records, and I replied with a quick quip, "Send them to Jack Kevorkian."

There was a pause on the other end of the line, and then he said dryly, "Very funny, Michael." But after a beat, the joke registered, and he started to chuckle. I gave him the name of the actual doctor, and he was still laughing when he hung up the phone.

The new doctor, referred to us by a close friend, came to the house to examine Dad and give his second opinion. He said Dad was suffering from a serious depression and should have seen a psychiatrist immediately after Kathryn had lost her eyesight. He believed that Dad simply hadn't been able to cope with the extent of Kathryn's physical and mental decline—and that he was burdened by guilt for not being able to help her.

He also agreed with Dr. Brody that Dad was exhibiting signs of dementia and expressed concern about Dad's ability to care for himself, let alone manage Kathryn's care.

We immediately hired an estate planning and probate attorney, who petitioned the court to have Dad examined by one of their doctors to assess his mental capacity. It took some time, but eventually the court-appointed doctor determined that Dad was no longer capable of managing his own affairs. We began the process of establishing a Conservatorship and a Trust to protect him and his estate.

I was appointed Conservator of his estate and Trustee of the Pandro S. Berman Trust. My sister Sue was named Conservator of his person. She continued to visit the house every day, making sure everything was in order. Cindy helped by doing the weekly grocery shopping, and all of us did our best to bring some joy into Dad's life—which was now becoming terribly bleak.

I found him different from week to week. Sometimes he would greet me warmly. Other times, he didn't seem to recognize me at all.

On one of those days, I asked him gently, "Who am I?"

He gave me a strange look and said, "You're the fellow that comes around here all the time."

I said, "Dad... don't you know me? I'm your son, Michael. I spent my childhood at the house on Mountain Drive—with you and Mom and Sue and Cindy."

He narrowed his eyes, squinting at me. "Did I know you back then?"

Moments like that were incredibly painful—but thankfully, they didn't happen too often. Most of the time, when I visited, he was lucid and recognized me right away.

I wanted to recreate the best of times with him, so I started sitting with him in the library, playing classical music from my collection at home. The old $33\frac{1}{3}$ wax recordings we used to listen to were long gone. Instead, I brought cassette tapes and CDs, which had far better sound quality.

Dad was fascinated by the CDs and the player I brought over. He didn't understand how it worked, but he loved the richness of the sound. He turned the CD player upside down, examining it inside and out.

"How can it play anything, when it doesn't even have a needle?" he asked.

It made me smile—but it also made me profoundly sad. The once-brilliant mind of the man who had helped bring sound technology to RKO Studios, could no longer comprehend a simple piece of modern technology like a CD player.

It was a telling signpost along the road of his decline.

Dad wasn't doing much reading at this point, aside from the newspaper. But he still enjoyed listening to music with me, just like in the old days, when we would sit together in the library of the old house, reading while music played softly in the background.

Lately, I'd been listening to some newer composers—post-minimalist John Adams, and the dissonant Toru Takemitsu, who composed cutting-edge classical music as well as electronic scores for Japanese horror films. My new favorite was the incredible French modernist composer Olivier Messiaen.

Dad seemed to enjoy everything I played for him. I think he especially appreciated not having to make conversation. He had always been fond of the old masters, and I could tell he still preferred them to the modern ones. So, I would mix in some Mozart and Beethoven and occasionally, a piano concerto we had both loved.

We would sit there in companionable silence, just listening, and it was deeply comforting for both of us.

When he found a piece to his liking, he always thanked me for introducing him to something new—and asked me to come back soon with more music.

KATHRYN'S SILENT GOODBYE

One Friday night, I took Beverly out to dinner and then to the airport. She was flying to Phoenix to visit her son Kenny and her grandchildren, Emily and Ryan. I usually went with her on those trips, but this time she would be gone for almost a week, and I was just too busy to take the time off.

By the time I got home from the airport, it was after 10:00 p.m., and there were several messages on my answering machine—including a shocking one from my nephew Cory, who was living in Dad's guest house on Roxbury Drive. It was the same house I had moved into years earlier when my wife Nancy and I separated.

The message was rather cryptic: *"Kathryn Berman passed away earlier this evening."*

I was stunned. I immediately called the house. My sister Sue answered and confirmed it was true. I asked how Dad was handling it, and she told me he didn't know—he was asleep. When I asked when she planned to tell him, she didn't have a clear answer. She said she was waiting to see if he woke up on his own, because she didn't want him to be alone when he found out.

I told her I'd come down and sit with her, just in case, and I drove over right away.

When I arrived, there was a strange-looking black vehicle in the driveway with curtained windows. I realized it was a hearse—sent by Forest Lawn to collect Kathryn's remains. As I walked through the front door, a man and a woman were carrying Kathryn downstairs on a stretcher. I wanted one last look at her, but she was already covered by a large blanket.

Sue was sitting in the library, visibly in shock—and I'm sure I was, too. I asked if she had spoken to Cindy, and she said Cory had notified her. But Cindy and her husband, Sy, didn't want to come up to the house at that hour. They said they would come by tomorrow to visit Dad.

I asked Sue what had happened. She told me Kathryn hadn't come down for dinner, so the cook, Eunita, had prepared a tray and brought it upstairs. When she found Kathryn apparently sleeping, she called out several times to wake her—but Kathryn didn't respond. Eventually, Eunita tried to take her pulse but couldn't feel anything. When she realized Kathryn wasn't breathing, she understood that Kathryn had passed away—but she didn't know what to do.

She went back downstairs, poked her head into the dining room, and silently motioned for Sue to come into the kitchen.

Sue was shocked by the news, but she returned to the dining room and finished her dinner. Then she walked Dad upstairs to his den, which had become his private bedroom. He had moved out of the master bedroom a couple of years earlier because he was a very light sleeper, and Kathryn's nighttime movements and snoring had been keeping him awake.

Normally, Dad would stop by her room at the top of the stairs to say goodnight, but Sue said that tonight he was especially tired and had gone straight to his room without stopping.

I asked what she would have done if Dad had wanted to go into Kathryn's room. She said she was prepared to tell him that Kathryn was already asleep and not to disturb her. I agreed that would work for the night—but asked, "What are you going to do in the morning?"

Sue said she didn't want to tell Dad right away. She'd been thinking about it for a couple of hours and was afraid the news would devastate him—possibly even kill him or send him into a deep depression from which he might never recover.

I had to agree with her on that. But I also had no idea how she could keep it from him for any length of time.

After giving it a great deal of thought, Sue had come up with a potentially risky plan: she would tell Dad that Kathryn had gone to Florida to visit her son Robby, and that she would be away for several weeks on an extended visit. The idea was to buy us some time—time to prepare Dad emotionally in ways that might help soften the eventual blow.

I told her I didn't think she'd be able to pull it off. Dad would likely remember that there had been no plans for Kathryn to travel—especially not in her condition. But Sue insisted he was so disoriented and forgetful these days that she was convinced he would accept the story.

The next morning, we returned early and shared Sue's plan with everyone in the house, including Gingi, who was in shock over the loss of her mother. We also called Kathryn's son Robby in Florida to break the news, and we informed the entire household staff of Sue's plan—warning them not to breathe a word of Kathryn's passing. If Dad asked about her, they were to tell him she had gone to Florida to visit her son.

Dad's bookkeeper, Henriette, was there for her weekly visit. Sue explained that Dad would not be aware of the funeral, which we were planning to hold in about three days. Henriette agreed to return and stay at the house with Dad while the rest of us attended the service and paid our respects at the cemetery.

I called Frank at school to tell him about Kathryn, and he asked about the funeral. I told him it would be on Friday, but I knew he was studying for final exams, and I told him not to come. I assured him I would make excuses for him, if necessary, but the truth was, I knew he wouldn't really be missed—and school was far more important.

I spent the day at the house, going over the books with Henriette. What surprised me most was that Dad didn't seem to notice Kathryn's absence—not at the lunch table, nor at any other point throughout the day. He didn't mention her name until that evening, after dinner. When he and Sue reached the top of the stairs, he said he wanted to go in and say goodnight to Kathryn.

Sue gently replied, "Don't you remember, Daddy? She went to Florida to visit Robby."

Dad looked a little confused for a moment, but then said, "Yes... that's right... I forgot," and turned to go into his bedroom.

I was concerned that one of his friends might call and offer condolences, inadvertently revealing the truth. But Sue had thought of that too. She went through his phone book and called every old friend he still had contact with, explaining the situation and asking them not to reach out to him.

Of course, doing so meant she had to reveal Dad's mental condition—which I initially thought was a bit demeaning. But Sue was right. It was far better to protect him than risk letting him collapse under the emotional weight of losing his wife.

Still, I always feared that one day he'd find out the truth—that Kathryn had died, and the entire family had kept it from him. If that happened, I imagined his reaction would be a painful mix of betrayal and humiliation. He might explode with anger and lash out in some way that would diminish his dignity.

But Sue stuck to her guns. Every so often, Dad would ask about Kathryn, and she'd calmly repeat that she was in Florida.

Eventually, he stopped asking altogether—which was both a relief and a heartbreak. It was a blessing that he didn't have to confront Kathryn's death, but it also confirmed what we had all begun to suspect: his dementia had progressed significantly. We were never going to see him again as he once was.

And we missed him—his sharp mind, his wit, his humor. We missed *him*.

· · * · * · * · * · · * ·

MOMENT BY MOMENT

However, Dad still had moments of surprising lucidity—times when he seemed entirely like his old self. He would recall things from the past with such clarity that I began to wonder if he had somehow overcome his dementia. I also found myself questioning how he could live on without ever mentioning or missing Kathryn. We were all careful not to bring up her name, but it occurred to me that he might have known—or at least suspected—that she had died and simply didn't want to face that reality.

One day, he shocked me by asking if I was still angry with him.

I asked him why he thought that, and he brought up the morning I had come to the house and confronted him with all my grievances. I reminded him that nearly twenty years had passed since that day—and that I had forgiven him long ago.

He went on to say that, in retrospect, he felt he had been too tough on me while I was growing up. He said he was sorry—and wanted to apologize. I had to fight off tears as I told him I always knew he was doing what he thought was best for me, and that he didn't need to apologize.

I also remembered what he had said to me that day as I left the house: *"The only thing that matters is that we all love each other."*

I excused myself to go to the bathroom because I didn't want him to see me in such an emotional state. I splashed cold water on my face and tried to compose myself. It was a poignant moment that my father could remember something so many years in the past, and that he cared enough to ask if I was still angry. That kind of reflection, that vulnerability, moved me deeply.

I thought about what Mom used to say when we were kids when Dad yelled at us: *"His bark is worse than his bite."* And in that moment, I realized how much I loved him—and always would.

Watching Dad's investments wasn't easy for me in my role as Conservator, but I was grateful to have Beverly's sound advice. A major portion of the MGM film library had been sold to Ted Turner, including all of Dad's independent films, which he co-owned with MGM. There were numerous new contracts we had to review and sign, and I had to study each one carefully and consult the attorneys to ensure I wasn't inadvertently signing away anything important. It took a great deal of time and concentration.

I also found it increasingly difficult to explain the financial matters to Dad in a way he could follow. In many cases, I made the decisions without consulting him, just to avoid causing him any confusion or distress.

However, one offer came in that I felt was worth sharing with him, partly because I thought it might cheer him up. An independent producer wanted to buy an option to adapt *Jailhouse Rock* into a stage musical, either for Broadway or a regional theater production.

I waited some time to tell him about it, wanting to pick a day when he seemed more coherent than usual.

And finally, that day came.

I entered the house and went upstairs to his den to say good morning. He was having his coffee and reading the paper, and I could tell he was in a particularly jovial mood. So, I began explaining the deal to him—going slowly and speaking clearly—and he was very enthusiastic.

He told me to go for it, but not to sign any contract that didn't include hiring me as the writer/producer of the project. He said he was sure I had the talent to write it. I pointed out that they might not want to hire me in that capacity, but he waved it off. "If they don't," he said, "someone else will. It's such a valuable property—

someone will eventually option it with you involved in the production."

I thanked him for his confidence in me, though I was rather skeptical about landing that kind of deal. I had very limited experience in live theater.

Dad's 90th birthday came and went. He spent much of his time in bed after that, but Sue made sure the household staff took him outside every day—either for a walk or a ride in his wheelchair—so he could get some fresh air. She also sat with him at the dinner table every night and encouraged him to eat, usually managing to coax him into eating more than he wanted.

She continued to oversee his medications, occasionally adding vitamins, and ensured he was getting daily showers with the help of the kind Filipino women who worked at the house.

Sue took him to see Dr. Brody for a regular check-up. When Brody asked how Dad was doing, Sue replied, "He's fine."

Brody shook his head and said, "His dementia has reached a deplorable state. He must be in real misery. And you call this *fine*? You've done too good a job taking care of him."

Sue didn't think much of it at the time, but when she told me about it later, I thought it was a rather strange remark. I interpreted it to mean that she had kept Dad alive too long—prolonging his suffering with dementia—and that, in Brody's opinion, she should have let him die naturally.

I never spoke to Dr. Brody about it, but if that's what he'd meant, I couldn't disagree more. My belief is—and always will be—that you hold onto life until the very last moment. And I'm sure most people in the world feel the same way.

I often thought about asking Dr. Brody what he'd *really* meant by that remark: *"You've done too good a job taking care of him."* But eventually, I let it go. In hindsight, I'm glad I didn't confront him. It might have gotten ugly and what would it have resolved?

It was March 28, 1996—Dad's 91st birthday. Sue was still taking excellent care of him, and I continued managing his affairs. He was in reasonably good spirits as we gathered around the table for his birthday celebration.

The cook had made his favorite dish—leg of lamb—but he didn't eat much of it. He did have some of his chocolate birthday cake and opened his presents, but soon he grew tired and asked to go to bed.

We had installed a chair lift because it had become too difficult for him to manage the stairs. His dementia had now progressed to the point where he was rarely coherent, and his hearing was fading—we had to raise our voices and speak directly into his ear to be understood. In many ways, we were all captives of his illness, and it reminded me of those emotionally difficult days we spent at the hospital with Mom while she was in a coma.

There was nothing more to do but wait. We knew he wasn't feeling well, and we began to wonder if maybe Dr. Brody had been right. Maybe Dad had lived too long. We started to wish that the powers that be would take him to a better place.

I was surprised—really surprised—that we were even thinking that way. Especially Sue, who continued to care for him with such devotion. But she believed he was suffering too much, and that it was time to let him go.

Still, none of us truly wanted to say goodbye. He was the last of his generation. Once he was gone, we would become the elders of the family, and none of us felt ready for that.

In the second week of July, Ching and Anastasia, the Filipino caretakers, traveled home to Manila to visit their ailing mother, who was also in her nineties. Sue brought in a substitute caregiver and personally instructed her on Dad's routine—how to manage his medications, how to bathe him, how to take him out for walks in his wheelchair. She stayed the entire day to make sure the new woman followed her directions.

Within a day or two, the caretaker developed an upper respiratory infection and passed it on to Dad. When Sue arrived the next day, she found him coughing. She immediately called Dr. Brody and asked him to come to the house right away.

But Dr. Brody told her he no longer made house calls because Medicare wouldn't cover them.

Sue said she would pay him herself, but she needed him to come as soon as possible. He continued to argue that he wasn't allowed to visit patients at home anymore.

Sue reminded him that he had been Dad's primary physician—and friend—for over forty years. She told him she feared Dad was dying and pleaded with him to stop by, if only to honor their long-standing friendship.

Dr. Brody finally consented to make a house call, probably because my sister shamed him into it. He came to the house and went directly upstairs to Dad's bedroom. Dad looked as though he didn't recognize him, so Brody said, "Who am I...?"

Dad answered immediately, "You're Mel Brody, my doctor."

Brody examined him for a few minutes and told us that Dad wouldn't last more than a day or so. Before leaving, he wrote a prescription for morphine to ease Dad's passing.

47

A HEARTBREAKING GOODBYE

Dad struggled but made it through the night, and we were all back early the next morning to say our final goodbyes.

At about 10:00 a.m., he closed his eyes for the last time. Even though we were expecting his passing, it was still a tremendous shock. As much as we had prayed for him to be released from his suffering, the tragedy of his loss was overwhelming. It also happened to be Cindy's birthday, and losing her father on that day was certainly not the kind of birthday gift anyone would want.

Sue was almost inconsolable, and even more upset with Mel Brody after I shared my thoughts about his earlier comment, the one about having "kept Dad alive too long" during his decline. It struck us as deeply ironic that, on the day before he died, Dad was still lucid enough to recognize Brody by name at his bedside.

We all sat in Dad's house, feeling helpless and completely drained from the emotional and physical toll of caring for him. His passing left us utterly exhausted. None of us even had the strength to get up and go home.

Sue seemed to have been hit the hardest. She didn't have the energy to get out of her chair. When she finally did, she went straight home, got into bed, and didn't get up for a couple of days.

Shortly after Sue left, Cindy went home as well and canceled her birthday dinner plans.

I stayed behind to wait for the staff from Hillside Mortuary to arrive and collect Dad's remains. I had to be there to sign the release, authorizing the removal of his body from the premises.

I remember lying down on the couch and dozing off, only to be awakened by the sound of the doorbell.

When it was all done, I realized I hadn't yet told Beverly that my dad had passed away. I called her at work and gave her the bad news. She wanted to rush home to be with me, but I told her I was emotionally exhausted and just going home to bed. There was no reason for her to come home just to watch me sleep.

I knew I was trying to escape the misery, and that sleep was one of the best ways to do it. But I also knew it would only bring temporary relief. I'd wake up with a feeling that something was terribly wrong, and for a fleeting moment, I wouldn't know what it was. Then I'd remember—that the man who had been with me every day of my life, including today, would not be with me tomorrow... or any day after.

I went straight to bed and didn't wake up until 7:00 p.m. At first, I thought it was the middle of the night, but then I heard Beverly downstairs in the kitchen. I put on a robe and went down.

She had made a pot of soup, which wasn't quite ready yet, and she rushed over to give me a big hug.

"Would you like a glass of wine... or some vodka?" she asked.

I told her vodka sounded pretty good, and I said I liked the smell of the soup. She told me it wouldn't be ready for another half hour, then poured me a glass of vodka over ice and cut a lime for me to squeeze in, just the way I liked it. She poured herself a glass of Chardonnay, and we sat down at the breakfast table.

I told her everything that had happened that morning, and she looked at me with sad eyes, not knowing what to say. I could see she was concerned, so I reassured her that I would get through it.

Then it hit me—I hadn't told Frank that Dad had died.

He was traveling in Europe with one of his friends from school, and he had left me phone numbers for every place he'd be visiting, along with the dates. I got out the list and found the number I needed. But once again, I had second thoughts about calling him.

He was having a wonderful time, and this news would ruin his vacation. He'd been very close with his grandfather and enormously proud of him. This would hurt him terribly. I hung up the phone and put the itinerary back in the top drawer of my desk. I decided to tell him everything when he got home.

The next morning, I called Sue. She told me she'd had a terrible night and didn't have the strength to get out of bed. I reminded her that we had a lot to do—we needed to make the arrangements for Dad's funeral and shop for all the food and liquor we'd need for the people who would be coming to sit Shivah with us.

She told me she wasn't up to handling any of it, and there were tears in her voice as she apologized. I told her I understood. Sue had been Dad's primary caregiver for so long that I suspected she needed some time to herself. I told her I would take care of it, and that Cindy would help me, and we'd get it all done. Hopefully, completing the tasks, would give us a sense of closure by the end of the week.

I phoned Cindy, who was in better spirits than Sue. She said she was glad Dad was out of his misery, and that he had certainly lived a wonderful life. Ninety-one years, filled with accomplishments, and he had done everything he'd ever wanted to do, and more.

I had to agree with everything she said, but I reminded her that we had a lot of work ahead of us. I told her I planned to go over to Hillside to make the funeral arrangements, that we'd need to choose a burial plot, and deal with a long list of other details. I asked if she could come with me to the mortuary, and she said she would. I was genuinely relieved I didn't have to do it all alone.

I picked up Cindy and we drove to Hillside Cemetery that

morning and took care of everything. We chose a rather expensive casket that we felt was fitting for a man of Dad's stature. We scheduled the time and date of the funeral service and selected a gravesite on a hill near the entrance to the Al Jolson Memorial Structure—a location we thought was a suitable and dignified final resting place.

With the help of the funeral director, we also arranged for a Rabbi from the Wilshire Boulevard Temple to conduct the service.

We left the cemetery around 1:00 p.m. and went to Nate 'n Al's Delicatessen in Beverly Hills for lunch, and to order enough food for about a hundred people to be delivered to Dad's house on the morning of the funeral. We estimated at least that many people would attend, including some members of the celebrity media.

Then we stopped at a market and bought liquor, wine, beer, and soft drinks in quantities to accommodate a crowd that size. Later, when we returned to Dad's house, we realized we'd also need a bartender to assist the three women already on staff—his longtime house employees—who would be serving food and cleaning up after the guests.

We decided they should all stay on through the end of the week, until things quieted down.

We also arranged for parking attendants, anticipating a great deal of cars—many driven by elderly guests who might find it difficult to park blocks away and have to walk such a distance to the house.

By mid-afternoon, my phone started ringing. Word had spread quickly about Dad's passing, and media outlets began reaching out to confirm the news.

The Hollywood Reporter and *Variety* were the first to call, followed by *The Los Angeles Times*, *The New York Times*, and *The New York Post*, along with several other newspapers.

There were also calls from the Academy of Motion Picture Arts and Sciences, and from Rick Jewell at the University of Southern California, who offered condolences on behalf of the film school faculty. The head of the American Film Institute called as well.

Danny Selznick called me from New York and kept me on the

phone, trying to cheer me up, and Richard Zanuck called from Malibu to offer his personal condolences. How the news about Dad had gotten out so fast amazed me, especially since nothing had appeared in print yet.

By the time Beverly got home, I was exhausted from answering so many phone calls, so we got in the car and went out to dinner. When we returned, there were several new messages on the answering machine—but it was now after 9 p.m., and there was no way I was returning those calls until the next day.

In the morning, I returned fifteen or eighteen calls, then sat down to write a eulogy for my father. It was Wednesday morning, and the funeral was scheduled for Friday—just two days to write the most important words I would ever say about my dad. And honestly, I had no idea where to begin.

I thought about all his accomplishments in the film industry, but those were well documented. Everyone already knew about his movies. People would be coming to the funeral to hear about the man himself—what he was like as a father, a friend, a humanitarian. The things they didn't know and were curious to understand.

I knew I needed to say something true and meaningful, something that would reflect who Pandro S. Berman really was and give closure to a remarkable life.

I wanted to give him a send-off worthy of a man of his stature. But the right words didn't come easily. I struggled through that entire day and much of the next, discarding page after page of attempts that didn't feel right.

It wasn't until Thursday night that the right words finally came. I got them down on paper as quickly as I could, afraid they might slip away if I didn't write them immediately.

I read the eulogy to Beverly, and she liked it a lot. She said I had captured Dad's essence in a way that would be both poignant and illuminating for those attending the funeral. I went to sleep that night at peace with myself, ready to face what I knew would be a difficult day.

48

A FUNERAL TO REMEMBER

We all gathered at my father's house at 9:00 a.m., and the limousines arrived at 9:30 to take the entire family to Hillside. When we arrived, the chapel was nearly full. Folding chairs were being set up outside on the large patio, along with speakers, so those who couldn't get seats inside could still hear the service.

As I stood there, I had to focus on what I was about to say to all these people about my father. Some of them had known him as long as I had known him.

When we entered the chapel, I noticed that the floor in front of the podium was filled with beautiful white flowers. In addition to the ones we'd ordered, there were several arrangements from relatives on my mother's side of the family. Fox Studios had sent an enormous spray of white roses with a card signed by Dick Zanuck, and there was an equally extravagant arrangement of white hydrangeas from Steven Spielberg, who had tremendous respect for Dad and his films and wanted the family to know that.

We went directly into the curtained-off family section at the front of the chapel and greeted the Rabbi, who had been waiting for us. He told me that he hadn't known my father well in his later years and didn't have any personal stories to share. He planned to speak about how charitable Dad had been—his generous donations to the temple each year—and things of that nature.

I told him that would be fine, and that the family would share plenty of personal stories.

My sister Sue told me she wouldn't be speaking. I could see she was very emotional, and she likely would have burst into tears if she tried to deliver a eulogy. Cindy also wasn't planning to speak, though for a different reason. She had helped her daughter, Kerry, prepare her eulogy and had contributed many of her own thoughts and feelings, so she felt she didn't have much more to add herself.

The Rabbi began the service with the religious portion of his sermon, which included some responsive reading. The number of voices joining in told me there was a large crowd present, so I peeked out from behind the curtain and saw a full house—people standing in the back of the room, and many more outside.

I was sure it would be intimidating to speak in front of such a crowd, especially for the grandchildren, all of whom had spent a great deal of time preparing their eulogies, just as I had.

Cindy's son, Cory, was the first family member to speak. He shared kind words about his grandfather and managed to get through his entire eulogy without losing his nerve. I could see how relieved he was when he came back and sat down.

His sister Kerry followed, sharing stories about how much she had loved spending time with her grandfather as a little girl, and how sweet he had been to her. She teared up a bit at the end, but like her brother, she got through it without any real trouble.

Sue's daughter, Michele, gave a wonderful eulogy, which she had spent hours preparing. She spoke with strength and conviction. Though she had to pause several times to fight back tears, her words were powerful, and everyone in the chapel could see how much she loved her grandfather.

I was the last to speak, and I was a little nervous as I walked up to the podium. I looked around the room and recognized many familiar faces—including a group of executives from 20th Century Fox and some from MGM. They were there not as official envoys from the studios, but because they genuinely admired my father.

I spoke about how he had left New York with nothing and had landed an entry-level job at RKO, and how he would send half of his earnings home every week to support his mother and little brother. I could see from the audience's expressions how impressed they were by that.

I went on to talk about his high school friendships with Irving Thalberg and David Selznick, and how he used to run and fetch oxygen for Thalberg when he collapsed on the playground and couldn't breathe.

I also spoke about his generosity—especially toward members of my mother's side of the family. One of my mother's cousins was married to a man who became seriously ill and couldn't work for more than a year. My father stepped in and supported the entire family with weekly checks until the man was able to return to work.

I shared how Dad had given me a deep appreciation for fine music when I was a child, and how we'd spent countless hours over the years listening to classical music—something that brought me a lifetime of joy.

I told them how Dad had taken great pains not to spoil me, insisting I work for the things I wanted—starting with a bicycle when I was twelve years old. I told the audience how much I resented having to earn that bike, which got a laugh, but then I explained how effective it had been. It taught me how difficult it was to earn money and gave me the drive to work hard in my own life. What Dad really wanted was peace of mind—knowing that after he was gone, I'd always be able to take care of myself.

Finally, I told them about something my father had said to me many years ago, during a conversation when I had aired some long-held grievances. He had apologized for being too tough on me while I was growing up, admitting he may have gone too far at times. But he said it was only because he loved me. Then I repeated the statement he'd made that day—one I've never forgotten: *"The only thing that really matters is that we all love each other."*

It was one of the most insightful things he had ever said, and I've thought about those words hundreds of times since.

When I finished giving my eulogy, I returned to the family section and took my seat, just in time to break down in tears. I hadn't cried yet over the loss of my father, but now the floodgates opened. I cried all the way through the Mourner's Kaddish and beyond.

I could barely compose myself by the time the service ended, and we were ushered back into the limousines and taken up the hill for the interment.

I would have to toss the first shovelful of dirt onto the coffin as it was being lowered into Dad's final resting place. I was dreading it more than anything else. It was the final act of goodbye, and for me, it would be the most difficult moment of the day.

I stood there, waiting for the graveside service to end, as images from my entire life with Dad—starting with my earliest memories—flashed through my mind.

I remembered him picking me up as I was sitting on the staircase in my pajamas when I was a little kid and taking me downstairs to meet celebrities at one of the elite Hollywood parties my mother loved to host. I met people like the Gershwins, Fred Astaire, and George Stevens—but I don't really remember *them*. I just remember flashes of tuxedos and beautiful women in fancy dresses, pinching my cheeks.

I remembered Dad the way I used to think of him—as Jupiter—and later, when I realized he was only human. I remembered hunting ducks with him in Bakersfield and watching baseball games with him in Brooklyn.

Dozens of other memories came to me in the back of the limo on our way back to Dad's house. I was sitting next to Beverly, my face buried in a handkerchief, and I cried most of the way back. The memories were beautiful to me, and painfully sad at the same time.

As soon as we arrived, I asked the bartender to fix me a large glass of vodka with a tiny splash of vermouth, and I tried to swallow away the aftermath of my tears.

Guests began arriving for the Shivah, and many of them came up to hug me or pat me on the back. One after another, they told me how much they appreciated the eulogy—that I had given them real insight into a man whom many had thought of as cold as steel. They were touched to discover that he had been human after all.

Someone even said, "You said it all, kid... Your father can now go to his final resting place with dignity."

Another person gave me a stunning compliment: "He was very lucky to have a son like you."

When the last of the mourners had finally left, and my sisters and I were sprawled out in the living room—exhausted and emotionally drained—I remembered what my father had once said to his brother Henry when their mother died. I turned to my sisters and repeated his words:

"That's it... We are all that's left of the old family now."

And that really was it.

My father had outlived all the other pioneers of the movie industry—including Goldwyn, Mayer, Zanuck, DeMille, Selznick, Thalberg, Laemmle, Adolph Zukor, Jesse Lasky, Jules Stein, and all the Warner brothers. Hollywood was now a different town, with a digital face, an ever-changing industry, and an ever-shifting view.

In many ways it had lost the magic and glow of that golden era. And its pioneers... all just memories.

EPILOGUE

POSTSCRIPT

It took eight years of hard work and many disappointments—watching deals fall through and waiting for new ones to materialize—but *Jailhouse Rock*, the theatrical musical production, finally opened at the Piccadilly Theatre in London's West End in 2004. I was the American producer, and I also wrote the first draft of the libretto—exactly what my dad had always wanted for me.

Beverly and I moved to London for several months, and I worked closely with the English producers in preparation for opening night. I had the feeling that my dad was watching all of it unfold from somewhere high above the clouds. I could almost feel his presence in the theater that night.

It's ironic that my father had never managed to get his Broadway show off the ground during the war, when we were living in New York, yet I was able to make it happen in London. Beverly and I dedicated the production to him on opening night with a champagne toast. If he *was* truly up there watching, I'd like to think there was a big smile on his face—because the show ran for a solid year.

I wish he had been alive and with us in London that night. All his concerns about me being too soft and living a failed life would have finally—and thankfully—been put to rest.

Pandro S. Berman Filmography

#	Year	Title	Studio	Genre
1	1931	Men of Chance	RKO	Drama
2	1932	The Half-Naked Truth	RKO	Comedy
3	1932	Men of America	RKO	War/Drama
4	1932	Symphony of Six Million	RKO	Drama
5	1932	The Age of Consent	RKO	Drama
6	1932	What Price Hollywood?	RKO	Drama
7	1933	The Monkey's Paw	RKO	Horror
8	1933	Christopher Strong	RKO	Drama
9	1933	The Silver Cord	RKO	Drama
10	1933	Morning Glory	RKO	Drama
11	1933	One Man's Journey	RKO	Drama
12	1933	Ann Vickers	RKO	Drama
13	1933	Aggie Appleby, Maker of Men	RKO	Comedy
14	1934	Man of Two Worlds	RKO	Drama
15	1934	Spitfire	RKO	Drama
16	1934	This Man Is Mine	RKO	Romantic Drama
17	1934	Where Sinners Meet	RKO	Comedy/Drama
18	1934	Strictly Dynamite	RKO	Comedy
19	1934	Stingaree	RKO	Adventure
20	1934	The Life of Vergie Winters	RKO	Drama
21	1934	Murder on the Blackboard	RKO	Mystery
22	1934	Let's Try Again	RKO	Romance
23	1934	Of Human Bondage	RKO	Drama
24	1934	Cockeyed Cavaliers	RKO	Comedy
25	1934	We're Rich Again	RKO	Comedy
26	1934	His Greatest Gamble	RKO	Drama

#	Year	Title	Studio	Genre
27	1934	Bachelor Bait	RKO	Comedy
28	1934	Hat, Coat, and Glove	RKO	Crime/Drama
29	1934	Their Big Moment	RKO	Comedy/Mystery
30	1934	The Fountain	RKO	Drama
31	1934	Down to Their Last Yacht	RKO	Comedy
32	1934	The Age of Innocence	RKO	Period Drama
33	1934	The Richest Girl in the World	RKO	Romantic Comedy
34	1934	The Gay Divorcee	RKO	Musical
35	1934	Wednesday's Child	RKO	Drama
36	1934	Gridiron Flash	RKO	Sports Comedy
37	1934	By Your Leave	RKO	Comedy
38	1934	The Little Minister	RKO	Romantic Drama
39	1935	Romance in Manhattan	RKO	Romantic Drama
40	1935	Roberta	RKO	Musical
41	1935	Laddie	RKO	Family/Drama
42	1935	Star of Midnight	RKO	Mystery
43	1935	Break of Hearts	RKO	Drama/Romance
44	1935	Top Hat	RKO	Musical Comedy
45	1935	Alice Adams	RKO	Drama
46	1935	Freckles	RKO	Drama
47	1935	In Person	RKO	Comedy/Romance
48	1935	I Dream Too Much	RKO	Musical
49	1935	Sylvia Scarlett	RKO	Comedy/Drama
50	1936	Muss 'Em Up	RKO	Crime/Drama
51	1936	Follow the Fleet	RKO	Musical
52	1936	Mary of Scotland	RKO	Historical Drama
53	1936	Swing Time	RKO	Musical Comedy
54	1936	The Big Game	RKO	Sports Drama
55	1936	A Woman Rebels	RKO	Period Drama
56	1936	Winterset	RKO	Drama
57	1936	That Girl from Paris	RKO	Musical
58	1937	Quality Street	RKO	Romantic Comedy

59	1937	The Soldier and the Lady	RKO	Adventure
60	1937	Shall We Dance	RKO	Musical Comedy
61	1937	Stage Door	RKO	Drama
62	1937	A Damsel in Distress	RKO	Musical Comedy
63	1938	Carefree	RKO	Musical Comedy
64	1939	The Hunchback of Notre Dame	RKO	Historical Drama
65	1939	Gunga Din	RKO	Adventure
66	1941	Ziegfeld Girl	MGM	Musical Drama
67	1941	Love Crazy	MGM	Romantic Comedy
68	1941	Honky Tonk	MGM	Western/Drama
69	1942	Rio Rita	MGM	Musical Comedy
70	1942	Somewhere I'll Find You	MGM	War/Drama
71	1943	Slightly Dangerous	MGM	Comedy/Romance
72	1944	Song of Russia	MGM	Drama/Musical
73	1944	Dragon Seed	MGM	War/Drama
74	1944	The Seventh Cross	MGM	Thriller/Drama
75	1944	Marriage Is a Private Affair	MGM	Romantic Drama
76	1945	The Picture of Dorian Gray	MGM	Horror/Drama
77	1946	Undercurrent	MGM	Thriller
78	1947	The Sea of Grass	MGM	Western/Drama
79	1947	Living in a Big Way	MGM	Musical/Comedy
80	1947	If Winter Comes	MGM	Drama
81	1948	The Three Musketeers	MGM	Adventure
82	1949	The Bribe	MGM	Film Noir
83	1949	Madame Bovary	MGM	Literary Drama
84	1949	The Doctor and the Girl	MGM	Medical Drama
85	1950	Father of the Bride	MGM	Comedy
86	1951	Father's Little Dividend	MGM	Comedy
87	1951	The Light Touch	MGM	Crime/Romance
88	1951	Soldiers Three	MGM	Military Adventure/Comedy

89	1952	Ivanhoe	MGM	Historical Adventure
90	1952	The Prisoner of Zenda	MGM	Historical Adventure
91	1953	Knights of the Round Table	MGM	Historical Epic
92	1953	All the Brothers Were Valiant	MGM	Seafaring Adventure
93	1953	Battle Circus	MGM	War Drama
94	1954	The Long, Long Trailer	MGM	Comedy
95	1955	Blackboard Jungle	MGM	Social Drama
96	1955	The Adventures of Quentin Durward	MGM	Swashbuckling Adventure
97	1956	Bhowani Junction	MGM	Political Drama
98	1956	Tea and Sympathy	MGM	Social Drama
99	1957	Jailhouse Rock	MGM	Musical/Drama
100	1957	Something of Value	MGM	Colonial Drama
101	1958	The Brothers Karamazov	MGM	Literary Drama
102	1958	The Reluctant Debutante	MGM	Romantic Comedy
103	1960	Key Witness	MGM	Crime/Drama
104	1960	BUtterfield 8	MGM	Drama
105	1960	All the Fine Young Cannibals	MGM	Musical Drama
106	1962	Sweet Bird of Youth	MGM	Southern Gothic Drama
107	1963	The Prize	MGM	Political Thriller
108	1964	Honeymoon Hotel	MGM	Romantic Comedy
109	1965	A Patch of Blue	MGM	Social Drama
110	1969	Justine	20th Century Fox	Psychological Drama
111	1970	Move	20th Century Fox	Dark Comedy

BIBLIOGRAPHY

Pandro S. Berman Filmography is compiled from the following sources:

Turner Classic Movies (TCM). "Filmography: Pandro S. Berman." *Turner Classic Movies.* Accessed May 2025. https://www.tcm.com

IMDb. "Pandro S. Berman – Filmography by Year." *IMDb.com, Inc.* Accessed May 2025. https://www.imdb.com

AFI Catalog of Feature Films. "Berman, Pandro S." *American Film Institute.* Accessed May 2025. https://catalog.afi.com

Wikipedia contributors. "Pandro S. Berman." *Wikipedia, The Free Encyclopedia.* Last modified May 2025. https://en.wikipedia.org/wiki/Pandro_S._Berman

ABOUT THE AUTHOR

Michael Berman is the son of Pandro S. Berman, the noted producer and head of production at RKO and MGM studios . He grew up during the golden era of Hollywood and became an award-winning film editor and 2nd unit director. He worked on many American television series and movies including *Magnun P.I.*, *Battlestar Galactica*, and *Air Wolf* before turning to writing. He was the American producer and contributing writer of the theatrical musical production of "Jailhouse Rock," which ran for one year in London's West End.

www.ingramcontent.com/pod-product-compliance
Lightning Source LLC
Chambersburg PA
CBHW031323230426
43670CB00006B/219